AF778188

Integrating the Practice of Medicine

A Decision Maker's Guide to Organizing and Managing Physician Services

Integrating the Practice of Medicine

A Decision Maker's Guide to Organizing and Managing Physician Services

Ronald B. Conners, PhD, *Editor*

American Hospital Publishing, Inc.,
An American Hospital Association company
Chicago

This publication is designed to provide accurate and authoritative information in regard to the subject matter covered. It is sold with the understanding that neither the author nor the publisher is engaged in rendering legal, accounting, or other professional service. If legal advice or other expert assistance is required, the services of a competent professional should be sought.

The views expressed in this publication are strictly those of the authors and do not necessarily represent official positions of the American Hospital Association.

AHA is a service mark of the American Hospital Association used under license by American Hospital Publishing, Inc.

© 1997 by American Hospital Publishing, Inc., an American Hospital Association company. All rights reserved. No part of this publication may be reproduced, stored in a retrieval system, or transmitted, in any form or by any means, electronic, mechanical, photocopying, recording or otherwise, without the prior written permission of the publisher. Printed in the United States of America.

Cover design by Studio Montage

Library of Congress Cataloging-in-Publication Data

Integrating the practice of medicine : A decision maker's guide to organizing and managing physician services / Ronald B. Conners, editor.

p. cm.

Includes bibliographical references and index.

ISBN 1-55648-206-X

1. Medicine—Practice—United States. 2. Integrated delivery of health care—United States. 3. Physician management companies—United States. I. Conners, Ronald B.

[DNLM: 1. Professional Practice—organization & administration. 2. Delivery of Health Care, Integrated—organization & administration—United States. 3. Models, Organizational. 4. Managed Care Programs—economics—United States. W 87 I61 1997]

R728.I48 1997

362.1'068—dc21

DNLM/DLC

for Library of Congress 97-17762

CIP

Discounts on bulk quantities of books published by American Hospital Publishing, Inc. (AHPI), are available to professional associations, special marketers, educators, trainers, and others. For details and discount information, contact AHPI, Books Division, 737 North Michigan Avenue, Suite 700, Chicago, Illinois 60611-2615 (Fax: 312-951-8491).

CONTENTS

ABOUT THE AUTHOR-EDITOR

Ronald B. Conners, PhD, is president/CEO of CareSouth, a large integrated home care management company in Macon, GA, serving the Southeast. He is also clinical professor of public health in the Division of Health Policy and Management of the School of Public Health at Columbia University and adjunct professor of public health at The Rollins School of Public Health at Emory University in Atlanta. He teaches graduate MPH courses in strategic management, health economics, physician practice management, and outpatient reimbursement. Previously, he was president of Health Reimbursement Systems, Inc., an alternate site delivery system consulting firm. Dr. Conners is the author of *Understanding Ambulatory Surgery Reimbursement: A Comprehensive Guide to Maximizing Reimbursement* and an editor of *Home Infusion Therapy,* published by American Hospital Publishing, Inc., in 1995. He received his MA and PhD with honors in economics from the Graduate Faculty of the New School for Social Research.

CONTRIBUTORS

W. David Bradford, PhD, is an associate professor of economics in the Whittemore School of Business and Economics at the University of New Hampshire. His research focuses primarily on three areas of health economics: contracting issues for physician practices, substance abuse issues and pregnancy, and the role of technology in providing health care services (especially for cardiology services). He has also investigated the role of Medicaid in physician and individual decision making and the nature of the employment-based health insurance market, among other issues. Professor Bradford has been at the University of New Hampshire for six years and recently was a visiting professor at the Yale School of Medicine. He has authored numerous peer-reviewed journal articles and book chapters. He received his PhD from Louisiana State University.

Gordon D. Brown, PhD, is professor and director of the Health Services Management Program, School of Medicine, at the University of Missouri-Columbia, where he is also a senior fellow and faculty chair of the Executive Program, National Center for Managed Health Care Administration. Dr. Brown speaks and publishes frequently in the area of managed care and organization strategy. He has led the development of both executive short courses in managed care and an Executive Master's Program in Health Services Management at the University of Missouri. He is chairman of the Accrediting Commission on Education for Health Services Administration and chairman of the board for the Network for Healthcare Management, a consortium of university programs in health services management. He has consulted with health care providers throughout the United States and internationally and was formerly a scientist with the World Health Organization, Geneva. He received his PhD and MA from the University of Iowa, Program in Hospital and Health Administration.

Lawton R. Burns, PhD, MBA, is associate professor of health care systems in The Wharton School at the University of Pennsylvania, Philadelphia. He teaches courses on health care strategy, organization, and management and integrated delivery systems. Previously, he taught in the Graduate School of Business at the University of Chicago and the College of Business Administration at the University of Arizona. He has conducted research on physician-organization arrangements over the past 12 years. He has conducted numerous surveys of physicians at the hospital system, county, state, and national levels and analyzed the trajectory of physician-hospital relationships over time. In recognition of this research, he was named the Edwin J. Crosby Memorial Fellow by the Hospital Research and Educational Trust in 1992. During the past few years he has helped design national surveys of hospital-physician integration activity for the Prospective Payment Commission, the American Hospital Association, and the Center for Health Management Research. More recently, he has received grants from the Agency for Health Care Policy & Research to examine the market forces that favor the development of IDSs and the internal mechanisms used by them to promote physician alignment. He has also received grants to study emerging topics in integration, including methods to right-size physician panels, incentivize physicians under capitation, and develop physician leadership. Currently, Dr. Burns is conducting case studies of six IDSs in Illinois for the Illinois Hospital and HealthSystems Association to identify common problems and problem-solving approaches in the integration process. He is also conducting research on medical groups and networks and is examining the market forces that shape the growth of group practices and investor-owned networks. He has published several papers on the structure and performance of the physician practice management industry. He is also teaching management seminars designed to prepare physicians and administrators for managing IDSs. Dr. Burns sits on the editorial boards of *Health Services Research* and *Health Care Management Review* (where he is associate editor). He is a member of the Grant Review Study Section for the Agency for Health Care Policy & Research and is the director of research for the Leonard Davis Institute of Health Economics. Dr. Burns received his doctorate in sociology and his MBA in health administration from the University of Chicago.

Jeffrey F. Chase-Lubitz, JD, is a partner in the health law practice of Brown, Rudnick, Freed & Gesmer, located in Boston, Providence, and Hartford. His practice focuses on individual and institutional health care providers for whom he provides legal and strategic advice concerning health care affiliation and network development. He has been selected to be included in the Healthcare Law Section of *The Best Lawyers in America* on the basis of peer evaluations. He received his JD from Vanderbilt University School of Law.

Russell C. Coile Jr., MBA, is a futurist specializing in the health care industry. He is senior vice president of the Dallas, TX, office of Chi Systems, based in Ann Arbor, MI. As an independent consultant, he provides market forecasts and strategic advice to a wide range of U.S. hospitals, medical groups, managed care organizations, and suppliers. He has written four books in the past ten years on the future of the health care field, and his newest book, *The Five Stages of Managed Care,* was published in January, 1997. His monthly newsletter, *Russ Coile's Health Trends,* is now in its eighth year. His prediction rate on "Top 10 Trends" was 90 percent accurate for 1995 and 100 percent accurate for 1996. In the past year Mr. Coile has participated in more than 100 seminars for such groups as the American Hospital Association, American College of Physician Executives, the Governance Institute, and Rand Healthcare Roundtable. He is a member of the editorial advisory boards of *Managed Care Outlook, Healthcare Systems Strategy Report, Nurse Week,* and the *Medical Network Strategy Report.* He received his BA from Johns Hopkins University and his MBA in health services administration from George Washington University.

William J. DeMarco is a 20-year veteran in the health plan development, marketing, and management business. Since 1980 he has led in the design, development, and restructuring of physician-owned health plans and various IPAs. He was the initial CEO for the Rockford (IL) Clinic-Sponsored Clinicare Health Plan and was the principal developer of Community Health Plan of Manitowoc, WI; Multimed Health Plan in Oklahoma City, OK; MDS IPA in Wichita, KS; Fox Valley IPA in Aurora, IL; Lake County Medical Society IPA in Libertyville, IL; and Midsouth Health Plan in Memphis, TN. He has also been asked to be the development advisor to start the Connecticut State Medical Society-owned HMO, MD Health Plan, and The Independent Physicians of New Jersey, a statewide physician-driven plan. He is currently an advisor for Physicians of Wisconsin, a statewide physician-owned multi-IPA organization. In 1980, Mr. DeMarco ran the Minneapolis district for HMO Minnesota, and in 1974, he was a member of a team of managers who developed the SHARE health plan (a community plan created with private and public funds). Mr. DeMarco is on the editorial advisory board for several publishers, including Aspen Systems, Healthcare Consultants, and is a visiting instructor at Loyola University College of Law, where he teaches courses on organizational development of health plans. He received his MA in organizational development of health care enterprises from DePaul University and is licensed as a Certified Management Consultant by the International Association of Management Consultants.

Paul R. DeMuro, JD, MBA, CPA, is a partner in the San Francisco and Los Angeles offices of the international law firm of Latham & Watkins. He specializes in mergers and acquisitions, managed care, Medicare reimbursement, and fraud and abuse. His clients include international, national, and regional health care companies, health plans, physicians and physician groups, physician practice management companies, hospitals and hospital systems, investment banks, laboratories, pharmaceutical companies, home health agencies, and ancillary service providers. He has been listed in *Who's Who in American Law* and *The Best Lawyers in America* and was named in 1997 one of "40 Health Care Attorneys Who Have Made Their Mark" by the *National Law Journal*. He has authored more than 30 articles, books, and book chapters and delivered almost 200 presentations throughout North America. He has been on the national board and the executive committee of the Healthcare Financial Management Association and is a member of the National Health Lawyers Association, the Health Law Section of the American Bar Association, the IPA Association of America and its legal steering committee, The Medical Group Management Association, the Board of the School of Health at California State University at Doninquez Hills, and the AICPA. He is on the advisory board for Aspen's *Managed Care Law Manual* and for the *Report on Medicare Compliance* newsletter produced by Atlantic Information Systems.

David W. Emmons, PhD, is director of policy research studies at the American Medical Association's Center for Health Policy Reseach in Chicago. He is responsible for developing and implementing a broad-based program of research on the financing and delivery of medical care. His own research has focused on the organization of physican practices, managed care, and issues pertaining to the uninsured. He has contributed articles to such journals as *Health Affairs, Medical Care, Journal of the American Medical Association, Journal of Health and Hospital Law, Journal of Human Resources, Medical Care Research,* and *Journal of Economic Theory*. Previously, Dr. Emmons taught economics at Goucher College, Virginia Polytechnic Institute and State University, and Wayne State University. He received his PhD in political economy from Johns Hopkins University, his MA in mathematics from the University of Texas at Austin, and his BA in mathematics from Drake University.

Allan Fine, MBA, BBA, is a senior manager in Ernst & Young LLP's Health Care Strategy Consulting Practice. He serves in a leadership role in the firm's managed care and integrated delivery systems practice. He has assisted clients in developing managed care strategic plans, conducting market and medical staff assessments, and developing and implementing integrated systems and regional and national networks and affiliations. In addition, he has helped clients in designing and implementing direct contracting arrangements, developing marketing and sales strategies for various managed care initiatives, conducting new product development, negotiating managed care contracts, and conducting managed care operational assessments. He is a prominent speaker and writer on topics related to managed care, IDSs, relationships between providers and employers, and marketing and sales strategies. Mr. Fine is the editor of the newsletter, *Allan Fine's Trends in Integrated Health Care,* and the journal, *Managed Care Quarterly,* published by Aspen Publishers, and is editor in chief of the newsletter, *Integrated Health Care Delivery Systems.* He is editor and coeditor, respectively, of the books, *Integrated Health Care Delivery Systems: A Guide to Successful Strategies for Hospital and Physician Collaboration* and *Integrated Health Care Delivery Systems: Business and Legal Forms,* both published by Thompson Publishing Group. He is coauthor of *Dealing Direct: A Strategy for Business-Provider Partnerships,* published in 1997 by American Hospital Publishing. Prior to joining Ernst & Young, Mr. Fine was vice president and director of a national consulting practice focused on managed care and physician-hospital integration strategy development and implementation. He has also held management positions with a provider-sponsored PPO and a major insurance carrier. He received his MBA in health care administration from Bernard M. Baruch College–Mount Sinai School of Medicine, City University of New York, and his BBA, cum laude, in marketing from Temple University in Philadelphia.

Eli Ginzberg, PhD, is A. Barton Hepburn Professor Emeritus of Economics, Graduate School of Business, Columbia University, New York, where he has been a member of the faculty since 1935. He is also director of The Eisenhower Center for the Conservation of Human Resources, director of The Charles H. Revson Fellows Program on the Future of the City of New York, and special lecturer in economics, Graduate School of Business and School of Public Health, all at Columbia University. During World War II, he served as chief logistical advisor to the Surgeon General of the Army, overseeing all medical resource allocations, human and hospital. He has written more than 100 books in the field of human resources and health policy, the most recent entitled *Tomorrow's Hospital: A Look to the 21st Century,* published by Yale University Press in 1996, and *Improving Health Care of the Poor: The New York City Experience,* published by Transaction Publishers this year.

Peter N. Grant, JD, PhD, is a partner in the law firm of Davis Wright Tremaine in their San Francisco and Seattle offices and is cochair of the firm's health law department. He is general counsel for the American Medical Group Association, IPA Association of America, the California Integrated Health Association, and the Hospital Council of Northern and Central California. He is past president of the California Society for Health Care Attorneys and the Northern California Chapter of the Healthcare Financial Management Association.

Rick W. Griffin, JD, is senior vice president and general counsel to Central Georgia Health System in Macon. He has more than 15 years of experience in health care law. Previously, he was in private practice as a partner with Sell & Melton, also in Macon, specializing in health care law. At Central Georgia Health System, Mr. Griffin is responsible for the delivery of legal services to all entities within the system, including a large tertiary care not-for-profit community teaching hospital, several managed hospitals, rural health clinics, a physician management organization, a managed care organization that includes an HMO, and a large home health management company. He is directly involved with all business development for the system, manages all insurance and risk management functions, and handles all legal aspects of physician recruitment and contracting with the hospital and the physician management organization. He is a member of the American Bar Association and the State Bar of Georgia, the National Health Lawyers Association, the American Academy of Health Care Attorneys, and the Georgia In-House Health Care Attorneys. He also serves on the board of directors of the Georgia Association of Health Care Attorneys. Mr. Griffin received his JD from Mercer University, Macon, GA, and his BBA from the University of Georgia, Stetson School of Business.

Nicole C. Hall, JD, is an associate in the Healthcare Practice Group at King & Spalding in Atlanta, GA. She regularly advises healthcare providers and other healthcare industry clients on a variety of health care regulatory and corporate issues. Ms. Hall received her JD from the University of Chicago Law School. She is a member of the American Academy of Healthcare Attorneys, the Georgia Academy of Hospital Attorneys, and the American Bar Association.

Kenneth M. Hekman, MBA, FACMPE, is president of Hekman & Associates, Inc., Holland, MI. His 20-year career in health care includes roles as a health planner, retirement center executive, medical group administrator, and consultant. He is the author of *Buying, Selling and Merging a Medical Practice,* published in 1996 by Richard D. Irwin Inc. He often speaks at national meetings on strategic planning, integration, and cutting-edge medical management concepts. He is a fellow in the American College of Medical Practice Executives.

Patrick M. Hurst is a national director of the Health Care Group and a managing director in the Chicago office of Houlihan Lokey Howard & Zukin. He has managed a wide variety of corporate finance, valuation, and financial restructuring engagements in the health care industry, ranging from M&A and securities valuation to strategy formulation and implementation. Mr. Hurst has been involved in numerous assignments involving medical practices, home health care agencies, nursing homes, hospitals, managed care companies, and other health care providers. Mr. Hurst has extensive experience with primary care, single-specialty, and multispecialty groups and physician-owned HMOs. Prior to joining Houlihan Lokey he worked in the Valuation and Bankruptcy Groups of Ernst & Young LLP and at a national consulting firm specializing in litigation support. He earned his BA in business administration from Marquette University and his MBA in finance from the University of Wisconsin-Madison.

Paul H. Keckley Jr., PhD, is vice president, strategic development, of PhyCor, Inc., the nation's largest and best-known practice management company, with operations in more than 70 markets. His responsibilities include corporate strategy development and affiliations with integrated health systems. Founded in 1988, PhyCor is widely recognized as the pioneer in the practice management industry. It was the first company of its kind to be traded publicly and continues to innovate aggressively as markets change and opportunities appear. Currently, the company is affiliated with 49 multispecialty groups, including 3,370 physicians in 28 states and 23 managed care networks with more than 15,800 physicians. Before joining PhyCor in 1994, Dr. Keckley was the principal of The Keckley Group, a national consulting firm that specialized in integration strategies involving physicians and hospitals. He received his PhD in business from Ohio State University and did additional graduate work in economics at Oxford University.

Phillip R. Kletke, PhD, is senior social scientist in the Center for Health Policy Research at the American Medical Association in Chicago. He has written numerous articles and several books on various aspects of health resource analysis, including demographic projections of the supply and distribution of physicians, the demand for their services, and the changing organization of physician practices. In addition, he has authored a number of articles on physician participation in Medicaid and other aspects of access to physician services. Recent articles by Dr. Kletke have appeared in such journals as the *American Journal of Kidney Disease, Journal of Health Policy, Politics and Law, Health Services Research, Inquiry, Medical Care,* and *Journal of the American Medical Association*. Previously, he was a research associate at the American Academy of Pediatrics. He received his MA and PhD in sociology from the University of Chicago and his BS in mathematics from Oklahoma State University.

Jennifer M. Marx is consulting analyst for DeMarco & Associates, Inc., in Rockford, IL. She specializes in the research, design, and development of physician compensation plans, including capitation budget design and fee schedule preparation, RBRVS relative value reimbursement systems, and performance pay programs for physician networks and integrated care delivery and financing systems. She is also executive director for the multi-IPA network, Physicians of Wisconsin. She has coauthored several monographs, including *Understanding Capitation, Management Services Organization, The Difference Between MSOs and PPMs, Physician-owned HMOs,* and most recently, *Medicare Strategy,* published by Inter-Study. Her book, *Provider Sponsored Organizations in a Rural Setting,* will be published in 1997. Ms. Marx received her BS in pre-med from the University of Notre Dame and her MBA from the University of Illinois–Champaign. She is a member of the American Association of Health Plans and The IPA Association of America.

Stephen A. Norton, MPP, is a research associate in the Health Policy Center of The Urban Institute in Washington, DC. His major areas of research are physician and hospital payment and health care for the medically indigent. He is currently involved in an evaluation of the devolution of power from the federal to the state level and its implications for the health status of low-income women and children. In addition, he has studied the variation in Medicaid fees across the United States and the impact of this variation on access to obstetrical services for low-income women, helped develop alternative approaches to measuring malpractice costs used for the Medicare Fee Schedule Geographic Adjustment Factors, and explored the potential effects of extending the Medicare physician payment system to state Medicaid programs. Mr. Norton has written a number of articles on the implications of physician and hospital payment on health care providers and on access to care for low-income individuals.

Kirsten A. Nyrop has served as vice president for government relations for Coastal Physician Group, Inc., Durham, NC, and was a management consultant with KPMG Peat Marwick. She has also held high-level public policy and administrative positions with various federal, state, and municipal agencies. She has undergraduate and Masters degrees from the University of North Carolina at Chapel Hill and has completed the course work and comprehensive exams for a doctorate through the university's School of Public Health.

Brian J. Passante, JD, is a partner in the law firm of Sell & Melton, LLP, in Macon, GA. His legal practice includes corporate formation, sale, and acquisition for health care providers and the representation of physicians and physician groups. He received his JD, cum laude, from Mercer University, Walter F. George School of Law. He was a member of the Mercer University Law Review.

Glen A. Reed, JD, is a partner in King & Spalding's Atlanta office and chair of the Healthcare Practice Group. His practice concentrates on the general representation of health care systems and on specialized projects involving health care industry restructuring, reimbursement, fraud and abuse, antitrust, managed care, and new service development. He serves as a director and president-elect of NHLA/AAHA, Inc., the organization recently formed by a merger of the National Health Lawyers Association and the American Academy of Healthcare Attorneys. He has served as president of the Georgia Academy of Hospital Attorneys and chair of the Thirtieth Annual Meeting of the American Academy of Healthcare Attorneys. Mr. Reed has lectured extensively on health care industry legal matters and served for six years as chair of the annual seminar *Fundamentals of Healthcare Law.* Mr. Reed has been listed in *The Best Lawyers in America* and *Who's Who in America.* He is a graduate of Yale Law School.

Uwe E. Reinhardt, PhD, is James Madison Professor of Political Economy at Princeton University, NJ. He is a member of the Institute of Medicine of the National Academy of Sciences and of the Council on the Economic Impact of Health Systems Change and a board member of the *Journal of the American Medical Association.* He was commissioner of the Physician Payment Review Commission from 1986 to 1995.

Steven M. Scott, MD, is chairman of the board and CEO of Coastal Physician Group, Inc., Durham, NC. Founding the company in 1977, he evolved the business from a small contract management firm to one of the largest physician management companies in the United States. His strategic vision and work ethic have positioned Coastal to consult with physicians and organize them into efficient medical care networks. A physician foremost, he believes the best solution for managing and controlling health care costs is to organize a system where physicians are the leaders. Dr. Scott is board certified in obstetrics and gynecology and is a member of the clinical faculty at Duke University Medical Center in Durham. He also serves on the board of visitors of the Babcock Graduate School of Management of Wake Forest University. He received his undergraduate degree and medical education from Indiana University and completed his residency in the Department of Obstetrics and Gynecology at Duke University Medical Center where he was chief resident. He participates regularly in seminars and is an active member of the American Medical Association, North Carolina Medical Society, American College of Obstetrics and Gynecology, American College of Emergency Physicians, American Academy of Medical Directors, Southern Medical Association, and the Carter Society. In addition, Dr. Scott has contributed articles to medical publications, including the *American Journal of Emergency Medicine.*

Jacque J. Sokolov, MD, is the chief executive officer of Advanced Health Plans, Inc., and AHP Development Corporation. Advanced Health Plans develops, finances, and implements advanced integrated health systems. Clients include physician organizations, hospital systems, insurance companies, managed care organizations, and health care system vendors in more than 150 U.S. markets, 40 states, and 3 foreign countries. AHP Development Corporation was formed more recently to accommodate client requests to evaluate and identify equity participation in strategic alliances, joint ventures, investor partnerships, and merger/acquisition activities. It actively seeks and assists the development of health plans, integrated delivery systems, and physician networks through equity participation and long-term managerial contracts. Dr. Sokolov previously was vice president and medical director at Southern California Edison Company. Advanced Health Plans created and implemented that company's highly successful managed care program, HealthFlex, which integrated its self-insured medical plans with an in-house claims payment system, a utilization management program, a preferred provider network, and primary care clinics. Dr. Sokolov serves on the boards of the Washington Business Group on Health, the National Fund for Medical Education, the National Health Foundation, and California Health Decisions, and on the advisory boards of the National Health Policy Council, the National Resource Center of Worksite Promotion, the White House Health Project, and the Health Care Advisory Committee for California Insurance Commissioner. He received a BA in medicine from the University of Southern California and an MD with honors from the USC School of Medicine. He completed his internal medicine residency at the Mayo Graduate School of Medicine and his fellowship in cardiovascular diseases from the University of Texas-Southwestern Medical School. He previously held and currently holds academic appointments and advisory board responsibilities including positions in the Schools of Medicine, Business, Public Health, and Pharmacy at Harvard University, the Massachusetts Institute of Technology, the University of Pennsylvania, the University of California-Los Angeles, and the University of Southern California.

Peter F. Straley is CEO of Baycare Health Partners, Springfield, MA, the largest PHO serving the western Massachusetts market. A joint venture between the Greater Springfield IPA and Baystate Health System, Baycare Health Partners represents three hospitals and nearly 700 physicians. Prior to joining Baycare, Mr. Straley was vice president at Jennings Ryan & Kolb and vice president, research & development, at Amherst Associates Inc. With more than 18 years of health care experience as a management consultant and in information systems, he has assisted numerous organizations in the development of strategic and financial plans, PHOs, and other forms of integrated system development. Mr. Straley was the lead author and editor of *Developing a Successful Physician–Hospital Organization,* published by American Hospital Publishing, Inc., in 1995. He received his MBA from the University of Massachusetts and his BA from Middlebury College, VT.

Darrell P. Thorpe, MD, is president and CEO of HealthPartners of Southern Arizona in Tucson. HPSA is a not-for-profit integrated health care organization that brings together previously separate health care providers and insurance operations into one organization. The goal of HPSA is to provide superior service and value and to improve the health status of the community. Dr. Thorpe has also been senior vice president for strategic services at Tucson Medical Center as well as HPSA since 1986. In that role, he was responsible for strategy formulation for the HealthPartners System. Before joining HPSA, he was vice president and senior consultant for Chi Systems, Inc., and president of Health Planning Associates in Tucson, where he consulted with hospitals throughout the United States and the Middle East in the areas of long-range planning, program development, facilities planning, and hospital organization and management.

Dewayne E. Ullsperger, FSA, MAAA, is a principal with Reden & Anders, Ltd., an actuarial consulting firm in Minneapolis, MN, that specializes in managed health care. He has served as consultant to numerous HMOs and provider organizations throughout the country. He specializes in pricing, product development, and provider reimbursement strategies for managed care programs. Mr. Ullsperger is a member of the American Academy of Actuaries and the Society of Actuaries and a fellow of the Society of Actuaries.

Stephen Zuckerman, PhD, is a principal research associate in the Health Policy Center of The Urban Institute in Washington, DC. His major areas of research are physician and hospital payment and health care reform. Currently, he is directing a major evaluation of five Medicaid waiver programs that are attempting to expand program eligibility with savings achieved through greater reliance on managed care. In addition, he has studied the impact of the Medicare Fee Schedule for physician services on service volume and intensity growth, developed alternative approaches to the Medicare Volume Performance Standard Policy, and explored the potential effects of extending the Medicare physician payment system to other payers. He also codirected the development of the Geographic Practice Cost Indices used in the Medicare Fee Schedule. Prior to joining the Urban Institute, Dr. Zuckerman worked at the American Medical Association's Center for Health Policy Research. He has published extensively on a variety of health economics issues.

PREFACE

The defeat of the Clinton health care reform proposal in 1994 reflected a revolution in Americans' perception of the proper role of government in health care. At the same time, another revolution in health care was taking place—the managed care revolution, which has brought rapid and sweeping changes to the country's health care delivery system. Physician services are no exception. Changes in the delivery of physician services are being driven by general market forces as well as by lifestyle preferences of physicians themselves. This book explores how these forces and preferences have shaped, and will continue to shape, the way medicine is practiced.

This book grew out of my teaching experience at Columbia University where, in 1995, I developed and taught physician practice management, a graduate course for students interested in the management of these special types of health care organizations. The course, the first of its kind at Columbia's School of Public Health, focused on how physicians organize to render care and how physician organizations are evolving in response to revolutionary changes in the health care delivery system.

While doing research in preparation for the course syllabus and reading list, I discovered a dearth of relevant literature. Nothing covered the field of practice management at a level beyond that of simple practice administration. To provide students with the interdisciplinary background needed to understand complex structural changes as well as other contemporary issues in physician practice management, I called on a number of experts in accounting, health administration, law, and economics. This partnering has led to the development of *Integrating the Practice of Medicine: A Decision Maker's Guide to Organizing and Managing Physician Services.*

This book is intended to be a comprehensive yet practical guide for health care executives, practice management executives, and students of health care administration. Balancing theory with practice, it examines emerging developments in the physician practice industry, explains essential methods of delivering physician services, and provides physician-hospital integration models. To facilitate its use, the book is divided into seven parts: Changes in Physician Supply and Practice Organizations; Physician Compensation and Reimbursement Mechanisms; Physician Services Organization and Delivery; The Valuation and Sale of Physician Practices; Evolving Physician Practice Organizational Models; Management Services Organizations; and The Future of Physician Services in the Managed Care Environment.

All of us who participated in this book's development hope it will clarify current trends in the organization and management of physician services.

This book would not have been possible without the help of two people. Christin Caryl was an MPH student at Columbia who participated in Physician Practice Management, first as a student, and then as a research assistant, helping with the administrative and research activities that are a necessary part of a project such as this. Eleanor Conners provided a vast amount of support—focusing initially on the administrative aspects of this project, and later, helping to create the needed time to complete the manuscript. To Ellie, without whose help and continuing support this project would never have been completed—thank you.

1

The Current State of the Physician Services Market

Ronald B. Conners, PhD

A dominant feature of the current health care environment is the ongoing revolution in the way physician services are organized and managed. Beginning with the introduction of the resource-based relative value scale (RBRVS) in 1993, the physician services market continues to undergo accelerating change reflected in the growth of managed care organizations (MCOs), the decline of fee-for-service (FFS) reimbursement, the growth of discounted FFS and capitation as a method of physician reimbursement, and the shift in delivery system focus to population-based services.

These paradigm-breaking changes are resulting in an ongoing transformation of the practice of medicine, moving the industry from an atomistic market structure to increasing levels of concentration, integration, and consolidation. The physician services market has been transitioning from a solo to a group practice structure for some years, but recently its transformation has accelerated—stimulated by the tremendous structural changes occurring within the delivery system. This chapter identifies some of the most significant changes and their impact on the physician services market.

EMERGENCE OF MANAGED CARE AS A MARKET DISCIPLINE

The introduction of Medicare and Medicaid together with retrospective cost reimbursement resulted in a dramatic upward shift in the demand for health care services. This rising demand for health care services, together with inflationary tendencies in the external economy, resulted in rapid escalation of health care prices. For many years, growth in the medical care component of the consumer price index has exceeded growth in the consumer price index for the overall economy.

A significant portion of inflationary growth in medical care prices is reflected in the rising health care insurance premiums paid by businesses. The growth in employee health benefit costs and their seemingly uncontrollable nature played an important role in the development of health care cost containment strategies by businesses.

Historically, businesses provided health benefits to their employees through indemnity insurance plans. As premiums for these plans continued to rise, firms sought to control costs by "managing care"—using self-insurance strategies, such as direct contracting, converting from indemnity insurance programs to HMO plans, or placing more pressure on existing insurers to monitor and control utilization. As these cost control strategies evolved, patient care would become more closely managed by the firms paying the bill. Utilization of services would be controlled through preauthorization requirements, monitoring of care plans, and limitations on the use of specialist care.

The success of these cost-control strategies reflects a shift in market power from the producers of health care to its consumers, increasing their control over pricing. Consumers of health care services are able to impose discipline within the marketplace by focusing on the specific details of the care process—defining who the acceptable providers are and placing limits on the care to be provided. In short, managed care emerged from the efforts of business to control health care costs.

The emerging and accelerating force of managed care as a market discipline has placed significant economic pressures on individual practitioners who may find themselves with insufficient market power to compete effectively (that is, to maintain an adequate level of referrals paying FFS prices). In many instances, long-established solo practices find increasing problems in a market more frequently dominated by HMOs, preferred provider organizations (PPOs), large integrated delivery systems (IDSs), and other organizational forms that have the primary effect of reducing the availability of patients.

Managed care has made the market for physician services far more competitive, emphasizing providers who have the ability to organize the practice of medicine into groups large enough to engage in areawide contracting and to provide physician services to ever larger population groups. Historically, physicians practiced in solo practitioner models and were paid a fee for each service rendered (FFS payment model). In the managed care environment, reimbursement is no longer on an FFS basis, but more commonly on a discounted FFS or capitation basis. A further change in the practice model is the shift from care of individual patients to a more population-oriented focus. Physicians now seek contracts for the care of large groups of patients, not individual patients. This shift from an FFS, private practice orientation to a more population-focused, discounted FFS or capitated payment method of organizing and providing care is a major revolution in the physician services marketplace.

Moreover, MCOs (defined as HMOs, PPOs, and IDSs) continue to increase in market share, evolving into new forms and expanding into new geographical areas. These organizations, which are themselves undergoing substantial consolidation, are experiencing increasing enrollments because they have proved their ability to lower the cost of hospital and physician services. As long as they continue to show they can maintain or lower health care costs, they will continue to be a significant force in the marketplace.

Physicians in active practice have been faced with tremendous external environmental change over the past decade. These macroenvironmental forces (that is, growth in MCOs, shift to capitation, and growth in population focus) have had a massive impact on the day-to-day operation of medical practices—directing physicians toward concentrating their market power, focusing on information systems and outcome measures, and concurrently stimulating the development of management services organizations (MSOs) and physician practice management companies (PPMCs).

BENEFITS OF MEDICAL PRACTICE CONSOLIDATION

The structure of the physician services market is influenced by the presence of economies of scale, defined as a decline in average cost per visit as practice size increases. The presence of scale economies in the practice of medicine has become more economically significant as buyers of physician services exercise growing amounts of power in this marketplace.

Reinhardt has presented evidence of economies of scale in group practices.[1] Physicians who are members of a group practice generate more visits and more revenue while functioning in a more efficient setting than the traditional solo practitioner.[2] Frech and Ginsburg also have provided evidence that the solo practice model is inefficient.[3]

Group practices have greater market power because they can lower the cost per visit. It is this market power that is critical in the managed care environment, providing the economic incentive for physician practices to become ever larger and to seek modifications in organizational form as a part of the quest to control referrals and lower costs. Buyers increasingly prefer to contract with a single provider of physician services to efficiently render care to their insured populations.

It is a combination of the economic incentive of lowering unit cost and the organizational preferences of buyers that has stimulated the development of group practice models such as independent practice associations, group practices without walls, and physician hospital organizations.

Significant economic and organizational benefits can be gained from consolidating physician practices. These benefits (in the form of lowered unit costs and higher quality) will accrue to the purchasers of physician service, primarily MCOs and, downstream, patients. To the extent that the lower average cost per patient visit materially increases the consolidated physician practices' ability to obtain more or larger managed care contracts, the participating physicians will benefit through increased patient volume.

The following are some of the economic and organizational benefits of consolidating physician practices:

- Lower cost per visit in the form of reduced overhead costs, increased purchasing power, and improved staffing ratios
- Increased physician productivity
- Enhanced marketing capability
- Improved access to capital and the potential for greater financial stability
- Improved educational and training opportunities
- Greater ability to enter risk-bearing contractual arrangements
- Ability to support improved billing and information systems
- Capability to engage in standardized care plan development, benchmarking, improved peer review processes, and other quality- and cost-enhancing programs

Viewed alternatively, physicians participating in group practice models do so at a substantial loss in autonomy, sacrificing the freedom of solo practice for the benefits of a collective form of practice. However, some evidence indicates that physicians in group practices receive higher compensation, so there may be a significant economic cost associated with practice autonomy.

In most physician practices, the cost of physician salaries and benefits typically ranges from 40 to 60 percent of total practice costs. Consequently, the per-unit cost of solo practice physician services will not decline unless physician compensation falls or practice overhead is reduced. Practice consolidation is, therefore, one of the important strategies for lowering per-unit cost because it allows practice overhead to be spread over a larger number of physicians.

THE NEED FOR MEDICAL PRACTICE MANAGEMENT

The complexity of managing and administering medical practices continues to escalate as regulators and payers place greater demands on physician providers.

Administrative Burdens

MCOs, as well as Medicare and Medicaid payers, have developed specific criteria that are preconditions of payment. It has long been common for physicians rendering care to specify on the bill the exact nature of the service provided, coding both the diagnosis and specific services in an alphanumeric coding scheme, using the diagnosis-oriented *International Classification of Diseases,* 9th revision (called the ICD-9 coding system)[4] or the procedure-oriented *Current Procedural Terminology,* 4th edition (called the CPT-4 coding method).[5]

The requirement that each incidence of service be coded in detail and that the codes used have internal consistency and be able to survive the computerized edits within the payer's claim-processing system, together with the unique billing formats required by each payer, makes the physician billing activity complex. Each payer has specific data requirements that must be met before payment, with little standardization among payers. Moreover, payers increasingly demand preauthorization before procedures may be done, require extensive documentation to medically justify an intervention, and reject or otherwise delay claims for failure to submit materials in the required format. These administrative requirements place continually increasing demands on practice managers, raising costs, generating larger receivables, and otherwise imposing serious burdens on the practice of medicine. Particularly in the solo practice setting, this increased complexity forces physicians to focus on administrative issues to ensure economic viability.

Increased Price and Quality Competition

Concurrent with the increase in administrative burdens, physicians also are being pressured by external forces to engage in both price and quality competition. Price competition occurs in the form of discounting the customary charges of the physician, called discounted FFS pricing, or of accepting the risks associated with a prospective flat pricing per member, per month system in return for high-volume contracts covering many lives. As a component of this increased pricing pressure, payers often demand information on outcomes from the practice, which is a form of nonprice competition.

For the physician to shift emphasis from price to quality, large information system investments are needed. These are required not only to reduce the administrative burdens associated with claims processing and billing management, but also to enable the acquisition and analysis of provider-specific data on outcomes and practice effectiveness. Access to information on quality of care by consumers and payers will increasingly be a mandate for physician providers, and the focal point of this must be physician-specific profiles.

These complexities in the management of medical practices may induce physicians to consider working with an MSO to reduce day-to-day practice management concerns or compel them either to seek alternative forms of practice, or, in some cases, to sell their practice.

The sale of a physician practice, in its more common current form, is to an MSO; which can itself be owned by an integrated delivery system or, possibly, is a publicly traded for-profit company offering an equity type model to the selling physician. From the physicians' point of view, the sale of the practice is accompanied by a long-term employment agreement, often with specific productivity requirements. The physician is then able to shift focus to the practice of medicine, leaving the business elements of the practice to the MSO.

EMERGENCE OF PHYSICIAN CORPORATIONS AND FOR-PROFIT HEALTH PLANS

The most striking developments of the current revolution in the way physician practices are organized and managed is the emergence of local, regional, and national physician corporations. On a local or regional level, hospitals or other IDSs develop MSOs to provide physician practice management services on a fee basis or actually purchase physician practices to establish control over the referral stream. In the case where the MSO purchases the physician practice, it then engages in the direct management of that practice.

On a regional or national level, physician practice management companies (PPMCs) have brought enormous amounts of investment capital to the industry through private placements or public offerings. Thus PPMCs have, almost overnight, become a serious force in the physician services market.

PPMCs develop market power by managing or purchasing physician practices and installing standardized administrative systems within them. This reduces the time spent by the physician in administrative activities, thus raising physician productivity by enabling him or her to focus primarily on patient care. Physician billing and profiling systems are provided by the PPMC, which often simultaneously manages the practice's nonclinical staff. Further economies are achieved by consolidation of purchasing, control over malpractice liability insurance premiums (because a regional or national risk-sharing pool may be developed), and the ability to seek regional and national managed care contracts. A common business practice among PPMCs is to develop a large organization of physicians and then contract with an HMO for the provision of physician services, sometimes using capitation for payment.

At the same time that regional and national physician corporations (such as PhyCor, MedPartners, Caremark, FPA Medical Management, InPhyNet, Coastal, and so on) emerge, for-profit health plans (such as Aetna, Cigna, Wellpoint, FHP, U.S. Healthcare, and so on) also are becoming national in their scope. These integration developments extend the opportunity for cost savings through the availability of enormous scale economies.

To appreciate the rapid growth of PPMCs, figure 1-1 shows the number of physician practices acquired by public companies between 1993 and 1996. The industry itself grew from $1.1 billion in revenues in 1992 to an estimated $5.1 billion in 1995. Amazingly, the 1995 PPMC market

FIGURE 1-1. Number of Practices Acquired by Public Companies

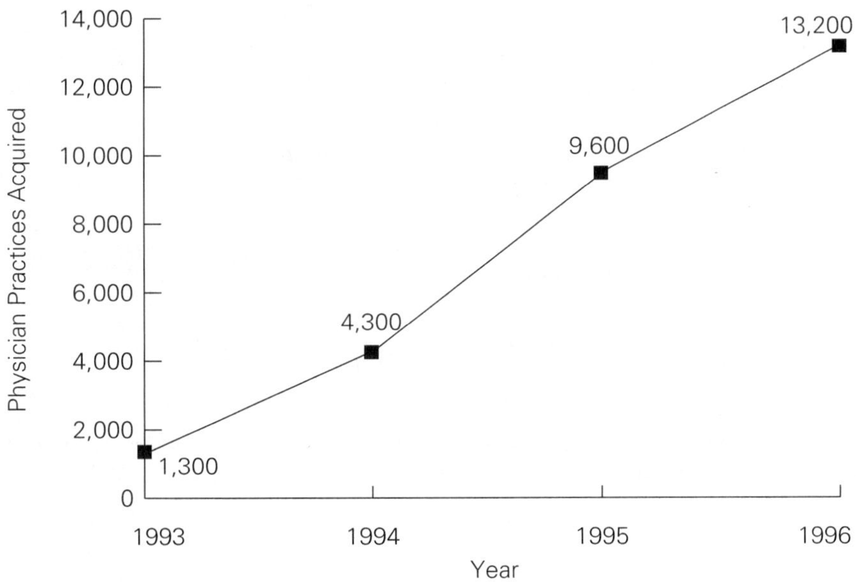

Source: The Advisory Board, *The Rising Tide: Emergence of a New Competitive Standard in Health Care* (Washington, DC: The Advisory Board Co., 1996), p. 10.

share has been estimated at only about 2 percent. This market share is growing, with Volpe, Welty & Co. projecting a 20 percent share by the year 2000.[6] Whether these projections are accurate remains to be seen. However, it is clear that the physician services market will not be the same in the years to come.

CONCLUSION

The practice of medicine within the past 10 years has undergone revolutionary change, primarily as a result of the cost containment initiatives inherent in a managed care environment. From the perspective of physician services, the most prominent features of this new model are the rising dominance of the consumer, the decline in the economic power of the physician, and the increased emphasis on value in physician services market transactions. To respond effectively to these changes in the physician services market, physicians are reorganizing and restructuring the way they practice medicine.

References

1. Uwe E. Reinhardt, "A Production Function for Physician Services," *Review of Economics and Statistics* 54 (Feb. 1972): 55–56.

2. Douglas M. Brown, "Do Physicians Underutilize Aides?" *Journal of Human Resources* 23, no. 3 (1988): 342–55.

3. H. E. Frech and P. Ginsburg, "Optimal Scale in Medical Practice: A Survivor Analysis," *Journal of Business* 47 (1974): 23–26.

4. *International Classification of Diseases,* 9th rev. (Los Angeles: Practice Management Information Corp., 1994).

5. *Current Procedural Terminology,* 4th ed. (Chicago: American Medical Association, 1996).

6. The Advisory Board, *The Rising Tide: Emergence of a New Competitive Standard in Health Care* (Washington, DC: The Advisory Board Co., 1996).

PART I

Changes in Physician Supply and Practice Organizations

The first step toward comprehending the organization and management of physician services is to understand the changes in physician supply and the distribution of physicians with regard to practice size. This section consists of two chapters. Chapter 2, "The Supply of Physicians," describes those forces affecting the current physician supply and examines future supply in light of expected reductions in the need for specialists. Chapter 3, "Physician Practice Size, 1991–1995," examines the decline in the number of solo practitioners and the rapid increase in the number of physicians practicing in group or institutional settings, particularly within the past few years. The consequences of this growth are explored within the framework of a managed care environment, with particular emphasis on management of the continuum of care.

2

The Supply of Physicians

Uwe E. Reinhardt, PhD

By virtue of their technical expertise and the authority vested in them by the state, physicians form the core of any modern health system. Thus, the supply of physicians has long been a concern of public policy in this country and elsewhere.

During the four decades preceding World War II, it was widely believed that the United States suffered from a surplus of physicians. However, following the war and until about the mid-1970s, it was generally assumed that there were too few physicians, especially after the introduction in the mid-1960s of the Medicare program for the elderly and the Medicaid program for the poor. In 1970, for example, there were approximately 156 physicians per 100,000 population, of which only about 115 per 100,000 population were so-called patient care physicians—those who had finished their graduate medical education and devoted their time fully to direct patient care.[1]

At that time, the United States embarked on an ambitious program of medical school expansion, largely with funds made available by both the state and federal governments. By the late 1970s, the expansion program had more than doubled the number of first-year places in American allopathic and osteopathic medical schools, from about 9,500 in the mid-1960s to 19,000.[2] In addition, the United States admitted an ever larger influx of international medical graduates (IMGs) into its residency programs, in many instances simply to staff inner-city teaching hospitals that were consistently shunned by American medical school graduates.

The sudden but sustained jump in the number of physicians graduating from residency has the effect each year of adding more physicians to the national pool than those retiring from it. Because the resulting net addition is small relative to the pool's size, the overall effect of the policy on the physician-population ratio is gradual, but inexorable, and its full effect will not be felt until several decades after the expansion program.

Figure 2-1 illustrates these long-term effects. It shows that the ratio of patient care physicians per 100,000 population has gradually risen from 115 in 1970 to 182 in 1990, and is expected to continue to rise until about the year 2010, when it will peak and then decline slightly. A fundamental question confronting policy makers and, most certainly, American physicians already in the field or in the pipeline is whether this growing supply of physicians per 100,000 population is actually needed and, if not, what the government or anyone else ought to do about a projected surplus.

Other things being equal, the gradual aging of the American population would naturally require a proportionate increase in the nation's

FIGURE 2-1. Actual and Projected Supply of Physicians in the United States, 1950–2020

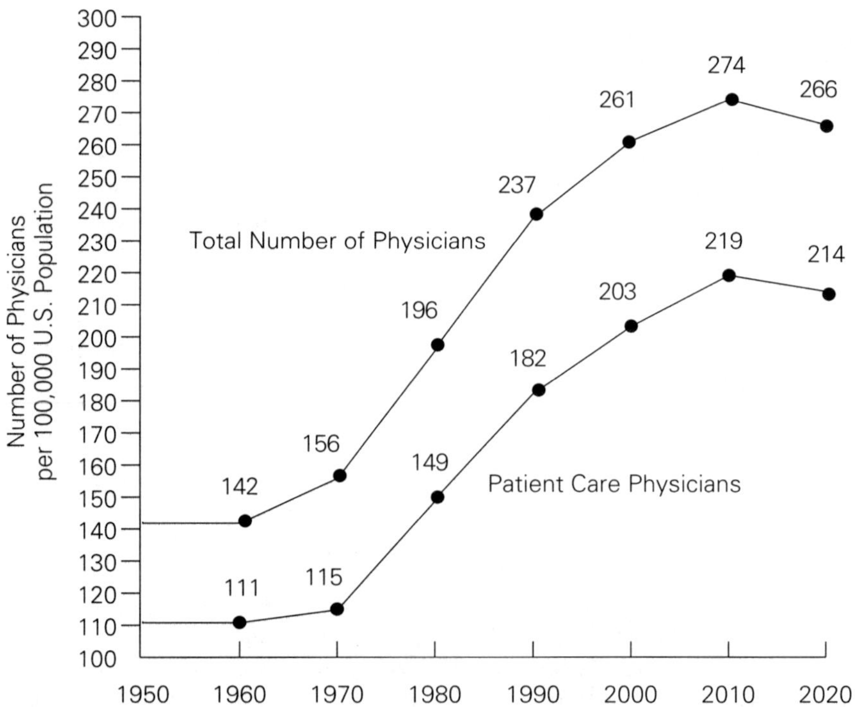

Source: From David A. Kindig, "Strategic Issues for Managing the Future Physician Workforce," in *Strategic Choices for a Changing Health System,* ed. Stuart H. Altman and Uwe E. Reinhardt (Chicago: Health Administration Press, 1996), p. 55; and Institute of Medicine, *The Nation's Physician Workforce: Options for Balancing Supply and Requirements* (Washington, DC: National Academy Press, 1966), p. 25.

physician-population ratio. The currently projected time path of that ratio, however, appears by all estimates to exceed those requirements. Furthermore, "other things" have not remained equal since the 1960s and 1970s. As the supply of physicians in this country grows, the American health system is shifting from the erstwhile open-ended, uncontrolled, fee-for-service system toward novel clinical, economic, and organizational arrangements generally lumped together under the ill-defined catchall term *managed care*. This shift is expected to accelerate the move toward a sizable physician surplus, because managed care systems typically require far fewer physicians per 100,000 population than does the open-ended, unmanaged, fee-for-service system.

However, if history is any guide, any forecast of the future physician workforce must be viewed with some caution. Because the U.S. health care system is highly dynamic, the demand-and-supply side of the market tends to interact to either overcome what was predicted to be a shortage or absorb what was predicted to be a surplus. Part of this continual adaptation is nothing other than basic economics. If a resource is scare, its price tends to be high and production technology changes to economize on its use; thus, the demand for it falls. Similarly, when a resource becomes plentiful, its price tends to fall and society finds added uses for that relatively cheaper resource; thus, the demand for it rises. It is so with human labor, just as it is with lumber and crude oil. Physicians are no exception to this basic law of demand and supply.

This chapter explores these trends and speculates about their impact on the future economic position of the American medical profession. It presents a very simple forecasting model that highlights the tenuous nature of such exercises; examines managed care as one major driver of future physician requirements; discusses how government ought to react to the sizable surplus of physicians predicted by virtually all recent studies of the American health workforce; focuses on one particularly inviting target of public health–workforce policy (the influx of IMGs into the U.S. health system); and, finally, offers some thoughts on the future economic conditions of American medicine.

FRAMEWORK FOR ASSESSING FUTURE PHYSICIAN REQUIREMENTS

The following basic steps in forecasting the future supply of and requirements for physicians are always the same:

1. The forecast begins with a projection of changes in the size and sociodemographic composition of the population to be served by physicians.

2. The forecast is translated into a projection of that population's "need" or "demand" for physician services.
3. On the basis of an assumed physician-productivity ratio (defined as the average number of physician services procured per year per physician), the projected service requirement is then translated into the corresponding number of full-time equivalent (FTE) physicians needed to produce the required services.
4. The projected requirement of physicians is compared to the supply of patient care physicians likely to be yielded by the projected population and by additional physicians recruited from abroad. This comparison points out potential future imbalances that may require remedial public policy.

Figure 2-2 distills these tasks into a compact physician-forecasting equation. The point of presenting this equation here is to identify the numerous factors that drive a health workforce projection and to highlight the complex interaction among them. Because many of the terms in the equation are multiplicative, the effect on the projected physician surplus or deficit caused by a forecasting error in one factor may be either amplified or tempered by the other variables in the equation. Thus, such forecasting errors can easily throw even the most carefully prepared forecast off the actual future trajectory of physician supply. That circumstance alone can explain why past health workforce forecasts have so often missed the mark ex post. A second reason for missing the mark, of course, is that any projected or real imbalance in the health workforce can trigger reactions from within the health system and sometimes from policy makers.

Supply of Physicians

The summary variable A_t in figure 2-2 denotes the projected supply of physicians expected to devote their time fully to direct patient care activities in some future year t. It is the product of the number of physicians projected to be alive in that year (S_t), the fraction of that supply not in retirement in that year (a_t), and the fraction of professionally active physicians in year t who devote all their time to patient care (c_t). None of these variables can be projected with a high degree of accuracy.

Number of Physicians Alive in the Future In a closed economy with a stable flow of annual graduations from medical school, the number of physicians expected to be alive in year t could be projected with reasonable accuracy, even a decade or more into the future. Because the number of medical school places in the United States has been more or less constant since the mid-1970s, and because there is perennial excess

FIGURE 2-2. Sample Forecasting Model for the Physician Workforce

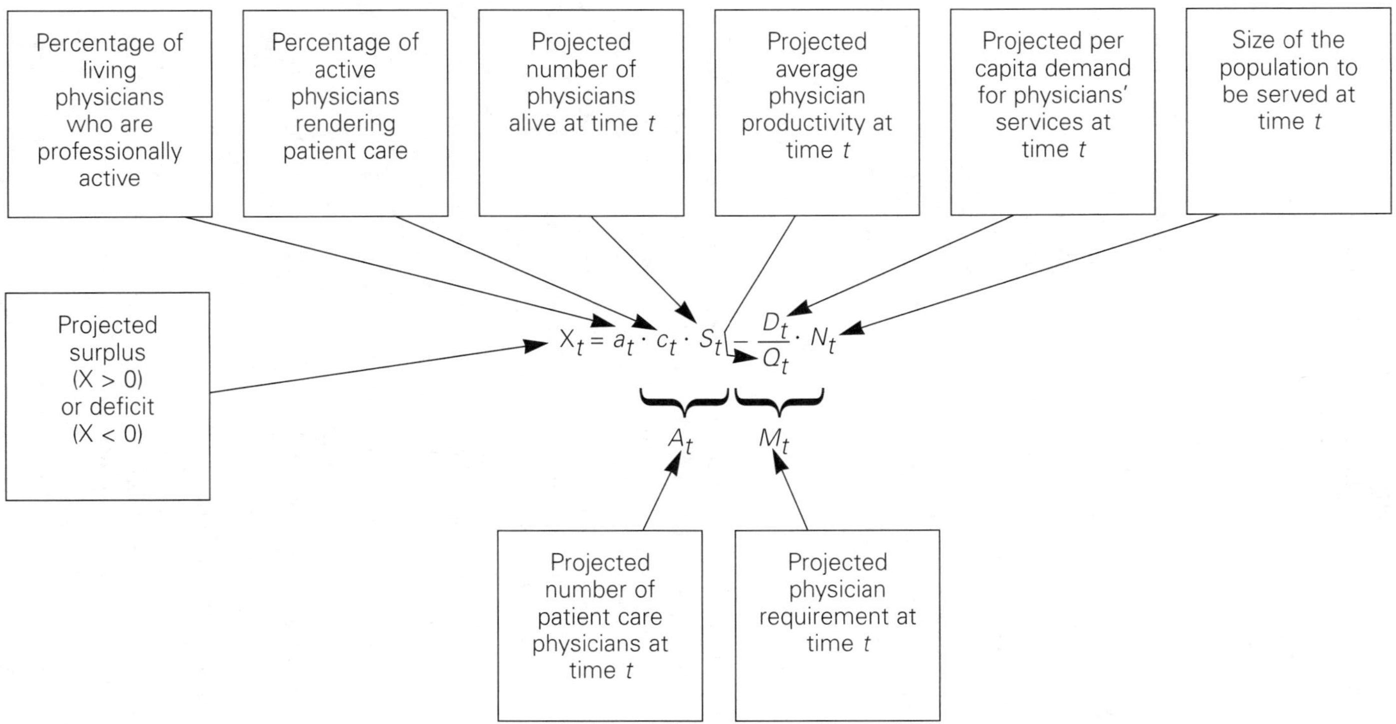

Source: Uwe E. Reinhardt, "Health Manpower Forecasting: The Case of Physician Supply," in *Health Services Research: Key to Health Policy*, ed. Eli Ginzberg (Cambridge, MA: Harvard University Press, 1991), p. 252.

demand for admission to these places, the homegrown contribution to the pool of physicians can be predicted with remarkable precision. In the United States, however, the number of homegrown additions to the physician supply has long been supplemented by a sizable inflow of IMGs. In 1993, for example, IMGs represented 22 percent of all medical graduate residents in the United States, a ratio that has continued to grow.[3]

Percentage of Professionally Active Physicians The fraction of living physicians who are professionally active depends on the age composition of the physician supply in year *t* and on economic factors that drive the decision of older physicians to retire. For example, it now is widely believed that the spread of managed care will drive into early retirement many older American physicians who developed their ideal conception of medicine under traditional, open-ended, unmanaged, fee-for-service (FFS) medicine. However, a recent survey of physicians suggests that, despite their growing frustrations, many worry about the adequacy of their retirement funds and thus continue to work.[4] Because the factors triggering early retirement are balanced by those triggering postponement of retirement, the actual future pattern of exits from the physician pool remains highly uncertain at this time.

Percentage of Active Physicians in Direct Patient Care In the past, the fraction of professionally active physicians working mainly in direct patient care was relatively stable. However, it is unlikely to remain so because the demands of the managed care model will simultaneously push many physicians out of patient care and into the added corps of administrative personnel needed by managed care systems. This will be particularly so if the U.S. Congress makes it easier for physicians and hospitals to form so-called provider-sponsored networks (PSNs) capable of offering the full range of health care services against receipt of an annual capitation—that is, capable of functioning as an insurance carrier and a health care delivery system under one organizational roof. How successful PSN development will be is anybody's guess at present.[5] Similarly, little is known about how massive the predicted migration of physicians from patient care to other health care–related tasks will be in the future.

Demand for Physicians

Summary variable M_t in figure 2-2 represents the demand side of the market for physicians. It is driven by three variables:

1. The size of the population to be served in future year *t* (variable N_t)

2. The per capita demand for the kind of services physicians provide (variable D_t)
3. The degree of productivity with which physicians provide these services (Q_t)

It may be noted in passing that the ratio D_t/Q_t in figure 2-2 reduces to nothing other than the physician-to-population ratio projected to be required in the forecast year *t*. This is so because, conceptually, variable D_t denotes total physician services divided by total population, whereas Q_t denotes total physician services divided by the total number of patient care physicians, and the term *total physician services* cancels out. As discussed later in this chapter, many health workforce forecasters who do not wish to bother making separate projections about the future per capita demand for physician services and future physician productivity simply posit normative physician-population ratios—so-called benchmark ratios—to estimate future physician requirements.

Future Population to Be Served For periods as short as a decade, the size of the U.S. population can be predicted with reasonable accuracy, although the U.S. Bureau of the Census usually projects several population scenarios to hedge its bets. In practical applications, adjustments must be made, of course, for the demographic composition of the population because the need for and use of health care is known to vary predictably with age and gender. That adjustment is not made in figure 2-2, solely to keep the display simple. To adjust for demographic shifts in practice, a separate physician requirement figure usually is projected for each distinct age-gender group in the forecasting model. That composition, too, can be projected reasonably accurately for horizons within a decade or two.

It is a popular but erroneous belief that the steady increase in the average age of the American population has been a major driver of the use of health services in this country and, therefore, of health spending. Actually, that demographic trend has hitherto been so slow as to have had only a minor impact on the use of health services and on health spending. For example, in their projection of health spending through the year 2000, Sonnefeld and colleagues observe that although Americans aged 65 and over spend an average of more than four times as much on health care as do those under age 65, the aging of the population is so gradual that "changes in the age-sex composition of the population will contribute only 4.7 percent to the 147 percent increase in total personal health care expenditures from 1990 to 2000."[6] This observation applies not only to the period 1990–2000, but it will remain valid roughly until the year 2015, when the first baby boomers reach age 65. Only thereafter will the average age of the population increase more rapidly. Year-to-year changes in the age composition of the population then will become a much more dominant driver of physician requirements and of overall health spending than they will be in the next two decades.

Per Capita Demand for Physician Services The projected future per capita use of physician services within each age-gender cohort is a highly problematic variable. At the conceptual level, the question arises whether this variable should be defined as the need for physician services identified by panels of objective, clinical experts or, alternatively, as the demand for physician services likely to present itself in year *t*. The needs-based projection is driven mainly by purely demographic and clinical factors. It depends on not only clinical and demographic factors, but also a whole host of socioeconomic and political factors that characterize the economic circumstances faced by American families during the forecast horizon.

Prominent among the economic variables driving the demand for physician services is the extent of health insurance coverage in the American population and the nature of that coverage (that is, whether it is tightly controlled managed care coverage, more loosely controlled managed care, or, say, the traditional indemnity insurance now being promised under the so-called medical savings accounts [MSAs]). The extent and nature of health insurance coverage, in turn, are driven by the average per capita family income of the American population and, more important, by the distribution of family income above and below this average. Finally, the extent of insurance coverage in any nation is driven by the prevailing social ethic and the political climate that this social ethic begets.

Currently, only about 85 percent of the American population has health insurance of any sort (although not all these have comprehensive coverage) and about 15 percent has no health insurance at all.[7] The latter percentage is projected to grow inexorably in the future as American business continues to reengineer its workforce. Practically, the reengineering of the nation's private sector causes people to be laid off and thus to lose their health insurance coverage. Even if the discarded employees find new employment elsewhere, they may be either rehired only on a contract basis (but without fringe benefits) or work for small companies that do not offer health insurance.

At present, it is anybody's guess whether Congress will eventually move to extend insurance coverage to all American families and, if so, when. Evidently, a decision to move toward universal coverage would have some impact on the future requirement of physicians because uninsured Americans tend to use only about 60 percent of the health services used by similarly situated, insured Americans.[8]

From the perspective of health workforce forecasting, however, much more important than universal coverage is the general nature of health insurance coverage in the United States—that is, how extensively that coverage will be structured predominantly around managed care and how tightly the delivery of care will in fact be managed. Because that facet of health insurance is likely to dwarf any impact that a move to universal coverage per se could have on the future demand for physicians, the role of managed care in health workforce forecasting is explored more fully in the following section.

Physician Productivity The average number of services produced annually by a physician is the product of the hours worked per year by the physician and the number of services produced per hour. The average annual number of hours worked by physicians depends on age and especially gender. For example, health services researchers have found that, on average, female physicians tend to work fewer hours than their male colleagues. Additionally, female physicians tend to see fewer patients per hour, although the differential appears to have shrunk somewhat over time.[9]

A major source of variation in a physician's hourly productivity is the extent to which the tasks he or she may perform are delegated to qualified support staff. Research shows that the degree of task delegation within medical practice can have a pronounced effect on the number of physicians required to care for a given population.[10] That circumstance alone introduces a high element of uncertainty into future physician workforce projections. Further, there is as yet little formal research on the impact of computers on measurable physician productivity.

Thus, as this simple forecasting model for the physician workforce demonstrates, any longer-term projection of the future supply of, and demand for, physicians is a highly uncertain undertaking whose product should always be taken with a grain of salt. This point will become visibly apparent in an exploration of physician staffing patterns in the managed care system.

MANAGED CARE AND FUTURE PHYSICIAN REQUIREMENTS

Although there does not yet exist a universally accepted definition of *managed care,* typically that arrangement involves selective contracting by those who pay for health—insurers—with those who provide it. Selective contracting allows insurers to either reward a favored provider with large numbers of insured patients or punish a recalcitrant one by shifting insured patients away from that provider toward more compliant providers. In that economic power resides the sway that insurance carriers have over providers under managed care.

Impact of Managed Care on Physician Decision Making and Productivity

Vis-à-vis the practicing physician, the economic power inherent in managed care arrangements is used to not only extract price concessions from the physician, but also directly influence his or her clinical decisions. The latter is achieved either indirectly, through statistical practice profiles, or directly, through application of clinical practice guidelines to individual medical cases, along with the requirement that the physician obtain the insurer's prior authorization for certain high-cost interventions. Failure on the physician's part to either produce an acceptable practice profile or play along with more direct interventions into his or her clinical decisions can trigger the economic weapon in the insurer's hand—expulsion of the physician from the selective insurance contract.

Managed care impacts the future requirement of physicians through both the annual per capita demand for physician services and the annual number of physician services produced per physician—in short, physician productivity. On the one hand, managed care serves to directly reduce the number of physician services going into the responses to given medical cases—especially inpatient services and the more expensive services of medical specialists. On the other hand, however, it also tends to induce medical groups or individual physicians who contract with HMOs or other forms of integrated systems to enhance physician productivity through tighter scheduling or the delegation of certain tasks to nonphysician personnel. That response tends to increase the productivity variable in the forecast equation (see figure 2-2).

HMO Staffing Levels Used as Benchmarks

At present, managed care is still evolving. Thus, it appears in many guises, with distinct regional flavors. On average, however, most managed care systems require fewer physicians per 100,000 population at risk than does the traditional, unmanaged, fee-for-service system. According to a recent study of staffing patterns in managed care systems, physicians in staff or group model HMOs tend to number below 120 per 100,000 enrollees.[11] For some large HMOs, that ratio has been found to be as low as 77. By contrast, the ratio of patient care physicians per 100,000 population for the United States as a whole already exceeds 180 (see figure 2-1).

However, before observed staffing ratios in HMOs can be used as benchmarks for the country as a whole, they need to be adjusted for differences between the mix of enrollees in those HMOs and the composition of the U.S. population. Figure 2-3, adapted from the same study, shows these adjusted staffing ratios. Weiner used them to project physician requirements in the year 2000, under various assumptions about the

FIGURE 2-3. Number of Physicians Required per 100,000 Population under Different Health Systems

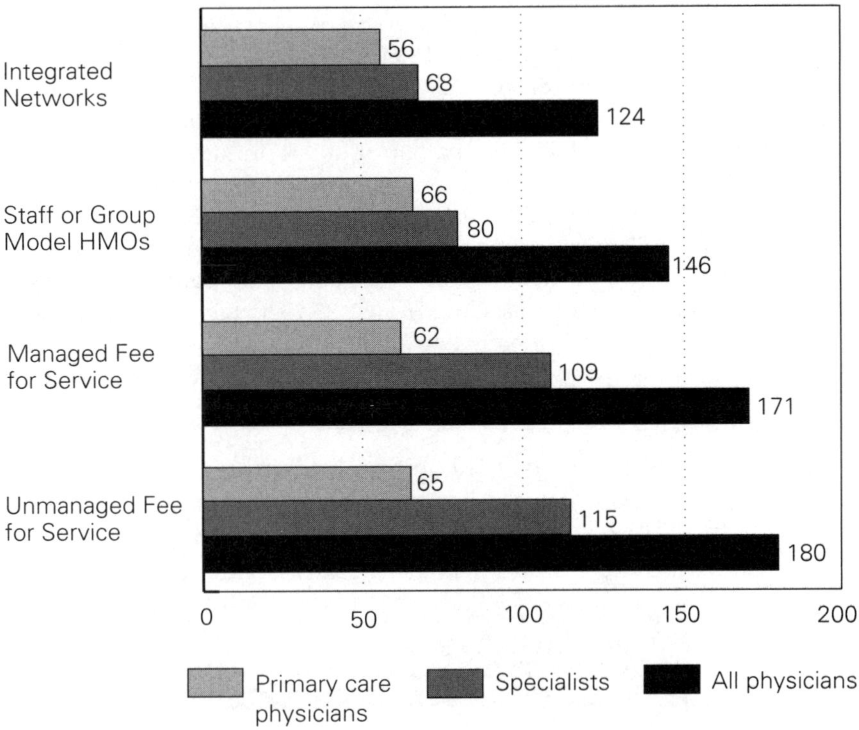

Source: Data from Jonathan Weiner, "Forecasting the Effects of Health Reform on U.S. Physician Workforce Requirement: Evidence from HMO Staffing Patterns," *JAMA* 272, no. 3 (1994): table 6.

future growth of managed care in the United States. For example, he estimates that if 40 to 65 percent of Americans were to receive their health care through integrated, managed care networks, by the year 2000 the supply of, and demand for, primary care physicians would be more or less in balance whereas the supply of specialists would outstrip requirements by as much as 60 percent. Overall, Weiner predicts that the supply of physicians in the year 2000 will exceed requirements by about 165,000 physicians, which means nearly one-third of the entire physician supply in the year 2000 would not be needed.

A more recent (1996) study of physician requirements by Goodman and colleagues points in the same direction, although it uses the following different normative benchmarks.[12]

- The average staffing pattern of a sample of not-for-profit HMOs
- The observed physician-to-population ratio in the hospital referral regions of Minneapolis

- The analogous ratio observed in the hospital referral area of Wichita, Kansas

The observed benchmark staffing patterns, once again adjusted for the age-gender composition of the U.S. population, are shown in figure 2-4. Interestingly, the observed, adjusted physician-population ratios for Wichita (with an HMO penetration rate of less than 5 percent) are lower for both generalists and specialists than they are in Minneapolis, where the HMO penetration rate is about 40 percent.

Depending on the particular benchmark used for comparison, Goodman and colleagues find that the ratio of the actual U.S. physician supply in 1993 to the normative ratio implied by the benchmark ranges from 0.93 to 1.35 for generalists and from 1.23 to as high as 1.57 for specialists. For the United States as a whole, these ratios translate into an estimated surplus of 46,099 generalists and 60,927 specialists relative to

FIGURE 2-4. Number of Physicians Required per 100,000 Population, Alternative Benchmarks (Age Adjusted)

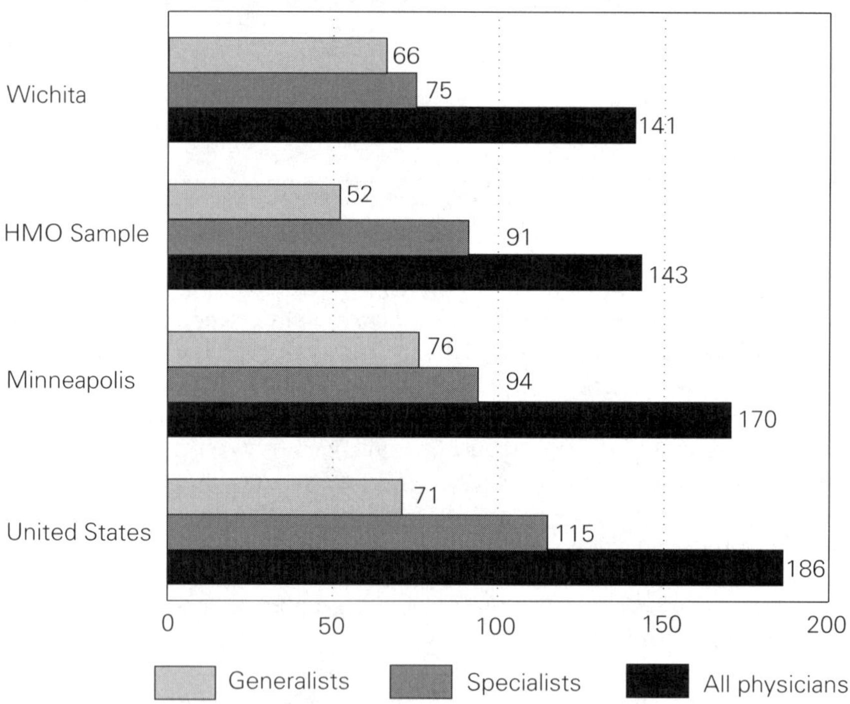

Source: American Medical Association Socioeconomic Monitoring System (SMS), 1991–1995 surveys.

the HMO benchmark; a surplus of 13,067 generalists and 99,619 specialists relative to the benchmark of Wichita; and a shortage of 12,588 generalists coupled with a surplus of 53,350 specialists relative to the benchmark of Minneapolis.

For a given benchmark, the relative size of the estimated excess supply varies by region. Naturally, it is particularly high in areas long favored by physicians. Against the benchmark staffing pattern furnished by the sample of HMOs, for example, Baltimore is estimated to have a surplus of about 2,500 physicians; Boston more than 5,000; Chicago about 2,500; New York City about 6,000; San Francisco about 2,100; and Washington, D.C., about 3,000.

Two important points must be noted in connection with this study. First, it illustrates once again just how sensitive the projected surplus or deficit of physicians is to the benchmark used as the normative benchmark physician-population ratio. Depending on the benchmark used by the authors, for example, their estimate points to either a deficit of 12,588 generalists for the United States as a whole, or a surplus of 46,099. This range of estimates represents about 30 percent of the total supply of generalists in the United States in 1993. Although this circumstance does not render such health workforce projections useless, it does highlight the need for extreme care in selecting the normative benchmarks used in such studies.

Second, it bears emphasizing that the estimated surplus or deficit for a particular hospital referral area is entirely hypothetical. The surplus or deficit would only occur if all the physician services rendered in the hospital referral region in question were produced with the assumed benchmark staffing pattern (here the average of the staffing patterns in the authors' benchmark sample of HMOs). In fact, the practice style still employed in the various hospital regions listed above is such as to absorb, so far, the bulk—if not all—of the estimated latent surpluses. Unless sustained pressure by employers and government on health plans forces the health system in those regions to adopt the more stringent benchmark staffing patterns assumed by Goodman, these latent surpluses may never become manifest in the form of unemployed physicians or drastically lowered physician incomes. Instead, they may remain purely hypothetical.

PUBLIC POLICY ON THE PHYSICIAN WORKFORCE

With the aid of the forecasting model presented earlier, it was shown how precariously dependent any projection of the future supply of or requirement for physicians is to numerous factors whose future time path must be projected as part of any such forecast. The sensitivity of projected surpluses and deficits to assumptions also was pointed out. Even so, despite the variance mere assumptions can induce in health workforce forecasts, by now the findings of several health workforce projections published in recent years have forged the broadly shared consensus that, in many regions of the United States, there soon will be a sizable surplus of medical specialists and, possibly, generalists. The migration of physicians from areas with high physician-to-population ratios to areas with relatively lower ratios cannot absorb the regional surpluses because most areas with relatively lower ratios nevertheless appear to have an abundant supply of physicians.

In short, the conventional wisdom at this time is that a sizable overall physician surplus looms for the United States as a whole.[13] This raises the question of what, if anything, government should do about it.

Government Controls on the Physician Supply

One school of thought advocates a highly interventionist public policy for one of two distinct reasons. First, there is a widely shared hypothesis that a surplus of physicians can be harmful to the patient's physical health and the nation's fiscal health. Within the context of traditional fee-for-service medicine, it is argued, a surplus may induce physicians to raise their fees, where possible, or to create an artificial demand for services that may be of dubious clinical merit. Alternatively, if the constraints of managed care prevent physicians from doing either of the above, a sizable surplus will severely depress physician income, which will demoralize the profession and thereby detract from the quality of patient care.

The second rationale is that government, both state and federal, directly or indirectly shoulders a large share of the cost of undergraduate and graduate medical education. Thus, it is only reasonable that if government pays for something, it has not only the right but the duty to control how much of that something it procures—whether airplanes for the Pentagon or physicians for the nation's health system.

These considerations have led to the view that the federal government ought to exercise tight control over the overall size of the nation's physician supply and the mix of specialties within it. That view was clearly articulated by Congress's influential Physician Payment Review Commission (PPRC) in its *Annual Report to the Congress, 1993*.[14] (See chapter 4.)

Evidently, the PPRC's recommendations inspired remarkably similar provisions contained in President Clinton's ill-fated Health Security Act (H.R. 3600, S.1557, Title III, Subsection A).[15] The act would have created a new National Council on Graduate Medical Education within the U.S. Department of Health and Human Services. The council would have been endowed with vast regulatory powers to direct the size and composition of the nation's health workforce, albeit after close consultation with the private accrediting bodies that have traditionally supervised the training of that workforce.

Finally, in a report published in 1995, the privately funded Pew Health Professions Commission went so far as to call for a reduction of first-year medical school places by 20 to 25 percent over the next decade, along with sharp cutbacks in the number of residency positions and restrictions on the number of IMGs allowed to immigrate into the United States.[16]

Central to the regulatory powers envisaged by the PPRC was creation of a national fund for graduate medical education to which all health insurance programs, both public and private, would contribute a percentage of their payments for health care. Congress would then set limits on the total number of residents to be supported by this national fund. In the PPRC proposal, first-year residency positions would not exceed the annual number of graduates from U.S. medical schools by more than 10 percent. (By contrast, in 1996, residency positions represented about 145 percent of the total number of MD and DO graduates from U.S. schools.[17]) A new federal body was to be created to allocate the limited total number of residency slots to the various medical specialties. Only approved residency positions in each specialty would be financially supported by the central fund. Although the PPRC did not formally recommend a particular specialty mix, it agreed with the general consensus that the proportion of residency slots in primary care specialties ought to be increased substantially from its current level, about 30 percent of all residencies, to perhaps as much as 50 percent.

Because the PPRC continued to support the tradition that payments for residency positions be made not to the residents directly but, rather, to the facilities employing the residents, the proposed policy would inevitably have required an explicit allocation of residency positions, by specialty, to different regions in the country and different teaching hospitals within each region. The PPRC stipulated that this allocation should be made strictly on the basis of the educational quality of training facilities and by the bodies that accredit graduate training. However, sooner or later, the politics of funding graduate medical education most probably would have drawn government directly into the intricacies of making this allocation, mainly on political criteria. It also would inadvertently have maintained the autonomy that the supply side in medical education has traditionally enjoyed in this country.

Reliance on the New Health Care Market

In a nutshell, proponents of government-regulated quotas for the size and mix of the health workforce argue that the supply side of the health sector always has been, and always will be, impervious to market signals emanating from the demand side. Although few students of American health care would take issue with the proposition as it relates to the past, the growth of selective contracting in health care during the past half-decade or so has led to a massive shift of economic power from the supply side to the demand side of the market. This shift in market power has made direct government controls over the health workforce obsolete, because selective contracting constrains the power of both the individual physician at the level of practice and the academic health center—the main source of the U.S. physician supply.[18]

At the level of medical practice, selective contracting effectively converts the economic status of patient care physicians from that of self-employed professionals and entrepreneurs into either formally employed professionals or self-employed subcontractors whose economic fate is in the hands of one or a few health plans. Unless the medical profession finds a way to erode (if not destroy) selective contracting, individual physicians will find it increasingly difficult to dictate either the volume of their services or the size of their fees.

It is hoped that the economic pressures described earlier will soon become apparent to prospective entrants into the medical profession. Given that they are among the best and brightest of the nation's young, the government ought, perhaps, to trust them to make the right decision in juxtaposing the probable pecuniary and psychic benefits from a future career in medicine against the risks faced by all employed professionals thrust into conditions of periodic surplus. If government wishes to intervene in that decision, it ought to confine itself to the assembly and dissemination of accurate information about the current and future market for physicians.[19]

The fact that health insurers can exclude academic health centers from their selective contracts threatens the autonomy of the institutions that train physicians. Rare and only temporarily fortunate is the academic health center that still enjoys the freedom to devote whatever real resources it chooses to treat particular illnesses, to charge whatever fee it wishes for each unit of real resource, and to subsidize from patient care revenues whatever other nonprofitable endeavors it fancies. Academic health centers that wish to survive and thrive in the new market environment must develop a high sensitivity for the signals emanating from the demand side of the health care market. In the process, they will reengineer themselves into a conglomerate that more separately operates the three enterprises within the academic health center: teaching, research, and patient care. Each of these enterprises will be operated with its own cost-accounting system, managerial goals, and corporate culture. The teaching enterprise will be financed by the traditional mix of private and public sources. The research enterprise also will be financed by a mix of public and private sources but will increasingly rely on commercial research contracts and joint ventures with commercial enterprises.

Finally, where feasible, the patient care arm of the conglomerate will be an integrated health care system that is capable of competing head-on with other for-profit or not-for-profit integrated health care networks in the marketplace. Inevitably, the nature of that competition will force this patient care enterprise to become organized and managed on principles that may be not-for-profit de jure but, in effect, will be commercial de facto. Such an enterprise may be viewed as a homegrown, for-profit philanthropist—fully owned by a not-for-profit conglomerate that maximizes health care market profits to fund the conglomerate's other two enterprises: education and research.[20] Given the leaner staffing pattern evidently preferred by well-managed health care systems, it is reasonable to believe that the reengineered academic health center, too, will move in the direction of this staffing pattern. That adaptation will automatically shift the academic health center away from the traditional, heavy reliance on specialty training toward greater emphasis on training in the primary care specialties.

To be sure, at this stage, these predictions are hypotheses rather than established facts. However, they are plausible enough to justify waiting a half-decade or so before subjecting the education and training of physicians to the heavy regulatory apparatus widely favored in this country only a few years ago.

Arguing that government ought not impose numerical quotas on medical education does not imply, of course, that it should take a hands-off approach to the issue. It cannot adopt that posture for the simple reason that it is already so deeply enmeshed financially with medical education. State governments now subsidize medical education directly through institutional grants to the states' public universities, including public medical schools. For its part, the federal government directly or indirectly subsidizes medical education and training at all levels. Indeed, the federal Medicare program is not just a health insurance program; it now is a major source of financing for graduate medical education in the United States, paying about $2 billion in 1995 in the form of subsidies to hospitals, specifically for the training of interns and residents.[21]

If it is accepted that the United States currently faces a growing surplus of physicians—especially medical specialists—and that current methods of financing physician training endows medical schools and teaching hospitals with too much autonomy over the size and composition of the nation's physician workforce, government must consider the following troublesome questions:

- Does it make sense to subsidize so heavily, and in so general a way, the production of something of which the nation has an excess supply?

- If the current general subsidies to undergraduate and graduate medical education cannot be justified any longer, do subcategories of medical trainees or specialties warrant encouragement through more carefully targeted subsidies?
- Should whatever subsidies government grants undergraduate and graduate medical education be funneled to students indirectly through payments made directly to medical schools and teaching hospitals, or should that flow of subsidies be redirected to the trainees themselves in the form of uniform, portable stipends, for which educational institutions would have to compete?

Limitations of space preclude a thorough exploration of these question within this chapter.[22] Suffice it to add that, ideally, graduate medical education should be structured and financed so that the teaching hospitals and ambulatory care facilities serving this function lack powerful economic incentives to impose their own narrow economic imperatives on the students' or society's interests. To that end, the facility should be financed strictly on a break-even basis—that is, in a way that does not make residents a source of cheap labor to be exploited for the benefit of either the facility or the physicians who supervise them, or both. A soul-searching question for the leaders of academic medicine is whether they agree with this basic principle and, if so, whether graduate medical education in this country has actually been run on it. If not, the time seems ripe for a major revision in the structure of public support for medical education in the United States.

ISSUE OF INTERNATIONAL MEDICAL GRADUATES

Whether or not government ought to impose direct quotas on medical education, there remains the question of whether the American health sector ought to remain as hospitable as it now is to the influx of IMGs. Figure 2-5, taken from the 1995 report of the Council on Graduate Medical Education (COGME), illustrates the growing importance of IMGs in the total pool of residents in this country. An estimated 80 percent tend to remain in the United States at the completion of their residency training.[23]

Reasons for the Influx of IMGs

The influx of IMGs into the United States is driven by the interplay of two distinct factors. On the supply side, a huge pool of talented professionals in other countries would like to match their skills and talents with the wondrously equipped American health sector, doing well in the

FIGURE 2-5. IMGs as a Percentage of the Total U.S. Residency Population

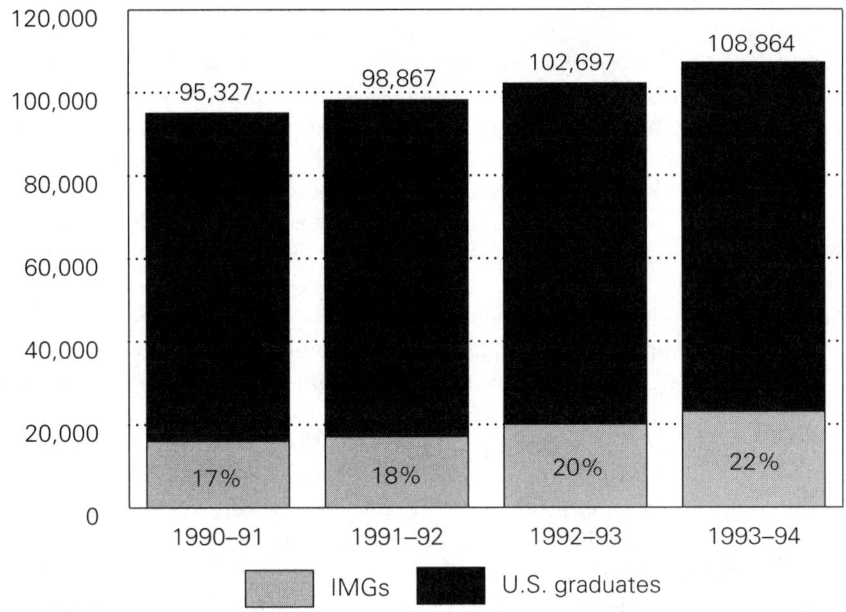

Source: Adapted from Council on Graduate Medical Education, *COGME 1995 Physician Workforce Funding Recommendations for Department of Health and Human Services Programs,* Seventh Report to Congress and the Department of Health and Human Services (Rockville, MD: U.S. Department of Health and Human Services, Health Resources Administration, June 1995), figure 3.

process by doing what they perceive to be good. On the demand side, numerous, inner-city teaching hospitals, especially in the Northeast, had hitherto been shunned by the fussier graduates from American medical schools and thus were forced to look to IMGs as a pool of cheap, skilled labor. That labor, by the way, is cheap not because IMGs often come from low-wage countries but, rather, because resident-trainees of any origin are made to work an enormous number of hours per week, at a remarkably low hourly wage. Further, as noted earlier, through direct and indirect subsidies for graduate medical education, the federal Medicare program now subsidizes that training so heavily on a per-resident basis that, for many teaching hospitals, additional residents might even function as a source of incremental profits. In 1965, for example, the average subsidy payment to teaching hospitals made by the federal Medicare program for graduate medical education amounted to an average of $65,000 per resident nationwide—although the actual payment varied from hospital to hospital, from a low of $20,000 per resident to a high of $120,000.[24]

If, indeed, the nation now faces a growing surplus of physicians, does it makes sense to permit this influx of IMG residents or, in any event, to let them remain in the country upon completion of their residency training? In a recent forum at the joint meeting of the American Medical Association and the American Osteopathic Association, a consortium of hospitals and physician groups issued a manifesto advocating the end of the federal waiver program that now allows IMGs to stay in the United States.[25] That manifesto echoes the report by the previously cited Pew Health Professions Commission that called for a tightening of U.S. immigration laws to ensure that IMGs return home once their training is completed. As an argument for this recommendation, the commission held that "it will be essential to give preference for these prestigious and lucrative positions [in medicine] to American citizens."[26]

Remarkably, the PPRC did not take an explicit stand on this issue. And in its more recent report, the Institute of Medicine did not include a formal recommendation on IMGs either, although it touched on the issue in passing.[27] (See chapter 4.) In this connection, it may be mentioned that the National Academy of Sciences, of which the Institute of Medicine is a part, has long defended the principle of a free global flow of intellectual resources and probably would find it difficult to make an exception for one such flow—the influx of IMGs into the United States. In general, the nation's higher education establishment shares the academy's view. Unbeknownst perhaps to the average citizen, the very scarce resources of higher education in this country have long been accessible to anyone in the world through a raw academic competition among talented people worldwide. Many of the foreigners seeking higher education in the United States ultimately remain in this country.

In its 1995 report, the Council on Graduate Medical Education did address the issue of IMGs explicitly and recommended that the federal government's direct medical education (DME) and indirect medical education (IME) payments to teaching hospitals per resident be reduced by 25 percent below 1995 levels for IMGs. The council also recommended that a transition program be established to assist hospitals that now rely primarily on IMGs for providing essential medical services.[28] A similar idea also appears in the Medicare Preservation Act (H.R. 2425) proposed by Congress in 1995. Had that bill passed, it would initially have reduced federal support for residents who are not citizens of the United States or of Canada, and would have completely eliminated any federal subsidies for IMG residents by 1999.[29]

Free Trade versus Protectionism

At war in the ongoing controversy over the issue of IMGs are two distinct principles that clash here as well as elsewhere in the economy. On the one hand is the principle of free trade, be it in goods and services or in the flow of financial capital and human resources. The free-trade principle rests on the normative proposition that consumers worldwide ought to be offered the widest possible choice among goods and services. In the present instance, the principle favors the unfettered inflow of IMGs if it affords Americans better access to health services or helps depress the fees for health services and the insurance premiums American consumers must pay. (As noted earlier, under selective contracting with managed care, an increase in the supply of physicians might well have that effect.) The heavy reliance on IMGs by certain teaching hospitals is based in part on this principle.

On the other hand is the popular protectionist principle that certain economic privileges offered by a nation ought to be preserved for its own citizens. This principle is advanced whenever American manufacturers and their workers clamor for protection from foreign competition, much to the chagrin of economists, consumer groups, and politicians who espouse the free-trade principle. Stripped to its core, the call for government restrictions on the influx of IMGs into the United States, either directly through quotas or indirectly through reductions in federal subsidies for IMGs only, is a classic protectionist argument not different at all from those made by textile workers, auto workers, or other interest groups seeking private economic advantage through government-enforced barriers against unwanted competition. An alternative rationale for such restrictions, that IMGs tend to be of inferior professional quality, is implausible in view of the fact that they must jump the same academic and clinical hurdles as their American colleagues. Besides, that concern would be more properly addressed simply by better-quality controls.

CONCLUSION

Given the economic forces now descending on American medicine, what central message can an economist offer American physicians? It is not exactly a cheerful message nor is it one of total gloom.

The formative years of many practicing American physicians coincided with a remarkable historical aberration—a decision by this nation literally to set aside the laws of demand and supply for its health care system. This was achieved through the combination of first-dollar, FFS health insurance with a virtually complete lack of any economic or administrative controls on the prices and volume of physician or other health services—controls that always had been imposed on health care providers in other countries that had achieved universal, first-dollar health insurance coverage. Perhaps inevitably, that felicitous environment fostered unrealistic expectations among this nation's physicians and other care providers.

It was, after all, predictable that such an open-ended arrangement could not last forever, for it carried with it its own seeds of destruction.

The virtually unconstrained flow of money into the American health system encouraged a very rapid expansion in the size of the health workforce and in the physical capacity of health care facilities. To maintain that capacity at the customary incomes expected by the providers of health care inevitably drove up national health spending at a rate and to levels that eventually were judged intolerable by both government and the business community. Thus, it was entirely predictable that, sooner or later, the demand side of the health sector would seek to recoup the power it had relinquished so thoughtlessly. The only question was whether government or the private sector would take the first bold step in that campaign.

In the end, the private sector took the initiative, but it is being followed closely by the public sector. Unbeknownst apparently to many American physicians, who had long looked on government as their nemesis, the managed care executives who now regulate health care need not and do not observe the niceties of due process and fairness that make government regulation at once so lumbering, but also relatively more tolerable than the swift and powerful dicta of the private regulators. Probably the only solace American medicine can take from its current predicament is that it chose the new market environment itself, through the political process, presumably with open eyes.

A fundamental insight from the laws of demand and supply is that excess supply of anything or anyone, at a prevailing price, eventually will drive the price down. Because the law of supply and demand can never be set aside for very long, not even for health care, it seems reasonable to expect sustained downward pressure on the average real (inflation-adjusted) income of American physicians, at least for the next decade or so. There is likely to continue to be a considerable variance around that average income level, as there always has been, but that variance is likely to shrink at the hands of the large managed care systems now seeking to standardize both the volume of physician services for given illnesses and the compensation paid physicians.

Whether the latent physician surplus described earlier will ever become manifest in the form of visibly unemployed physicians—the legendary taxi driver with the MD degree—is not at all clear and can be doubted for a number of reasons. First, as noted, the fundamental law of demand applies to anything at all, be it a widget or an hour of human labor. As the price (hourly or annual income) of a given type of labor falls, those who would use that labor will seek to employ more of it, other things being equal. That law is one potential silver lining in any major future decline of average physician income. As physician income falls, society is likely to find added uses for physicians.

However, the law works in both directions. As physician incomes rise, society will seek to economize on the use of physicians. That implication of the law should stand as a stark warning for those who now seek to protect physician incomes through unionization of the medical profession. In effect, such a policy would exacerbate the physician surplus. It would make the executives of managed care systems cast about for means of substituting less costly forms of labor, or even capital, for the services of physicians. Physicians contemplating unionization might do well to study the history of the United Auto Workers of America (UAW) whose *working* members enjoy among the highest wages in American manufacturing—wages that cannot be explained with appeal to the skills of auto workers—but who enjoy them at the cost of perennial high unemployment among their ranks. The tendency to trade employment for higher wages is particularly pronounced in unions that accord preferred status to seniority. In such unions, workers with seniority can vote for high-wage strategies in the secure knowledge that junior workers will foot the bill through added unemployment. That prospect ought to give pause to physicians in general, but especially to young physicians about to enter the medical profession.

A second reason why the legendary, taxi-driving American physician probably will remain a mere legend lies in the many alternative economic opportunities beckoning anyone in the United States who shares certain characteristics typical of physicians: high intelligence, discipline, and a demonstrated taste for hard work. The ever growing needs of managed care itself will offer physicians countless exciting and financially rewarding alternatives to patient care, should their drive and skills not be wanted in that sphere. But for bright, energetic people, there will always be countless economic opportunities in many other sectors of the economy.

Third, telemedicine remains a major sleeper in the evolution of American health care. At the moment, telemedicine is still in its infancy and remains expensive. However, it may well follow the path of electronic computation and become ubiquitous as well as economic, and therein lies a potential new economic frontier for American physicians. To say that few, if any, nations educate and train their physicians as well as the United States may appear boastful, but probably is quite true. If telemedicine does one day own up to its current billing, American medicine probably will go global on its back. If so, American physicians may become the core of yet another major new American knowledge-based export: the sale of American medical know-how worldwide.

Once a secure and lucrative investment of money and time, the study of medicine has become the same risky proposition faced all along by most other employed professionals. In the end, one might even wonder, given the menacing forces brewing within the forward march of managed care, whether any American youngster ought to be dissuaded from choosing a career in medicine. However, for the bright and ambitious, medicine remains an exciting career based on a solid body of technical know-how, forever challenged by new bodies of knowledge, and forever holding forth the uncertain, but nevertheless enticing prospect that a good physician will continue to do reasonably well by doing good.

References

1. Uwe E. Reinhardt, "Health Manpower Forecasting: The Case of Physician Supply," in *Health Services Research: Key to Health Policy,* ed. Eli Ginzberg (Cambridge, MA: Harvard University Press, 1991), p. 259.

2. Reinhardt, p. 260.

3. David A. Kindig, "Strategic Issues for Managing the Future Physician Workforce," in *Strategic Choices for a Changing Health System,* ed. Stuart H. Altman and Uwe E. Reinhardt (Chicago: Health Administration Press, 1996), p. 161.

4. Mark Holoweiko, "Which Doctors Are Quitting Medicine?" *Medical Economics* 73, no. 23 (Dec. 9, 1996): 176–91.

5. Uwe E. Reinhardt, "Will Physicians Take Back Medicine?" *Physician Executive* 22, no. 8 (Aug. 1996): 10–15.

6. Sally T. Sonnefeld and others, "Projections of National Health Expenditures through the Year 2000," *Health Care Financing Review* 13, no. 1 (Fall 1991): 3.

7. Employee Benefit Research Institute, *Health Insurance Probability Access and Affordability,* EBRI Issue Brief No. 173, May 1996, p. 1.

8. Congressional Budget Office, *Behavioral Assumptions for Estimating the Effect of Health Care Proposals* (Washington, DC: Congressional Budget Office, Nov. 1993), table 3, p. viii.

9. Reinhardt, "Health Manpower Forecasting: The Case of Physician Supply," pp. 270–73.

10. Reinhardt, "Health Manpower Forecasting," pp. 234–83.

11. Jonathan Weiner, "Forecasting the Effects of Health Reform on U.S. Physician Workforce Requirement: Evidence from HMO Staffing Patterns," *JAMA* 272, no. 3 (1994): 222–30.

12. David C. Goodman and others, "Benchmarking the U.S. Physician Workforce: An Alternative to Needs-Based or Demand-Based Planning," *JAMA* 276, no. 22 (1996): 17.

13. See, for example, Council on Graduate Medical Education, *First Report of the Council to the Congress and the U.S. Department of Health and Human Services* (Rockville, MD: U.S. Department of Health and Human Services, Health Resources Administration, 1988); Physician Payment Review Commission, *Annual Report to Congress, 1993* (Washington, DC: PPRC, 1993); Steven A. Schroeder, "Training an Appropriate Mix of Physicians to Meet the Nation's Needs," *Academic Medicine* 68, no. 2 (1993): 118–22; Steven A. Schroeder, "Specialty Distribution of U.S. Physicians: The Invisible Driver of U.S. Health Care Costs," *New England Journal of Medicine* 328 (1993): 961–63; Pew Health Professions Commission, *Reforming Graduate Medical Education: A Report from the Commission* (San Francisco: UCSF Center for the Health Professions, Sept. 1995); and Institute of Medicine, *The Nation's Physician Workforce: Options for Balancing Supply and Requirements* (Washington, D.C.: National Academy Press, 1996).

14. Physician Payment Review Commission, *Annual Report to Congress, 1993*.

15. *Health Security Act,* President Clinton's Health Reform Proposal and Health Security Act as presented to Congress on October 27, 1993 (Chicago: Commerce Clearing House, 1993).

16. Pew Health Professions Commission, *Critical Challenges: Revitalizing the Health Professions for the Twenty-First Century. The Third Report of the Pew Health Profession Commission* (San Francisco: UCSF Center for the Health Professions, Nov. 1995), pp. 44–45.

17. Institute of Medicine, *The Nation's Physician Workforce: Options for Balancing Supply and Requirements* (Washington, DC: National Academy Press, 1996), p. 83.

18. Uwe E. Reinhardt, "Planning the Nation's Health Workforce: Let the Market In," *Inquiry* 31 (Fall 1994): 250–63.

19. See Reinhardt, "Planning the Nation's Health Workforce."

20. See Uwe E. Reinhardt, "Grow Your Own For-Profit Philanthropist," in *The Academic Health Center in the 21st Century,* ed. Ralph Snyderman and Vicki Y. Saito (Durham, NC: Duke University Medical Center, 1996), pp. 2–15.

21. Prospective Payment Assessment Commission, *Medicare and the American Health Care System. Report to the Congress* (Washington, DC: PPAC, June 1995), p. 47.

22. See Reinhardt, "Planning the Nation's Health Workforce."

23. Kindig, "Strategic Issues for Managing the Future Physician Workforce," p. 154.

24. Prospective Payment Assessment Commission, *Medicare and the American Health Care System,* p. 47.

25. Jon Hamilton, "Medical Educators Finger IMGs as Solution to Glut," *Physician's Weekly: Highlights and Analysis of Medical News* 14, no. 1 (Jan. 6, 1997): 1.

26. Pew Health Professions Commission, *Critical Challenges,* pp. 44–45.

27. Institute of Medicine, *The Nation's Physician Workforce.*

28. Council on Graduate Medical Education, *COGME 1995 Physician Workforce Funding Recommendations for Department of Health and Human Services Programs,* Seventh Report to Congress and the Department of Health and Human Services (Rockville, MD: U.S. Department of Health and Human Services, Health Resources Administration, June 1995), p. iii.

29. U.S. Congress, House of Representatives, Committee on Ways and Means, *Medicare Preservation Act of 1995: Report on H.R. 2425* (Washington, DC: U.S. Government Printing Office, 1995).

3

Physician Practice Size, 1991–1995

David W. Emmons, PhD
Phillip R. Kletke, PhD

The U.S. health care system is evolving toward organizations of greater size and complexity—a change fueled by competition among providers and by pressures to curb health expenditures.[1] In this regard, physician practices have proved to be no exception to the forces of change. Current discussions of medical practice organization often are focused exclusively on physician-hospital organizations (PHOs), hospital and insurer acquisitions of physician practices, and other emerging forms of vertical integration. However, long before these organizational forms came into vogue, market forces were actively reshaping the physician services market.

This chapter examines the distribution of physicians with respect to practice size between 1991 and 1995. The analysis documents a significant decrease in the proportion of physicians in solo practices over this period and a corresponding increase in the proportion of physicians in institutional settings. The chapter also analyzes trends, by practice size and specialty, in the amount of time physicians spend providing care, in selected measures of physician output, and in physician earnings. This information should help physicians and group practice administrators (and others interested in physician practices) understand some of the

---

Opinions expressed in this chapter are those of the authors and should not be attributed to the American Medical Association.

changes in their practice environment over the past five years and, it is hoped, will be of value to them in formulating competitive strategies for the future.

Finally, the chapter presents 1995 data on physician distribution with respect to practice size, by a variety of physician and geographic characteristics of interest to policy makers. In particular, there are data on practice size with respect to physician specialty, community size, census division, board certification, age, sex, country of medical school graduation, and a state-level measure of the degree of managed care penetration. Because of its implications for physician productivity, the information should be of use to policy makers grappling with a variety of physician workforce issues.

BACKGROUND

Conventional wisdom embraces a number of unsubstantiated notions about current trends in physician practice organization. Included among these are the following:

- The shift away from solo practice is a new phenomenon that has been caused by either managed care generally or capitated payments to physicians.
- Solo practice is incompatible with certain forms of managed care.
- The transition from solo to group practice has skyrocketed in the past few years.

Discussion or expression of these notions can be found in, for example, Rice;[2] Shortell, Gillies, and Anderson;[3] and Johnsson.[4]

However, in contrast to conventional wisdom, the shift away from solo practice is hardly a new phenomenon. Jensen observed that the proportion of physicians in group practice grew from approximately 3 percent in 1946 to 12 percent in 1965 and 25 percent in 1980.[5] This trend clearly predates any significant levels of managed care participation or managed care growth among physicians.[6] In addition, the research literature is replete with studies of the advantages and disadvantages of group practice relative to solo practice that offer more fundamental, and more compelling, explanations for the structure of physician practices. (See, for example, the studies identified in the next section.) Finally, although managed care contracting is more common among group practice physicians than solo practitioners, Emmons and Simon found that, in 1995, more than 60 percent of solo practitioners had managed care contracts and nearly half of them had at least one capitated contract.[7] Evidence of the true profitability of these contracts—for practices of any size—remains to be seen.

Theoretical Considerations

The research literature identifies a number of ways in which practicing in a group might afford physicians economic or other advantages relative to practicing alone. Graham discusses enhancements to productivity through the division of labor and the advantage of a more regular work schedule.[8] Freshnock and Goodman point to cost advantages in a group setting in obtaining information on new medical techniques.[9] Pope and Burge[10] and Held[11] offer evidence suggesting that solo practitioners may be unable to fully utilize certain capital acquisitions. Reinhardt offers similar evidence concerning the ability of physicians to substitute nonphysician personnel for their own time in the delivery of care.[12] Lorant and Kimbell suggest that environmental factors may encourage greater productivity in a group setting.[13]

In a paper reminiscent of Satterthwaite's[14] and Pauly and Satterthwaite's[15] notion that physician services are a reputation good (that is, one for which consumers rely on information provided by relatives or other personal acquaintances whose judgment is trusted), Getzen argues that all medical care is transacted by "brand name" and group practice enables physicians to reduce the cost of establishing a market identity and to transfer reputation more efficiently.[16] In essence, Getzen suggests that group practices exist because they offer physicians a cost advantage in marketing their services to patients. Gaynor and Gertler highlight the role of risk spreading in self-employed group practice.[17]

However, the research literature also clearly indicates that group practice is not without limitations. Goodman and Wolinsky discuss a preference among physicians for autonomy.[18] Kimbell and Lorant conclude that economies of scale exist, but only over a limited range of practice sizes.[19] Pauly[20] and Newhouse[21] discuss the problem of shirking or "free riding" in the context of a group medical practice, particularly where the division of profits is defined ex ante. Because they neither bear the full cost of nor reap the full reward for their actions, individual physicians in a group with predefined profit shares have an incentive to produce less than they would otherwise. Lee suggests that group practices address the shirking problem by monitoring its members to ensure that the group's resources, including physician time, are used to their fullest.[22] Clearly, however, the group must bear the costs of monitoring, and these are likely to increase with practice size. Gaynor and Pauly examine productive efficiency among group practices and conclude that practice size is inversely related to productivity.[23] Gaynor and Gertler analyze the same group practice data and conclude that physician work effort is inversely related to the extent of revenue sharing.[24]

Empirical Research

"Survivor analyses" of medical practice size generally have found large groups to be more efficient at the margin than solo practices. Such analyses presume that changes in the distribution of practice sizes reflect movement toward an equilibrium distribution characterized by efficiency. Firm sizes whose share is growing are said to be efficient at the margin relative to firm sizes with constant or declining shares. Frech and Ginsburg found groups to be more efficient at the margin than solo practices over the period 1965 to 1969.[25] Moreover, they reported the greatest gains in market share among practices with more than 25 physicians. In a study of practice size from 1965 to 1980, Marder and Zuckerman found evidence of the efficiency of practices with 100 or more physicians but also concluded that solo practices were efficient in some regions of the country.[26]

More recent evidence of the trend away from solo practice toward larger practice size has been provided by Emmons;[27] Marder and others;[28] Havlicek, Eiler, and Neblett;[29] Kletke, Emmons, and Gillis;[30] and Havlicek.[31] Emmons examined the distribution of physician practice sizes in 1983 and 1986, and found a slight decline in the proportion of the smallest practices (including solo) and an increase in the proportion of practices with 25 or more physicians. Marder and colleagues examined the proportion of solo practitioners between 1983 and 1988, and reported a 1.8 percentage point drop in the proportion of solo practitioners between 1987 and 1988, but they noted that all other yearly changes in that proportion were statistically insignificant. Kletke, Emmons, and Gillis analyzed trends in physician practice arrangements from 1983 to 1994, and found an increase in the number of physicians practicing as employees concomitant with an 11 percentage point decrease in the proportion of self-employed patient care physicians in solo practice.

In an analysis of group practice census data for the years 1965 to 1991, Havlicek, Eiler, and Neblett found that mean group size had increased from 6.6 to 11.5 physicians. They also reported that 65 percent of medical groups planned to add physicians over the next five years. Finally, Havlicek analyzed data from a 1994–1995 group census survey, and found that, in 1995, 32 percent of all nonfederal physicians were practicing in groups and the average group size was 10.5 physicians.

DATA AND METHODS USED IN THE ANALYSIS

This analysis is based on data from the American Medical Association's Socioeconomic Monitoring System (SMS) surveys for the years 1991 to 1995. The SMS data were collected using telephone surveys of random samples of nonfederal, postresident, patient care physicians. Each survey collected data from more than 4,000 physicians on a variety of organizational, financial, and performance characteristics. Response rates to the surveys ranged between 60 and 70 percent. All descriptive statistics reported in this analysis have been weighted to correct for nonresponse bias. Detailed discussions of the SMS survey methodology and the construction of the yearly weights are contained in Gonzalez.[32]

The measure of practice size is based on responses to a question concerning the number of physicians in the physician's main medical practice. Because the question was not asked of independent contractors, HMO employees, or hospital employees, those physicians are categorized in the analysis as "institutional" physicians. Use of this category differentiates this analysis from the empirical studies identified earlier. Although there is no evidence on the average number of physicians practicing together in institutional settings, the category is important in illustrating changes in physician practice arrangements during the early 1990s.

In addition to data on practice size, the SMS surveys provide information on the specialty in which the physician practices, the nature of the community in which he or she practices (nonmetropolitan, small metropolitan, or large metropolitan), the census division in which the physician practice is located, whether the physician is board certified, the physician's sex and age, whether the physician is a U.S. medical graduate, and the 1991 level of managed care penetration in the state in which he or she practices. The index of managed care penetration was derived from information in the 1991 SMS survey on the proportion of physicians with HMO, preferred provider association (PPO), and individual practice association (IPA) managed care contracts, and the extent of their revenues derived from such contracts. States with too few respondents to permit reliable statistical estimation of the extent of managed care penetration are included in the analysis in a "not classified" category. Most of the "not classified" states are unlikely to have significant levels of managed care.

Finally, SMS data on physician net earnings, after expenses but before taxes, were used to gauge the financial rewards of practice. As with the other variables analyzed, these data were obtained from the 1991 and 1995 SMS surveys. However, the SMS surveys collected information on the prior year's earnings and expenses so that measures were confined to 1990 and 1994 earnings. The specific measures considered here are inflation-adjusted physician net income, after expenses but before taxes, and inflation-adjusted effective hourly wages. Effective hourly wages were estimated by dividing the physician's net income by the product of total hours worked per week and the number of weeks worked during the previous year. Wages were computed only for physicians who indicated they worked at least 20 hours per week and 20 weeks per year.

EMPIRICAL FINDINGS

Following are the empirical findings of this analysis. An appendix to this chapter provides definitions for the terms used in the tables, including specialty categories (tables 3-2 through 3-5), census divisions (table 3-5), and percentage of managed care penetration (table 3-5).

Distribution of Practice Size, 1991–1995

Changes in the distribution of physician practices with respect to size between 1991 and 1995 are shown in table 3-1. The percentage of solo practitioners fell over the period from 34.1 to 26.5 percent. Similarly, the share of physicians in groups of two to four physicians fell from 22.0 to 19.1 percent. The data show only very modest increases in the share of physicians in the other three group settings—5 to 9 physicians, 10 to 24 physicians, and 25 or more physicians. The share of physicians practicing in institutional settings, however, increased by more than 8 percentage points.

TABLE 3-1. Distribution of Practice Size, 1991–1995

	1991	*1992*	*1993*	*1994*	*1995*
Practice Size					
1 MD	34.1%	33.6%	32.1%	30.0%	26.5%
2 to 4 MDs	22.0	22.4	21.2	20.4	19.1
5 to 9 MDs	10.2	10.2	11.5	10.9	11.1
10 to 24 MDs	5.5	5.5	6.4	6.1	6.4
25 MDs or more	5.8	5.8	6.3	6.6	6.5
Institutional	22.3	22.5	22.6	26.1	30.4
Total	100.0%	100.0%	100.0%	100.0%	100.0%
N	4,054	3,955	4,114	4,107	4,024

Source: American Medical Association Socioeconomic Monitoring System (SMS), 1991–1995 surveys.

Hours Worked, 1991 and 1995

Table 3-2 presents information on the number of hours physicians spent in a variety of settings in 1991 and 1995. Total hours of practice per week, patient care hours per week, office hours per week, hours on hospital rounds per week, and weeks worked per year are detailed by practice size and specialty. Percent changes between 1991 and 1995 and their statistical significance are also indicated in the table.

The total number of hours worked per week by physicians fell by 4.0 percent between 1991 and 1995, from 59.1 to 56.7 hours. The largest declines were reported by solo practitioners and physicians in small- to medium-sized groups. The number of hours spent in patient care fell by nearly the same amount (3.9 percent), from 53.3 to 51.3 hours. The number of office hours worked per week was essentially stable, at 26.5 hours in 1995. Declines in the number of hours per week spent on hospital rounds, from 8.7 hours in 1991 to 7.7 hours in 1995, account for about half the decline in patient care and total hours per week. Physicians did work about a half-week longer in 1995 than they did in 1991, working 47.2 weeks on average. This change was statistically significant among solo practitioners, physicians in small- to medium-sized practices, and institutional physicians.

The largest declines in total hours worked per week occurred among radiologists, anesthesiologists, and pathologists (RAPs) (7.1 hours) and obstetricians and gynecologists (4.6 hours). Significant declines in hours worked per week and patient care hours were seen among solo practitioners in medical/pediatric subspecialties, obstetrics/gynecology, and radiology/anesthesiology/pathology. However, the decline in hours worked among RAPs occurred in virtually all practice settings. The size of the decreases in the number of hours worked per week among RAPs was inversely related to practice size.

No clear relationship existed between the number of hours spent on hospital rounds per week and practice size for the population of patient care physicians as a whole. However, significant changes were observed among some of the specialties. Physicians in general internal medicine reduced the number of hours spent on hospital rounds per week by 24.8 percent, from 12.3 to 9.3 hours. General/family practitioners reported 21.5 percent fewer hours on hospital rounds in 1995 compared to 1991, 5.1 versus 6.5 hours. Statistically significant decreases were observed among general/family practitioners in small groups, groups of 10 to 24, and institutional settings. The other specialties in which statistically significant declines in the number of hours on hospital rounds were observed were medical/pediatric subspecialties and obstetrics/gynecology.

Table 3-2 supports the hypothesis that larger practices afford physicians greater leisure opportunities. In both 1991 and 1995, the number of weeks worked per year was inversely related to practice size both

TABLE 3-2. Hours Worked, 1991 and 1995

	Total Hours Worked per Week			Patient Care Hours per Week			Office Hours per Week			Hospital Rounds Hours per Week			Weeks Worked per Year		
	1991	1995	% Change	1991	1995	% Change	1991	1995	% Change	1991	1995	% Change	1991	1995	% Change
Total	59.1	56.7	−4.0!!	51.3	51.3	−3.9!!	26.8	26.5	−1.4	8.7	7.7	−11.4!!	46.8	47.2	0.8!!
1 MD	61.3	59.3	−3.3!	55.4	53.9	−2.6	30.7	30.5	−0.7	8.7	7.7	−11.7!	48.0	48.4	1.0!
2 to 4 MDs	60.6	58.4	−3.6!	55.8	53.7	−3.9!	28.5	29.7	4.1	9.7	8.3	−14.4!	46.8	47.5	1.6!!
5 to 9 MDs	60.2	56.3	−6.4!!	55.4	52.5	−5.3!	24.4	26.8	10.2!	9.4	8.5	−9.4	45.9	46.5	1.3!
10 to 24 MDs	59.4	58.0	−2.4	54.9	53.2	−3.2	27.2	23.9	−12.0	8.4	7.0	−16.9	45.2	46.0	1.6
25 MDs or more	57.1	56.2	−1.4	52.4	50.5	−3.5	29.8	27.2	−8.8	7.9	7.9	0.8	45.9	46.0	0.3
Institutional	54.2	53.3	−1.6	46.7	46.6	−0.2	17.5	19.7	12.8!	7.6	7.1	−6.0	46.3	46.8	1.1!
Gen/Family Practice	60.1	57.3	−4.6!	54.7	52.9	−3.3	35.1	34.7	−1.1	6.5	5.1	−21.5!!	47.3	47.3	−0.1
1 MD	63.0	61.7	−2.1	56.8	57.5	1.3	37.8	39.3	3.8	6.4	6.5	0.5	48.2	48.4	0.4
2 to 4 MDs	60.3	56.8	−5.9	55.1	52.3	−5.2	35.0	36.1	3.1	7.7	5.6	−27.4!	46.9	47.8	1.9
5 to 9 MDs	61.9	56.2	−9.2!	58.4	52.3	−10.5!	34.9	37.0	5.9	6.1	5.3	−13.8!	46.7	47.2	1.0
10 to 24 MDs	57.8	55.4[a]	−4.1	56.8[a]	52.8[a]	−7.1	40.0	33.6[a]	−16.0	5.4	2.1[a]	−61.3!	44.8	48.4[a]	8.0
25 MDs or more	56.0	56.2	0.2	52.3	50.4	−3.7	35.8	34.9	−2.4	4.0	4.4	9.1	46.6	45.1	−3.1
Institutional	54.0	54.6	1.1	48.4	49.9	3.0	27.9	29.4	5.4	6.4	4.0	−37.2!	46.5	46.3	−0.3
Gen Internal Med	60.6	58.8	−2.9	55.3	53.4	−3.3	29.1	30.5	4.8	12.3	9.3	−24.8!!	47.4	47.4	−0.0
1 MD	65.7	65.5	−0.2	60.0	59.9	−0.2	31.8	34.2	7.5	14.2	10.9	−23.4!	48.8	49.0	0.4
2 to 4 MDs	63.2	58.1	−8.0	58.4	54.2	−7.2	33.5	31.6	−5.8	12.0	9.1	−24.3	47.6	48.2	1.3
5 to 9 MDs	62.2	59.2	−4.8	54.9	53.3	−2.8	29.0	31.0	7.0	11.7	8.8	−24.6	47.3	46.6	−1.6
10 to 24 MDs	59.6	57.5	−3.6	55.9	51.2	−8.3	29.0	29.9	2.9	14.2	6.7	−52.6!	45.8	44.6	−2.6
25 MDs or more	55.1	56.9	3.4	53.4	52.0	−2.6	31.9	31.2	−2.1	10.4	8.6	−17.8	46.0	47.5	3.1
Institutional	51.5	53.6	4.2	44.5	47.8	7.5	18.6	26.5	42.4!!	9.9	8.6	−13.1	46.0	46.1	0.3
Gen Pediatrics	57.6	56.7	−1.6	52.8	51.0	−3.3	34.4	33.6	−2.6	7.4	7.3	−1.6	47.4	47.7	0.5
1 MD	62.3	61.4	−1.5	56.4	56.3	−0.1	39.2	40.1	2.4	6.8	7.3	7.4	49.1	49.0	−0.2
2 to 4 MDs	62.0	61.4	−0.9	58.3	55.6	−4.5	39.9	37.6	−5.8	6.9	7.8	13.9	47.4	48.1	1.6
5 to 9 MDs	55.7	49.8	−10.6	50.6	46.2	−8.8	36.1	34.1	−5.5	6.5	5.8	−10.8	46.1	48.1	4.4
10 to 24 MDs	51.4[a]	55.9[a]	8.8	48.1[a]	52.7[a]	9.6	35.6[a]	36.5[a]	2.7	4.8[a]	4.2[a]	−13.3	46.9[a]	47.6[a]	1.4
25 MDs or more	50.3	52.9	5.1	47.3	49.1	3.9	35.2	35.8	1.6	5.0	5.2	4.7	44.1	45.7	3.7
Institutional	50.0	53.0	6.0	44.6	45.1	1.2	18.4	23.0	25.2	11.3	8.8	−22.5	47.3	46.6	−1.3
Med/Ped Subspecs	62.8	60.2	−4.2!	56.8	53.7	−5.5!	23.3	21.4	−8.2	17.8	15.0	−15.6!	46.7	47.9	2.5!!
1 MD	65.6	59.3	−9.7!	58.7	53.1	−9.5!	27.2	27.6	1.7	16.2	11.0	−32.1!	47.4	48.9	3.1!
2 to 4 MDs	64.0	63.1	−1.4	59.1	57.7	−2.3	25.4	22.9	−9.9	18.9	17.5	−7.2	46.9	48.2	2.7!
5 to 9 MDs	61.5	65.2	6.0	57.6	60.7	5.5	19.2	22.7	18.7	23.2	20.5	−11.5	45.8	47.0	2.6
10 to 24 MDs	59.5[a]	64.6	8.5	55.2[a]	60.5	9.5	23.9[a]	23.4	−2.0	14.6[a]	15.6	7.4	44.1[a]	45.4	3.0
25 MDs or more	65.4	60.5	−7.5	59.0	54.0	−8.5	27.5	19.6	−28.7	15.5	18.5	19.4	46.9	47.6	1.6
Institutional	55.7	55.7	0.1	48.0	46.6	−2.8	13.3	13.9	4.7	16.7	13.5	−18.8	46.2	47.9	3.7!

Obst/Gynecology	63.9	59.3	−7.2!	59.5	54.6	−8.3!!	27.9	28.2	0.9	5.6	4.7	−15.9!	46.9	47.1	0.4
1 MD	66.6	59.2	−11.2!	62.5	54.6	−12.7!	30.2	28.5	−5.7	5.9	4.9	−17.9	48.0	48.1	0.2
2 to 4 MDs	67.2	62.1	−7.6	62.9	58.7	−6.7	29.5	32.1	8.8	6.0	4.9	−17.8	46.4	46.5	0.2
5 to 9 MDs	58.6	61.3	4.6	54.7	58.3	6.5	25.4	30.8	21.1!!	4.9	4.5	−7.5	46.6	47.3	1.5
10 to 24 MDs	58.5[a]	67.1[a]	14.6	53.1[a]	56.1[a]	5.6	28.7[a]	31.1[a]	8.5	3.9[a]	3.4[a]	−11.9	47.2[a]	46.9[a]	−0.5
25 MDs or more	62.0[a]	59.9[a]	−3.4	56.5[a]	54.6	−3.4	29.9[a]	26.1[a]	−12.8	5.7[a]	4.9[a]	−14.8	46.0[a]	45.8[a]	−0.3
Institutional	58.8	52.0	−11.5	54.2	45.3	−16.5!	21.7	19.5	−9.9	4.9	4.3	−11.5	45.9	46.0	0.3
Surgery	58.8	58.7	−0.2	53.4	53.2	−0.4	23.0	22.9	−0.3	6.5	6.2	−4.9	46.5	47.4	1.9!!
1 MD	58.8	60.0	2.1	53.1	54.5	2.5	24.8	24.4	−1.6	6.2	6.3	1.9	47.5	48.3	1.6!
2 to 4 MDs	57.8	58.3	0.7	53.6	53.6	−0.0	22.7	25.5	12.2!	6.8	6.0	−12.7	46.2	47.1	1.9!
5 to 9 MDs	62.2	56.5	−9.2!	56.4	52.3	−7.3	23.4	23.2	−1.1	7.0	6.0	−14.2	44.6	46.4	3.9
10 to 24 MDs	59.0	59.0	0.1	55.8[a]	53.8	−3.5	21.7	21.5	−1.0	6.6	5.6	−14.8	45.8[a]	46.5	1.5
25 MDs or more	56.0	59.5	6.2	51.6	51.8	0.4	24.3	23.0	−5.4	5.7	4.9	−14.8	45.4	47.5	4.8
Institutional	59.7	58.0	−2.9	50.8	50.7	−0.1	15.6	16.1	3.0	7.0	7.1	0.9	45.7	47.0	2.8
RAPs	59.6	52.5	−11.8!!	53.4	48.3	−9.6!!	.	.	.	.	.	..	45.3	45.3	−0.1
1 MD	60.7	45.5	25.1!!	54.6	43.6	−20.0!	.	.	.	.	.	..	47.2	47.5	0.8
2 to 4 MDs	59.8	49.9	−16.5!!	55.0	44.8	−18.6!!	.	.	.	.	.	..	46.2	46.7	1.1
5 to 9 MDs	60.2	53.9	−10.6!!	56.9	51.4	−9.6!	.	.	.	.	.	..	45.1	44.1	−2.3!
10 to 24 MDs	62.1	56.0	−9.8!!	56.7	52.8	−6.8	.	.	.	.	.	..	44.6	45.3	1.6
25 MDs or more	58.1	53.5	−7.9	51.8	49.8	−4.0	.	.	.	.	.	..	45.7	42.8	−6.3!
Institutional	57.7	52.0	−9.9!!	49.3	46.2	−6.3	.	.	.	.	.	..	44.8	45.5	1.6
Other Specs	52.7	51.6	−2.2	45.5	45.1	−1.0	17.4	19.1	9.8	4.2	4.8	13.6	47.5	47.8	0.6
1 MD	54.4	53.1	−2.5	48.0	46.9	−2.3	31.2	30.9	−0.7	7.5	6.9	−7.1	47.8	47.8	0.1
2 to 4 MDs	53.6	54.8	2.3	46.3	49.6	7.1	23.3	37.2	59.8!!	7.4	7.6	2.2	47.2	48.0	1.6
5 to 9 MDs	55.8	50.7	−9.0	50.2	46.2	−8.0	7.4	19.5	163.4!!	2.1	7.1	234.9!	48.0	48.1	0.2
10 to 24 MDs	53.3	54.0	1.2	46.7	45.5	−2.5	11.9[a]	9.0	−24.4	2.1[a]	0.8	−61.9	46.0	47.7	3.7
25 MDs or more	52.4	50.8	−3.0	45.8	42.9	−6.3	24.5[a]	20.4	−16.5	2.9[a]	3.9	34.2	46.3	46.6	0.5
Institutional	50.6	50.0	−1.2	42.4	43.0	1.4	10.5	9.9	5.7	2.5	3.0	20.0	47.5	47.8	0.7

!! Denotes significance at p = .01.
! Denotes significance at p = .05.
[a] Denotes that the statistic is based on fewer than 20 observations

Source: American Medical Association Socioeconomic Monitoring System (SMS), 1991 and 1995 surveys.

overall and by specialty. Overall, solo practitioners worked nearly two and a half more weeks per year than physicians in practices of 10 or more. The extent to which weeks worked per year varied by practice size differed across specialties, ranging from one week among physicians in "other" specialties to four and a half weeks among physicians in radiology/anesthesiology/pathology.

Output, 1991 and 1995

Summary measures of physician output by practice size and specialty for 1991 and 1995 are shown in table 3-3. RAPs are not included because they were not asked the SMS questions on which the output measures are based. Physicians had 107.6 patient visits per week in 1995, down 9.1 percent from 1991. Decreases in the number of total visits per week were observed for all practice sizes, from solo practitioner to practices of 10 to 24 physicians. Among physicians in practices of 1 to 24, the magnitude of the decreases and the percent decline were inversely related to practice size. These changes reduced the difference between output of the most productive practice sizes and that of the least productive practices between 1991 and 1995.

The decline in total visits per week between 1991 and 1995 was principally composed of a 6.9 percent decrease in office visits per week (73.7 in 1995) and a 19.8 percent decrease in visits per week on hospital rounds (18.9 in 1995). No change was observed in the overall number of surgical procedures per week (3.7). Significant changes in office visits overall were found among solo practitioners and physicians in groups of 10 to 24. Significant decreases in visits on hospital rounds were observed for solo practitioners and physicians in small group practices, each of whom reported greater-than-average decreases in that output measure.

Among the specialties analyzed, the number of total visits per week decreased significantly in general/family practice (7.4 percent), general internal medicine (11.5 percent), general pediatrics (9.1 percent), obstetrics/gynecology (16.2 percent), and surgery (9.1 percent). Among obstetricians and gynecologists, the decline in total visits was especially large among solo practitioners and physicians in small group practices. Obstetrics/gynecology was the only specialty to experience a statistically significant decline in the number of office visits per week.

Statistically significant decreases in visits per week on hospital rounds were reported by physicians in general/family practice (30.8 percent), general internal medicine (30.7 percent), obstetrics/gynecology (35.7 percent), and surgery (25.2 percent). Decreases in visits per week on hospital rounds also were statistically significant in obstetrics/gynecology and surgery among physicians in solo practice and those in groups of two to four.

Table 3-3 also reveals differences by specialty in the change in surgical procedures per week between 1991 and 1995. Although the numbers themselves are small (still less than one per week per physician in 1995), both physicians in general internal medicine and physicians in general pediatrics reported statistically significant increases in the number of surgical procedures performed per week. Obstetricians and gynecologists, on the other hand, reported a 19.4 percent decline (to 7.1 procedures per physician in 1995) in the number of surgical procedures performed per week.

Financial Rewards to Practice, 1990 and 1994

Table 3-4 presents information on physician earnings by practice size and specialty for the years 1990 and 1994. Consistent with the previous tables, the data reported in table 3-4 were obtained from the 1991 and 1995 SMS surveys. The SMS surveys, however, collect information on the prior year's earnings and expenses.

Overall, physicians reported inflation-adjusted net earnings of $186,300 in 1990 and $181,000 in 1994. The difference between the two figures (−2.9 percent) is not statistically significant. Average 1994 net earnings in family practice, general internal medicine, and general pediatrics were $120,300, $133,700, and $120,000, respectively. Physicians in medical and pediatric subspecialties reported 1994 average net earnings of $208,100. Physicians in obstetrics/gynecology reported 1994 net earnings of $199,300, a statistically significant 15.2 percent decrease from their inflation-adjusted 1990 earnings. As a group, RAPs reported a statistically significant decrease of 6.9 percent in their inflation-adjusted net earnings between 1990 and 1994.

The detailed tabulations of physician earnings by practice size and specialty indicate that net income is positively correlated with practice size. The *apparent* discrepancy in that relationship occurs among physicians in groups of 25 or more and institutional physicians (assuming the latter are in large practices). This exception is attributable to the fact that these practices have, on average, a greater proportion of employee physicians, who typically earn less than their self-employed counterparts.[33]

Physicians' inflation-adjusted effective hourly wage remained stable between 1990 and 1994 ($70.81/hour in 1994). Most specialties reported no significant change in their inflation-adjusted effective hourly wage between 1990 and 1994. The one exception was obstetrics/gynecology, which experienced a statistically significant decrease of 12.6 percent. Physicians' effective hourly wages generally exhibited the same curvilinear relationship with practice size as net earnings, with the decrease in wages among those in practices of 25 or more being driven, again, by the share of employee physicians in those practices.

TABLE 3-3. Output, 1991 and 1995

	Total Visits per Week			Office Visits per Week			Hospital Round Visits per Week			Surgical Procedures per Week		
	1991	1995	% Change	1991	1995	% Change	1991	1995	% Change	1991	1995	% Change
Total	118.4	107.6	−9.1!!	79.2	73.7	−6.9!!	23.6	18.9	−19.8!!	3.7	3.7	0.3
1 MD	117.6	107.7	−8.4!!	87.7	82.1	−6.3!	21.0	16.1	−23.1!!	3.7	4.0	9.7
2 to 4 MDs	128.3	116.2	−9.4!!	89.2	89.2	−0.0	29.3	20.6	−29.7!!	4.8	4.9	2.6
5 to 9 MDs	129.8	113.4	−12.6!!	82.5	79.6	−3.6	26.9	21.9	−18.4	4.7	4.0	−14.8
10 to 24 MDs	128.7	108.1	−16.0!!	81.9	65.3	−20.3!	22.7	16.6	−26.9	3.2	4.2	34.3
25 MDs or more	115.4	107.5	−6.8	82.8	75.9	−8.4	19.4	18.7	−3.6	3.1	3.4	10.7
Institutional	101.2	98.3	−2.8	46.8	51.3	9.6	21.4	19.9	−7.0	2.1	2.2	5.2
Gen/Family Practice	144.4	133.7	−7.4!	111.8	108.3	−3.1	17.2	11.9	−30.8!!	0.9	0.6	−30.6
1 MD	151.4	147.5	−2.6	119.7	120.9	1.0	17.1	13.4	−21.6	1.0	0.8	−25.0
2 to 4 MDs	144.9	141.8	−2.2	111.3	117.9	5.9	21.1	14.7	−30.0!	0.9	0.5	−39.6
5 to 9 MDs	159.0	133.5	−16.0!	119.4	116.8	−2.1	20.2	13.6	−32.5	1.3	0.6	−58.2!
10 to 24 MDs	168.6	118.7[a]	−29.6!!	133.2	82.5[a]	−38.1!!	14.1	6.5[a]	−53.5	0.7	0.9[a]	25.9
25 MDs or more	125.8	121.7	−3.3	106.3	103.9	−2.3	7.2	8.7	21.6	0.7	0.8	20.0
Institutional	122.7	119.9	−2.3	88.0	91.9	4.5	15.4	9.4	−38.9!	0.5	0.5	−9.1
Gen Internal Med	118.3	104.7	−11.5!!	74.0	71.4	−3.4	30.1	20.9	−30.7!!	0.2	0.7	323.8!
1 MD	120.8	108.5	−10.2	80.5	72.3	−10.2	29.9	22.8	−23.7	0.2	0.3	62.6
2 to 4 MDs	129.0	112.8	−12.6	80.7	81.9	1.4	35.7	20.2	−43.4!!	0.1	0.9	834.6!
5 to 9 MDs	120.1	114.5	−4.7	80.5	76.5	−5.0	29.0	20.8	−28.3	0.3	0.3	−4.2
10 to 24 MDs	126.5	98.3	−22.3	73.7	68.6	−6.9	40.3	12.7	−68.6	0.5	0.0	−100
25 MDs or more	126.7	109.6	−13.5	86.8	80.2	−7.6	24.0	19.3	−19.5	0.0	4.1	.!
Institutional	94.9	95.3	−0.4	47.6	62.6	31.4	24.1	21.4	−11.3	0.1	0.2	177.8
Gen Pediatrics	140.7	127.9	−9.1!	115.3	107.5	−6.8	17.5	14.6	−16.2	0.4	0.8	94.9!
1 MD	141.8	137.3	−3.2	124.9	123.3	−1.3	13.5	10.9	−19.6	0.5	0.4	−24.8
2 to 4 MDs	164.5	148.4	−9.8	143.4	137.4	−4.2	17.1	14.4	−15.5	0.7	0.4	−37.8
5 to 9 MDs	150.9	124.1	−17.7!	130.3	111.5	−14.4	18.5	11.3	−38.5	0.4	0.5	22.7
10 to 24 MDs	140.5[a]	147.1[a]	4.7	120.0[a]	123.8[a]	3.2	11.2[a]	14.5[a]	29.8	0.7[a]	2.3[a]	245.2
25 MDs or more	131.0	130.0	−0.7	117.1	113.5	−3.0	8.0	12.0	50.1	0.1	1.6	1886.0!
Institutional	102.6	100.7	−1.9	50.6	63.5	25.4	28.2	20.4	−27.7	0.0	1.2	.!
Med/Ped Subspecs	100.4	96.6	−3.8	51.8	48.1	−7.2	41.1	36.4	−11.4	3.1	3.7	20.2
1 MD	98.9	100.1	1.2	58.0	66.6	14.8	34.9	24.3	−30.3!	2.9	4.2	44.7
2 to 4 MDs	109.6	103.3	−5.8	61.2	52.1	−14.9	43.0	41.4	−3.6	2.5	5.1	103.6!
5 to 9 MDs	113.4	115.1	1.5	48.2	51.2	6.2	57.6	56.6	−1.7	5.4	4.2	−23.0
10 to 24 MDs	97.6[a]	92.0	−5.7	61.1[a]	56.9	−6.8	37.9[a]	33.6	−11.4	2.6[a]	6.4	149.8
25 MDs or more	104.7	98.1	−6.3	56.8	38.9	−31.4	32.1	40.3	25.5	3.4	1.8	−46.9
Institutional	76.9	81.9	6.5	21.6	26.5	22.9	42.9	36.4	−15.2	2.8	1.8	−37.3

Obst/Gynecology	112.2	94.0	−16.2!!	86.6	78.0	−9.9!	18.9	12.1	−35.7!!	8.8	7.1	−19.4!
1 MD	104.7	86.1	−17.8!	85.6	70.8	−17.3!	16.7	9.0	−45.9!!	8.0	6.2	−22.5
2 to 4 MDs	129.5	102.6	−20.7!!	102.0	92.3	−9.5	21.7	12.0	−44.6!!	9.5	7.6	−19.8!
5 to 9 MDs	136.2	121.8	−10.5	110.8	107.3	−3.2	21.2	14.2	−33.1	10.2	8.2	−20.5
10 to 24 MDs	111.2[a]	127.7[a]	14.8	95.2[a]	102.9[a]	8.1	15.8[a]	16.1[a]	1.9	12.1[a]	10.7[a]	−11.2
25 MDs or more	104.1[a]	103.0[a]	−1.1	81.7[a]	85.3[a]	4.5	20.3[a]	17.1[a]	−15.9	7.5[a]	7.3[a]	−2.8
Institutional	94.0	65.3	−30.5!!	55.5	40.1	−27.7	18.1	14.6	−19.1	8.3	6.2	−25.1
Surgery	106.9	97.2	−9.1!!	75.4	70.4	−6.7!	24.1	18.0	−25.2!!	8.7	8.3	−4.4
1 MD	99.5	90.7	−8.8	74.3	68.5	−7.7	18.8	14.4	−23.6!	7.8	8.0	2.9
2 to 4 MDs	117.9	106.9	−9.3!	81.5	83.3	2.3	30.3	18.4	−39.2!!	10.2	9.0	−12.2!
5 to 9 MDs	116.7	103.5	−11.3	87.5	77.3	−11.7	24.2	17.0	−30.0	9.4	8.9	−5.9
10 to 24 MDs	101.3[a]	102.6	1.3	78.3	75.0	−4.2	18.5[a]	17.0	−8.3	9.9[a]	8.9	−9.8
25 MDs or more	105.7	89.6	−15.2	75.6	64.2	−15.1	24.0	15.3	−36.2	9.1	8.3	−8.8
Institutional	97.1	90.8	−6.5	47.5	49.6	4.5	29.6	26.3	−11.0	6.8	7.5	9.6
Other Specs	112.9	109.2	−3.3	45.1	47.8	6.1	10.3	11.1	7.6	0.5	0.8	67.4.
1 MD	101.4	107.8	6.3	80.1	85.1	6.2	13.9	14.4	3.8	0.7	1.7	122.7
2 to 4 MDs	136.9	121.7	−11.1	74.7	92.4	23.7	19.4	15.1	−22.2	0.6	0.9	50.7
5 to 9 MDs	143.1	97.8	−31.6!!	18.1	47.5	163.3!	2.7	13.7	399.6!	0.0	0.6	.
10 to 24 MDs	134.1[a]	117.7	−12.2	29.6[a]	21.8	−26.2	3.1[a]	2.9	−6.4	0.0[a]	0.1	.
25 MDs or more	105.7[a]	106.3	0.6	61.8[a]	61.4	−0.6	6.0[a]	9.6	60.2	0.6[a]	0.4	−30.6
Institutional	104.7	109.0	4.1	24.9	20.6	−17.3	9.1	9.3	1.6	0.4	0.5	40.7

!! Denotes significance at p = .01.
! Denotes significance at p = .05.
[a] Denotes that the statistic is based on fewer than 20 observations

Source: American Medical Association Socioeconomic Monitoring System (SMS), 1991 and 1995 surveys.

TABLE 3-4. Physician Earnings by Practice Size and Specialty, 1990 and 1994

	Net Income (1000s) in 1994 Dollars			*Hourly Wage in 1994 Dollars*		
	1990	*1994*	*% Change*	*1990*	*1994*	*% Change*
Total	186.3	181.0	−2.9	70.29	70.81	0.7
1 MD	180.0	176.8	−1.8	64.84	64.68	−0.3
2 to 4 MDs	220.4	211.7	−3.9	80.58	81.50	1.1
5 to 9 MDs	235.7	216.9	−8.0	89.20	84.90	−4.8
10 to 24 MDs	213.4	213.7	0.1	82.42	85.75	4.0
25 MDs or more	167.4	172.1	2.8	65.58	69.79	6.4
Institutional	142.7	149.2	4.6	59.07	61.60	4.3
Gen/Family Practice	116.4	120.3	3.3	42.98	46.31	7.7
1 MD	120.4	121.6	1.0	42.18	42.73	1.3
2 to 4 MDs	118.8	131.3	10.5	43.67	51.35	17.6
5 to 9 MDs	133.7	123.1	−7.9	47.77	46.88	−1.9
10 to 24 MDs	135.1[a]	137.0[a]	1.4	51.39[a]	53.18[a]	3.5
25 MDs or more	110.1	122.6	11.4	44.61	50.93	14.2
Institutional	98.9	110.8	12.0	40.49	44.32	9.5
Gen Internal Med	128.3	133.7	4.2	47.34	52.07	10.0
1 MD	130.4	127.9	−2.0	42.88	41.60	−3.0
2 to 4 MDs	141.3	166.9	18.2	47.72	68.64	43.8!
5 to 9 MDs	149.1	141.9	−4.8	56.19	55.64	−1.0
10 to 24 MDs	146.1	134.3[a]	−8.1	59.40	53.42[a]	−10.1
25 MDs or more	130.4	134.5	3.2	51.35	54.39	5.9
Institutional	92.9	120.0	29.2!	42.90	50.76	18.3!
Gen Pediatrics	118.6	120.0	1.2	44.45	46.12	3.8
1 MD	123.6	117.0	−5.4	40.36	39.08	−3.2
2 to 4 MDs	125.1	132.8	6.2	43.85	48.80	11.3
5 to 9 MDs	138.3	126.6	−8.5	57.14	53.21	−6.9
10 to 24 MDs	136.6[a]	171.3[a]	25.4	55.08[a]	71.12[a]	29.1
25 MDs or more	111.5[a]	109.6	−1.7	53.48[a]	52.21[a]	−2.4
Institutional	92.0	104.9	14.0	38.69	41.01	6.0
Med/Ped Subspecs	216.0	208.1	−3.6	75.40	75.37	−0.0
1 MD	212.4	214.2	0.8	68.73	78.84	14.7
2 to 4 MDs	265.1	244.1	−7.9	89.92	82.97	−7.7
5 to 9 MDs	250.0	275.5	10.2	92.78	95.39	2.8
10 to 24 MDs	196.4[a]	211.3	7.6	83.75[a]	82.05	−2.0
25 MDs or more	163.8	181.8	11.0	55.12	66.42	20.5
Institutional	154.3	155.5	0.7	61.32	58.63	−4.4

TABLE 3-4. *(Continued)*

	Net Income (1000s) in 1994 Dollars			*Hourly Wage in 1994 Dollars*		
	1990	*1994*	*% Change*	*1990*	*1994*	*% Change*
Obst/Gynecology	235.1	199.3	−15.2!	83.25	72.73	−12.6!
1 MD	232.1	188.2	−18.9	74.78	64.90	−13.2
2 to 4 MDs	273.2	186.1	−31.9!!	90.97	70.97	−22.0!
5 to 9 MDs	264.3	253.3	−4.1	99.31	89.05	−10.3
10 to 24 MDs	236.0[a]	289.7[a]	22.7	93.08[a]	91.08[a]	−2.2
25 MDs or more	233.1[a]	224.8[a]	−3.6	92.20[a]	82.24[a]	−10.8
Institutional	181.7	159.9	−12.0	74.47	67.63	−9.2
Surgery	268.1	251.7	−6.1	102.68	95.08	−7.4
1 MD	246.1	243.9	−0.9	94.04	89.20	−5.1
2 to 4 MDs	293.0	273.5	−6.7	112.85	104.59	−7.3
5 to 9 MDs	345.7	267.5	−22.6!	132.31	102.80	−22.3!
10 to 24 MDs	346.4[a]	240.0	−30.7	133.42[a]	92.82	−30.4
25 MDs or more	212.4	215.5	1.4	82.73	79.09	−4.4
Institutional	209.6	232.8	11.0	80.23	90.86	13.2
RAPs	232.9	216.8	−6.9!	89.14	94.96	6.5
1 MD	237.0	222.2	−6.3	84.38	89.73	6.3
2 to 4 MDs	257.7	230.4	−10.6	94.48	105.02	11.2
5 to 9 MDs	284.1	251.2	−11.6!	107.57	108.17	0.6
10 to 24 MDs	265.1	245.3	−7.5	97.22	104.87	7.9
25 MDs or more	238.5	223.3	−6.4	90.59	104.34	15.2
Institutional	185.7	183.2	−1.4	76.00	80.78	6.3
Other Specs	148.6	144.8	−2.5	61.60	60.64	−1.6
1 MD	151.6	133.4	−12.0!	60.76	54.60	−10.1
2 to 4 MDs	189.8	186.5	−1.7	78.88	74.74	−5.2
5 to 9 MDs	159.3	166.9	4.8	62.61	73.84	17.9!
10 to 24 MDs	162.9[a]	201.5	23.7	66.93[a]	78.86	17.8
25 MDs or more	158.4	164.1	3.6	67.46	70.90	5.1
Institutional	131.2	132.1	0.7	56.62	56.28	−0.6

Source: American Medical Association Socioeconomic Monitoring System (SMS), 1991 and 1995 surveys.

Distribution of Practice Size, 1995

Table 3-5 reports information on the distribution of physicians by practice size in 1995 across a variety of physician and geographic characteristics. In particular, data are presented on the practice size distribution of physicians by specialty, community size, census division, board certification, age and sex, country of graduation, and a state-level measure of the degree of managed care penetration.

Primary care physicians are somewhat more likely than non–primary care physicians both to be in solo practice and to practice in institutional settings. There is considerable variation in the practice size distribution among the non–primary care specialties, however, with the proportion of solo physicians ranging from 6.3 percent among RAPs to 35.5 percent among surgeons. Strong similarities exist between the practice size distributions of general/family practice and general internal medicine, and between those of obstetrics/gynecology and surgery.

Table 3-5 reveals that physicians in nonmetropolitan areas are more likely than physicians in metropolitan areas to be in solo and small group practice. Approximately 56 percent of physicians in nonmetropolitan areas practice in either a solo setting or a group with two to four physicians, in contrast to 44 percent of physicians in metropolitan areas. Physicians in large metropolitan areas are more likely than nonmetropolitan physicians to practice in an institutional setting.

Physicians in New England are more likely than physicians in other regions of the country to practice in an institutional setting. Physicians in the West North Central and Pacific census divisions are more likely to be in practices with 25 or more physicians. The proportion of solo physicians in the Pacific census division is among the highest in the country while the proportion in the West North Central area is among the lowest—even though both areas are widely recognized as having high managed care penetration.

Table 3-5 also shows that physicians who are not board certified are more likely to be in solo practice and more likely to practice in an institutional setting than those who are. Male physicians are more likely than female physicians to be in solo and small group practices. A preponderance of female physicians practice in institutional settings (43 percent).

Older physicians are substantially more likely to practice as solo practitioners than younger physicians. Only 12.5 percent of physicians age 35 and under are in solo practice, in contrast to 45.0 percent of those over the age of 65. Younger physicians are more likely than older physicians to practice in group settings of all sizes, and are at least 10 percentage points more likely to practice in an institutional setting. More than a third of international medical graduates practice in solo settings, in comparison to fewer than one fourth of U.S. medical graduates. International medical graduates also are more likely to practice in institutional settings.

Finally, table 3-5 presents information on the distribution of practice size by a state-level measure of managed care penetration. Differences in the share of physicians in solo practice by this measure are essentially indiscernible. However, physicians in states with more than 25 percent managed care penetration are more than twice as likely to be in large group practices than physicians in any other region of the country.

TABLE 3-5. Practice Size by Physician Characteristics and Geography, 1995

	1 MD	*2 to 4 MDs*	*5 to 9 MDs*	*10 to 24 MDs*	*25 MDs or More*	*Institutional*	*Sample Size*
All Physicians	26.5	19.1	11.1	6.4	6.5	30.4	4024
Type of Specialty							
Primary care	28.1	18.8	8.6	4.2	8.0	32.3	1213
Nonprimary care	25.9	19.2	12.2	7.3	5.8	29.5	2811
Specialty Group							
Gen/family practice	28.6	19.7	8.6	3.1	6.2	33.8	501
Gen internal med	29.9	15.7	6.9	5.8	8.6	33.1	441
Gen pediatrics	24.2	22.3	11.4	3.4	10.5	28.2	271
Med/ped subspecialties	25.3	20.9	10.3	7.7	7.3	28.4	537
Obst/gynecology	32.9	25.1	14.7	3.7	4.9	18.7	278
Surgery	35.5	28.4	10.2	3.5	4.6	17.8	822
RAPs	6.3	12.6	18.5	17.7	8.6	36.2	530
Other specialties	27.1	9.1	10.1	4.9	4.3	44.5	644
Community Size							
Nonmetro	35.4	20.5	8.3	3.6	6.2	26.0	478
Small metro	23.7	20.5	13.7	8.6	5.8	27.7	1263
Large metro	26.3	18.1	10.3	5.7	6.9	32.7	2283
Census Division							
New England	25.4	13.7	11.9	5.1	4.7	39.2	275
Middle Atlantic	28.2	20.1	11.5	4.1	2.0	34.0	659
E North Central	23.5	19.6	11.2	7.3	7.2	31.3	622
W North Central	16.0	18.6	14.9	6.6	10.1	33.9	270
South Atlantic	30.0	18.9	11.8	8.0	3.2	28.2	739
E South Central	23.7	29.1	10.2	6.4	6.0	24.5	220
W South Central	28.8	19.2	8.6	5.7	7.6	30.2	348
Mountain	24.9	20.5	12.7	7.8	5.9	28.1	219
Pacific	29.0	16.6	9.2	6.4	12.8	26.0	673
Board Certification							
Not certified	33.1	15.3	6.6	4.1	3.8	37.0	791
Certified	24.9	20.0	12.2	6.9	7.1	28.7	3233
Sex							
Male	27.8	19.5	11.5	6.8	6.3	28.1	3416
Female	19.4	16.9	9.2	4.0	7.5	43.0	608
Age							
35 and under	12.5	20.1	13.6	7.5	6.4	39.8	412
36 to 45	19.0	20.2	12.4	7.1	8.4	32.9	1571
46 to 55	29.1	19.7	11.0	6.7	5.9	27.7	1194
56 to 65	43.4	17.4	8.3	3.6	3.9	23.5	607
Over 65	45.0	11.7	6.5	4.9	3.9	28.0	241
Country of Med School Graduation							
USMG	23.8	20.3	12.7	6.8	6.9	29.5	3202
IMG	37.2	14.5	5.0	4.8	4.8	33.5	822
State-Level Managed Care Penetration							
0 to 15%	26.7	22.0	11.9	6.6	4.9	27.9	833
15 to 20%	26.0	19.7	11.1	5.5	3.7	33.9	1129
20 to 25%	27.8	20.5	10.9	7.2	5.8	27.7	655
Over 25%	26.3	16.4	9.9	6.2	12.2	29.0	990
Not classified	26.5	16.0	12.8	7.3	4.6	32.8	418

Source: American Medical Association Socioeconomic Monitoring System (SMS), 1995 survey.

IMPLICATIONS OF THE ANALYSIS

The data presented here indicate that, between 1991 and 1995, there was a significant decrease in the proportion of physicians in solo practices and a corresponding increase in the proportion in institutional settings. In addition, they show that the share of solo practitioners fell at an increasing rate during those years. However, the data also clearly show that there was no wholesale abandonment of solo practice. Percentage point changes in the share of patient care physicians in solo practice did not show any consistent pattern of increases or decreases over the five years studied.

Viewed from a historical perspective, the observed movement from solo to group practice is a continuation of a trend evident as early as the 1960s—well in advance of any significant managed care presence or growth. Early growth in group practice undoubtedly aided insurers in the development of managed care by reducing the transaction costs of establishing and monitoring a managed care panel. Naturally, the fact that the transition to group practice was not precipitated by managed care does not preclude it as an important determinant of physician practice choice today.

The analysis of the 1991–1995 SMS data indicates that physician input and practice output have changed in recent years and that these changes are correlated with practice size and specialty. Overall, both the total number of hours worked per week and the number of hours in patient care per week declined by about 4 percent. The total number of visits per week among patient care physicians fell by more than 9 percent, and the number of office visits per week fell by nearly 7 percent. Moreover, physicians in larger practices and those in institutional settings work fewer hours per week and fewer weeks per year than their counterparts in solo practice. Clearly, if the current trend toward group practice continues, the lower work effort of physicians will absorb some of the projected physician surplus. (See chapter 2.)

The number of visits on hospital rounds fell by more than 19 percent between 1991 and 1995. (See table 3-3.) Physicians in surgery and obstetrics/gynecology reported declines of 25 and nearly 36 percent, respectively. Physicians in general/family practice and general internal medicine reported declines in visits on rounds in excess of 30 percent.

The number of surgical procedures performed per week was stable between 1991 and 1995 for physicians overall. However, the data revealed important differences by specialty. Where obstetricians/gynecologists reported a more than 19 percent decline in the number of surgical procedures performed per week over the five-year period, physicians in general internal medicine and in general pediatrics reported an increase. Physicians in obstetrics/gynecology and physicians in radiology, anesthesiology, and pathology also reported significant decreases in the number of hours they worked per week. (See table 3-2.)

Although the cause of the changes observed for RAPs is more difficult to assess, the reduction among obstetricians/gynecologists in the number of visits per week between 1991 and 1995, and to some extent the reduction in their hours worked, were likely the result of widespread implementation of recovery guidelines by insurers. Highly controversial, the guidelines are promoted by insurers as being necessary to move patients out of the hospital as early as possible. In addition to widely publicized guidelines for obstetrics/gynecology, insurers in some areas have issued guidelines for general surgery, oncology, cardiology, and orthopedics.[34]

Guidelines developed by the actuarial firm of Milliman & Robertson called for reducing hospital stays following an uncomplicated C-section from the 1992 national average of 6.7 days to 2.[35] Public outcry over changes taking place in hospital stays for maternal care prompted legislators in most states to pass legislation mandating minimum lengths of stay following delivery. Furthermore, federal legislation was passed in 1996 that incorporated minimum length of stay rules for insurers and prohibited insurers from offering incentives to encourage shorter hospital stays for maternity care.[36]

In addition to insurers' recovery guidelines, equalization of payment rates for vaginal and C-section deliveries by at least one major insurer[37] and implementation of clinical profiling systems providing feedback to physicians by hospitals in some areas of the country[38] undoubtedly contributed to the observed trend. However, the question remains as to the magnitude of the effects of these changes on the number of surgical procedures per week among obstetricians and gynecologists. A corollary question centers on the extent to which the differences in surgical procedures per week observed by specialty—the decline for obstetricians/gynecologists and the increase among physicians in general internal medicine and in general pediatrics—are the result of managed care firms actively steering patients away from surgical specialists.

In general, physicians' inflation-adjusted earnings, both annual and hourly, remained fairly stable between 1991 and 1995. However, this stability did not hold for all specialties. Physicians in obstetrics/gynecology and in radiology, anesthesiology, and pathology had significant decreases in their inflation-adjusted net income. Obstetrics/gynecology also experienced a statistically significant 12.6 percent decrease in its mean inflation-adjusted effective hourly wage.

Finally, the SMS data for 1995 revealed substantial differences in the practice size distribution of physicians by age. In particular, younger physicians are far less likely to be in solo practice than older physicians. The differences observed by age are a consistent extension of a pattern identified by Kletke, Emmons, and Gillis. Although many physicians change practice arrangements during their careers, the growing disparity between practice size distribution of young and old physician cohorts and the effects of cognitive dissonance suggest yet another reason to expect the distributional transition from solo to group practice to continue.

CONCLUSION

Between 1991 and 1995 there was a significant movement away from solo practice and a concurrent increase in the proportion of physicians practicing in institutional settings. Contrary to conventional wisdom the movement away from solo practice was not precipitated by the recent growth in managed care. Practice sizes were already increasing by the 1960s, long before managed care had made any significant inroads into the U.S. health care system.

Notable among the empirical results in this chapter is the decline in hours worked per week—a decrease of 4 percent overall. This change was particularly dramatic for hours spent on hospital rounds, which decreased by 11 percent. The data also reveal significant declines in patient visits—in both inpatient and outpatient settings. Decreases in work hours and patient visits per week were generally smaller in large practices, suggesting that greater practice size can insulate physicians against an increasingly competitive marketplace.

The data on financial rewards to practice, however, make it clear that simple prescriptions for physician practice size are fraught with danger. After controlling for inflation, neither net income nor hourly wages changed significantly over the period of study. Viewed from this perspective, greater practice size has not constituted a buffer against the market. Furthermore, differences in the financial rewards to practice show no consistent pattern with regard to practice size.

APPENDIX VARIABLE DEFINITIONS

Specialty

Primary Care

Gen/family practice:	Family practice, general practice
Gen internal med:	General internal medicine
Gen pediatrics:	General pediatrics

Non–Primary Care

Med/ped subspecs:	Adolescent medicine, allergy and immunology, cardiovascular disease, diabetes, endocrinology,

	gastroenterology, geriatric medicine, hematology, infectious diseases, medical oncology, neonatal-perinatal medicine, nephrology, nutrition, pediatric allergy, pediatric cardiology, pediatric emergency medicine, pediatric endocrinology, pediatric gastroenterology, pediatric hematology/oncology, pediatric nephrology, pediatric pulmonology, pulmonary diseases, rheumatology
Obstetrics/gyne:	Gynecological oncology, gynecology, maternal and fetal medicine, obstetrics and gynecology, reproductive endocrinology
Surgery:	Cardiovascular surgery, colon and rectal surgery, facial plastic surgery, general surgery, head and neck surgery, hand surgery, neurological surgery, ophthalmology, orthopedic surgery, otolaryngology, pediatric surgery, plastic surgery, traumatic surgery, thoracic surgery, urology, vascular surgery
RAPs:	Anesthesiology, anatomic/clinical pathology, diagnostic radiology, forensic pathology, neuropathology, nuclear medicine, nuclear radiology, pathology, pediatric radiology, radiation oncology, radiology
Other specialties:	Child neurology, child psychiatry, critical care medicine, dermatology, emergency medicine, general preventive medicine, neurology, occupational medicine, physical medicine and rehabilitation, psychiatry, psychoanalysis, public health, other specialty, unspecified

Census Division

New England:	Connecticut, Maine, Massachusetts, New Hampshire, Rhode Island, Vermont
Middle Atlantic:	New Jersey, New York, Pennsylvania
East North Central:	Illinois, Indiana, Michigan, Ohio, Wisconsin
West North Central:	Iowa, Kansas, Minnesota, Missouri, Nebraska, North Dakota, South Dakota
South Atlantic:	Delaware, District of Columbia, Florida, Georgia, Maryland, North Carolina, South Carolina, Virginia, West Virginia
East South Central:	Alabama, Kentucky, Mississippi, Tennessee

West South Central:	Arkansas, Louisiana, Oklahoma, Texas
Mountain:	Arizona, Colorado, Idaho, Montana, Nevada, New Mexico, Utah, Wyoming
Pacific:	Alaska, California, Hawaii, Oregon, Washington
Managed Care Penetration	
0 to 15%:	Georgia, Illinois, Iowa, Kentucky, Louisiana, New Jersey, North Carolina, South Carolina, Virginia
15 to 20%:	Connecticut, Indiana, Michigan, Missouri, New York, Oklahoma, Pennsylvania
20 to 25%:	Alabama, Florida, Maryland, Ohio, Oregon, Tennessee, Texas
Over 25%:	Arizona, California, Colorado, Massachusetts, Minnesota, Washington, Wisconsin
Not classified:	Alaska, Arkansas, Delaware, District of Columbia, Hawaii, Idaho, Kansas, Maine, Mississippi, Montana, Nebraska, Nevada, New Hampshire, New Mexico, North Dakota, Rhode Island, South Dakota, Utah, Vermont, West Virginia, Wyoming

References

1. P. Starr, *The Social Transformation of American Medicine* (New York: Basic Books, 1982).

2. B. Rice, "Don't Count Soloists Out," *Medical Economics* 71, no. 24 (Dec. 26, 1994): 74–86.

3. S. M. Shortell, R. R. Gillies, and D. A. Anderson, "New World of Managed Care: Creating Organized Delivery Systems," *Health Affairs* 13, no. 5 (1994): 46–64.

4. J. Johnsson, "Solo Practice: Down, Not Out," *American Medical News* 39, no. 7 (Feb. 19, 1996): 3.

5. L. E. Jensen, "The Development of Group Medical Practice in the United States of America: 1929–1980," in *5th International Congress on Group Medicine* (Tokyo: Japan Medical Association, 1982).

6. D. W. Emmons, "Changing Dimensions of Medical Practice Arrangements," *Medical Care Review* 45, no. 1 (1988): 101–28.

7. D. W. Emmons and C. J. Simon, "Managed Care: Evolving Contractual Arrangements," *Socioeconomic Characteristics of Medical Practice 1996* (Chicago: American Medical Association, 1996).

8. F. E. Graham, "Group versus Solo Practice: Arguments and Evidence,"*Inquiry* 9, no. 2 (1972): 49–60.

9. L. J. Freshnock and L. J. Goodman, "The Organization of Physician Services in Solo and Group Medical Practices," *Medical Care* 18, no. 1 (1980): 17–29.

10. G. C. Pope and R. T. Burge, "The Marginal Practice Cost of Physicians' Services: Final Report," (Waltham, MA: Center for Health Economics Research, 1993).

11. P. J. Held, "Group Practice and the Ownership of Medical Laboratory and X-ray Facilities," in *Analysis of Economic Performance of Medical Group Practices,* ed. P. J. Held and U. Reinhardt, Report 79-05 Mathematic Policy Research (Princeton, NJ: Mathematic Policy Research, 1979).

12. U. E. Reinhardt, "A Production Function for Physician Services," *Review of Economics and Statistics* 54, no. 1 (1972): 55–66.

13. J. H. Lorant and L. J. Kimbell. "Determinants of Output in Group and Solo Medical Practice," *Health Services Research* 11, no. 1 (1976): 6–20.

14. M. A. Satterthwaite, "Consumer Information, Equilibrium Industry Price, and the Number of Sellers," *Bell Journal of Economics* 10, no. 3 (1979): 483–502.

15. M. V. Pauly and M. A. Satterthwaite, "The Pricing of Physicians' Services: A Test of the Role of Consumer Information," *Bell Journal of Economics* 12, no. 3 (1981A): 488-506.

16. T. E. Getzen, "A 'Brand Name Firm' Theory of Medical Group Practice," *Journal of Industrial Economics* 33, no. 2 (1984): 199–215.

17. M. Gaynor and P. Gertler, "Moral Hazard and Risk Spreading in Partnerships," *Rand Journal of Economics* 26, no. 4 (1995): 591–613.

18. L. J. Goodman and F. D. Wolinsky, "Conditional Logit Analysis of Physicians' Practice Mode Choices," *Inquiry* 19 (Fall 1982): 262–70.

19. L. J. Kimbell and J. H. Lorant, "Physician Productivity and Returns to Scale," *Health Services Research* 12, no. 4 (1977): 367–79.

20. M. Pauly, "Efficiency, Incentives and Reimbursement for Health Care," *Inquiry* 7, no. 1 (1970): 114–31.

21. J. P. Newhouse, "The Economics of Group Practice," *Journal of Human Resources* 8, no. 1 (1973): 37–56.

22. R. H. Lee, "Monitoring Physicians: A Bargaining Model of Medical Group Practice," *Journal of Health Economics* 9, no. 4 (1990): 463–81.

23. M. Gaynor and M. V. Pauly, "Compensation and Productive Efficiency in Partnerships: Evidence from Medical Group Practice," *Journal of Political Economy* 98, no. 3 (1990): 544–73.

24. Gaynor and Gertler.

25. H. E. Frech and P. B. Ginsburg, "Optimal Scale in Medical Practice: A Survivor Analysis," *Journal of Business* 47, no. 1 (1974): 23–36.

26. W. D. Marder and S. Zuckerman, "Competition and Medical Groups: A Survivor Analysis," *Journal of Health Economics* 4, no. 3 (1985): 167–76.

27. Emmons.

28. W. D. Marder and others, "Physician Employment Patterns: Challenging Conventional Wisdom," *Health Affairs* 7, no. 5 (1988): 137–45.

29. P. L. Havlicek, M. A. Eiler, and O. T. Neblett, eds., *Medical Groups in the U.S. 1993* (Chicago: American Medical Association, 1992).

30. P. R. Kletke, D. W. Emmons, and K. D. Gillis, "From Owners to Employees: Current Trends in Physicians' Practice Arrangements," AMA Center for Health Policy Research Discussion Paper 96-1, Mar. 1996.

31. P. L. Havlicek, ed., *Medical Groups in the U.S. 1996: A Survey of Practice Characteristics* (Chicago: American Medical Association, 1996).

32. M. L. Gonzalez, ed., *Physician Marketplace Statistics 1995* (Chicago: American Medical Association, 1996).

33. Kletke, Emmons, and Gillis.

34. Bureau of National Affairs, Inc., "Guidelines Issued to Medical Specialists by Ill. Blues Plan Angers Medical Society," *BNA's Health Care Policy Report* 2, no. 5 (Jan. 31, 1994): 170–71.

35. G. Borzo, "R.I. Doctors Face 'Absurd' Inpatient Limits," *American Medical News* 37, no. 11 (Mar. 21, 1994): 1; and M. Millenson, "Blues Plan Lays Guideline Mandate on Specialists," *Report on Medical Guidelines & Outcomes Research* 4, no. 23 (Dec. 2, 1993): 1–3.

36. Bureau of National Affairs, Inc., "President Signs Bill to Expand Maternity, Mental Health Coverage," *BNA's Health Care Policy Report* 4, no. 39 (Sept. 30, 1996): 1531–32.

37. Bureau of National Affairs, Inc., "N.J. Blues to Equalize Payment for Vaginal, C-Section Deliveries," *BNA's Health Care Policy Report* 3, no. 30 (July 24, 1995): 1180.

38. Bureau of National Affairs, Inc., "C-Section Rates Declining at Three Denver Hospitals," *BNA's Health Care Policy Report* 2, no. 46 (Nov. 21, 1994): 1948.

PART II

Physician Compensation and Reimbursement Mechanisms

This section consists of four chapters. Chapter 4, "Reimbursement for Physician Services," explains fee-for-service physician payment systems, comparing past and current methodologies. Chapter 5, "Reimbursement for Physician Services in a Capitated Environment," outlines typical capitation arrangements and explains the basic principles and structure for developing a physician reimbursement mechanism in a capitated environment. Chapter 6, "National Trends in Physician Income," examines current trends in physician income, with a review of income by specialty. Chapter 7, "Legal and Financial Considerations of Physician Compensation in the Institutional Setting," focuses on the "business" arrangements between physicians and institutions, especially on the impact on those arrangements of the laws and regulations governing health care fraud and abuse and those governing tax-exempt organizations.

4

Reimbursement for Physician Services

Stephen A. Norton
Stephen Zuckerman, PhD

The growth of managed care may lead to a fundamental shift in the way physicians are paid for their services. Traditional fee-for-service (FFS) arrangements may gradually give way to systems based on capitated monthly payments covering, for example, all office care provided to a panel of patients. In fact, recent reports suggest that in California more than 60 percent of payments to physicians from HMOs come through capitation.[1] Although fixed monthly fees may be the future, the current reality is that Medicare, Medicaid, and private insurers still pay for most physician services on an FFS basis.[2] Within the physician services market, Medicare is the dominant payer, accounting for 28 percent of physician revenues in 1995.[3]

This chapter focuses on Medicare's approach to FFS payment systems. It discusses the history of Medicare physician payment and describes the current methodology, which establishes payment based on a resource-based relative value scale, a geographic practice cost adjustment, and fee updates established by comparing actual spending to a preestablished target. The chapter also reviews possible changes in the system's components, compares the system to methods used to pay physicians under state Medicaid programs, and assesses the extent to which Medicare has influenced private payers.

HISTORY OF MEDICARE PHYSICIAN REIMBURSEMENT

When the Medicare program was enacted in 1965, the physician payment methodology mirrored systems used by private insurers. At that time, private insurers paid physicians their actual charges for a service up to a prespecified percentile of the charge distribution in a given market area. This customary, prevailing, and reasonable (CPR) payment methodology was inherently inflationary because physicians had the incentive to increase their charges in order to increase the insurer's allowed fees. In addition, because payments in some localities were based on specialty-specific charge screens, physicians in different specialties in the same locality could be paid different amounts for the same service. Moreover, although the CPR approach limits what the Medicare program would view as allowable charges for services, there were virtually no restrictions on a physician's ability to bill the patient directly for any amount not covered by the insurance plan, a situation known as *balance billing*. Finally, by basing allowed amounts on physicians' actual charges, the CPR system institutionalized a system in which payment rates were based on neither the costs of providing services nor patient valuation of services.

Beginning in 1975 with the Medicare economic index (MEI) and culminating most recently with the 1992 Medicare physician payment reforms, the Medicare program implemented a series of programs designed to mitigate the impact of these problems. The MEI was an index of prices for physician practice services that served as an upper limit on the rate of increase in the maximum amount the program would pay. It established the principle that, at a minimum, growth in what the program pays for services should be linked to growth in what it costs to produce those services, as opposed to what physicians charge. In the mid and late 1980s, further controls on fees were implemented, including fee freezes, limits on MEI updates, and targeted reductions in the rates of increase for selected services.

As Medicare began this process of strengthening its price controls, concerns emerged about possible shifts in costs to beneficiaries, in the form of increases in balance billing. Those concerns were addressed through the Participating Physician program, under which physicians could voluntarily agree to forego balance billing for all Medicare patients, and by explicit limits on the extent of balance billing that nonparticipants could impose. (In essence, by giving beneficiaries clear financial incentives to seek out participants, the Participating Physician program was a forerunner of private-sector preferred provider organizations [PPOs].)

Despite all these changes, however, the Medicare physician payment methodology was still characterized by the vestiges of the CPR system, with its inherent problems. From the policy maker's perspective, perhaps the biggest problem was that CPR had resulted in payments for surgeries and other procedures that were high relative to payments for visits and other primary care services.[4] To break the link between Medicare's rates and CPR, Congress undertook a series of major reforms of the Medicare payment methodology in 1992. This reform initiative consisted of a number of related changes. First, the Health Care Financing Administration (HCFA) adopted the Medicare fee schedule (MFS), which based relative payments across services on the relative resource costs of producing those services. By doing so, HCFA hoped to replicate the workings of a competitive market.[5] In addition, the 1992 reforms included the Medicare Volume Performance Standard (MVPS) policy, which linked fee updates to growth in the volume and intensity of services. Finally, to ensure that beneficiaries were not required to make up for the reductions in many high-priced services whose Medicare payment rates were cut as a result of reform, limits were tightened on the amount of balance billing physicians could impose.

1992 MEDICARE PHYSICIAN PAYMENT REFORM INITIATIVE

As adopted by Congress, payments for a given service under the MFS are computed as the product of (1) the relative value of the service based on the Medicare relative value scale (RVS), which determines how much to pay for a given service relative to other services; (2) a geographic adjustment factor, which determines how much to pay for a given service in a specific area relative to other areas;[6] and (3) a conversion factor that assigns a dollar value to the geographically adjusted relative values, which determines the basic level of payment. Originally, the conversion factor (CF) was set so that implementation of the Medicare RVS was budget neutral, that is, did not result in program expenditures greater or less than they would have been if the CPR methodology had continued in place. CF updates are based on the Medicare Volume Performance Standard (MVPS) mechanism, discussed later in this chapter.

Medicare Relative Value Scale Mechanism

The key component of the MFS—the RVS—assigns a relative resource cost to each physician service, incorporating three major components of the costs required to produce the service: the physician's work, practice expenses, and the cost of professional liability insurance. Between 1986 and 1992, researchers at Harvard University developed physician work relative value units (RVUs) by surveying approximately 3,300 physicians on the amount of work required for the most commonly performed services (approximately 500) in 33 specialties.[7] With the assistance of practicing physicians, the Harvard researchers then established relationships between surveyed and nonsurveyed services and assigned work values to the remaining physician services reported in the current procedural terminology (CPT).[8] In total, the Harvard study produced work values for more than 5,000 services.[9] For a number of services, however, work RVUs were not based on surveys of physicians. For example, work RVUs for radiology and anesthesiology services were derived from previously developed scales.

For the practice expense and malpractice components of physician costs, HCFA used Medicare physician charge data to compute RVUs.[10] Despite the interest in basing the RVS on relative resource costs, this level of data was not achievable for practice expenses or malpractice insurance at the time the MFS was implemented, and the decision was made to accept the relative charge approach for these components. Amendments to the Social Security Act passed in 1994 mandated the development and implementation of resource-based practice expense relative values as part of the MFS. (Although no congressional mandate exists to develop resource-based malpractice liability expense RVUs, the Physician Payment Review Commission [PPRC] has recommended that it do so.) The current charge-based method of determining practice expense relative values will be repealed as of 1998. Work by the PPRC, however, suggests that such a payment reform could redistribute approximately 26 percent of practice expense payments.[11]

To make the RVS meaningful, it was necessary to ensure that the services for which payment rates were being established were defined consistently across the country. To accomplish this goal, the MFS also included nationally uniform physician payment policies aimed at clarifying service definitions and establishing rules for setting payments for modified services (for example, when only the technical or professional component of a service is provided). Although HCFA guidelines on payment policies existed prior to implementation of the MFS, they were often applied differently depending on the carrier. For example, although all Medicare carriers under the previous CPR payment system based payment for surgical services on a global package, definition of the package varied extensively.[12] (These payment policies are discussed in greater detail in a review of Medicaid payment systems later in this chapter.)

Geographic Practice Cost Adjustments

To incorporate justifiable differences in the costs of providing services across localities, Congress required that each of the components of total RVUs—work, practice expense, and malpractice—be adjusted by a geographic practice cost index (GPCI). The *work GPCI* reflects variation in the earnings of professional workers and can be viewed as a cost-of-living adjustment for physicians; the *practice expense GPCI* measures differences in the costs of hiring practice employees and renting office space; and the *malpractice GPCI* is an index of the costs of a comparable professional liability insurance policy in different areas of the country. (The original development of these indices are discussed in detail by Welch and others.[13] As established by Congress, the practice cost and liability GPCIs adjust for the full differences in these costs between Medicare localities. Only a quarter of the differences between localities is recognized in the work GPCI. These indices have been revised as new data have become available.[14]

Medicare Volume Performance Standard Policy

Another significant portion of the 1992 physician payment reform initiative was implementation of the MVPS policy. The MVPS provides HCFA with a mechanism to reduce (or increase) physician payment levels through the CF update when the volume and intensity of services grow more quickly than recent historical trends. In essence, the MVPS allows for reductions or increases in the conversion factor when overall spending falls above or below an expenditure growth performance standard. Currently, performance standards are computed for three different service categories (surgical, primary care, and other nonsurgical services) in a given year. Actual expenditure growth in each service category is compared to the performance standard as data on actual expenditure growth become available to determine future updates to the conversion factor. For example, the MVPS for 1996 is compared to actual spending for 1996 during 1997, and this comparison determines how large the CF update will be in 1998. The 1998 CFs are then increased or decreased, depending on whether the growth in actual 1996 expenditures exceeded or fell below the 1996 performance standard. Under this policy, if the resulting CF update leads to too low a level of payment, the likelihood that future spending will be below the target is increased and the potential for future increases in the update is greater.

The performance standard is set equal to the sum of the adjusted historical trend in the volume and intensity of physician services for the preceding five years, the growth in beneficiaries, changes in prices, and the effect of other changes in laws and regulations that might affect expenditure growth. The policy is designed only to hold physicians accountable for growth in the volume and intensity of services beyond adjusted historical trends. Historical volume and intensity trends are reduced by a specified deduction because there was a general perception that volume and intensity included a certain amount of inefficient and inappropriate care. However, the size of the volume and intensity reduction is inevitably somewhat arbitrary and has been an issue of concern among policy makers.[15]

Since its implementation, the formula for computing performance standards has met with considerable criticism, particularly from the PPRC. First, by applying the same spending targets to all physicians, the MVPS provides very weak incentives to any individual physician to change behavior.[16] Because individual physicians cannot believe that their responses to the policy can have a significant impact on the size of bonuses or penalties, the policy may have little effect on the aggregate volume and intensity of services.

Second, it is argued that separate performance standards for different categories of services lead to distortions in relative payments, which undermines the basic principle underlying the RVS—the internal consistency of the scale of relative work values. The PPRC has recommended that a single performance standard be used to update the conversion factors, regardless of service category.[17] Although this regularization would maintain the internal consistency of the scale of relative work values, it would not allow different types of services to grow at different rates.

Finally, concerns have been raised regarding the fixed deduction from historical volume and intensity growth rates. Currently, the performance standard takes a fixed deduction of 4 percentage points, which is an inflexible and arbitrary approach. A constant 4 percent deduction might not account for significant changes in medical practice that may have considerable health benefits or in the economy as a whole. Because growth in the gross domestic product (GDP) represents the economy's capacity to pay for additional health spending, the PPRC has recommended that performance standards be linked to growth of real GDP per capita plus 1 or 2 percentage points to allow for higher rates of growth due to advancements in medical capabilities.

Balance Billing

To ensure that beneficiaries were not required to make up for the reductions in many high-priced services whose Medicare payment rates were cut when the MFS was implemented, limits that had been in place since the mid-1980s were tightened on the amount of balance billing physicians could impose. Physicians were able to collect less than 10 percent above the fee schedule amount when they chose not to assign the claim. By 1995, almost three out of four physicians seeing Medicare patients agreed to become formal participants and accept Medicare's allowed fee as payment in full. This acceptance rate resulted in more than 90 percent of all Medicare charges being provided without balance billing. These limits on balance billing may reduce out-of-pocket spending by beneficiaries but do nothing to control Medicare's costs. In fact, they may make it more difficult for Medicare to control its payments because the

Medicare fee has to seem reasonable to a large number of physicians and their representatives.[18]

MEDICAID ADOPTION OF THE RVS AND OTHER MEDICARE PAYMENT REFORMS

Despite the extensive research and planning that went into the Medicare payment reforms, no states have adopted the full range of these reforms for their Medicaid programs. However, a number of state Medicaid programs, almost 40 percent in January 1995, have implemented the RVS.[19] (The states that have adopted these programs include Arizona, Delaware, Florida, Georgia, Indiana, Kentucky, Massachusetts, Michigan, Mississippi, North Carolina, Ohio, Oklahoma, Oregon, Rhode Island, South Carolina, Texas, Utah, Washington, and West Virginia.) Although these Medicaid programs have adopted the RVS to pay physicians, many of the states have adapted the RVS to meet their specific budgetary or access goals. For example, Texas established access-based fees for services that were considered undervalued and, as a result, represented a potential access risk. Oregon and Washington have separate conversion factors for obstetrics/gynecology services.[20] Obstetrics/gynecology and pediatrics were the areas most affected by RVS relativity adjustments designed to ensure access for Medicaid eligibles.[21] Similarly, states adopting the RVS to pay physicians generally set their own CF to reflect their objectives regarding overall levels of payments.

Although states may adopt the Medicare RVS, they may not adopt other components of the Medicare payment methodology, such as budget neutrality in implementation, the mechanism for updating the CF, or any of the uniform payment policies. In their 1992 survey of state Medicaid programs, McCormack and colleagues found that states that adopted the RVS exhibited considerable variation in what other Medicare policies the states adopted. Although almost 50 percent of the 13 states indicating they had adopted the RVS had adopted surgical service definitions and the payment methodology for assistants at surgery, only 20 percent had adopted budget neutrality as a constraint against payment levels and none had adopted volume performance standards.[22]

The following subsections explore in detail two dimensions in which Medicare and Medicaid reimbursement methodologies differ: payment levels and payment policies.

Implicit Conversion Factors for Medicaid Reimbursement

The current level of Medicaid payments in a state is determined using the Medicare RVS, calculating CFs that could be applied to the RVS to generate fees that would be revenue neutral relative to current Medicaid payment methodologies in that state. Table 4-1 includes state-specific budget-neutral CFs for 49 Medicaid programs based on information from a 1993 Medicaid fee survey.[23] These CFs are those that might be used intuitively by any state implementing an RVS-based payment system of its own. The state results are presented in descending order. There is a substantial amount of variation in the estimated CFs, ranging from a high of $60.80 (Alaska) to a low of $13.91 (New Jersey). Using the 1993 Medicare CF for primary care services ($33.72) as a baseline for comparison, 48 states have implicit Medicaid CFs below the Medicare CF. Several states with large Medicaid populations are well below Medicare. For example, California ($20.01), New York ($15.41), and New Jersey ($13.91) all have CFs that are more than 40 percent less than Medicare.

These implicit CFs are consistent with previous work that has illustrated considerable variation in Medicaid fees across states and suggest that if each state implemented its own revenue-neutral RVS-based Medicaid system, considerable variation across states in Medicaid payments for services would remain. Across the United States, Medicaid programs exhibited more than a twofold variation in fee levels in 1993.[24] Fees in Alabama were roughly one and a half times as high as the average Medicaid fee, and fees in New Jersey were roughly 50 percent of the average Medicaid fee.

Medicaid Adoption of Other Medicare Payment Policies

In addition to using the Medicare RVS to determine payments, state Medicaid programs might consider using the other payment policies that accompanied the Medicare reforms. These rules are intended to ensure that carriers apply uniform policies when computing allowed fees for surgical services, anesthesia payments, services provided in hospital outpatient departments, multiple procedures, certain services rendered by nonphysician providers, and payment of physicians who assist at surgery. However, of those Medicaid programs using the Medicare RVS to set fees in 1993, few were using its payment rules to determine payments. Because of the importance of these payment policies for defining the services associated with the RVUs (for example, the RVUs for surgical procedures are based on a predetermined global time period), the extent to which Medicaid payment rules differ from Medicare may necessitate revisions of the RVS or changes in Medicaid rules. Without these changes, Medicaid fees computed from the Medicare RVS could differ greatly from those intended by Medicaid policy makers. If current Medicaid payments are based on global periods that are shorter than those used by Medicare, for example, movement toward an RVS fee for Medicaid would likely cause changes in the way physicians bill for surgical

TABLE 4-1. Implicit Conversion Factors for Medicaid Based on 1993 Fee Data

State	*1993 Revenue—Neutral CFs*	*State*	*1993 Revenue—Neutral CFs*
Alaska[a]	60.80	Florida	25.27
West Virginia	38.55	New Hampshire	25.05
Georgia	32.44	Wisconsin	24.96
Nevada	32.42	North Dakota	24.91
Wyoming	31.51	Kansas	23.90
Massachusetts	31.47	South Dakota	23.29
Nebraska	30.93	Colorado	23.13
Kentucky	30.84	Delaware	23.07
Arkansas	30.59	Pennsylvania	22.54
Washington	29.58	Iowa	22.16
Idaho	28.89	Utah	22.10
Alabama	28.82	Vermont	22.08
Louisiana	28.67	Connecticut	21.81
Virginia	28.49	Mississippi	21.24
Tennessee	28.20	Michigan	21.08
Maryland	27.83	Oregon	21.08
North Carolina	27.82	South Carolina	20.95
Minnesota	27.72	California	20.01
Montana	27.22	Maine	19.94
Texas	26.90	Illinois	19.74
Hawaii	26.82	Ohio	19.19
District of Columbia	26.70	Missouri	18.43
Oklahoma	26.66	Rhode Island	16.33
Indiana	25.94	New York	15.41
New Mexico	25.66	New Jersey	13.91

[a]Fee data used in computation of the implicit CF are for Anchorage, Alaska, only.

services. Of course, the extent of these changes would vary depending on how much Medicaid payment policies currently resemble Medicare rules.

Following is a comparison of Medicaid physician payment policies to the rules established under the MFS, with regard to a number of individual reforms within three general areas of payment: global surgical package definitions, payments for multiple procedures, and site-of-service differentials.[25]

Global Surgical Package Definitions Major Medicare surgical services are paid on the basis of a global fee that includes the preoperative evaluation and management visits beginning the day before the surgery, the surgery itself, and postoperative services related to the surgery. The consultation in which the decision to undergo surgery is made is reimbursed separately. The length of the postoperative period included in the global payment package varies by four broad types of procedures, including major, minor, ambulatory, and endoscopic. For major and ambulatory procedures, postoperative services related to the surgery cannot be billed separately by a physician for 90 days after the surgery itself. For minor procedures, the length of the postoperative payment period is 10 days. For endoscopic procedures, physicians can bill separately for services immediately after the procedure is completed. To allow assessment of how Medicaid rules compare to this approach, states provided information on the global surgical payment package for nine procedures that spanned these four types of services.[26]

Although nearly all Medicaid programs have developed a global surgical payment policy, there is considerable variation in what is included in the global package. Table 4-2 indicates that more than half of the states surveyed follow Medicare and do not include payment for the surgical consult in the global package for any of the procedures surveyed. For the remaining states that bundle payment for the surgical consult into the global package, there is considerable variation across broad service groups and even across procedures within these groups. In Illinois, for example, physicians are paid separately for the surgical consultation in which the decision to undergo destruction of a benign facial lesion (CPT 17000) and a cystourethroscopy (CPT 52000) is made but are not paid separately when the consult involves major procedures such as an arthroplasty of the knee (CPT 27447) and a coronary artery bypass (CPT 33512).

Overall, most Medicaid programs have adopted a postoperative payment period that is different from Medicare. As table 4-2 shows, only 8 of the 44 states surveyed have a postoperative period that replicates Medicare's policy. Of the 31 states with other postoperative payment periods, 13 have periods that are longer than Medicare, with one state (New York) defining its postoperative period for an arthroplasty of the

TABLE 4-2. Comparison of Medicare and Medicaid Physician Payment Policies

	Same as Medicare		Different from Medicare		No Information—Unclear	
Medicare Policy	*Number*	*Listing of States*	*Number*	*Listing of States*	*Number*	*Listing of States*
Global Surgical Payments						
The surgical consult is not included in the global payment package.	23	AK, AL, AZ, CO, CT, DE, GA, ID, KY, MA, ME, MI, MN, MS, MT, NC, ND, NY, OR, SC, VT, WA, WY	17	AR, CA, FL, HI, IA, IL, IN, LA, MO, NH, NJ, OK, PA, TX, UT, VA, WI	4	MD, NH, OD, SD
Postoperative Period Length Major—90 days Ambulatory—90 Days Minor—10 Days Endoscopic—0 Days	8	AK, AZ, FL, GA, KY, MI, OK, WI	31	AL, AR, CO, IA ID, IL, ME, MN, MO, MS, MT, NC, ND, NH, NJ, NM, NY, OR, PA, SC, SD, TX, UT, VT, VA, WY, AL, CT, MA, CA, IN	5	LA, MD, MT, NM, SD
Payment for Multiple Procedures						
100% of first procedure, 50% of second, and 25% of all subsequent procedures	14	FL, GA, HI, IA, ID, MA, MI, ND, NH, NM, OH, UT, VT, WA	29	AL, AK, AR, CA, CO, CT, DE, ID, IL, IN, KY, LA, ME, MD, MN, MS, MO, MT, NJ, NY, NC, ND, OK, OR, PA, SC, TX, VA, WI, WY	1	MO
Site-of-Service Differential						
Payment limits based on site of service	8	CA, IL, MN, MO, MT, NC, OH, TX	36	AL, AK, AZ, AR, CO, CT, DE, FL, GA, HI, ID, IN, IA, KY, LA, ME, MD, MA, MI, MS, NH, NJ, NM, NY, ND, OK, OR, PA, SC, SD, UT, VT, VA, WA, WI, WY	0	

Source: S. Norton, D. Verrilli, and S. Zuckerman, "Medicaid Physician Payment: Current Policies and the Potential Impact of the MFS RVS," Urban Institute Working Paper 06375-04, 1995.

knee (CPT 27477) as 180 days. The remaining states have postoperative payment periods ranging from 5 to 62 days.

Multiple Procedures Multiple procedures are those performed by a physician on the same patient on the same day for which Medicare allows separate payment. Currently, if more than one procedure is provided on the same patient during a single operative session, Medicare will pay 100 percent of the global fee only for the highest-valued procedure, 50 percent for the second most expensive procedure, and 25 percent for the third, fourth, and fifth most expensive procedures. Special rules apply to endoscopic and dermatologic procedures. (In the case of multiple endoscopic procedures, the full value of the higher-valued endoscopy is recognized plus the difference between the next highest endoscopy and the base endoscopy. Medicare also has identified some dermatology services for which the multiple-procedure rules do not apply because the RVUs for these codes reflect the multiple nature of the procedure.)

As table 4-2 illustrates, 14 of the 44 states surveyed have a multiple-procedure payment policy similar to Medicare's. However, the majority of states are more generous than Medicare. Twenty states recognize 100 percent of the payment for the most expensive procedure and 50 percent for all subsequent procedures. One state (Montana) paid 100 percent for all procedures. Four states were less generous than Medicare, and two states (New York and New Jersey) limit the total amount payable rather than payments for individual procedures.

Site-of-Service Differential The 1993 MFS includes a list of procedures that are subject to a site-of-service differential limiting payments when provided in an outpatient setting. The basic idea is that physicians incur fewer practice expenses when they provide a service in a hospital outpatient department and that Medicare is already paying for these costs by reimbursing the hospital for facility charges. Therefore, Medicare applies a site-of-service differential for selected services by reducing practice expense RVUs by 50 percent. In the 1992 MFS, for example, HCFA estimated that this RVU adjustment resulted in an average payment reduction of 21 percent.[27] This reduction occurs mostly among evaluation and management services, such as office visits.

As table 4-2 shows, site of service has no impact on payment rates in 36 Medicaid programs. A small number of states, however, do differentiate payment on the basis of site of service. In California, for example, common office procedures such as acne surgery (CPT 10040), excision of a benign tumor (CPT 11421), a breast biopsy (CPT 19100), and application of an ambulatory-type cast (CPT 29450) are paid 80 percent of the fee when the service is provided in an outpatient or surgical clinic. Similarly, in Illinois, ambulatory services such as cast application, suture repair of a skin wound, and endoscopies are paid at a lower rate in the outpatient setting than in the physician's office. In Michigan and Ohio, payments for evaluation and management services provided in the outpatient or inpatient setting are reduced by 40 and 30 percent, respectively, relative to services provided in a physician's office. In Texas, payments for nonemergency services provided in the emergency room are reduced by 40 percent.

PRIVATE PAYERS' ADOPTION OF THE MEDICARE RVS

The factors leading private payers to adopt the RVS are similar to those that motivated Medicare and Medicaid programs to adopt it. The RVS allows them to move away from their own charge-based payment systems, which had many of the same problems as the Medicare system. In particular, the RVS underwent extensive scrutiny and debate and is now widely viewed as a rational cost-based payment system with uniform standards. Private payers, however, face two additional incentives for adopting the RVS. First, the system is maintained by the federal government and thereby reduces administrative costs to the insurer. Second, adoption of the RVS focuses any potential negotiations over payment levels on the conversion factor and thus simplifies negotiations and fee discounting. The simplifications are particularly useful at a time when many payers are seeking discounts from providers. In fact, once some payers begin using the RVS, its adoption by other payers may be important in order to remain competitive.

Two studies have found that private payers are adopting the RVS. One has shown that a number of the leading indemnity insurers in 1992, with a range of health insurance products and national geographic coverage, either were considering adopting or had adopted an RVS-based payment system for physician services.[28] According to that study, the payers most likely to adopt the RVS were Blue Cross/Blue Shield plans, IPA-model HMOs, and PPOs. These results are corroborated by a more recent review by the American Medical Association (AMA).[29] Moreover, payers with a concentration of business in the Midwest and West were more likely to adopt the RVS.

As with Medicaid, payers that adopt the RVS system pick and choose among the Medicare payment policies to suit their particular needs and the circumstances of the market. Although these payers were likely to adopt an RVS-type system, they did not adopt the Medicare RVS as is. Many insurers adopted Medicare's global surgical payment policies outright. However, many of the payment policies of the MFS (for example, site-of-service differentials, geographic fee adjustments, and performance standards) were rejected by private payers. Moreover, a significant portion of those payers that adopted the RVS modified RVUs in some specialties. For example, Blue Cross/Blue Shield plans frequently modified obstetrics/gynecology RVUs.

In addition to variation across companies in what components of the MFS the companies adopted, there is significant variation in how individual companies implemented their payment systems across product lines and geographic areas. For example, one national company indicated that approximately 50 percent of the markets in which it conducted business would be reimbursed on the basis of RVS by 1993. In the non-RVS segment of its market, the payer continued to use the CPR method of payment.[30] Finally, the RVS-type payment system was most likely used for reimbursement for PPO products and least likely for traditional indemnity lines.[31]

Private FFS Reimbursement

Medicare fees were roughly 71, 62, and 66 percent of private payer fees in 1989, 1992, and 1994, respectively.[32] However, recent increases in Medicare fees resulting from CF updates and the growth of fee discounts in the private sector indicate that this gap may be closing.[33] The closing of the gap between Medicare and private fees may in part be a function of the rising share of the private market receiving care through PPOs.

PPOs are a form of managed care in which providers agree to accept discounted fees with the expectation that their patient volume will remain constant or potentially increase, and they are becoming an increasingly important provider of services in the private insurance market. Between 1987 and 1994, the number of PPOs increased sevenfold, from 100 to more than 700 plans.[34] Growth in the number of individuals enrolled with PPOs reflects these trends. In 1993, the share of all individuals with private insurance enrolled in PPOs increased from an estimated 10.4 to 43.0 percent.[35] A recent study of 30 PPO plans indicates that the predominant payment method for PPO providers was discounted FFS and that none of the PPOs surveyed used capitation as a basic form of physician reimbursement.

The available evidence suggests that private payers have been able to establish heavily discounted rates with PPOs, but even discounted FFS rates in the private market remain well above those paid by Medicare. Using data from two large national insurers, Verrilli and Zuckerman found that, on average, payments were 20.8 percent higher for indemnity than for PPO products in one insurer and 11.5 percent in the other.[36] Despite these sizable discounts achieved by both payers in their analysis, PPO rates were still well above those paid by Medicare in 1993. Again, across all services, 1993 Medicare fees were 35.2 and 33.2 percent below the PPO rates for the two payers.[37] However, the process of discounting observed among the PPOs in the Verrilli and Zuckerman study did not suggest that relative fees within the PPOs were rapidly moving in the direction of those embodied in the Medicare RVS.

CONCLUSION

The Medicare program, in part reacting to the perceived flaws in the CPR methodology, introduced a major innovation in FFS physician payment. Implementation of the RVS and the MVPS in 1992 attempted to rationalize payment methodologies by basing allowed fees on the resource costs of providing services. Given Medicare's dominance in the physician services market, it is not surprising that many other payers have begun to adopt the reforms developed by that program. As of 1995, approximately 40 percent of state Medicaid programs had adopted the RVS. Moreover, surveys indicate that a number of private payers, including Blue Cross/Blue Shield plans and national insurance carriers, also have adopted the RVS.

However, although non-Medicare payers are adopting the RVS, they are adopting neither Medicare's payment levels nor the MFS reforms in their entirety. In 1993, reimbursement by Medicaid programs was, on average, 73 percent of that provided by Medicare.[38] In 1995, Medicare reimbursement levels were estimated to be roughly 70 percent of private levels.[39] Moreover, although many payers have adopted the RVS, they have not adopted other components of the Medicare payment methodology, such as the mechanism for updating the conversion factor.

References and Notes

1. E. Rosenthal, "Reduced HMO Fees Cause Concern about Patient Care," *The New York Times,* Nov. 25, 1996, section A.

2. A recent study of 30 PPOs found that the dominant method of payment was discounted FFS. See M. Gold and others, *Arrangements between Managed Care Plans and Physicians* (Washington, DC: Physician Payment Review Commission, 1995).

3. C. Simon and P. Born, "Physician Earnings in a Changing Managed Care Environment," *Health Affairs* 15, no. 3 (1996): 124–33.

4. S. Jencks and A. Dobson, "Strategies for Reforming Medicare's Physician Payments," *New England Journal of Medicine* 312, no. 23 (1985): 1492–1500.

5. W. Hsiao and others, "Results and Policy Implications of the Resource-Based Relative-Value Study," *New England Journal of Medicine* 319, no. 13 (1988): 881–88.

6. The geographic basis for payment is the Medicare payment locality. Localities were established by Medicare carriers for the purpose of developing charge profiles for use as screens in the CPR payment methodology the MFS replaced. Although carriers varied in their approaches to defining localities (they range from entire states to parts of individual counties), localities have been, and continue to be, the basis for implementing pricing policy changes.

7. W. Hsiao and others, "An Overview of the Development and Refinement of the Resource-Based Relative-Value Scale," *Medical Care* 30, no. 11 (1992): NS1–NS12.

8. L. Leape and others, "Small-Group Judgement Methods for Determining Resource-Based Relative Value Scales," *Medical Care* 30, no. 11 (1992): NS28–NS39.

9. Since 1992, work values have been modified periodically to ensure they still accurately reflect physicians' work, either as a response to public comments on them or to accommodate changes in CPT. This annual review was required by the Omnibus Reconciliation Act of 1989. The act also requires a major review every five years. This five-year review now has been completed and is resulting in further redistribution in payments toward primary care and away from procedural services.

10. J. Levy and others, "Impact of the Medicare Fee Schedule on Payments to Physicians," *JAMA* 264, no. 6 (1990): 717–22.

11. Physician Payment Review Commission, *Practice Expenses under the Medicare Fee Schedule: A Resource-based Approach,* Background Paper No. 92-1 (Washington, DC: PPRC, 1992).

12. Physician Payment Review Commission. *Variation in Medicare Global Service Policies,* Background Paper No. 89-2 (Washington, DC: PPRC, 1989).

13. P. Welch, S. Zuckerman, and G. Pope, "The Geographic Medicare Index: Alternative Approaches," Urban Institute Working Paper, Washington, DC, 1989.

14. Office of the Federal Register, National Archives and Records Administration, "Medicare Program: Refinements to Geographic Adjustment

Factor Values and Other Policies under the Physician Fee Schedule," *Federal Register* 59, no. 121 (1994): 32755–94.

15. Physician Payment Review Commission, *Annual Report to Congress* (Washington, DC: PPRC, 1995).

16. J. Holahan and S. Zuckerman, "The Future of Medicare Volume Performance Standards," *Inquiry* 30, no. 3 (Fall 1993): 235–48; and T. Rice and J. Bernstein, "Volume Performance Standards: Can They Control Growth in Medicare Services?" *The Milbank Quarterly* 68, no. 3 (1990): 295–319.

17. Physician Payment Review Commission, *Annual Report to Congress.*

18. Holahan and Zuckerman.

19. Physician Payment Review Commission, *Annual Report to Congress.*

20. R. W. Whitten, "RVS Adoption by Non-Medicare State and Federal Health Programs," paper presented at an AMA conference titled "RVS Physician Payment: Choice, Fee-For-Service and Health System Reform," Chicago, May 1994.

21. L. McCormack and others, *Use of Medicare Payment Methodologies and Cost Containment Strategies by Medicaid Programs and Private Payers* (Boston: Health Economics Research, Inc., 1993).

22. McCormack and others.

23. In the spring of 1993, the Urban Institute surveyed 49 states (excluding Arizona) and the District of Columbia regarding their fees for a total of 20 high-expenditure and high-volume services, ranging from office visits to obstetrical services. (See Norton, below, for more details.) Implicit CFs are computed as the weighted average of service-specific CFs, computed as the payment for a given service divided by the RVUs for that service. The weights used in the computations are the shares of total RVUs the service accounts for within the surveyed services.

24. S. Norton, "Medicaid Fees and the Medicare Fee Schedule: An Update," *Health Care Financing Review* 17, no. 1 (1995): 197–82.

25. Information on Medicare physician payment policies is taken from Office of the Federal Register, National Archives and Records Administration, "Medicare Program: Fee Schedule for Physician Services," *Federal Register* 56, no. 227 (Jan. 1991): 59502–819. Updates were

identified in "Medicare Program: Fee Schedule for Physician Services for Calendar Year 1993," *Federal Register* 57, no. 228 (Nov. 1992): 55914–6167; "Medicare Program: Revisions to Payment Policies under the Physician Fee Schedule," *Federal Register* 58, no. 133 (July 1993): 37994–8019; "Medicare Program: Revisions to Payment Policies and Adjustments to the Relative Value Units under the Physician Fee Schedule for Calendar Year 1994," *Federal Register* 58, no. 230 (Dec. 1993): 63626–854; and "Medicare Program: Refinements to Geographic Adjustment Factor Values and Other Policies under the Physician Fee Schedule," *Federal Register* 59, no. 121 (Dec. 1994): 32755–94.

26. In June 1994, the Urban Institute conducted a survey of 50 Medicaid programs plus the District of Columbia to explore payment policies on the definition of global surgical periods for major, ambulatory, and minor procedures; supplemental payments for office medical supplies; payments for physicians who assist at surgery; payments for multiple procedures and payment differentials for sites of service, types of providers, and geographic areas; payments for the technical and professional component of radiology services and diagnostic tests; and payments for anesthesia services. Medicaid directors from 44 states responded. The Medicaid programs that did not reply within this specified time were the District of Columbia, Kansas, Nevada, Nebraska, Rhode Island, and West Virginia. The survey was not applicable to Tennessee because its Medicaid enrollees receive medical services through managed care arrangements. For more details, see S. Norton, D. Verrilli, and S. Zuckerman, "Medicaid Physician Payment: Current Policies and the Potential Impact of the MFS RVS," Urban Institute Working Paper 06375-04, 1995.

27. *Federal Register* 56.

28. McCormack and others.

29. American Medical Association, *Medical Practice Financing Systems* (Chicago: AMA, 1995).

30. McCormack and others.

31. McCormack and others; and American Medical Association.

32. Physician Payment Review Commission, *Annual Report to Congress* (Washington, DC: PPRC, 1996).

33. Physician Payment Review Commission, *Annual Report to Congress,* 1996.

34. American Association of Preferred Provider Organizations, *PPO Industry Profile 1995* (Washington, DC: AAPPO, 1995).

35. Employee Benefit Research Institute, "Sources of Health Insurance and Characteristics of the Uninsured: Analysis of the March 1994 Current Population Survey," Issue Brief 158, Washington, DC, Feb. 1995.

36. D. Verrilli and S. Zuckerman, "Preferred Provider Organizations and Physician Fees," *Health Care Financing Review* 17, no. 3 (1996): 161–70.

37. Verrilli and Zuckerman.

38. Norton.

39. Physician Payment Review Commission, *Annual Report to Congress,* 1996.

5

Reimbursement for Physician Services in a Capitated Environment

Dewayne E. Ullsperger

As enrollment in managed care plans continues to grow, physicians are increasingly being asked to accept risk as a condition of payment. Reducing cost is a major reason for the emergence of this trend, as purchasers, including employers and Medicaid programs, have succeeded in many markets in driving down the cost of sponsored health programs. As a result, health plans have become the messenger, where the message is to realign economic incentives to yield a fair price, real value, reasonable profits, and predictable growth in costs. Health plans pass risk on to physicians through a number of mechanisms, including:

- Use of physician "withholds," whereby the plan retains, or withholds, a portion of the physician's reimbursement to be returned based on the plan's financial results and/or individual provider performance
- Participation in the gains and/or losses of a "shared-risk" fund, which is based on target PMPM (per member, per month) expenses for a defined set of institutional, referral, and/or other services
- Capitation for a defined set of physician services, where physicians are compensated on a PMPM basis for services the physician(s) has the ability to provide
- Global capitation for all or most of the health care risk

This chapter provides an overview of the typical financial characteristics of a capitated arrangement and presents a framework for developing a reimbursement mechanism for physician services in a capitated environment.

OVERVIEW OF CAPITATION ARRANGEMENTS

In a capitated environment, significant risk is transferred to participating providers; the amount of money paid to capitated providers covers all costs associated with the capitated services, regardless of the actual number of services provided or their value. Figure 5-1 presents a typical flow

FIGURE 5-1. Flow of Funds under a Fully or Partially Capitated Arrangement

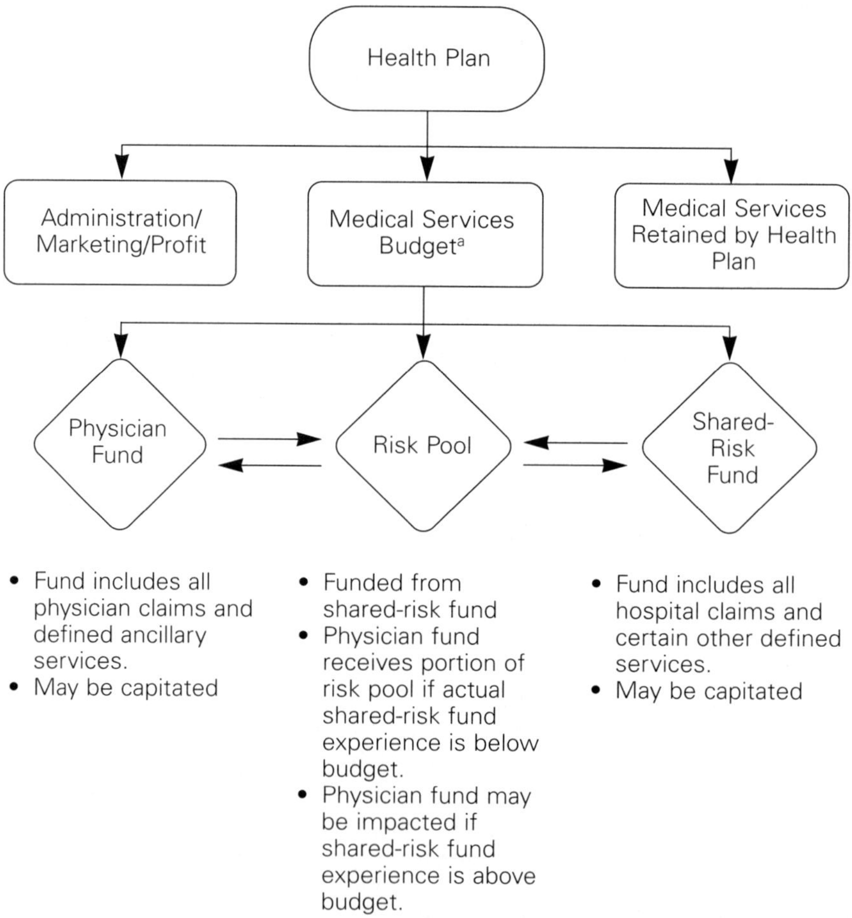

[a]May actually be a capitation to a provider organization.

of funds under a fully or partially capitated arrangement. Generally, health plans allocate the premium dollar into several funds, including:

- Plan administration, marketing, and profit
- Medical services risk retained by the plan
- Hospital/institutional services
- Physician services
- Other medical services

Any or all of the medical services funds may be capitated. Typically, physician services are capitated to a provider group. Also, a hospital/institutional fund, or shared-risk fund, budget is established. Moreover, there may be a fund for ancillary medical services that is treated separately. Gains and/or losses in the shared-risk fund(s) are shared between the provider group and the health plan.

In establishing PMPM budgets for each fund, a responsibility matrix is usually developed and is included in the provider agreement. (See table 5-1.) Figure 5-1 and table 5-1 can vary significantly for a given contract, often depending on the availability of capitation contracts for specific services (for example, mental health and substance abuse), the capabilities of the provider group, and the appetite for risk on the part of the plan or the provider group. In evaluating contracts with health plans, the provider group should understand the component costs of the various funds, or risk pools, established by the plan. This includes evaluating the utilization levels and reimbursement schedules underlying the proposed arrangement. Also, the provider group should evaluate the portion of premium retained by the plan for administration, profit, and medical services for which the plan is retaining the risk.

FULL-PHYSICIAN CAPITATION

In a full-physician capitation, all physician services are capitated to a provider group (for example, an independent practice association [IPA] or a multispecialty group). Additional incentives may or may not be present.

Generally, the health plan should develop a budget for physician services that is based on expected utilization and fee-for-service-equivalent reimbursement (although in some areas capitations appear to be based largely on market conditions). Typically, the target reimbursement levels will be no more than would be available under a modified fee-for-service (FFS) arrangement. For example, if an HMO can contract with area providers on a fee schedule consistent with 115 percent of RBRVS (Medicare's resource-based relative value scale), capitation contracts will likely be structured to compensate physicians at no more than 115 percent

TABLE 5-1. Matrix of Responsibility

Service	*Responsibility* Shared Risk Fund	*Physician Fund*	*Health Plan*
Hospital inpatient facility:			
Acute	X		
Mental health			X
Substance abuse			X
Detox			X
Skilled nursing facility	X		
Hospital outpatient facility:			
Outpatient surgical	X		
Emergency room	X		
Observation bed	X		
Radiology	X		
Laboratory/pathology	X		
Therapy	X		
Other diagnostic	X		
Other therapeutic	X		
Home health care agency	X		
Equipment/supplies	X		
Transplants (Phys & Hosp)			X
Ambulance	X		
Primary care physician		X	
Specialty physician		X	
Professional mental health/substance abuse			X
Office-based radiology		X	
Office-based laboratory		X	
Reference lab		X	
Therapy:			
Rendered by hospital facility or employees	X		
Rendered by physician		X	
All other services:			
Billed via HCFA 1500		X	
Billed via UB 92	X		
Pharmacy (if covered benefit)			X
OOA emergency services			X
Reinsurance:			
Premium	X	X	
Recovery	X	X	

of RBRVS. Table 5-2 presents an illustrative budget based on the following assumptions:

- 117 percent of national 1996 RBRVS schedule, excluding anesthesia
- Anesthesia reimbursement based on an anesthesia factor of $38
- Member copayment of $10 per office visit
- Commercial (employer group) population
- Transplants are excluded

These assumptions were chosen for illustrative purposes to result in a capitation target of $40 PMPM. Table 5-2 also presents illustrative rates on an age/sex basis for this benefit plan. Variations to this arrangement may be as follows:

- The capitation rates may be expressed as a percentage of premium.
- Certain services or specialties may be carved out of the capitation.
- Excess-loss coverage may be provided to limit the group's exposure to high-cost individuals.
- A risk corridor may be provided, whereby the physician group's gains or losses relative to a fee schedule may be shared between the plan and the capitated provider group.

Percentage of Premium Contracts

As premium levels become very competitive in some markets, there is a tendency for HMOs to attempt to pass some of the underwriting risk on to provider groups in order to preserve both market share and profit margins. Percentage-of-premium contracts are often used as the vehicle for this transfer of risk. In this type of contract, the HMO contracts for all or a portion of medical services based on an agreed-on percentage of premium. For example, the HMO may compensate a physician group based on 35 percent of the HMO's total premiums for members assigned to that group. It is common to see percentage-of-premium contracts developed for Medicare and Medicaid contracts where the premium is known in advance, but the HMO is newly entering the market.

Percentage-of-premium contracts increase risk to providers because premium levels become a variable and the provider group is at risk for the plan's ability to set appropriate premium rates. In negotiating a percentage-of-premium contract, the provider group should understand the plan's underwriting process for commercial groups as well as its current and projected premium yield. In addition, the provider group should

TABLE 5-2. Example Physician PMPM Budget

PMPM Budget

Service Category	*Utilization/ 1,000*	*Reimbursement/ Service*[a]	*PMPM*
Surgery			
Nonmaternity	374	$243.10	$7.58
Maternity—nondelivery	15	262.80	0.33
Maternity—deliveries	16	1,869.40	2.49
Venipuncture	372	10.50	0.33
Anesthesia	100	369.40	3.08
Radiology	747	57.40	3.57
Pathology/lab	2,587	13.30	2.87
Office visits	2,910	43.20	10.48
Preventive medicine	173	101.20	1.46
Inpatient visits	145	70.10	0.85
Consultations	139	109.50	1.27
Emergency room/critical care	70	97.30	0.57
Immunizations/injections	353	29.60	0.87
Psychiatry	258	85.50	1.84
Ophthalmology	116	74.10	0.72
Physical medicine	366	21.40	0.65
Other medicine	898	44.80	3.35
Miscellaneous	148	46.00	0.57
Total			$42.88
Copayments[b]			($2.88)
Net budget			$40.00

Illustrative Age/Sex-Adjusted Budgets

	Distribution of Members		*Age/Sex-Adjusted Budgets*	
Age	*Male*	*Female*	*Male*	*Female*
Under 2	1.7%	1.6%	$54.00	$54.00
2 to 14	10.8	10.3	19.40	19.40
15 to 19	3.4	3.2	21.70	29.10
20 to 44	22.6	25.2	26.40	55.10
45 to 59	8.0	8.9	48.60	59.90
60 and over	2.2	2.1	85.20	71.90
Subtotal/average	48.7%	51.3%	$31.79	$47.80
Grand total/average		100.0%		$40.00

[a]Reflects anesthesia factor of $38.00, other services at 117% of 1996 national RBRVS.

[b]Reflects a $10 copayment for office visits, preventive medicine, psychiatry, and ophthalmology.

understand the methodology used by the plan to assign premiums to each member—in particular, family members.

Many physician groups have negotiated some protection from the underwriting risk by negotiating a "floor." The floor represents the minimum PMPM capitation the group will receive. For example, a provider group may negotiate a 35 percent of premium contract, with a floor of $35 PMPM. With this floor provision, the minimum capitation would be $35 PMPM even if the premium yield falls below $100 PMPM.

Carve-outs

Carve-outs refer to specific medical services that are not included in the capitation agreement. The HMO retains the risk for these services. It is common to see certain services carved out of a physician capitation agreement, in particular the following:

- Reference lab
- Mental health and substance abuse
- Routine vision care
- Out-of-area or out-of-network services
- Transplants

Generally, PMPM carve-outs vary depending on the contracts that have been negotiated by the health plan. The physician group should become comfortable with the amounts carved out for these services. It is difficult to evaluate carve-outs to reflect the presence of point-of-service (POS) product, out-of-network benefits. When a health plan offers a POS benefit plan, the plan will generally adjust its capitation rates to reflect an estimate of the percentage of services to be rendered out of network or include these services in the provider group's capitation. Use of out-of-network providers can vary significantly depending on:

- Breadth of the plan's provider network
- Strength of, and access to, the provider group
- Richness of the out-of-network benefit to be offered relative to the in-network benefit
- Chance fluctuation

Because of these variations, there is a tendency for the health plan to be relatively conservative in making any adjustments to the capitation. Usually, however, this carve-out can be structured as a *risk pool,* where any dollars not used for out-of-network benefits are returned to the capitated provider groups.

Excess-Loss Coverage

Often the health plan will retain the risk for most or all of the claims exceeding a certain threshold per member per year. This retention of risk is referred to as *excess-loss,* or *stop-loss, coverage.* For example, the plan may reduce the capitation to fund protection for 80 percent of claims per member per year in excess of $10,000 (that is, the provider group retains the risk for 20 percent of a member's claims in excess of $10,000). If the plan does not offer such protection, coverage is available from a number of insurance carriers. Usually, the "claim" is calculated based on the underlying FFS-equivalent fee schedule. Table 5-3 shows actuarial-based claim cost estimates for several excess-loss coverage options for a commercial population.

Most plans load the expected claim costs for factors such as risk margin, administration, and profit. Some plans provide excess-loss coverage in their capitation agreements without specifically identifying the cost of this coverage. A provider group should request that the plan identify these costs and determine whether the contract allows the group to purchase excess-loss coverage from a private carrier. Although private carriers will add 25 to 45 percent to the expected claim cost to cover administration and profit, it is often worthwhile to seek quotes from private carriers as something to compare to what the plan is offering.

Risk Corridors

In markets where capitation is not common, HMOs often guarantee FFS-equivalent reimbursement until membership reaches a certain level (say, 500 members). In addition, some plans guarantee that the providers will receive no less than some percentage of an agreed-on fee schedule. This minimum fee schedule limits the provider group's risk within a defined risk corridor. Such provisions generally guarantee 70 to 85 percent of a reasonable or market-based reimbursement schedule.

TABLE 5-3. Actuarial-Based Claim Cost Estimates for Excess-Loss Coverage Options

Deductible	*Coinsurance*	*PMPM Claims Cost*[a]
$5,000	80%	$3.00
10,000	80	1.10
15,000	80	0.60

[a]Reflects 117 percent of national 1996 RBRVS, $38 anesthesia factor.

INTERNAL REIMBURSEMENT MECHANISM

Whether the plan is capitating an IPA or a medical group, a significant number of individual physicians may be participating under a full-physician capitation arrangement. When entering into such an agreement, there should be some discussion regarding a mechanism for reimbursing these individual providers for their services.

Basic Principles of the Reimbursement Mechanism

In developing an internal reimbursement mechanism, certain basic principles should be addressed, including:

- *The reimbursement mechanism should provide for an equitable distribution of the capitation dollars.* This is a challenge because each party tries to maximize its income within the constraint that the total capitation income is the upper limit for payments to individual providers.
- *The reimbursement mechanism should provide incentives to control overall utilization and reward efficiency and quality in the provision of medical care.* Likewise, it should not excessively harm individual providers because of circumstances beyond their control.
- *Adequate provision should be made for services the network or medical group will not provide.* For example, the mechanism should address the costs for out-of-area emergency care if these services are included in the capitation.
- *A risk-absorption approach should be established.* This is done to protect cash flow in the event that costs exceed the capitation.
- *The mechanism should not be so overly complex as to confuse participating providers or create an excessive administrative burden.* There is often intense pressure to create the perfect risk-sharing model, only to find that the provider group is unable to administer it.

General Structure of the Reimbursement Mechanism

The general structure of a reimbursement mechanism can be thought of as having two elements: provider payment, which defines how providers will be paid on a day-to-day basis; and risk sharing, which determines how providers are ultimately paid for services and defines the process of how surplus dollars are distributed (the settlement process).

The relative importance of these two components depends on the structure of the provider group. For IPAs, the independence of the practitioners requires that there be some type of risk-sharing mechanism in place to avoid cash flow problems. At a minimum, this may require a withhold (explicit risk sharing) or an aggressive fee schedule relative to the capitation level (implicit risk sharing). In either case, there should be expectations that the capitation is sufficient to cover the day-to-day payments to providers. Any surplus or withhold dollars can be distributed within the risk-sharing mechanism.

Depending on the physician compensation structure of a multispecialty clinic and its exposure to capitation, a risk-sharing approach may not be utilized. However, if capitation revenue becomes a significant portion of the clinic's revenue, the clinic should explore the need to structure appropriate internal risk sharing as a means of incenting individual physicians or departments to provide efficient, cost-effective care.

External Pool Allocations

In developing a budget for the apportionment of the physician capitation, several categories of expenses will likely fall outside the capabilities of the participating providers. Allocations for these external expenses should be established prospectively to avoid misunderstanding. Following are several items that should be considered in developing a budget:

- *Contribution to surplus.* In particular, an IPA may set aside moneys to fund a surplus reserve. These moneys can be used to retire start-up expenses, fund capital expenses such as computer software, or address statutory reserve (net worth) requirements.
- *Administrative expense allocation.* For an IPA, administrative costs will need to be funded.
- *Excess-loss coverage.* If the health plan does not provide coverage within the capitation contract, the provider group may purchase or self-fund excess-loss coverage. The premium to purchase this coverage (or allocation for self-funding) needs to be allocated from the capitation. Reinsurance recoveries would be allocated in a similar manner.
- *Nonnetwork medical service expenses.* A portion of the medical services will likely be performed by nonparticipating providers, including emergency care, referrals to nonparticipating subspecialists, and in the case of POS products, the costs of member self-referrals to nonnetwork physicians. Depending on the product, a portion of the capitation revenue should be set aside to cover these anticipated expenses. Unused funds would be available for distribution, and deficiencies in this allocation need to be funded during the settlement process.

- *Subcapitation payments.* The provider group may transfer responsibility for certain services to a third party in return for a per-member capitation. Services that are often capitated include mental health, substance abuse, and reference lab services. Specialty physician and disease management capitations are becoming more common, as well.
- *Shared-risk pool exposure.* The capitation agreement with the health plan may include a shared-risk incentive arrangement for hospital, pharmacy, and/or ancillary services. To the extent that the provider group may be liable for deficits in this fund, provision should be made to accommodate these potential losses. This exposure can be handled as an external pool allocation or within the settlement process of the risk-sharing mechanism.

Once external pool allocations have been defined, the remainder of the capitation is available for services provided by participating providers.

Provider Payment Options

The component of an internal reimbursement mechanism that receives the most scrutiny is the provider payment arrangement. Following is a summary of provider payment options, along with comments regarding each one.

Modified Fee-for-Service/Fee Schedule Under a fee schedule, physicians are paid on a per-procedure basis. If provider payments are made based on a fee schedule, there should be a withhold established to protect against deficits. Alternatively, the fee schedule should be low enough so that deficits are unlikely. The advantages to this approach are that it is easily understood by providers and reflects the status quo for most of them. Its major disadvantage is that individual providers have a financial incentive to overutilize, even if the threat of higher future withholds is present. In many markets, providers believe that the withhold is simply an additional discount, so the withhold loses its value as a financial incentive. Some health plans and provider groups use varying withholds based on a provider's or specialty's past performance. This is intended to help focus accountability toward individual physicians.

Floating Fee Schedule with a Budget A variation to the modified FFS/fee schedule is to implement a floating fee schedule. The fee schedule "floats" such that provider payments match capitation revenue. This method may be applied on an aggregate basis for all physicians or applied to specific specialties. Depending on the volume of capitation revenue, the group may want to implement budgets for as many specialties as is reasonable and combine the remainder into an "all other" category.

There are several advantages to this approach, including:

- The budgets introduce the concept of capitation because utilization of services impacts the ultimate fee schedule.
- Problem areas become easier to identify if specialty-specific budgets are developed.
- Specialists scrutinize the need for referrals, in effect assisting in the gatekeeping process.
- Physicians tend to self-police overutilizing physicians in the same budget pool.

The disadvantages to this approach include:

- It is relatively complex and requires a fairly sophisticated monitoring system.
- There is usually a time lag in acquiring the information needed to implement it.
- Reconciliation and budget realignments will need to be made over time.
- Budgets by specialty are fairly difficult to establish prospectively. Realignments are sometimes difficult, particularly if a realignment means reducing the budget for a particular specialty.

Provider groups often implement a target fee schedule and allow it to float within a certain range. This helps to avoid situations where a particular specialty is penalized or rewarded simply because the budget was too low or too high at the outset.

Primary Care Capitation One common example of physician capitation is to capitate primary care physicians for a defined scope of services. The capitation rates typically vary by member age and gender. Payments for services provided by the primary care physician that are not delivered under the capitation agreement are paid from a fee schedule. It is relatively easy to develop reasonable capitation rates for primary care services. The group will need to implement a reasonable referral authorization process because there is an incentive to overrefer services that could be provided by the primary care physician. For this reason, groups commonly develop an incentive mechanism that rewards primary care physicians based on:

- Adherence to quality and preventive care standards
- Access
- Open practices to new patients
- Financial indicators, such as referral and hospital costs

Specialty Capitation A specialty capitation is generally developed on a PMPM basis by product line (for example, Medicare, commercial), without adjustment for age and sex. It usually covers all services provided by the specialist; however, capitated services need to be appropriately defined. As with the floating fee schedule approach, specialists under capitation tend to scrutinize referrals.

For a multispecialty group, the specialist capitations tend to be developed at the department level, avoiding the complication of having more than one participating provider within the specialty. However, specialty capitation can be more difficult for IPAs. If one legal entity (for example, a group of five cardiologists) within an IPA can handle all of the IPA's members, the specialty group can be capitated fairly easily. Similarly, a specialty-specific IPA can be formed to accept capitation for a particular group of independent physicians. However, specialty capitation becomes more difficult when more than one legal entity is representing a particular specialty. Assigning subsets of members to various specialists is problematic for the following reasons:

- The assignment mechanism may be administratively burdensome.
- It may be confusing to primary care physicians (PCPs).
- There may be variations in the quality and/or focus of particular specialists.
- The same PMPM may not be appropriate for all specialists given these variations as well as variations in member demographics.

As a result of these concerns, many IPAs implement a specialty capitation methodology that is similar to the floating fee schedule approach. As an alternative to a fee schedule–based system, some IPAs will also use a point system, whereby each physician within the specialty receives one point for each unique patient. Alternatives may include use of risk adjusters to refine the point system. One concern regarding the nonclaims-based approaches is that they will require some administrative capabilities that are not presently in place for most health plans and IPAs.

Risk-Sharing Options

Risk sharing is fundamental to developing an internal reimbursement mechanism under capitation. The risk-sharing approach should be developed to encourage alignment of the incentives of participating providers. Consistent with the basic principles outlined above, the risk-sharing approach should provide cash flow protection to the capitated provider group (particularly if the group is an IPA or similar organization) and should promote the cost-effective delivery of high-quality health care.

Example of a Simple Risk-Sharing Approach A simple example of a risk-sharing approach would be to implement a withhold. Ideally, the withhold would be set at such a level that the likelihood of a cash deficit is fairly small. For example, if the physician capitation is $40 and the withhold is 15 percent, expected payments throughout the year would be $34 PMPM. Any gains could be distributed on the basis of payments withheld throughout the year. Table 5-4 illustrates potential results under this arrangement.

As a risk-sharing approach, this model has the advantage of being administratively simple and, in aggregate, provides some incentives to control utilization. Its biggest disadvantage is that the incentives for an individual provider to control utilization are diluted because utilization and ultimate reimbursement are still highly correlated on an individual basis. Also, specific problem areas are not highlighted by the use of this model.

Example of a Sophisticated Risk-Sharing Approach The risk-sharing approach described in this section provides a general framework from which to develop a more refined reimbursement and risk-sharing model based on the provider group's unique characteristics and objectives. It illustrates some of the decisions that will need to be made, as well as how the flow of funds may be structured in a risk-sharing mechanism. Variations of this approach have been used by a number of provider organizations. The following summarizes the provider payment structure underlying this approach:

- Anesthesia reimbursement is based on an anesthesia factor of $38.
- Reimbursement is based on 117 percent of national 1996 RBRVS for other physicians.
- There is a 15 percent physician withhold.

TABLE 5-4. Potential Results of PMPM Distribution Based on Payments Withheld throughout the Year

	Expected PMPM: $40		
	Scenario 1: Actual PMPM $38[a]	*Scenario 2: Actual PMPM $40*[a]	*Scenario 3: Actual PMPM $42*[a]
Gain/(loss)	$2.00	$0.00	$(2.00)
Withholds[b]	5.70	6.00	6.30
Distribution[c]	7.70	6.00	4.30

[a]Assuming reimbursement at target schedule (before withhold reduction).

[b]15% of actual PMPM. For simplicity, assumes all providers are subject to withhold. In reality, some providers (such as nonnetwork referrals) would not be subject to withholds.

[c]Sum of the withholds and the gain/(loss).

For ease of illustration, the withhold is applied to all services (although in practice, some services, such as out-of-area emergency, may not be subject to a withhold). This example is based on the budget developed in table 5-2 for a commercial population. PMPM budgets by specialty have been developed, which reflect expected claim costs given the provider payment structure described above. In this example, the provider withhold serves two purposes: It is both a tool for ensuring cash flow for the organization and a financial incentive for individual specialties, or departments, to provide cost-effective care.

Table 5-5 presents the resulting withhold and bonus distribution for a hypothetical scenario of actual claims by specialty. The withhold is returned and bonuses are distributed based on the following priorities:

- If aggregate losses for the organization exceed the withholds, the loss would need to be funded from the provider group's reserves, an increase in withholds, and/or a decrease in the reimbursement schedule.
- To the extent that aggregate losses are less than the amounts withheld, withholds are returned pro rata so that no specialty exceeds its budget.
- Half of any remaining monies are distributed pro rata as a bonus to those specialties that had a gain. This is referred to as the *specialty performance bonus.*
- The remainder is distributed based on the expected claim cost distribution by specialty. This is referred to as the *group performance bonus.*

Following is an explanation of table 5-5:

- Column A reflects the PMPM budgets by specialty. These reflect the expected FFS-equivalent costs for the provider group.
- Column B presents the resulting expected claim dollars. For example, the expected claims for urology total $72,000 ($0.60 PMPM multiplied by 120,000 member months).
- Column C presents a scenario of actual claims for the physician group.
- Column D presents the resulting gain or loss (expected minus actual).
- Column E shows those specialties that had a gain.
- Column F reflects withholds that have been implemented. The withholds equal 15 percent of actual claims. The total dollars to be distributed are the gain of $300,000 and the withholds of $675,000, for a total of $975,000.
- Column G shows the withholds to be returned by specialty. If a specialty's loss exceeds its withhold (as in the case of nephrology),

TABLE 5-5. Withhold and Bonus Distribution of Claims by Specialty

Member Months: 120,000	(A)	(B)	(C)	(D)	(E)	(F)	(G)	(H)	(I)
Specialty	*PMPM Budget*[a]	*Expected Claims*	*Actual Claims*	*Gain/ (Loss)*	*Specialty Gains*	*Withhold*	*Withholds Returned*	*Specialty Performance Bonus*	*Group Performance Bonus*
Allergy and immunology	$0.49	$58,800	$63,600	($4,800)	$0	($9,540)	$4,740	$0	$2,925
Anesthesiology	3.06	367,200	386,900	(19,700)	0	(58,035)	38,335	0	18,265
Cardiology and cardiovascular disease	1.05	126,000	133,900	(7,900)	0	(20,085)	12,185	0	6,267
Cardiovascular/thoracic/vascular surgery	0.57	68,400	87,500	(19,100)	0	(13,125)	0	0	3,402
Dermatology	0.54	64,800	75,000	(10,200)	0	(11,250)	1,050	0	3,223
Emergency medicine	0.49	58,800	66,900	(8,100)	0	(10,035)	1,935	0	2,925
Endocrinology	0.14	16,800	19,000	(2,200)	0	(2,850)	650	0	836
Gastroenterology	0.54	64,800	39,600	25,200	25,200	(5,940)	5,940	12,234	3,223
General surgery	1.57	188,400	133,600	54,800	54,800	(20,040)	20,040	26,604	9,371
Hematology/oncology	0.72	86,400	77,800	8,600	8,600	(11,670)	11,670	4,175	4,298
Infectious disease	0.13	15,600	16,400	(800)	0	(2,460)	1,660	0	776
Mental health	1.69	202,800	222,300	(19,500)	0	(33,345)	13,845	0	10,087
Neonatology	0.19	22,800	22,700	100	100	(3,405)	3,405	49	1,134
Nephrology	0.23	27,600	36,300	(8,700)	0	(5,445)	0	0	1,373
Neurology	0.39	46,800	51,200	(4,400)	0	(7,680)	3,280	0	2,328
Neurosurgery	0.37	44,400	39,200	5,200	5,200	(5,880)	5,880	2,524	2,208
Obstetrics and gynecology	4.26	511,200	386,300	124,900	124,900	(57,945)	57,945	60,635	25,427
Ophthalmology	1.33	159,600	122,900	36,700	36,700	(18,435)	18,435	17,817	7,939
Orthopedics/orthopedic surgery	1.66	199,200	231,800	(32,600)	0	(34,770)	2,170	0	9,908
Otorhinolaryngology (ENT)	1.10	132,000	158,600	(26,600)	0	(23,790)	0	0	6,566
Pathology/lab	1.82	218,400	208,100	10,300	10,300	(31,215)	31,215	5,000	10,863
Physical medicine and rehabilitation	0.75	90,000	77,200	12,800	12,800	(11,580)	11,580	6,214	4,477
Plastic and reconstructive surgery	0.23	27,600	21,300	6,300	6,300	(3,195)	3,195	3,058	1,373
Podiatry	0.27	32,400	31,500	900	900	(4,725)	4,725	437	1,612
Primary care	12.76	1,531,200	1,351,900	179,300	179,300	(202,785)	202,785	87,045	76,163
Pulmonary medicine	0.20	24,000	18,300	5,700	5,700	(2,745)	2,745	2,767	1,194
Radiology	2.72	326,400	348,200	(21,800)	0	(52,230)	30,430	0	16,235
Rheumatology	0.13	15,600	21,000	(5,400)	0	(3,150)	0	0	776
Urology	0.60	72,000	51,000	21,000	21,000	(7,650)	7,650	10,195	3,581
Total	$40.00	$4,800,000	$4,500,000	$300,000	$491,800	($675,000)	$497,490	$238,755	$238,755

[a]Reflects anesthesia factor of $38.00, other services at 117% of 1996 national RBRVS. Assumes a $10 office visit copayment.

no withhold is returned. Otherwise, withholds are returned so that the total payments for the specialty do not exceed its budget. (Table 5-6 shows the calculation for the withhold return for allergy and immunology.) After return of the withholds, $477,510 remains to be distributed (total distribution of $975,000 less withhold returns of $497,490). Half of this amount ($238,755) is to be distributed as a specialty performance bonus (column H) and half as a group performance bonus (column I).

- Column H shows the specialty performance bonus distribution. This is calculated based on the distribution of gains for those specialties that have a gain (column E). For example, the total gain for all specialties with a gain is $491,800. Urology represents $21,000 (4.27 percent) of the total gain. Thus, urology receives 4.27 percent of the total specialty performance bonus of $238,755, or $10,195.
- Column I shows the distribution of the group performance bonus. This reflects the specialty's expected share of the PMPM budget, applied to the total bonus of $238,755. For example, anesthesiology reflects 7.65 percent of the PMPM budget ($3.06 from column A divided by $40.00). Thus, anesthesiology receives 7.65 percent of the group performance bonus, or $18,265.

A number of variations to this model must be considered. For example:

- The group may want to distribute any monies remaining after the withhold return across either all specialties that had a gain or all specialties whether they had a gain or not.
- Withholds may be returned in their entirety to all specialties if funds are available in aggregate.
- PCPs or specific specialties may be capitated.
- A larger share of the bonus may be distributed to PCPs.
- Some of the "bonus funds" may be retained by the provider organization to fund reserve requirements.

The details of the approach for a particular provider organization depend on the areas the organization intends to emphasize.

TABLE 5-6. Withhold Return for Allergy and Immunology

Expected claims	$58,800
Actual claims	63,600
Less withhold	(9,540)
Net Claims	54,060
Withhold return[a]	4,740

[a]Expected claims minus net claims, but no more than the withhold.

CONCLUSION

To ensure reasonable long-term reimbursement levels in a capitated environment, a physician group should first ensure that, in aggregate, its capitated agreements provide for reasonable FFS-equivalent reimbursement rates. Several contractual variations ought to be reviewed and a framework created for developing a budget for physician services.

Internal reimbursement for the services of individual providers or departments should be structured to provide some cash flow protection to the provider group, as well as to promote the cost-effective delivery of medical care. There are a number of variations to consider in developing a provider reimbursement and risk-sharing mechanism; the example presented in this chapter may be used as a starting point for discussions within a particular provider organization.

As with most facets of managed care, a physician reimbursement mechanism cannot be developed in a vacuum. Care should be taken to coordinate efforts to develop such a mechanism with the provider group's utilization management, quality assurance, and information systems functions.

6

National Trends in Physician Income

W. David Bradford, PhD

The decade and a half since 1980 has been a period of rapid and radical change in health care in the United States. Much of this change has affected the way that physicians practice medicine and interact with the larger health care sector. Some researchers who have examined the period from the mid-1970s to the mid-1980s suggest a rather pessimistic outlook for physician income,[1] an outlook that has been reinforced by still more recent evidence.[2] Others find evidence of stronger performance.[3] A closer look at income in terms of revenue and cost trends over a more extended and recent period—1982 to 1993—offers a somewhat brighter view of how physicians are faring throughout this time of change.

This chapter examines the trends in income and the constituent changes in revenues and costs that make up physicians' net earnings, in an effort to understand the impact of the changes in the overall health care sector on physician welfare (at least as it is reflected in the "pocketbook"). It also briefly speculates on whether these trends are likely to continue.

BACKGROUND

Physicians are crucial players in the health care field. In 1993, they received just over 19 percent of all the dollars flowing into the health care sector (a proportion that has remained relatively stable over the past decade and a half).[4] Moreover, their influence reaches far beyond the $171 billion they receive in direct payments: Hospital services, most pharmaceutical products, and medical equipment all are used under the direct supervision of a physician. The incentives facing physicians to use or conserve these resources drive much of the trend in health care expenditures. If physicians can control the trends in their income by directing the use of nonphysician inputs into the health care production process, it is even more important to understand how their incomes are changing over time.

As mentioned earlier, the past 10 to 12 years have witnessed major structural changes in the health care sector. The following subsections discuss three of them.

Medicare's Move to a Prospective Payment System

One of the first major changes of the 1980s was the move by Medicare away from retrospective, cost-based fee reimbursement to a prospective payment system (PPS) for hospital services. This new system classified conditions into broad categories called diagnosis-related groups (DRGs) and based hospital reimbursement on these groups rather than on the actual costs of treatment. This had two potential effects on physicians. First, it increased the constraints on what physicians could do in a hospital treatment setting, as the potential for losses to the institution because of excessive use of resources rose dramatically. Second, because of the manner in which PPSs were implemented (applied to inpatient services but not outpatient), hospitals and physicians faced increasing incentives to shift production from an inpatient to an outpatient setting. This gave physicians greater control over the treatment of many patients, and allowed them to sell many services they had not previously provided. Equally important, many private third-party payers and individual state Medicaid programs adopted the Medicare PPS, increasing the effect of this change on physicians.

Medicare's Adoption of the Resource-Based Relative Value Scale

A second major change came toward the end of 1992 with the introduction, again by Medicare, of the resource-based relative value scale (RBRVS) for direct physician reimbursement. In 1986, the Physician Payment Review Commission (PPRC) was created to investigate what improvements could be made to the manner in which physicians were reimbursed under Medicare. At that point, Medicare still used the customary, prevailing, or reasonable reimbursement criteria that had received substantial criticism. The PPRC argued that a new fee schedule should attempt to capture true resource costs. (This recommendation was based on the belief that the medical market was characterized by market failures leading physicians to use inputs inefficiently). An additional policy goal was to adjust payments to providers so that the incomes of primary care physicians would rise, thereby encouraging more doctors to go into specialties.

The RBRVS consists of three parts:

1. An estimate of physician effort devoted to a particular procedure
2. An estimate of the physician costs associated with the effort devoted to each procedure
3. A monetary conversion factor that translates the RBRVS into an actual dollar reimbursement for each service

This approach places an emphasis on resource costs that vary according to specialty and geography. As implemented, the resulting fee schedule effectively increases the Medicare reimbursement rates for "cognitive"-type services and those services provided in more rural settings while decreasing the fees for services typically provided by many specialists and surgeons. As a result, primary care physicians are receiving relatively larger reimbursements, as are those physicians who treat patients in rural settings. Because published income data extend only one year beyond RBRVS implementation, it is impossible to fully discern any preliminary effect on gross income trends; however, careful comparison of the trend prior to 1992 with the 1993 data will be suggestive, particularly with respect to the redistribution of resources among specialties.

Managed Care Revolution

Perhaps the greatest shock to the medical profession since 1982 has been the accelerating managed care revolution. More and more individuals and families are selecting this new form of insurance over traditional indemnity plans. Much of the impetus behind this explosion in managed care enrollment is the promise of cost savings, a feature quite attractive to the businesses that shoulder a substantial portion of employees' health insurance premiums. This promise is grounded in the use of capitated payments to physicians, which provide a direct incentive for conservation and which may place a serious constraint on physicians' ability to control their income. Although the number of different contract types between physicians and managed care third-party payers is growing nearly as rapidly as the managed care industry itself, it is far from clear whether this transformation will harm or enhance the growth in physician income.

BROAD AVERAGES OF PHYSICIAN INCOME

The best-known characteristics of physician earnings are the broad averages. However, this is not to suggest that something important cannot be learned about what has happened, and what is likely to happen, in the physician services market by examining the trends in several measures of earnings—specifically, net income and hourly net income for the average physician and for physicians in several broad specialty classes.

However, before discussing the trends, a note on the numbers is in order. Frequently, time series for physician earnings and costs present these statistics in nominal dollar terms. For example, if one looks at the time series on net income from the American Medical Association's *Socioeconomic Characteristics of Medical Practice* (the primary source of data for this chapter), one finds that net income has risen from $97,000 in 1982 to more than $189,000 in 1993.[5] However, these figures do not reflect the impact of inflation. One dollar would have purchased a larger basket of goods in 1982 than in 1993. If only the undeflated figures are examined, the increase in physician earnings would be overstated because some of the increase in the number of dollars would not represent an increase in buying power. Thus, all figures presented in this chapter are deflated to represent the buying power of a constant dollar (in this case, indexed to the average value for 1982–1984). These constant dollars are called real dollars (to distinguish them from the unadjusted *nominal* dollars).

Finally, a brief note about how physicians receive their income is in order. Historically, income arrived via one source—fees received for services rendered. Today, this is no longer true; a wide variety of payment mechanisms exist. For example, physician reimbursement can be based on per-patient capitation. In this setting, the concept of a patient base (or pool), long implicit in the medical market, has been formalized so that patients are assigned to physicians with a variety of formal and quasi-formal contracts, and physicians receive fixed payments per month for each patient. Physicians also may receive bonuses and profit shares from third-party payers when they keep their utilization of specific resources below a specified level. Such incentives to reduce resource use is applied to physicians by managed care and traditional indemnity payers, and in conjunction with fee-for-service (FFS) or capitation payment mechanisms. Some physicians are paid based on a salary. Again, this mechanism exists in a number of practice and insurance mechanisms, from large multispecialty private practice to staff-model managed care organizations (MCOs). The main point is that the variety of payment mechanisms is enormous; there is no convergence toward one standard of remuneration.

Annual Real Income

With that in mind, this examination begins with the trend in real annual income (net of all practice costs, but before taxes). Figure 6-1 presents this trend for all physicians. Clearly, the decade from 1982 to 1993 was one of relative gains by the average physician in terms of earnings (buying power). In real terms, annual income rose from about $101,240 in 1982 to more than $131,000 by 1993, an increase that was relatively steady. There was a three-year period, between 1983 and 1985, when real income fell, but only slightly (less than $250 decrease for the entire three-year period, making it more accurate to say that incomes were stagnant). However, after 1985, income rose fairly rapidly.

It is interesting to note that the brief stagnation of average income coincided with PPS implementation for hospital reimbursement by Medicare. One hypothesis might be that there was a period of adjustment where physicians and hospitals had to learn how the PPS worked before they were able to use the DRG payment mechanisms effectively to maximize their reimbursement. As discussed earlier, the PPS encouraged changing the site of service from an inpatient to an outpatient setting. This change would take some time to fully implement. The lag in income following the advent of the PPS could be the result of "stickiness" in the shift toward outpatient treatment, a setting that may permit more physician flexibility in treatment. If this hypothesis is correct, one might expect to see less of a downturn during the 1983–1985 period for those classes of physicians who used hospitals less heavily in the practice of medicine. For that, it is necessary to examine the trend in annual real income for physicians in different specialties.

Figure 6-2 breaks out the trend in real net income for five specialty groupings: general practice, internal medicine, surgery, pediatrics, and obstetrics/gynecology. A cursory examination of this figure reveals several points of interest. First, there is a significant disparity in the level of income across specialties. Surgeons and obstetricians have the highest incomes, at almost $181,800 and $153,600 in 1993, respectively. General practitioners and pediatricians generally tie for the lowest annual earnings early in the time period, though pediatrics nudges slightly ahead with $93,700 in real income by 1993, in contrast to a lower income of $80,830 for general practice in the same year. Many of these distinctions in raw income are to be expected given the lengthier training of many specialists relative to general practitioners (that is, given their higher level of "human capital"). However, the relative ranking of obstetrics is somewhat at odds with the prediction of human capital models of physician income. Some hints of what may be going on with the obstetricians may be seen later in this chapter.

A second point to take from figure 6-2, not unrelated to the first, is that much of the increase in average annual earnings evidenced in figure 6-1

FIGURE 6-1. Real Annual Net Income, All Physicians

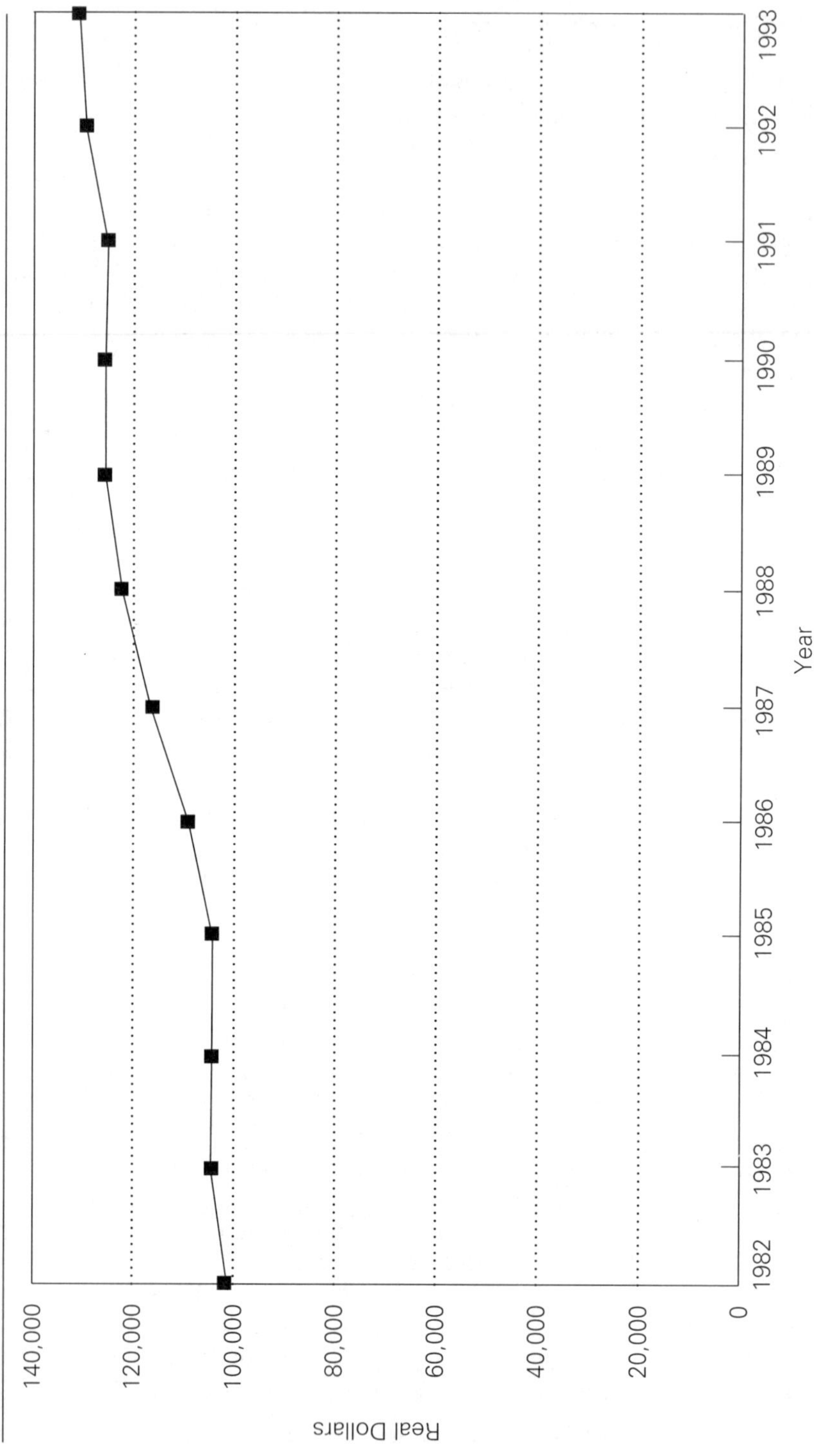

FIGURE 6-2. Real Annual Net Income, by Specialty

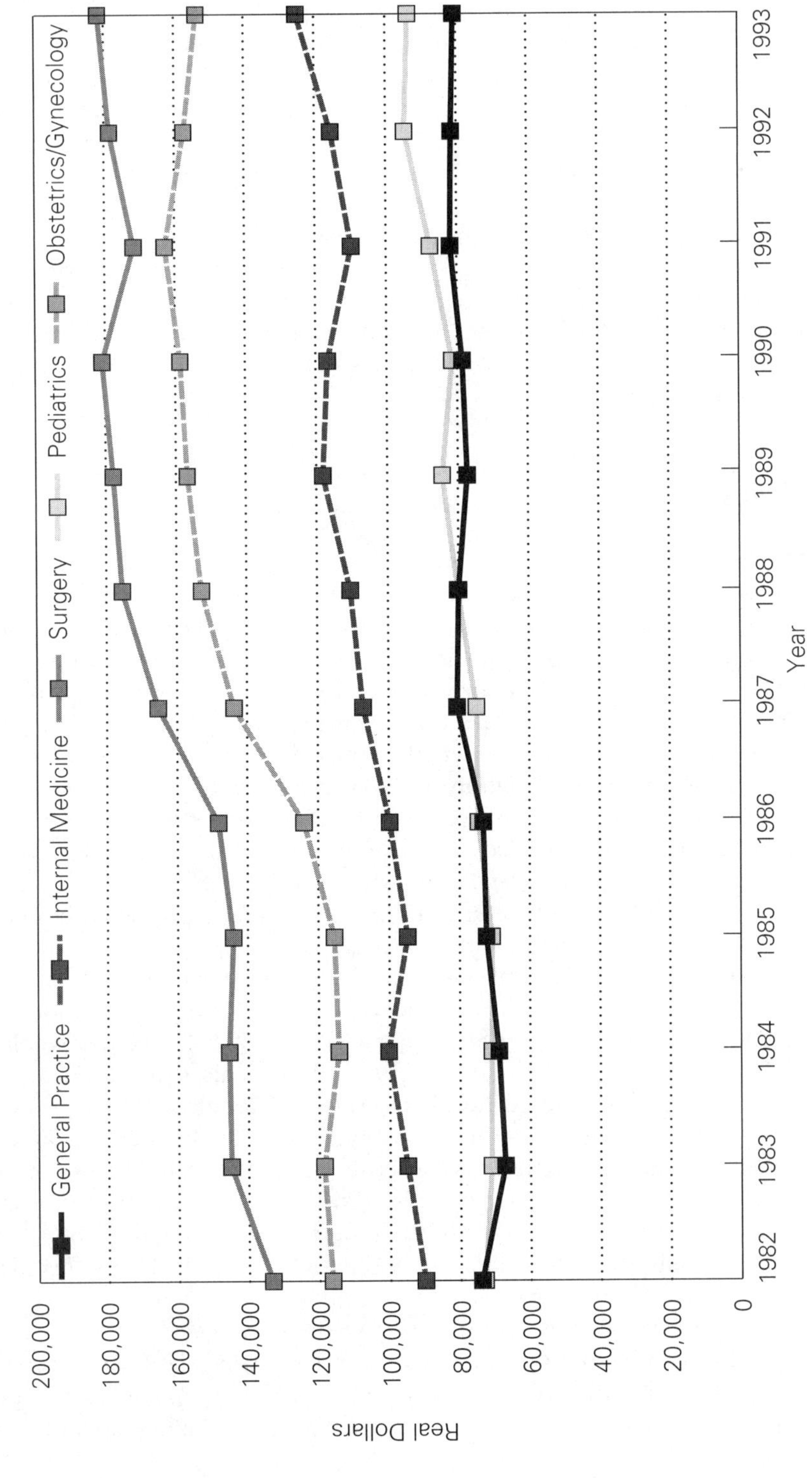

is going to the more highly trained specialties. For example, general practitioners end the 1982–1993 time period pretty much where they began, gaining only a few thousand dollars in real buying power. Pediatricians do not fare much better. On the other hand, surgeons and obstetricians have the fastest rate of growth during the 1986–1990 period. Specialists in internal medicine, as seems their fate, lie somewhere between the two extremes.

Finally, with respect to the PPS effect discussed earlier, the specialty least likely to practice medicine in a hospital setting—general practice—sees no decrease in real income during the 1983-1985 period of PPS start-up. Contrarily, surgeons' incomes fall somewhat during the three-year period. Again, these are the specialties that practice in a hospital setting much more frequently.

Hourly Real Income

Obviously, in any chapter on trends in physician income, one expects to find some indication of not only what is happening to income, in a broad sense, but also whether physicians are becoming "better off" with time. Certainly, the evidence presented to this point indicates that physicians (at least more specialized providers) are indeed making more money. However, income alone does not necessarily determine whether physicians are better off—that is, whether they would rather have their situation in 1982 or their situation in 1993. For example, if the increase in annual income is the result of an increased work effort, it is not at all clear that physicians would prefer more income and more time on the job to less income and less time on the job.

In fact, as is clearly seen in figure 6-3, average physician hours per year have been rising—and rising at a rather rapid rate—over the 1982–1993 period, from about 2,650 hours per year in 1982 (approximately 57 hours per week for 46.6 weeks out of the year) to more than 2,770 hours per year in 1993 (approximately 58.8 hours per week for 47.7 weeks out of the year). In 1993, the average physician worked almost two hours more per week and one additional week per year compared to the average physician 10 years earlier. Clearly, then, the increase in real income has come at some cost. Have physicians been compensated for this increase in work effort with an increase in hourly compensation, or have they actually seen their hourly rate fall? If the latter, it is more likely that physicians in 1993 would be willing to trade places with their 1982 counterparts.

The answer to this question is not foregone. Economists have long argued that one should expect to see an inverse relationship between hours of labor supplied and hourly pay. Frank Sloan made just this point a number of years ago.[6] To see if the inverse relationship holds, the

FIGURE 6-3. Hours of Professional Activity per Year, All Physicians

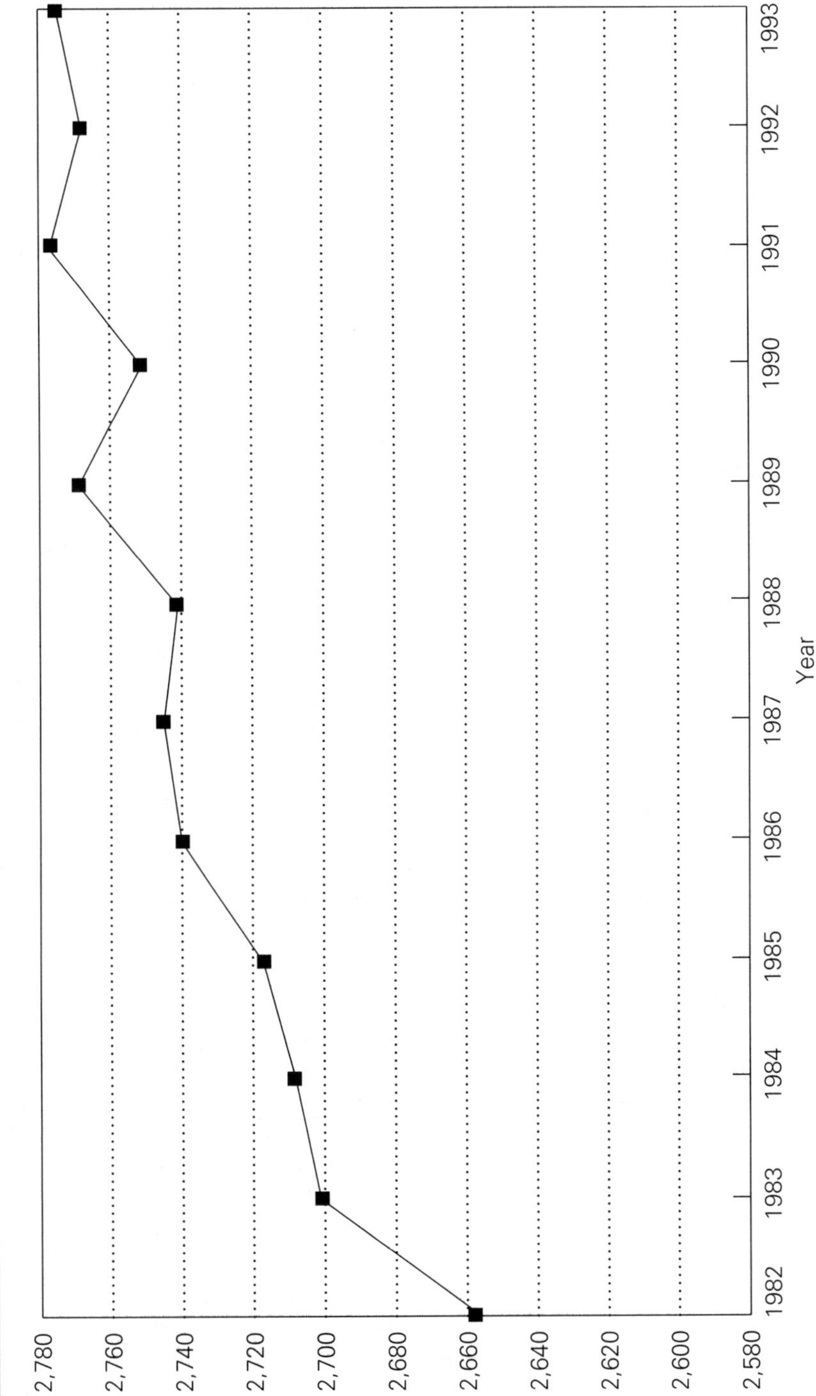

hourly compensation can be calculated for all physicians and for those in the five specialties charted in figure 6-2. It should be noted that this hourly rate is just the net real income divided by the hours per year; almost no physicians are truly hired "by the hour." Figure 6-4 presents the trend in hourly income for all physicians.

As the figure shows, the average physician's hourly pay has in fact increased over the years as the number of hours he or she supplies to the market has risen (figure 6-3). Not shown in the figures is the fact that the increases in hours of service have occurred for all specialties, with obstetricians consistently working the most and surgeons consistently working the fewest hours per year (until 1993 when general practice, which had been about average, suddenly became the specialty class that worked the fewest hours per year). In aggregate, then, it cannot be said that physicians are worse off due to the increase in work effort; income has risen faster than effort. Nor can it be said that physicians are better off; they may still prefer less income and less work. But because most established physicians likely have the ability to work fewer hours if they truly want to, the fact that they actually supply more hours and receive more compensation per hour indicates that, on average, they are probably better off.

However, just as with total real income, a somewhat different picture of the change in physician well-being is obtained if the trend in hourly earnings for each of the five specialties identified previously is examined. Figure 6-5 shows these trends. The disparity in the annual income trends is replicated in the hourly earnings trends. Surgeons do best in the hourly earnings race, as in the total net income race, whereas general practitioners and pediatricians fare worst. Surgeons were earning almost $64 per hour by 1993 whereas the lowest-paid general practitioners were earning less than $29 per hour during the same year. Moreover, the hourly compensation for general practitioners was not much more in real terms than the $27 they earned in 1982, though surgeons had gained more than $13 per hour over the same time period.

In fact, general practitioners received markedly smaller percentage increases in their hourly compensation over this time period (about 5.1 percent overall) than the other specialties. Internal medicine enjoyed a 29.1 percent rise; surgery received a 25.5 percent increase; and pediatrics and obstetrics both saw about a 20 percent increase in hourly earnings. Thus, when considering whether physicians are "better off" after 1993 than they were in 1982, the answer would seem to depend on which type of physician is being examined. It seems likely that most specialty types should consider themselves better off, at least within the realm of compensation for work. However, by and large, general practitioners have not shared in these gains in hourly returns. The reason for this lag remains unclear.

FIGURE 6-4. Hourly Real Net Income, All Physicians

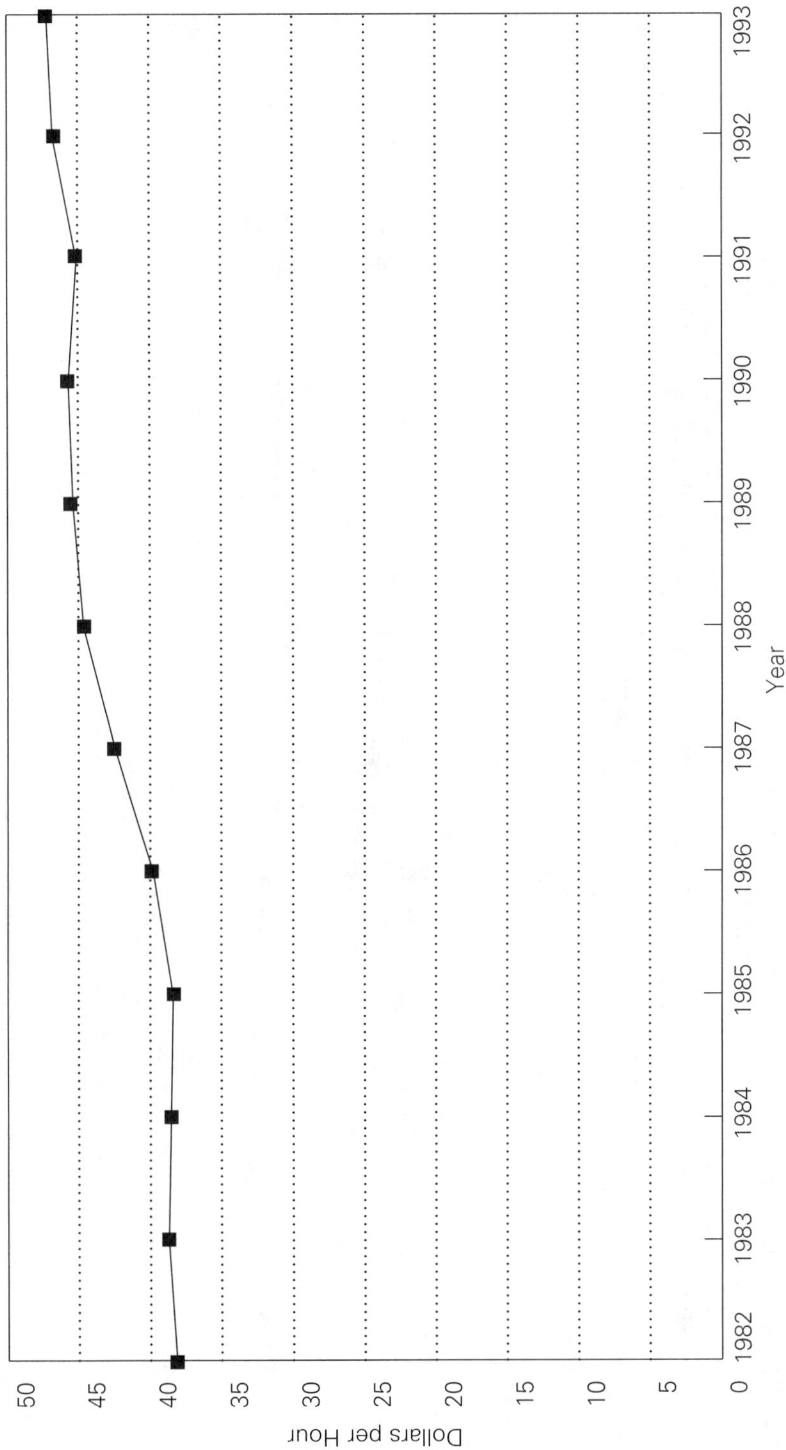

FIGURE 6-5. Hourly Real Net Income, by Specialty

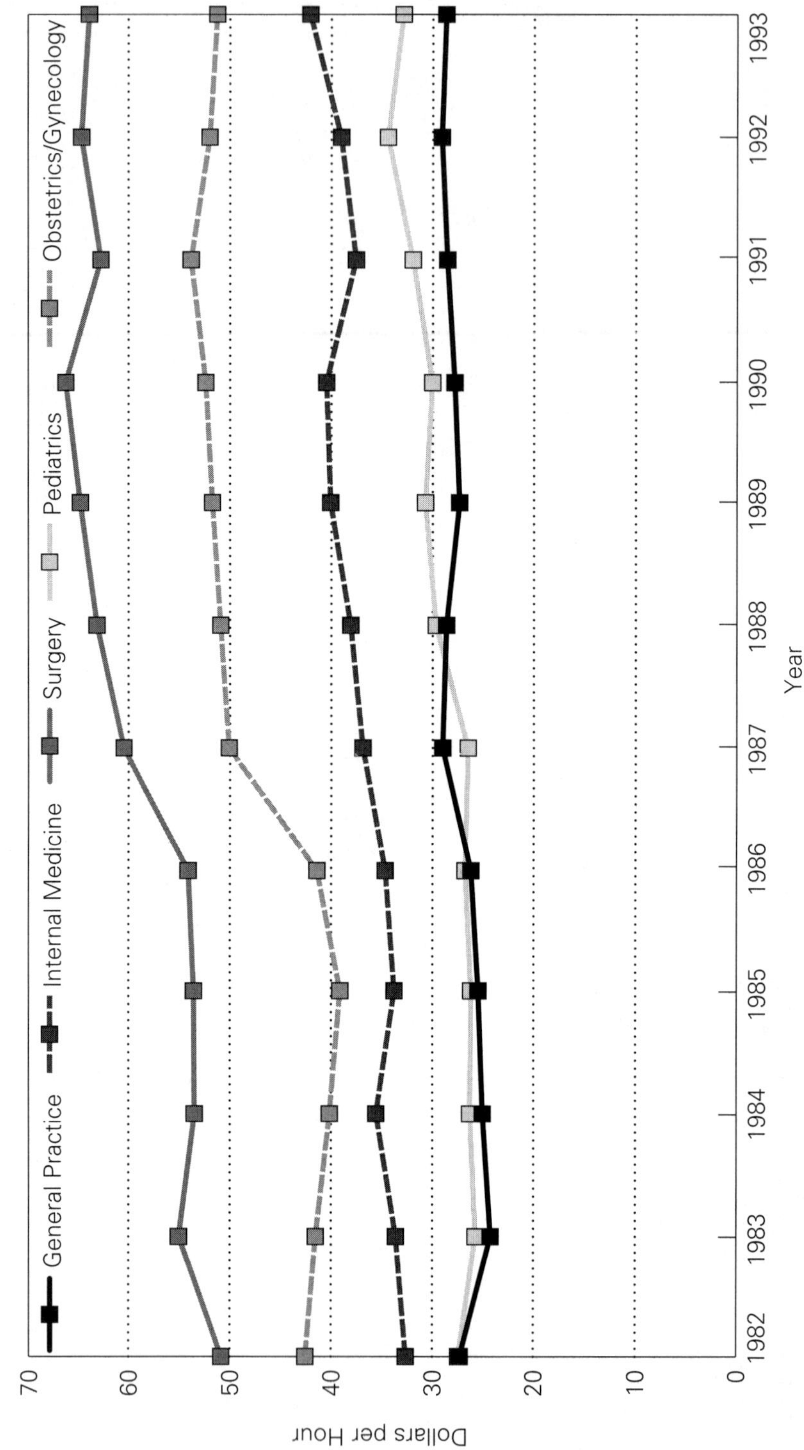

TRENDS, REVENUES, AND COSTS

To explain the general upward trend in physician income, and to begin to understand something of the disparities between the levels of income in the different specialties, it is necessary to look below the surface of the gross trend to see how the determinants of net income are changing. One way to do this is to examine the changes in revenue and costs over the 1982–1994 period.

Sources of Revenue

The changes in the level of income for physicians over the 12 years since 1982 were accompanied by changes in the sources of income, from both the perspective of what physicians were doing and who was paying for their services. With respect to the former, figure 6-6 indicates that the shifts in physician service provision that occurred over this period were reasonably minor. In 1982, physicians were supplying the bulk of their visits (63 percent) in their offices and 25 percent of their visits in hospital inpatient settings. In 1994, this distribution was much the same. There was a slight decrease in the percent of service supplied as hospital inpatient visits, down to 19 percent, and a commensurate increase in the percent of services supplied in an office (or outpatient) setting, up to 68 percent.

Part of the explanation for this shift is undoubtedly the switch to prospective payment for Medicare and other third-party payers in 1983. As discussed earlier, the PPS applied only to inpatient services, with outpatient visits reimbursed using the old "cost-plus" methodology. (The shift to prospective reimbursement for outpatient services only began in the early 1990s.) Thus, federal policy altered the relative profitability of outpatient care and encouraged many hospitals and physicians to shift the site of care appropriately. In addition, many innovations during this period (the dramatic improvements in orthoscopic surgery, for example) changed the technology of health care so that more procedures could be done on an outpatient basis. Whatever the cause, the change in site of service is a defining characteristic of the physician services market in the 1980s and early 1990s.

During the time period in question, the relative importance of different payers changed rather dramatically. Figure 6-7 shows that, in 1980, patients paid for a significant portion of their physician care out-of-pocket (about 32 percent) whereas private third-party payers picked up about 37 percent of the bill.[7] The two main government programs that pay for medical care, Medicaid and Medicare, together accounted for only 24 percent of the average dollar received by a physician. However, by 1993, patient out-of-pocket payments accounted for only 16 percent of the revenue flowing to physicians whereas the portion of physician

FIGURE 6-6. Distribution of Patient Visits by Type, All Physicians

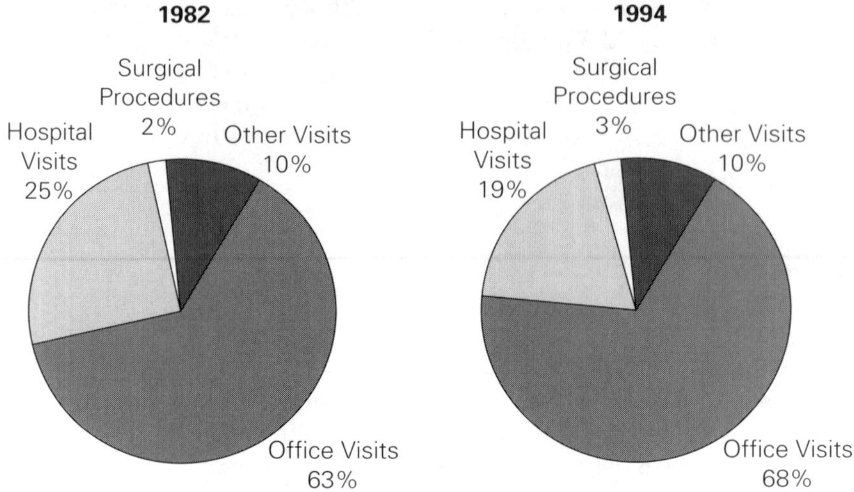

income paid directly by private insurers rose to 49 percent. This trend probably is quite significant because it demonstrates the spread of more generous insurance plans. This "generosity" (in terms of the amount patients must pay for the marginal unit of care) took two forms: the spread of HMOs, and the spread of traditional insurance plans with lower deductibles and copayments. Certainly much of the growth in total and hourly earnings over this period can be attributed to decreasing elasticities of demand for care that one would expect to be associated with lower out-of-pocket costs. To what degree the incentive structures and utilization oversight inherent in managed care restrained the growth in income is impossible to determine without more detailed analysis. However, it is clear that this shift of burden for the marginal episode of care is one of the more dramatic trends associated with the long secular increase in physician income.

Finally, one further aspect of the changing practice patterns that has led to a rise in revenue (and income) can be seen in the behavior of physicians with respect to the number of visits they provide and the fees they charge. Figure 6-8 shows that the average physician enjoyed a general decrease in number of visits supplied each week, despite a four-year period from 1985 to 1989 when the downward trend was reversed. As discussed earlier, this period also is characterized by slight increases in the number of hours of time supplied to the practice of medicine each week. This seems to indicate that physicians were spending increasing amounts of time in each visit with their patients over this 12-year period.

(It is perhaps interesting, though tangential, to note that general practitioners and pediatricians consistently supply more visits per week than the other three specialty groups considered.)

Coinciding with this general lengthening of an average office visit, figure 6-9 indicates that there is an increase in the fees charged for these visits. This increase in fees is rather more constant than the decrease in number of visits, with fees rising from an average real level of about $24 per visit to an average of nearly $37. Whether this reflects a perception on the part of patients and third-party payers that quality is rising, or whether this is the effect of falling out-of-pocket payments and thus falling elasticities of demand, cannot be ascertained at this level. Whichever of these effects is driving the increase in revenue, there is no apparent end to the trend in the data to date.

Sources of Costs

In general, the changes in the costs facing physicians are not particularly surprising. Figure 6-10 shows that the total costs facing the average physician have risen at a steady rate between 1982 and 1993. This trend is replicated fairly consistently for each of the specialty classes considered here. By comparing figure 6-10 to figure 6-1, it can be seen that costs per physician are comparable to average net income, though closer to average income by 1993 than in 1982. That is, physicians face an overhead rate that is about 50 percent of their revenue, certainly not out of

FIGURE 6-7. Sources of Payment for Physician Services

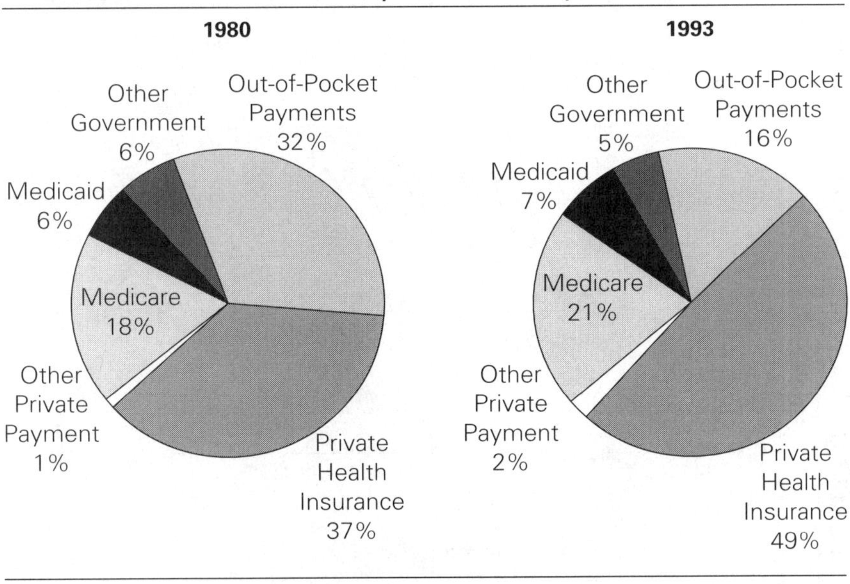

FIGURE 6-8. Average Number of Patient Visits per Week, All Physicians

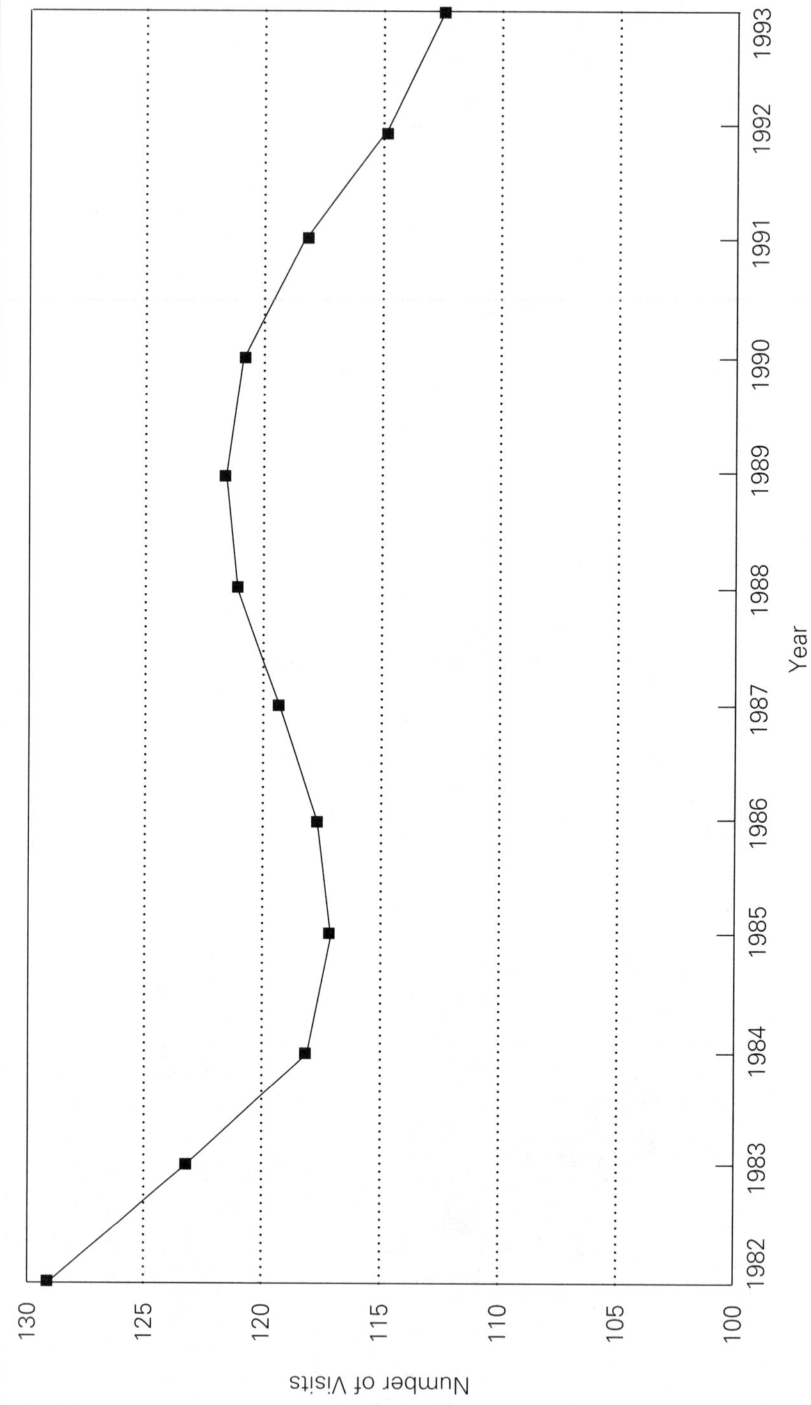

FIGURE 6-9. Average Fee for an Office Visit with Established Patient, All Physicians

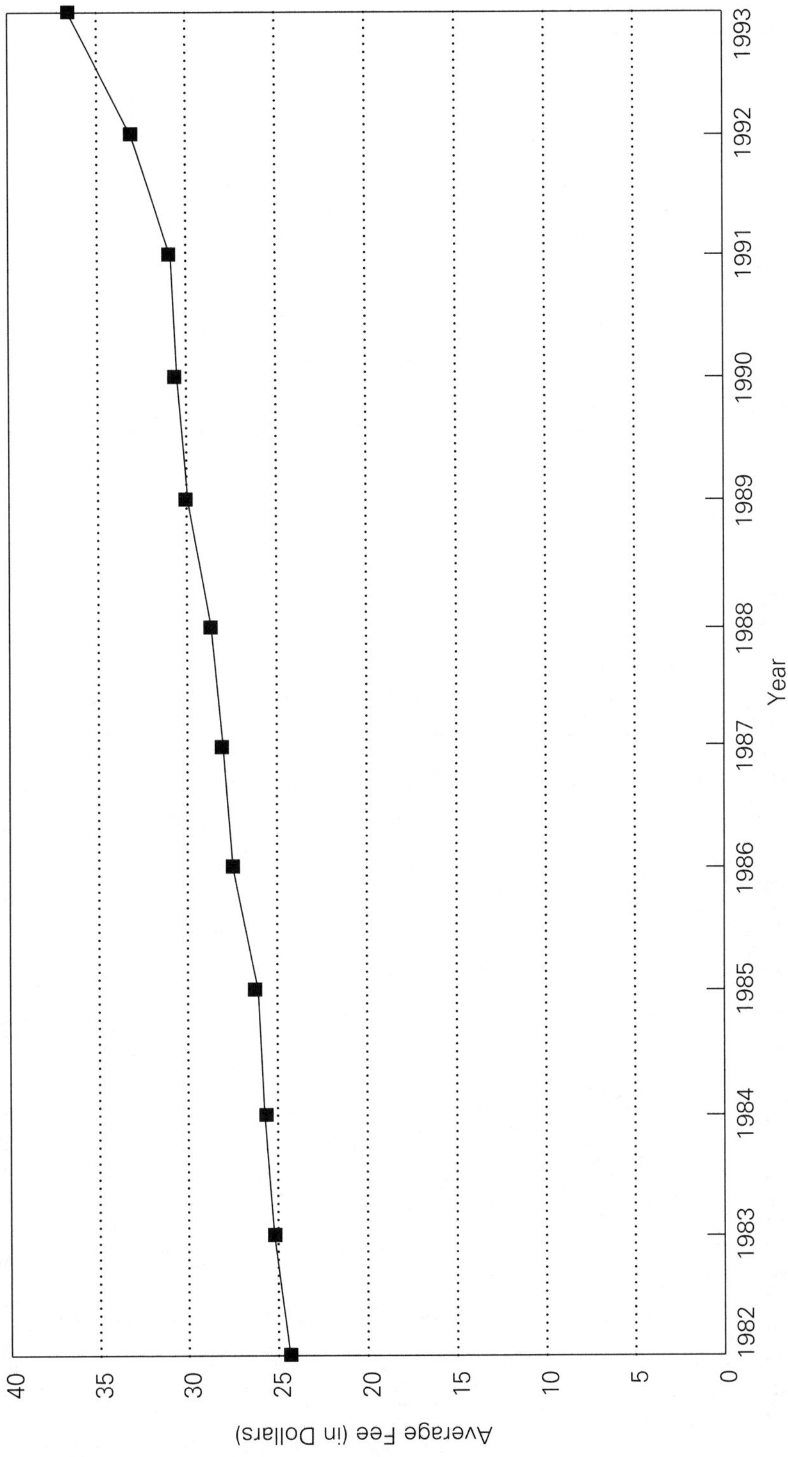

FIGURE 6-10. Average Total Expenses per Physician, All Physicians

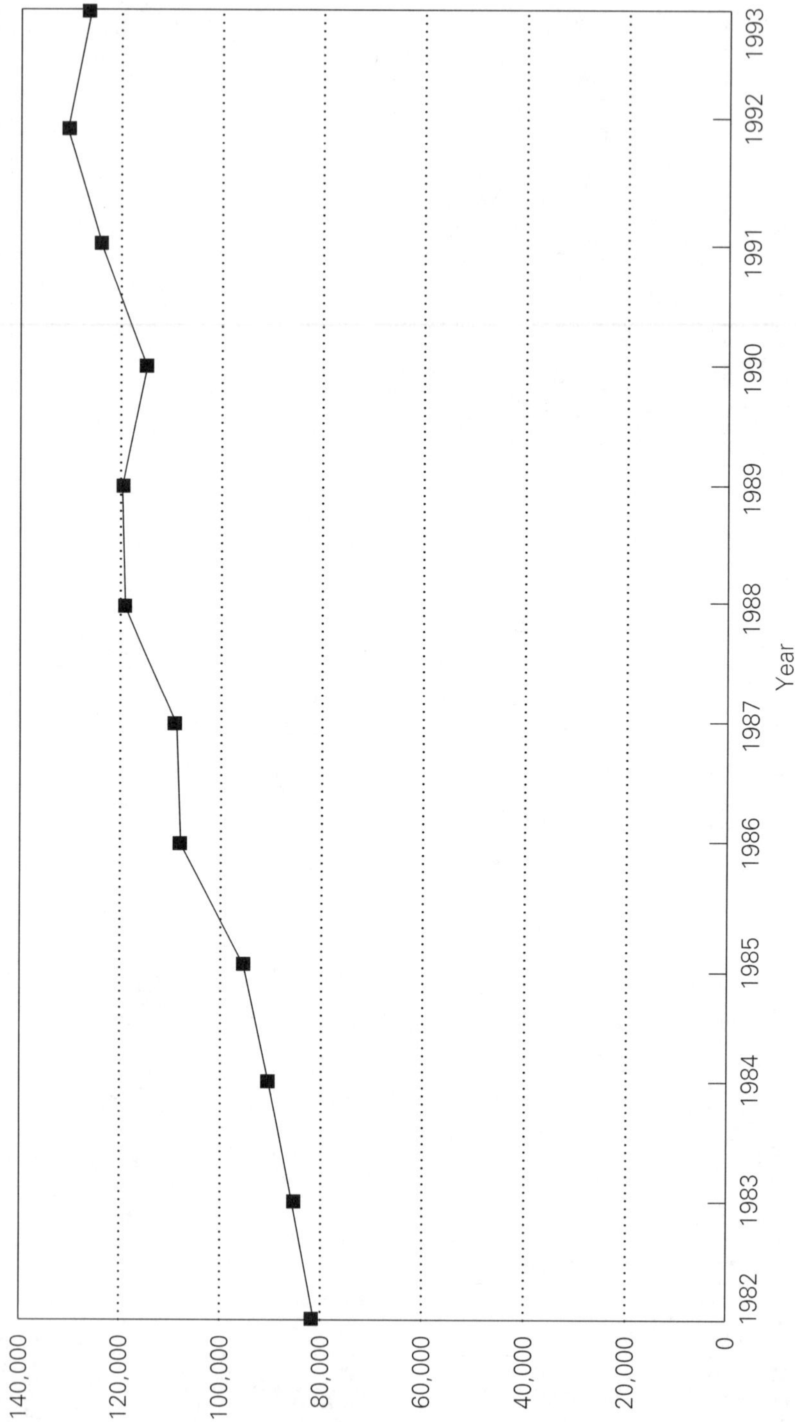

line with other firms in the economy. Figures 6-11 and 6-12 present information on two cost categories: payroll and equipment, respectively. Both factors of production became more expensive in real terms over the decade, though the increase in the burden of these costs did not fall disproportionally for any one specialty.

The interesting component of costs, in terms of the change and distribution by specialty, is professional liability expenses (malpractice insurance premiums). The trend in this component of costs is presented in figure 6-13. Malpractice costs are a frequent topic of debate in the popular and trade press, nearly universally demonized as a driving force behind the increasing flow of dollars to physicians. Figure 6-13 shows that malpractice costs exhibit two interesting behaviors over this time period. First, obstetricians and surgeons bear a significantly larger burden from liability insurance than do their colleagues in general practice, internal medicine, or pediatrics. That is clearly related to the riskiness of the activities in which they engage. Although it may be difficult to rationalize the dramatically higher costs for obstetricians over surgeons, given the generally lower medical risk associated with childbirth than most non-pregnancy-related surgeries, one need only recall that the risk being insured against is the risk of legal suit. Clearly American society is highly litigious when it comes to childbirth. This characteristic of liability costs is quite consistent with the popular view.

However, what is not so commonly recognized is that the long upward trend in malpractice premiums seems to have been reversed for all physician specialty groups. Since 1987 or 1988, malpractice costs have fallen at a rate that approximates their previous increase. This is particularly true for the high-cost specialties of obstetrics and surgery, but also is apparent in the other three groups (though less pronounced). That liability costs are falling so rapidly bodes particularly well for the future.

There appears to be a general and unabated increase in fees, which, despite the decrease in number of visits, has led to an increase in physician revenue. Further, despite the increase in most types of costs, revenue growth has outpaced cost growth (because net income is rising). Now there is a strong reversal in liability premium costs—one of the most worrisome categories of expenditure over the past decade. Given that there is no indication from the data to date of a reversal in the trend for revenue, the prospects for increased income growth, at least as evidenced in the trends, seems quite promising.

CONCLUSION

The period since 1982 seems to have been one of slowly growing prosperity for physicians in general, despite temporary setbacks in the early

FIGURE 6-11. Average Payroll Expenses per Physician, All Physicians

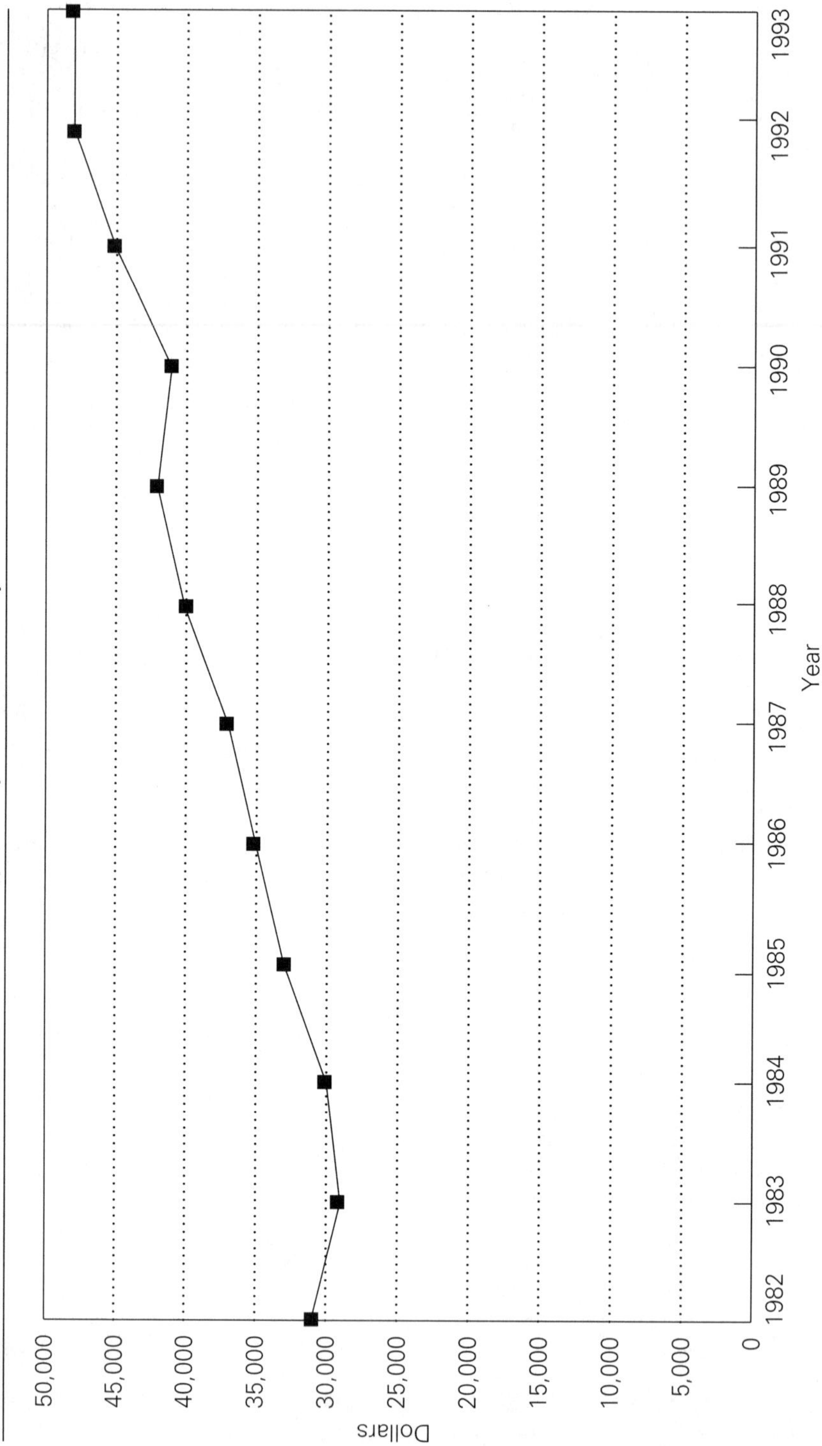

FIGURE 6-12. Average Equipment Expenses per Physician, All Physicians

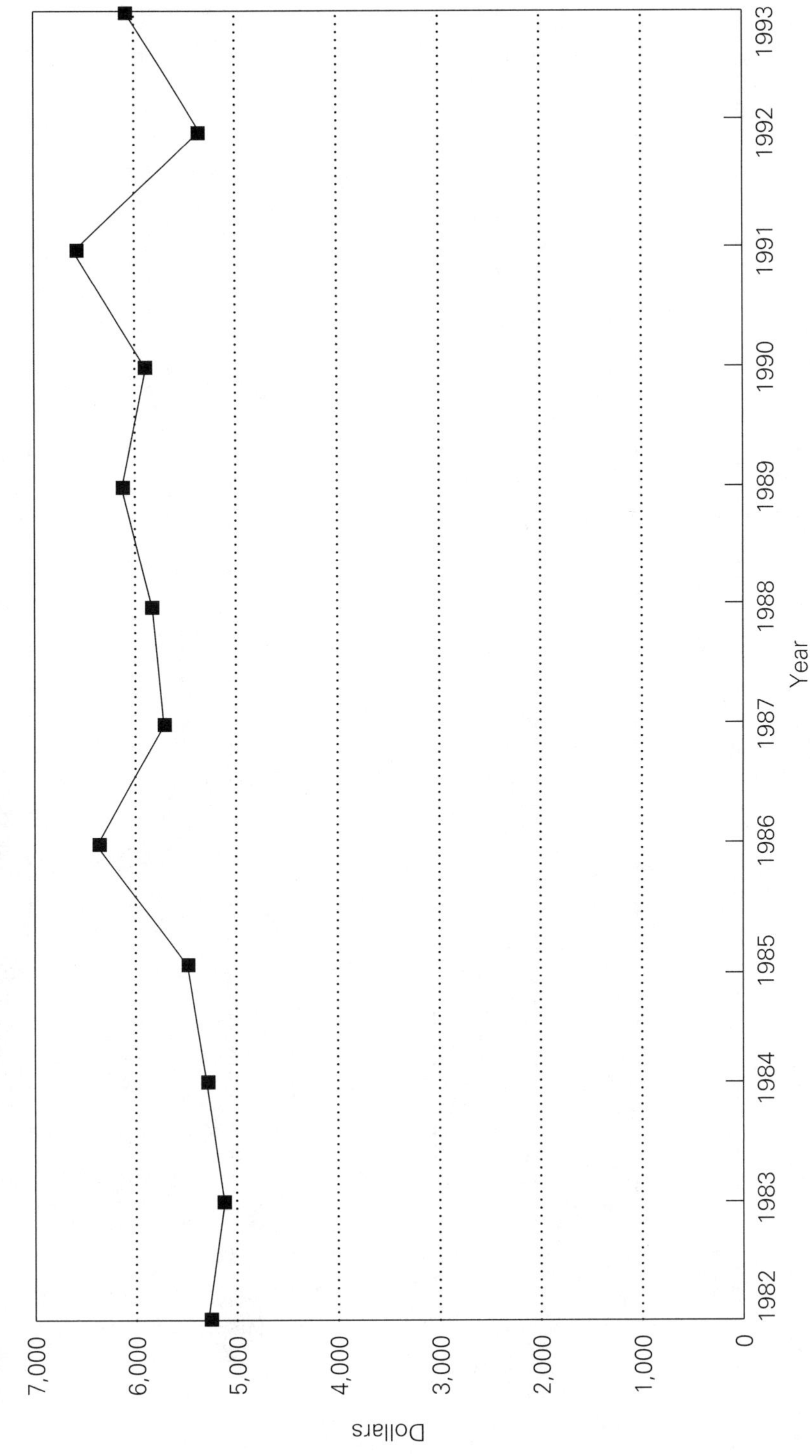

FIGURE 6-13. Average Professional Liability Expenses per Physician, by Specialty

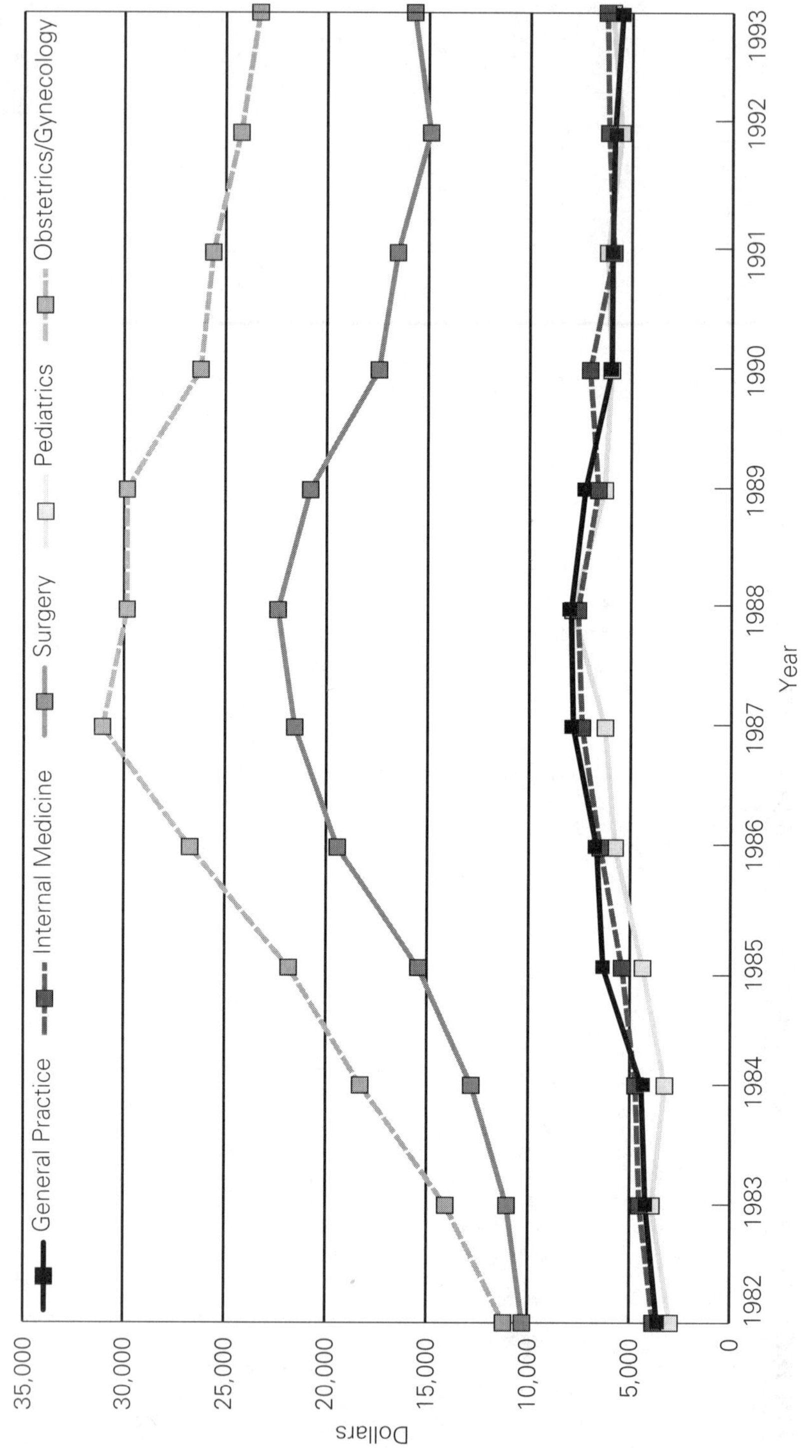

1980s. This stands in contrast to descriptions of income trends from the 1975–1984 period, when some physicians lost ground.[8] However, the general prosperity has not been distributed evenly, with some specialties (such as general practice) gaining very little and others (such as surgery) growing much faster than average. This growth in income has come despite structural changes such as the PPS, Medicare's RBRVS, and the spread of managed care, all of which are ostensibly aimed at reducing revenue flows into the medical profession. Physicians have been able to adapt to, and even prosper in, this period of change and dislocation—a fact that should provide some comfort as providers look forward to even more change and uncertainty.

In fact, several indicators bode well for the medical profession. As seen above, liability costs, long an anathema to physicians, broke a decades-long trend and began a significant decline in 1987 and 1988. Moreover, there has been no immediately perceptible impact of RBRVS on average physician income. Finally, physicians might take some comfort in the projections for the future. Currently, physicians receive just under 20 percent of each dollar spent on medical care in the United States (about $183 billion). However, projections to the year 2005 indicate that the proportion of health care dollars flowing to physicians should rise to more than 22 percent, or $483.6 billion.[9] If this is close to the mark, physicians will find themselves in an even better position with respect to income in the future. Despite recent negative press, the trends in physician incomes show a profession that is strong and secure.

References

1. J. C. Langenbrunner and others, "Physician Incomes and Work Patterns across Specialties: 1975 and 1983–1984," *Health Care Financing Review* 10, no. 2 (1988): 17–24.

2. L. Perry, "Physician Income Increases Drop Significantly—9AMA," *Modern Healthcare,* 20 (Nov. 19, 1990): 8; and J. Foreman, "In Focus: Trends in Physician Income," *Archives of Ophthalmology* 110 (Feb. 1992): 178.

3. G. E. Pope and J. E. Schneider, "Data Watch: Trends in Physician Income," *Health Affairs* 11 (Spring 1992): 181–93.

4. S. T. Burner and D. R. Waldo, "Data View: National Health Expenditure Projections, 1994–2005," *Health Care Financing Review* 16, no. 4 (1995): 221–42.

5. Center for Health Policy Research, *Socioeconomic Characteristics of Medical Practice 1995,* ed. M. L. Gonzalez (Chicago: American Medical Association, 1995).

6. F. A. Sloan, "Physician Supply Behavior in the Short Run," *Industrial and Labor Relations Review* 28 (July 1975): 549–69.

7. K. R. Levit and others, "National Health Expenditures, 1993," *Health Care Financing Review* 16, no. 1 (1994): 247–94.

8. Langenbrunner and others.

9. Burner and Waldo.

7

Legal and Financial Considerations of Physician Compensation in the Institutional Setting

Glen A. Reed, JD
Nicole C. Hall, JD

The method by which physicians in institutional settings are paid has both organizational and legal ramifications. Because current practices in the compensation of institution-based physicians are influenced significantly by the manner in which institutional providers are reimbursed by government program third-party payers for physician professional and administrative services, it is important to understand these reimbursement rules. Compensation practices and contract terms also are influenced by various regulatory considerations, particularly the laws and regulations governing health care fraud and abuse and those governing tax-exempt organizations.

This chapter focuses on the content of contractual arrangements between physicians and institutions as the basis for the analysis of the business arrangement. It also reviews the Medicare program rules governing reimbursement for the professional and administrative services of physicians in an institutional setting. Finally, it reviews the regulatory considerations that are relevant to the alternative methods of physician compensation used by institutional providers.

CONTRACTUAL ARRANGEMENTS BETWEEN PHYSICIANS AND INSTITUTIONAL PROVIDERS

The three most common types of contractual arrangement between physicians and institutional providers are provider-based physician agreements, agreements for the provision of administrative services by the physician, and employment agreements for the provision of professional services by the physician. Each of these arrangements is described below.

Provider-Based Physician Agreements

Typically, provider-based physician agreements are used for physician specialties that provide clinical services in the provider institution, such as pathology, radiology, anesthesiology, or emergency medicine. Often such agreements are exclusive in nature, meaning that they give the physician or physician group the right to provide particular medical specialty services in the hospital and exclude other physicians with the same specialty from practicing in the hospital. Provider-based physician agreements typically require physicians or physician groups to perform the following functions:

- Provide the specified services according to a predetermined coverage schedule, which includes the stipulation that physicians be available "on call" to provide services on weekends and weekdays at times outside the hospital department's normal operating hours
- Provide detailed administrative supervision of the entire department involved in provision of the institution's services in the physician's specialty, including supervision and training of technical personnel employed by the institution but integral to the department's clinical operations
- Establish policies and procedures (including quality assurance, utilization review (UR), and risk management) to ensure the quality and efficiency of all of services provided
- Assume responsibility for preparing and maintaining medical and business records relating to services provided in the department

Administrative Services Agreements

Institutional providers may enter into contractual arrangements with physicians for the provision of administrative services, such as medical director or unit director agreements. Under a typical medical director agreement, the physician may act as medical director of an inpatient provider unit, a hospital-based outpatient clinic, or an ancillary service program. In this role, he or she usually is responsible for supervising the delivery of clinical services in conformance with the provider's policies and procedures and the applicable licensure and accreditation standards. Unlike provider-based physician agreements, administrative services agreements typically do not relate to the provision or guaranteed availability of clinical services in the physician's specialty by the physician and members of his or her group.

The physician often will be responsible for such duties as the following:

- Overseeing the quality of the clinical services provided
- Developing training and educational programs for provider employees relating to the provision of clinical services
- Acting as a liaison with the provider's administration and medical staff
- Ensuring adequate coverage for the provision of clinical services
- Ensuring the maintenance of adequate records in connection with the clinical services provided
- Evaluating personnel employed in connection with the delivery of clinical services
- Advising the provider with regard to the equipment and technology necessary for the proper delivery of clinical services

Medical director agreements typically are part-time independent contractor arrangements, but part-time employment agreements also are sometimes used.

Employment Agreements

Physician employment agreements are becoming increasingly common as a growing number of health systems pursue a strategy of purchasing physician practices in the community and integrating them into the practice of medicine. Often a health system that wishes to acquire a physician practice will purchase it and subsequently employ its prior physician owner or owners to provide professional services in a clinic setting. Physician employment agreements typically are full-time arrangements for the provision of professional services by the physician. Often he or she must maintain active medical staff privileges at the hospital and participate in hospital quality assurance (QA), UR, risk management, medical staff, and managed care activities and programs. In addition, he or she may be required to abide by certain policies and operating procedures developed by the provider and applicable to the medical practices owned and operated by the provider.

Employment agreements also are used to secure the services of full-time physician administrators, such as medical directors of entire hospitals or health systems. If these agreements do not involve the rendering of professional clinical services, they are very similar to contracts with lay administrative personnel and do not raise most of the issues discussed in this chapter.

REIMBURSEMENT CONSIDERATIONS

The method of compensation provided a physician under any of the three types of contractual arrangements described above will be influenced, at least in part, by the relevant reimbursement rules relating to the types of services being provided by the physician. For reimbursement purposes, the Medicare program distinguishes between physician services provided to an individual provider's patient and services rendered to a provider. Physician services provided to an individual patient are paid under Part B of the Medicare title of the Social Security Act, according to the Medicare physician fee schedule. However, a provider will be paid under Part A for the costs it has incurred for compensation paid to a physician for services rendered to the institutional provider.

Part B Payments for Physician Services

Under the Medicare regulations, payment for physician services rendered to a provider's patient will be paid on the basis of the Medicare physician fee schedule if (1) the services are furnished to the patient personally by the physician, (2) they contribute directly to the individual patient's diagnosis or treatment, and (3) they ordinarily require performance by a physician.[1] Additional requirements apply in the case of anesthesiology, radiology, and pathology services.[2] For example, in the case of radiology services, payment will be made on a fee-schedule basis only if the services meet the three requirements described above and are "identifiable, direct, and discrete diagnostic or therapeutic services" furnished to an individual patient.[3] Fee schedule payment for radiology interpretations requires that a written report be prepared for inclusion in the patient's medical record maintained by the hospital.[4]

Medicare's Reassignment Prohibition In order for an institutional provider to directly receive the fee schedule payments due a physician, the provider must satisfy one of the exceptions to the general prohibition against reassignment of Medicare amounts due a physician or other supplier.[5] As a general matter, Medicare does not pay amounts that are due a physician under an assignment of benefits from a patient to any other person under reassignment, power of attorney, or any other direct payment arrangement.[6] However, there are several exceptions to the reassignment prohibition.

Payments to an Employer Medicare may pay amounts due a physician to his or her employer if the physician is required, as a condition of employment, to turn over to the employer the fees for his or her services.[7] For this exception to apply, there must be an employer-employee relationship between the physician and the person or organization hiring the physician to perform services; and the terms of the employment must provide that the employer, and not the physician, has the right to receive payment for all the physician's services within the scope of the employment relationship.[8] An employer may establish that it is qualified to receive payment for a physician's services by submitting a written statement certifying that it will bill the Medicare program for the physician's services only if he or she is an employee and has acknowledged in writing that the employer has the right to receive payment of his or her fees under the terms of employment.[9] The physician's written acknowledgment that the employer has the right to receive payment for his or her services may be in the form of a written employment contract that either expressly or "by clear implication" provides that the employer has the right to receive his or her fees.[10] Absent a written employment contract, the employer must have in its possession a signed and dated statement by the physician acknowledging that the employer has the right under the terms of the employment arrangement to receive payment for his or her services.[11]

Payments to a Facility An exception to the reassignment prohibition also exists for payments to the facility where the services were furnished (that is, the institutional provider entity) if there is a written agreement between facility and physician pursuant to which the facility bills for the physician's services.[12] For purposes of this exception, the term *facility* is limited to institutions that furnish services to individuals as inpatients (such as hospitals, university medical centers that own and operate hospitals, skilled nursing facilities, nursing homes, and so on).[13] The contractual arrangement between facility and physician may apply to all the services the physician furnishes in the facility or only to a particular category of his or her services that is clearly distinguishable from other categories (for example, services in the outpatient part of the facility by a physician who collects his or her own fees for the services he or she furnishes to inpatients).[14] A facility may qualify to receive payment for the services of physicians provided in the facility by submitting a written statement certifying that it will bill for the services of its physicians only as provided in the written contractual relationships with them.[15]

Although billing by the institutional provider for the professional services of hospital-based physicians is permitted by these provisions, for a variety of reasons the predominant practice in recent years has become direct billing by the physician or physician group for physician professional services. Under employment agreements in a clinic setting, however, the provider/employer is almost always responsible for billing, and compensation to the physician often is made on a basis not directly related to the amounts billed for the physician's services. Every physician contract should clearly state which party is responsible for billing and entitled to receive payment.

Indirect Contractual Arrangements It should be noted that a contractual relationship between the physician and the facility in which he or she furnishes services may exist indirectly by reason of a contractual relationship between the physician and some other entity (for example, a professional corporation) and a contractual relationship between that entity and the facility. However, a facility that has an indirect contractual arrangement with a physician is not entitled to bill and receive payment for his or her services merely on the basis of this arrangement. In order for the facility to bill and receive payment for the physician's services, it must enter into a direct contractual relationship with the physician and must certify to the Medicare program that it will bill and receive payment for his or her services only so long as it has this direct relationship.[16] For example, if a professional corporation enters into a contract with a hospital to provide physician emergency department (ED) services, pursuant to which the hospital bills and receives payment for the physician services provided by the corporation and the corporation receives payment directly from the hospital, in order for the hospital to bill and receive payment for the ED physician services, it also must enter into a direct contractual arrangement with the individual physicians.[17] Even if the professional corporation is not entitled to bill and receive payment for the physicians' services (that is, the physicians are independent contractors who bill for their own services), the hospital could receive direct payment for the physicians' services based on a direct contractual arrangement between it and each of the physicians.[18]

Part A Payments to Providers for Physician Services

An institutional provider entitled to cost reimbursement will be paid under Part A for the costs it incurs for physician services if (1) the services do not meet the conditions for payment under the physician fee schedule for physician services rendered to provider patients (discussed previously); (2) the provider has incurred a cost for the salary or other compensation paid to the physician for his or her services; and (3) the costs incurred by the provider for the physician's services meet the general requirements relating to reasonable, necessary, and proper costs related to patient care.[19] Particular rules, which are beyond the scope of this chapter, apply in the case of the costs incurred by a teaching hospital for the supervision of interns and residents.[20] Although certain costs allocable to hospital outpatient departments and certain types of cost-reimbursed units or services still affect reimbursement, hospital inpatient services have been paid on a fixed, prospectively determined basis for a number of years and the amounts of payment are not determined by the hospital's current costs for the services.

Physician Compensation Costs Physician compensation costs include monetary payments, fringe benefits, deferred compensation, and any other items of value (except for office space or billing and collection services) a provider furnishes to a physician in exchange for his or her services.[21] Only physician compensation costs allocated to physician services to the provider are allowable costs to the provider under Part A.[22] To receive payment for the physician compensation costs incurred by the provider, the provider must submit to its fiscal intermediary a written allocation agreement between provider and physician that specifies the amount of time the physician spends furnishing physician services to the provider, physician services to patients, and services that are not reimbursable under either Medicare Part A or Part B.[23] The compensation paid the physician by the provider for his or her services must be reasonable in terms of time devoted by the physician.[24] The total compensation received by a physician from a provider will be allocated among each of the three categories of services identified above unless the provider certifies to its fiscal intermediary that the physician's compensation is attributable solely to his or her services to the provider, and the physician bills and personally receives payment for all the physician services furnished to patients.[25] Absent a written allocation agreement, the intermediary assumes that 100 percent of the physician compensation costs incurred by the provider should be allocated to physician services rendered to provider patients.[26]

Record-Keeping Requirements The Medicare regulations also impose record-keeping requirements in connection with the payment to providers of allowable physician compensation costs. Any provider that does not accept the assumed allocation of all physician services to direct services to provider patients is required to maintain time records or other information used by the provider to allocate physician compensation in a form that facilitates validation of the information by the provider's fiscal intermediary or the Medicare carrier.[27] The provider also is required to report the information on which allocation of the physician's compensation is based to the intermediary or the carrier on an annual basis, and to promptly notify the intermediary or carrier of any revisions to the compensation allocation.[28] Records relating to physician compensation allocations, including any information on which the allocations are based, must be maintained by the provider for at least four years after the end of each cost-reporting period to which the allocations apply.[29]

Reasonable Compensation Equivalency Limits Medicare reimbursement of the costs incurred by a provider for compensation paid to a physician for services is subject to reasonable compensation equivalency limits.[30] The amount of the reasonable compensation equivalency limit is published in the *Federal Register*. If the amount of compensation paid by a provider to a physician exceeds the reasonable compensation equivalency limit, Medicare payment of the costs incurred by the provider for the physician's compensation is based on the level established by the limits.[31]

However, the reasonable compensation equivalency limits are subject to certain adjustments. For example, the provider's intermediary may adjust them to account for costs incurred by the physician or the provider related to malpractice insurance, professional society memberships, and continuing medical education (CME).[32] In addition, an intermediary may grant a provider an exception to the reasonable compensation equivalency limits if the provider is able to demonstrate to the intermediary that it is unable to recruit or maintain an adequate number of physicians at a compensation level within the limits.[33]

REGULATORY CONSIDERATIONS

Under the Medicare reimbursement rules described above, institutional providers can receive payment under Part A and Part B of the Medicare program for administrative and professional physician services rendered to patients in an institutional setting. As a result, institutional providers can enter into arrangements with physicians, as both employees and independent contractors, pursuant to which the provider agrees to be responsible for billing patients and collecting payment for the professional services rendered by the physician, and the physician receives compensation directly from the provider for his or her professional and administrative services. As discussed earlier, the three most common types of contractual arrangements between physicians and institutional providers are provider-based physician agreements, medical director or other administrative services agreements, and physician employment agreements. The institutional provider and the physician must take into account certain regulatory considerations when determining the method by which physicians are compensated under any of these three types of arrangements. The key regulatory considerations relevant to physician compensation in an institutional setting are outlined in the next pages, followed by a discussion of three alternative compensation arrangements and the regulatory issues raised by each.

Key Regulatory Considerations

The key regulatory considerations relating to the compensation of physicians in an institutional setting relate to the following prohibitions:[34]

1. The prohibitions against excessive private benefit and private inurement, set forth in IRS Section 501(c)(3) and related Treasury regulations
2. The prohibitions against certain physician referrals contained in the Ethics in Patient Referrals Act of 1989, as amended (Stark II)[35]
3. The prohibition on illegal remuneration contained in the Medicare and Medicaid Patient and Program Protection Act of 1987 (the Anti-Kickback Statute)[36]

Contractual arrangements between physicians and institutional providers for the provision of professional and administrative services by the physicians can be in the form of either employer-employee or independent contractor arrangements. The classification of the relationship between physician and institutional provider is relevant to the regulatory considerations discussed below and, in addition, has legal consequences of its own that are beyond the scope of this chapter.[37] The employment status of physicians is determined under generally applicable common-law rules. Under these rules, the critical determination is whether the purported employer has the right to control or direct the individual who performs the services, not only as to the result but also as to the means by which it is achieved.[38] In Revenue Ruling 87-41,[39] the Internal Revenue Service (IRS) set forth 20 factors it will apply in determining control. In addition, there are numerous rulings on worker classification in the health care context.[40] Although selection of either an independent contractor or an employment approach has been widely viewed as optional in the context of physician services, increased IRS scrutiny in this area has made it important to choose the employee model and pay all required employment-related taxes whenever the institutional provider will be directing the physician as to the means of accomplishing his or her work, particularly when the physician's full-time services will be obtained and other factors in the IRS criteria are present.

Compensation and the Private Inurement/Private Benefit Prohibition Compensation issues are receiving increasing scrutiny in the tax-exempt arena. Section 501(c)(3) of the Internal Revenue Code provides that an organization will not qualify for exemption unless "no part of the net earnings of [the organization] inures to the benefit of any private shareholder or individual." As a result, an exempt organization may pay no more than reasonable compensation without running afoul of the private inurement or private benefit prohibitions. Compensation includes not only salary and wages, but also contributions to pension and profit-sharing plans; unpaid deferred compensation; payment of personal expenses; rents, royalties, and fees; and personal use of the organization's property or facilities.[41]

Tax-exempt hospitals often rely on tax-exempt bond offerings to finance the construction of facilities or the purchase of equipment. Qualified private activity bonds, and qualified 501(c)(3) bonds in particular, are subject to certain restrictions, including those regarding the use of proceeds and issuance costs.[42] At least 95 percent of bond issue proceeds must be used for the exempt purpose of the issue. In other words, interest on the bonds will not be tax-exempt if more than 5 percent of the net proceeds are used directly or indirectly in an unrelated trade or business or by a "non-exempt" person.[43] Management and services contracts, including contracts with physicians, may give rise to private business use of bond-financed facilities. Revenue Procedure 93-19[44] sets forth the circumstances in which services rendered pursuant to such contracts will not constitute private business use of bond-financed facilities.

Physician Self-Referral Prohibitions Under the Stark II prohibitions on certain physician referrals, physicians with a financial relationship with an entity may not make referrals of Medicare or Medicaid patients to that entity for the furnishing of designated health services, unless a specifically defined exception to the prohibition is satisfied.[45] An entity may not bill any individual or government payer for designated health services furnished pursuant to a prohibited referral.[46] A *financial relationship* includes a direct or indirect relationship between a physician and an entity in which the physician has (1) an ownership or investment interest that exists in the entity through equity, debt, or other means and includes an interest in an entity that holds an ownership or investment interest in any entity providing designated health services; or (2) a compensation arrangement with the entity.[47] The Stark statute and regulations provide an exception to the statute's compensation arrangement referral prohibitions for bona fide employment relationships[48] and for personal service arrangements.[49]

Prohibition of Illegal Remuneration The Medicare and Medicaid Anti-Kickback Statute prohibits the offer or receipt of any remuneration, directly or indirectly, overtly or covertly, in cash or in kind, in return for, or which is intended to induce, the referral of patients for the furnishing or arranging for the furnishing of any item or service for which payment may be made in whole or in part under a federal health care program.[50] Violation of the statute is a felony, punishable by a fine of up to $25,000 or imprisonment for up to five years, or both.[51] Violation of the statute also is grounds for exclusion by the Department of Health and Human Services (DHHS) from participation in Medicare and state health care programs.[52]

Remuneration has been interpreted broadly to include anything of value.[53] In 1991, the Office of Inspector General (OIG) of the DHHS released a memorandum to the administrator of the Health Care Financing Administration (HCFA) which concluded that the Medicare Anti-Kickback Statute is violated if a hospital-based physician is required to pay more than the fair market value for services provided by the hospital or if he or she is compensated by the hospital for less than the fair market value of the goods and services he or she provides.[54]

The statute provides a statutory exception for "any amount paid by an employer to an employee (who has a bona fide employment relationship with such employer) for employment in the provision of covered items or services."[55] The so-called safe harbor regulations promulgated under the statute also provide that prohibited remuneration does not include "any amount paid by an employer to an employee who has a bona fide employment relationship with the employer, for employment in the furnishing of any item or service for which payment may be made in whole or in part under Medicare or a State health care program."[56] The regulations promulgated under the Anti-Kickback Statute also provide an exception to its prohibitions for certain payment arrangements between institutional providers and independent contractors.[57]

Methods of Physician Compensation

The compensation provisions of provider-based physician agreements, medical director or other administrative services agreements, and physician employment agreements typically provide for one of three types of financial arrangements:

1. A fixed-fee arrangement
2. A per-unit or per-service fee arrangement
3. A fixed-fee arrangement plus incentive compensation

Each method of compensation raises certain regulatory issues that must be considered when determining the appropriate financial arrangement between physician and institutional provider. These issues are discussed in the following subsections.

Fixed-Fee Arrangement Under a fixed-fee arrangement, the institutional provider typically is responsible for billing and collection for the professional services rendered by the physician pursuant to the employment or independent contractor agreement between provider and physician. The provider then pays the physician a salary of some fixed amount for all professional services rendered during the term of the agreement. For example, the contract may read as follows: "For all services that the Physician renders to the Hospital during the term of this Agreement, the Hospital agrees to pay the Physician annual compensation in the amount of $____." The physician's salary may include payment for administrative services provided, or the physician may receive any additional amount of fixed compensation for such services. A fixed-fee arrangement may be desirable from an administrative perspective because of its simplicity; however, such an arrangement is likely to be desirable from a financial perspective only to the extent that the pattern of services to be provided is such that an appropriate level of compensation for such services can be determined and fixed in advance.

Fixed-fee arrangements are permissible under the safe harbor guidelines for management and services contracts involving the use of property financed with tax-exempt bonds. Under Revenue Procedure 93-19,[58] a service contract will satisfy the safe harbor guidelines as a 50 percent periodic fixed-fee arrangement as long as the following conditions are fulfilled:

- At least 50 percent of the compensation for services for each annual period is based on a periodic fixed fee, where *periodic fixed fee* is defined as a stated dollar amount for services rendered under a specified period of time, such as a month or a year.
- The term of the contract, including all renewal options, does not exceed five years.
- The contract is terminable by the provider, without penalty or cause, upon reasonable notice at the end of the third year.[59]

If the business arrangement requires a commitment to the physician or physician group of more than three years, an ad hoc analysis of all the facts and circumstances of the arrangement will be necessary to determine whether "private use" will be found to exist without the ability to take advantage of the safe harbor provisions of the revenue procedure. For example, private use is a significant potential problem in the case of independent physicians operating a hospital ancillary service department but is unlikely to be a problem in the case of full-time employee physicians providing services in an outpatient clinic.

In addition, for a fixed-fee arrangement to avoid running afoul of the private inurement prohibition, compensation under the arrangement must be "reasonable."[60] In examining compensation arrangements for inurement of net earnings, the IRS and the courts traditionally have focused on three factors:

1. Whether the compensation was negotiated at arm's length
2. Whether the amount of compensation is reasonable in light of the services performed
3. Whether the arrangement is not merely a device to distribute profits to principals or to transform the organization's principal activity into a joint venture[61]

To the extent that a compensation package as a whole meets these three tests, it will not be considered to result in inurement of net earnings.

In determining whether compensation paid by an exempt organization is reasonable, the courts and the IRS have applied the standards concerning the deductibility of reasonable compensation by non-exempt organizations.[62] The tax court has noted that "[p]erhaps the most significant factor in passing upon the reasonableness of compensation in a tax case is a comparison between the compensation that is under consideration and the prevailing rates of compensation paid to the holders of comparable positions by comparable companies within the same industry."[63] Thus, the courts and the IRS generally turn to salary surveys and other comparable statistics as a first step in evaluating the reasonableness of compensation.

The Hospital Audit Guidelines of the IRS list the following factors as relevant in determining the reasonableness of compensation:

- Duties performed and amount of responsibility
- Time devoted to duties
- Special knowledge and experience
- Individual ability
- Previous training
- Compensation paid in prior years
- Prevailing general economic conditions (including wage levels for work of similar scope and nature, price levels, and inflation)
- Living conditions in the particular locality
- Comparability to similar positions in similar entities[64]

In general, tax-exempt organizations are not required to lose physician services to for-profit organizations that are willing to offer higher compensation. Meeting bona fide competition is a valid basis for arguing that the compensation paid to a particular physician is reasonable compensation.

As long as the physician's salary represents the "fair market value" of the services being provided, fixed-fee arrangements will satisfy the requirement of the Stark exceptions for bona fide employment arrangements and personal service arrangements. As noted above, both these exceptions require that the compensation paid pursuant to the arrangement not be determined in a manner that takes into account the volume of value of any referrals or other business generated between the parties.[65] Fixed-fee arrangements also satisfy the Anti-Kickback Statute safe harbor for employment arrangements, which, on its face, is very broad and does not include a requirement that the amounts paid to the employee be consistent with fair market value.[66] As discussed below, a fixed-fee arrangement may be required for compliance with the Anti-Kickback Statute in the case of independent contractor arrangements, given that the statute's safe harbor for personal services contracts requires not only that the compensation be consistent with fair market value and not take into account the volume or value of any referrals or business otherwise generated between the parties, but also that the *aggregate* compensation paid over the term of the agreement be set out in advance.[67]

Per-Fee Arrangements Contracts between an institutional provider and a physician involving a per-unit or per-service fee arrangement are most common for physician specialties that provide professional services primarily in a hospital or institutional setting. Examples would be agreements under which a physician will provide professional interpretations of a diagnostic test provided by the institutional provider, with the provider responsible for billing for both the technical and professional charges; or an agreement to pay for physician administrative time on a per-hour basis. Typically, this type of agreement provides that the physician will receive a specified amount for each professional service rendered. For example, a contract for radiology services may read as follows: "In consideration of the professional interpretation services to be provided by Physician pursuant to this Agreement, Hospital agrees to pay Physician the amount set forth on Exhibit 'A' for each service performed." A per-unit fee arrangement is likely to be preferred in situations where the total amount of services required to be performed by the physician over a specified period of time is difficult to determine in advance.

Per-unit fee arrangements fall within the safe harbor guidelines for management or service contracts between institutional provider and physician that may give rise to private business use of bond-financed facilities. Under the safe harbor guidelines of Revenue Procedure 93-19,[68] a services contract will satisfy the safe harbor guidelines as a per-unit fee arrangement if the following conditions are present:

1. All the compensation is based on a per-unit fee or a combination of a per-unit fixed fee and a periodic fixed fee.

2. The term of the contract, including all renewal options, does not exceed three years.
3. The contract is terminable by the institutional provider, without penalty or cause, upon reasonable notice at the end of the second year.[69]

With regard to the private inurement prohibition applicable to tax-exempt entities, the guidelines for determining reasonable compensation in light of the services being performed, described earlier, also apply in the case of compensation paid to a physician by a tax-exempt organization pursuant to a per-unit or per-service fee arrangement. As long as the physician's total compensation, including the per-unit fee arrangement, meets the IRS's tests of reasonableness, the compensation arrangement will not run afoul of the private inurement prohibition.

Per-unit fee arrangements do not comply with the technical requirements of the Anti-Kickback Statute safe harbor for personal service arrangements. As mentioned above, the safe harbor for personal service arrangements requires that the *aggregate* compensation to be paid over the term of the agreement be set out in advance. The OIG has acknowledged that, for various legitimate reasons, health care providers may be unable to specify the aggregate compensation to be provided for services rendered over the term of an agreement. As a result, the OIG has indicated that per-unit or per-service contracts are not violations of the Anti-Kickback Statute but will be analyzed on a case-by-case basis under the statute. However, according to the OIG, "the more the payments appear to reflect the volume of referrals from the financially-interested party, the more suspect the arrangement becomes and the more likely we will need to examine it carefully."[70] As a result, although per-unit fee arrangements in which the fair market value of the payments for the services rendered is appropriately documented may survive scrutiny under the Anti-Kickback Statute, they generally are not advisable.

On the other hand, per-unit fee arrangements are acceptable under the broad Anti-Kickback Statute safe harbor provision for employer-employee relationships. As noted above, this exception provides safe harbor protection for any amount paid by an employer to a bona fide employee for employment in the provision of covered items or services.[71] Unlike the safe harbor for personal services arrangements, the safe harbor provision for employer-employee relationships does not impose a requirement that the compensation be consistent with fair market value and not determined in a manner that takes into account the volume or value of business generated between the parties.[72] Part-time employment arrangements fall within this safe harbor provision, as long as a bona fide employer-employee relationship exists.[73]

A contractual arrangement between physician and institutional provider that involves a per-unit fee arrangement should be acceptable under the Stark exceptions for employment contracts and personal service arrangements. As noted above, both Stark exceptions require that the compensation to be paid over the term of the agreement must not exceed fair market value and must not be determined in a manner that takes into account the volume or value of any referrals or other business generated between the parties.[74] A per-unit fee arrangement should be acceptable under these exceptions even if the compensation paid over the term of the agreement varies based on the number of patient referrals by the physician, as long as the compensation does not literally "take into account" the volume or value of any such referrals. For example, this will be the case if there are no financial incentives in the agreement (such as increased per-unit rates) based on the volume of services performed.

The legislative history of Stark II indicates that Congress did not intend to prohibit per-unit compensation under Stark. According to both the House Report and the House Conference Report, "the requirement that the compensation be paid in advance is not intended to prohibit arrangements where entities pay [for services] on a per service basis, as long as the other requirements are satisfied."[75] Further, in an April 1994 speech to the OIG, the chief counsel of the OIG specifically stated that, under the Stark II personal services safe harbor, a per-service or per-hour payment is all that needs to be specified in order to satisfy the safe harbor.[76]

The Stark law also provides an exception for remuneration provided to a physician by a hospital if the remuneration is unrelated to the provision of designated health services.[77] Arguably, per-unit compensation arrangements between physician and hospital are permissible under this exception, as long as the payments are for administrative and physician services only and not related to the provision of designated health services.

Fixed-Fee Plus Incentive Compensation It is becoming increasingly common for contracts between institutional providers and physicians to include a compensation arrangement that involves both a fixed-base salary and the opportunity for the physician to earn additional or "incentive" compensation. Incentive compensation arrangements offer potential benefits to both provider and physician. Such arrangements may be used by an institutional provider as a means to recruit and retain qualified physicians and to encourage them to provide both high-quality and cost-effective care. Incentive arrangements are almost essential in certain physician practice settings to encourage the levels of productivity regularly occurring in small independent physician practices with which the health system will have to compete. Incentive compensation arrangements can take a variety of forms, including productivity bonuses that reward the physician for services personally performed by the physician and performance bonuses that reward the physician for improving the quality, efficiency, and coordination of services provided by the institution as a whole.

A productivity bonus may be calculated based on the revenues generated by a particular physician, minus certain operating and administrative expenses attributable to the physician, up to a specified amount. The amount of the productivity bonus, or the physician's eligibility to receive the bonus in the first instance, also may be based on the satisfaction of certain criteria by the physician, such as compliance with institutional rules and regulations, participation in institutional meetings and committees, and participation in managed care contracts of the institution. A performance bonus may be awarded solely on the basis of specified performance-related criteria (for example, the results of patient satisfaction surveys, QA/UR, compliance with institutional policies and rules, participation in managed care arrangements, and so on) that are not tied directly to the revenues generated by the individual physician.

Traditionally, the IRS's concern with respect to incentive or contingent compensation arrangements is that they can create a significant conflict between serving the personal interests of the one being compensated and maximizing the extent to which ongoing activities may otherwise serve the exempt purposes of a charitable organization.[78] However, the IRS has approved of such arrangements in certain contexts and has identified five safeguards, which, when present, tend to demonstrate that the compensation arrangement will not create relationships in which the one being compensated will be under any significant incentive to promote his, her, or its own interest at the expense of interfering with the charitable mission of the Section 501(c)(3) organization. These safeguards are as follows:

1. A completely arm's-length contractual relationship, with the service provider having no participation in the management or control of the organization.
2. The contingent payments serve a real and discernible business purpose of the exempt organization independent of any purpose to operate the organization for the direct or indirect benefit of the service provider (for example, achieving maximum efficiency and economy in operations by shifting the principal risk of operating cost to the service provider so as to alleviate the organization's need to carry large insurance-type reserves).
3. The amount of compensation is not dependent principally on incoming revenue of the exempt organization but, rather, on accomplishment of the objectives of the compensatory contract (for example, the success of the employer organization and the service provider in keeping actual expenses within the limits of projected expenses on which the ultimate prices of charitable services are based).

4. Review of the actual operating results reveals no evidence of abuse or unwarranted benefits (for example, prices and operating costs compare favorably to those of other, similar organizations) or safeguards exist to prevent such abuse (for example, provisions of the organic documents of the exempt organization or of the written agreement pursuant to which the compensation is being paid).
5. Presence of a ceiling or reasonable maximum so as to avoid the possibility of a windfall benefit to the service provider based on factors bearing no direct relationship to the level of service provided.[79]

A compensation arrangement will be suspect if it rewards physicians for the financial performance of a department or activity for which they perform no significant personal or supervisory services. The IRS has expressly recognized the legitimacy of properly structured net revenue incentive compensation arrangements for physicians where the incentive compensation formula is based on physician personal productivity, as distinguished from net revenues of the hospital or a net revenue stream joint venture for a hospital department.[80]

As a general matter, incentive compensation arrangements of the type described above are likely to be acceptable under the Anti-Kickback Statute's broad exception for amounts paid by an employer to an employee pursuant to a bona fide employment relationship. However, such arrangements between institutional provider and independent contractor physician raise the same issues as do per-unit fee arrangements, namely, that the aggregate compensation to be paid over the term of the agreement is not set out in advance. Although, based on the OIG's statements with regard to per-unit fee arrangements, it is likely that incentive compensation arrangements would be subject to a case-by-case analysis; the more the incentive compensation arrangement appeared to reflect the volume of referrals between the parties, the more likely the arrangement would result in scrutiny and enforcement under the statute.

Employment arrangements that offer incentive compensation in the form of productivity bonuses based on services personally performed by the physician specifically are permitted under Stark. Both the Stark statute and the final Stark I regulations provide that the requirement of the employment exception that the amount of compensation provided under an employment arrangement must be determined in a manner that does not take into account (directly or indirectly) the volume or value of any referrals by the physician does not prohibit payment of remuneration in the form of a productivity bonus based on services performed personally by the physician.[81]

With regard to independent contractor arrangements under Stark, the Stark exception for personal services arrangements provides that compensation paid to an independent contractor physician by an institutional provider may be determined in a manner that takes into account the volume or value of referrals or other business generated between the parties only in the case of a "physician incentive plan."[82] Under the final Stark I regulations, a *physician incentive plan* is defined as "any compensation arrangement between an entity and a physician or physician group that may directly or indirectly have the effect of reducing or limiting services provided with respect to individuals enrolled with the entity."[83] In the case of a physician incentive plan between a physician and an entity, the compensation may be determined in a manner that takes into account (directly or indirectly) the volume or value of any referrals or other business generated between the parties, if the plan meets certain requirements specified in the regulations.[84]

CONCLUSION

The recent changes in the health care system have altered the relationship between institutional providers and physicians by both increasing their interdependence and expanding the nature of their business relationship. The content of the contractual arrangements between institutional providers and physicians reflects this new relationship. The traditional forms of hospital-physician contracts may no longer serve the best interests of provider, physician, or community; and, as a result, providers should give careful consideration to the structure and content of the proposed contractual arrangement. An essential component of these contractual arrangements is the financial arrangement between physician and institutional provider. Because the method of physician compensation has both organizational and legal ramifications for an institutional provider, it is important that the provider clearly understand the alternative methods of compensation and both the reimbursement-related and regulatory considerations that may determine the appropriate method of compensation.

References and Notes

1. 42 C.F.R. §415.102.
2. See 42 C.F.R. §§415.110; 415.120; 415.130.
3. 42 C.F.R. §415.120(a).
4. 42 C.F.R. §415.120(a).

5. Social Security Act §1842(b)(6).

6. 42 C.F.R. §424.80.

7. 42 C.F.R. §424.80(b)(1).

8. HCFA Publication 14, *Medicare Carriers Manual,* Part III, §3060.1.

9. *Medicare Carriers Manual,* Part III, §3060.1.

10. *Medicare Carriers Manual,* Part III, §3060.1.

11. *Medicare Carriers Manual.* Part III, §3060.1. The manual recommends use of the following language: "I acknowledge that, under the terms of my employment, only [Name of Employer] is entitled to claim or receive any fees or charges for my services."

12. 42 C.F.R. §424.80(b)(2); *Medicare Carriers Manual,* Part III, §3060.2.

13. *Medical Carriers Manual,* Part III, §3060.2B. Physician services furnished outside the physical premises of a facility are considered furnished in the facility if they are furnished to an inpatient of the facility or if they represent tests performed on specimens obtained from the patient, or interpretations of tests performed, while the patient is within the physical premises of the facility.

14. *Medicare Carriers Manual,* Part III, §3060.2A.

15. *Medicare Carriers Manual,* Part III, §3060.2A. When the facility does not have an appropriate written contract, the following language may be submitted, if signed and dated by both facility and physician: "It is agreed that only [name of facility] will bill and receive any fees or charges for the services of [name of physician] furnished to patients at the above-named facility."

16. *Medicare Carriers Manual,* Part III, §3060.2D.

17. *Medicare Carriers Manual,* Part III, §3060.2D.

18. *Medicare Carriers Manual,* Part III, §3060.2D.

19. 42 C.F.R. §413.9.

20. See generally 42 C.F.R. §§415.150 through 415.190, and *CCH Medicare and Medicaid Guide,* §8000, et seq.

21. 42 C.F.R. §415.60(a).

22. 42 C.F.R. §415.60(c).

23. For example, funded research. See 42 C.F.R. §415.60(e),(f).

24. 42 C.F.R. §415.60(f)(ii).

25. 42 C.F.R. §415.60(d). If payments for physician services rendered to patients are received directly or indirectly by the provider or an organization related to the provider, these payments are not compensation for physician services furnished to the provider. 42 C.F.R. §415.60(d)(2).

26. 42 C.F.R. §415.60(f)(2).

27. 42 C.F.R. §415.60(g)(1).

28. 42 C.F.R. §415.60(g)(2).

29. 42 C.F.R. §415.60(g)(3).

30. 42 C.F.R. §415.70(a). The reasonable compensation equivalency limits do not apply to the costs of physician compensation attributable to furnishing inpatient hospital services that are paid for under the prospective payment system. In addition, compensation a physician receives for activities that are not reimbursable under either Medicare Part A or Part B is not considered for purposes of applying the compensation limits. See 42 C.F.R. §415.70(a)(2),(3).

31. 42 C.F.R. §415.70(c).

32. 42 C.F.R. §415.70(d). For the costs of membership in professional societies and CME, the intermediary may adjust the limit by the lesser of the actual cost incurred by the provider or the physician for these activities, or five percent of the limit. For the cost of malpractice expenses incurred by either provider or physician, the intermediary may adjust the reasonable compensation equivalency limit by the cost of the malpractice insurance expense related to the physician's services furnished to provider patients. See 42 C.F.R. §415.70(d)(1),(2).

33. 42 C.F.R. §415.70(e).

34. Although not addressed in this chapter, the structure of the contractual relationship between physician and provider (including method

of compensation) also may be affected by a state's corporate practice of medicine prohibition (see for example Tex. Rev. Civ. Stat. Ann. art 4495(b) 3.08); liability concerns, including tort and antitrust liability; state illegal remuneration statutes (see for example Kan. Stat. Ann. §65-2837(b); Tex. Health & Safety Code Ann. §161.091); and state law prohibitions or restrictions on physician referrals (see for example Ga. Code Ann. §§43-1B-1 through 8; Md. Health Occ. Code §§1-301 through 1-306).

35. 42 U.S.C. §1395nn.

36. 42 U.S.C. §1320a–7b(b).

37. For example, employers are required to withhold FICA, FUTA, and income taxes for all employees.

38. See Treas. Reg. 31.3121(d)-1(c); 31.3306(I)-1; 31.3402(c)-1(h).

39. 1987-1 C.B. 296.

40. See for example Rev. Rul. 73-417, 1973-2 CB 332; Rev. Rul. 70-629, 1970-2 C.B. 228; Rev. Rul. 66-274, 1966-2 C.B. 446.

41. Internal Revenue Service, "Reasonable Compensation," *Exempt Organizations Continuing Professional Education Technical Instruction Program for Fiscal Year 1992* at 194 (IRS); "Compensation," *Exempt Organizations Continuing Professional Education Technical Instruction Program for Fiscal Year 1990* at 171 (IRS).

42. See IRC §§141k(e)(1)(G); 145.

43. IRC §145(a).

44. 1993-1 C.B. 526.

45. 42 U.S.C. §1395nn(a)(1)(A). The term *designated health services* includes any of the following items or services: clinical laboratory services; physical therapy services; occupational therapy services; radiology services, including magnetic resonance imaging, computerized axial tomography scans, and ultrasound services; radiation therapy services and supplies; durable medical equipment and supplies; prosthetics, orthotics, and prosthetic devices and supplies; home health services; and outpatient services. 42 U.S.C. §1395nn(h)(6).

46. 42 U.S.C. §1395nn(a)(1)(B).

47. 42 U.S.C. §1395nn(a)(2); 42 C.F.R. §411.351.

48. Under this exception, a prohibited compensation arrangement does not include amounts paid by an employer to a physician who has a bona fide employment relationship with the employer for the provision of services if (1) the employment is for identifiable services; (2) the amount of the remuneration under the employment is consistent with the fair market value of the services and is not determined in a manner that takes into account (directly or indirectly) the volume or value of any referrals by the referring physician; and (3) the remuneration is provided pursuant to an agreement that would be commercially reasonable even if no referrals were made to the employer. 42 U.S.C. §1395nn(3)(2); 42 C.F.R. §411.357(c).

49. Under this exception, the contractual arrangement must meet the following requirements: (1) It must be set out in writing, be signed by the parties, and specify the services covered by the arrangement; (2) it must cover all the services to be provided by the physician to the entity; (3) the aggregate services contracted for must not exceed those that are reasonable and necessary for the legitimate business purposes of the arrangement; (4) the term of the agreement must be for a least one year; (5) the compensation to be paid over the term of the arrangement must be set out in advance, must not exceed fair market value, and must not be determined in a manner that takes into account the volume or value of any referrals or other business generated between the parties; and (6) the services to be performed under the arrangement must not involve the counseling or promotion or a business arrangement or other activity that violates any state or federal law. 42 U.S.C. §1395nn(e)(3); 42 C.F.R. §411.357(d).

50. 42 U.S.C. §1320a–7b(b). The Medicare and Medicaid Anti-Kickback Statute was recently amended by the Health Insurance Portability and Accountability Act of 1996 (P.L. 104-191, 110 Stat. 1937) to prohibit illegal remuneration in connection with all federal health care programs. The term *federal health care program* means any plan or program that provides health benefits, whether directly, through insurance, or otherwise, which is funded directly, in whole or in part, by the U.S. government (other than the Federal Employee Health Benefit Program); or any state health care program, including Medicaid, the Maternal and Child Health Services Block Grant Program, and the Social Services Block Grant Program.

51. 42 U.S.C. §1320a–7b(b).

52. 42 U.S.C. §1320a–7.

53. In May 1992, the OIG issued a Special Fraud Alert that identified "questionable practices" that would violate the statute if engaged in by hospitals in return for physician referrals, including the following: (1) payment of any sort of incentive by the hospital each time a physician refers a patient to the hospital; (2) use of free or significantly discounted office space or equipment (in facilities usually located close to the hospital); (3) provision of free or significantly discounted billing, nursing, or other staff services; (4) free training for a physician's office staffing areas such as management techniques, CPT coding, and laboratory techniques; (5) guarantees that provide that if the hospital's income fails to reach a predetermined level, the hospital will supplement the remainder up to a certain amount; (6) low-interest or interest-free loans, or loans that may be "forgiven" if a physician refers patients (or some number of patients) to the hospital; (7) payment of the cost of a physician's travel and expenses for conferences; (8) payment for a physician's CME courses; (9) coverage on hospital's group health insurance plans at an inappropriately low cost to the physician; and (10) payment for services (which may include consultations at the hospital) which require few, if any, substantive duties by the physician, or payment for services in excess of the fair market value of services rendered. See Department of Health and Human Services, Office of Inspector General, Special Fraud Alert, *Hospital Incentives to Physicians* (May 1992).

54. Department of Health and Human Services, Office of Inspector General, *Financial Arrangements Between Hospitals and Hospital-Based Physicians* (Oct. 1991) (OEI-09-89-00330). In a case arising out of a dispute that originally triggered this report, in December 1995, a Virginia circuit court awarded approximately $3 million in damages to a radiology group whose members lost their privileges after rejecting a hospital's exclusive service contract, which called for the group to buy certain equipment and obtain billing, collection, and practice management services from hospital-owned firms. The court found that the Anti-Kickback Statute was violated and, after a jury considering the damages issue only returned a verdict of no damages, the court overruled the verdict and granted an award it said was based on undisputed evidence. *Virginia Radiology Associates v. Culpepper Memorial Hospital,* Va. Circuit Court (Norfolk, 12129195). See *Health Law Reporter* 5: 240 (Feb. 15, 1996).

55. 42 U.S.C. §1320a–7b(b)(3)(B).

56. 42 C.F.R. §1001.952(I). For purposes of this exception to the statute, the term employee has the same meaning as it does for purposes of

26 U.S.C. §3121(d)(2). Section 3121(d)(2) provides that employee means "any individual who, under the usual common law rules applicable in determining the employer-employee relationship, has the status of any employee." 26 U.S.C. §3121(d)(2).

57. Under the safe harbor provision for personal services and management contracts, prohibited "remuneration" under the statute includes any payment made by a principal to an agent as compensation for the agent's services, as long as all of the following standards are met: (1) the agency agreement is set out in writing and signed by the parties; (2) the agreement specifies the services to be provided by the agent; (3) if the agreement is intended to provide for the agent's services on a periodic, sporadic, or part-time basis, rather than on a full-time basis for the term of the agreement, it specifies exactly the schedule of such intervals, their precise length, and their exact charge; (4) the term of the agreement is for not less than one year; (5) the aggregate compensation paid to the agent over the term of the agreement is set out in advance, is consistent with fair market value in arm's-length transactions, and is not determined in a manner that takes into account the volume or value of any referrals or business otherwise generated between the parties for which payment may be made in whole or in part under Medicare or a state health program; and (6) the services performed under the agreement do not involve the counseling or promotion of a business arrangement or other activity that violates state or federal law. 42 C.F.R. §1001.952(d).

58. 1993-1 C.B. 526.

59. 1993-1 C.B. 526.

60. See for example *Mabee Petroleum Corp. v. United States,* 203 F.2d 872 (5th Cir. 1953); *World Family Corp. v. Commissioner,* 81 TC 958 (1983), acq. in part, 1984-2 C.B. 2, nonacq. in part, 1984-2 CG2; *BHW Anesthesia Foundation, Inc. v. Commissioner,* 72 TC 681 (1979), nonacq., 1980-2 C.B. 2.

61. See for example Rev. Rul. 69-383, 1969-2 C.B. 113; Gen. Couns. Mem. 39670 (Oct. 14, 1987).

62. Internal Revenue Service, "Reasonable Compensation," *1992 Exempt Organizations Continuing Professional Education Technical Instruction Program Textbook* at 200 (IRS).

63. *John Marshall Law School v. United States,* 81-2 U.S.T.C. ¶9514m (Ct. Cl. Tr. Div.), aff'd, 228 Ct. Cl. 902(1981).

64. Internal Revenue Service Audit Guidelines for Hospitals, Manual Transmittal 7 (10) 69-38, Exempt Organizations Guidelines Handbook §331 (1) (Mar. 1992).

65. 42 U.S.C. §1395nn(e)(2); 42 C.F.R. §411.357(c); 42 U.S.C. §1395nn(e)(3); 42 C.F.R. §411.357(d).

66. However, the OIG has indicated that payments made by a hospital to a physician pursuant to an employment arrangement that are in excess of the fair market value for the items and services being provided may be viewed as payments for referrals and, as such, would not be covered under the employment exception, which only exempts payments for the provision of covered items and services. Letter from D. M. Thornton, associate general counsel, OIG, DHHS, to T. J. Sullivan, Office of the Associate Chief Counsel, IRS, Dec. 22, 1992.

67. 42 C.F.R. §1001.952(d).

68. 1993-1 C.B. 526.

69. Under the safe harbor guidelines, a *per-unit fee* is a fee based on a unit of service provided, such as a stated dollar amount for each specified procedure performed. The amount of the per-unit fee must be specified in the contract or otherwise specifically limited by the provider or an independent third party, such as the Medicare program.

70. 56 *Federal Register* 35952, 35973.

71. 42 U.S.C. 1320a–7b(b)(3)(B); 42 C.F.R. §1001.952(i).

72. However, as noted above, the OIG has indicated that payments made pursuant to an employment arrangement that are in excess of the fair market value for the items and services being provided may be viewed as payments for referrals and, as such, would not be covered under the employment exception, which only exempts payments that are for the provision of covered items and services. See letter from Thornton to Sullivan.

73. See 56 *Federal Register* 35952, 35981.

74. 42 U.S.C. §1395nn(e)(2); 42 C.F.R. §411.357(c); 42 U.S.C. §1395nn(e)(3); 42 C.F.R. §411.357(d).

75. House Rep. No. 103-11, 93rd Cong., 1st Sess. 3(1993), reprinted in *1993 USCCAN* at 780; House Conf. Rep. No. 103-213, 93rd Cong., 1st Sess. 3 (1993), reprinted in *1993 USCCAN* at 1503–4.

76. "Under the Stark II exception, a per-service or per-hour payment is all that needs to be specified. In other words, under Stark II, you may specify that the doctor [performing the personal services] will be paid $200 per hour for however many hours will be worked on A-B-C services in the coming year." See D. M. Thornton, "Impact of the Anti-Kickback Statute and the Stark Amendment on Vertically Integrated Delivery Systems in the Health Care Industry," Apr. 1994.

77. 42 U.S.C. §1395nn(e)(4); 42 C.F.R. §411.357(g)(2).

78. Gen. Couns. Mem. 38905 (Oct. 6, 1982); see also Gen. Couns. Mem. 39444 (Nov. 13, 1985).

79. Gen. Couns. Mem. 38905 (Oct. 6, 1982), citing Gen. Couns. Mem. 32453 (Nov. 30, 1962).

80. See, for example, the exemption ruling issued to Marietta Health Care Physicians, Inc., on Oct. 3, 1995, reprinted in *95 Tax Notes Today* (Oct. 17, 1995): 202–39.

81. 42 U.S.C. §1395nn(e)(2); 42 C.F.R. §411.357(c)(4).

82. 42 U.S.C. §1395nn(e)(3)(A)(v).

83. 42 U.S.C. §1395nn(e)(3)(B)(ii).

84. A physician incentive plan must meet the following requirements: (1) No specific payment is made, directly or indirectly, under the plan to a physician or physician group as an inducement to reduce or limit medically necessary services provided with respect to a specific individual enrolled with the entity; (2) in the case of a plan that places a physician or a physician group at substantial financial risk as determined by the secretary [of the Department of Health and Human Services] pursuant to 42 U.S.C. §1395mm(i)(8)(A)(ii), the plan complies with any requirements the secretary may impose pursuant to such section; and (3) upon request by the secretary, the entity provides the secretary with access to descriptive information regarding the plan in order to permit the secretary to determine whether the plan is in compliance with these requirements. 42 U.S.C. §1395nn(e)(3)(B)(i).

PART III

Physician Services Organization and Delivery

How physician services are organized and delivered depends not only on the preference of the individual physician, but also on a myriad of regulations to be found in business law, corporate law, and the tax code. In addition to legal, tax, and corporate practice of medicine considerations, effective physician practices must also consider a number of critical management issues.

This section consists of three chapters. Chapter 8, "Legal and Tax Consequences of Organizing Physician Practices," reviews the common choices of organizational form and compares their advantages and disadvantages. Chapter 9, "Physician Services Management Issues," evaluates current systems for monitoring quality and reviews the relationship between physician productivity and quality of care. Chapter 10, "The Corporate Practice of Medicine Doctrine," discusses the history, application, and impact of corporate involvement in the practice of medicine.

8

Legal and Tax Consequences of Organizing Physician Practices

Rick W. Griffin, JD
Brian J. Passante, JD

Health care administrators and executives are faced with the growing trend in physician practice organization toward group concentrations and group practices, increasingly in coordination or partnership with integrated health care delivery systems. Choosing the most appropriate legal entity for acquiring or forming such group practices is a complex process because there are so many variations, and the choice can have many ramifications on both the flexibility of the type of entity selected and the tax ramifications of the new enterprise, now and in the future. The clear goal is to maximize the selected entity's advantages and minimize its disadvantages in the changing health care landscape.[1]

The traditional choices of business entity include the solo private practice (referred to in legal parlance as *Sole proprietorship*), the partnership, and the corporation. However, more recently, variations of the newer limited liability partnership (LLP) have been instituted in many states. The principal legal factors and characteristics that distinguish one

---

The concepts and information presented herein are not intended to be construed as legal advice by the authors. The complexity of the issues overviewed in this chapter merit careful consideration in light of specific circumstances, location, and applicable law. One or more of the concepts discussed may not be applicable in a specific state, and the reader should consult with personal legal, tax, and professional advisors concerning any particular questions that arise.

form from another are governance, limitation of personal liability, taxation, continuity of existence, and free transferability of ownership interest. The lines between the choices have blurred because creative businesses and professionals use various mechanisms to lend to one type of entity the aspects and attributes of another.[2]

This chapter briefly examines the four types of business entity—limited liability company (LLC), corporation, partnership, and sole proprietorship—and groups their comparative characteristics into legal characteristics and factors and tax characteristics and factors, further categorizing each entity's characteristics by classifying and examining them as either advantages or disadvantages. (See table 8-1.) Finally, the chapter includes a checklist of questions that need to be asked when preparing to choose the most favorable business form in specific circumstances.

SOLO PRIVATE PRACTITIONER, OR SOLE PROPRIETORSHIP

One approach to selecting a business entity is not to form any formal entity at all. If a physician practices alone and has not incorporated, by default, he or she is a *sole proprietor.* Although many practitioners still operate as a sole proprietorship, use of this form of organization is decreasing. For a health care executive, the limitations and critical disadvantages of this older, more traditional form of physician service delivery highlight the significant advantages that can be offered by group practices acquired or supported by a structured hospital-physician partnership.

The distinguishing characteristics of a sole proprietorship are as follows:

- Governance is concentrated solely in the sole proprietor.
- The owner and his or her assets are subject to unlimited personal liability for the debts, taxes, and claims of creditors.
- There is no continuity of existence because the proprietorship ceases when the practice ceases.
- Taxes are the responsibility of the individual, which avoids the double-taxation concerns facing corporate shareholders.

Although sole proprietorship is the simplest form of business entity to establish and operate, it lacks some of the attractive features of other business entities, and its use is inconsistent with the present trends toward larger practice groups and concentrations. (See table 8-2 for an overview of this business entity's advantages and disadvantages.) Moreover, although adequate liability insurance may counterbalance some of

TABLE 8-1. Comparative Chart of Characteristics of Four Different Business Entities

	Type of Organization			
Factor	*Solo or Private Practice*	*Partnership*	*Corporation*	*LLC*
Formality of formation and operation	Simple to form and operate; generally no documents required	Relatively simple to operate and form; written partnership agreement not required, but often advisable	Requires the most formality in creation and annual operation; requires formal incorporation, articles of incorporation filing, and so on	Generally simple and informal; similar to general partnership except formal articles of organization required
Expenses of formation and operation	Minimal	Some costs in preparation of partnership agreement; no special filing fees or annual reports	Most expensive to operate, including incorporation fees, annual filing fees, intangible tax in some states, and tax on initial capitalization	Some filing fees on articles of organization, although generally less than a corporation
Extent of personal liability	Unlimited personal liability	Generally unlimited liability with partners jointly and severally liable for most debts, except for variations of limited partnership and limited liability partnership	All shareholders have limited liability (to capital investment) unless otherwise provided	All members have limited liability unless otherwise provided (except in states not recognizing LLC formally)

(Continued on next page)

TABLE 8-1. *(Continued)*

	Type of Organization			
Factor	*Solo or Private Practice*	*Partnership*	*Corporation*	*LLC*
Will personal liability shield be lost if formalities not observed?	Not applicable; no personal liability shield to lose	No; not applicable except for limited partnerships and limited liability partnership variations	Yes	No
Common control documents	None	None required, but partnership agreement common	Articles of incorporation, bylaws, rules, shareholder agreements	Articles of organization, membership operating agreement
Continuity of legal existence and duration	None; lapses upon resignation, retirement, or death of principal	Generally exists until member withdraws, unless the written partnership agreement provides otherwise; no continuity of existence applying federal income tax characteristics and tests	Long duration and generally uninterrupted continuity; entity continues until formal dissolution; transfer or withdrawal of ownership interest *does not* cause dissolution	No continuity of existence applying federal income tax characteristics and tests; however, upon withdrawal of member, remaining members cast vote to continue LLC rather than dissolve

Participation in management	No limitations	No limitations, except for LP variation	No limitations, except PC can only be by professionals	No limitations
Management body	No	No, except possibly managing partner, or in the case of LP where only general partner manages day-to-day operations	Board of directors	All members or a management board, or a combination; very variable control structure
Public filings required	None	Generally none, except for LPs and LLPs	Articles of incorporation and annual statement of officers	Articles of organization
Transferability of ownership interest	No	No, unless permitted by agreement; partners enjoy absolute right to select partners	Generally yes, except for professional corporations, closely held corporations, share transfer agreements, or restrictions imposed by articles or securities laws	Varies by state act; some membership interests are freely transferable to assignees; others are restricted by membership, operating agreement, or state or federal securities laws

(Continued on next page)

TABLE 8-1. *(Continued)*

	Type of Organization			
Factor	*Solo or Private Practice*	*Partnership*	*Corporation*	*LLC*
Ramifications of exit of partner or owner	Not applicable	Generally, dissolution unless the partnership agreement provides otherwise; except for LP, where exit of limited partner will not cause dissolution	None	Generally, dissolution unless the operating agreement provides otherwise or majority of remaining members vote to continue; exit of more than 50% of members can trigger liquidation for federal tax purposes per I.R.C. Sec. 708
Limits on the number of owners	Only one	At least two	Any number or types of owners	At least two to be considered for partnership tax treatment in most states
Qualifications for owners/types of owners	Only one type; licensed to practice medicine	Any type of owner	Any type of owner, except that S corporations restricted to U.S. citizens and certain trusts; PCs restricted to licensed professional	Any type of owner

Classes of ownership interests	Only one	Multiple classes are permitted	Multiple classes are permitted, except in S corporation and PC	Multiple classes are permitted
Rules for naming entity	No requirements; total flexibility, but may require a trade name filing	No restrictions, except limited partnership must include "LP," and limited liability partnership must include "LLP" or similar	Must contain "corporation," "company," "incorporated," or abbreviation; some other limitations may apply in certain states	Must contain "limited company," "LC," or "LLC"
Ramifications of doing business in multiple states	No special requirements, except possibly registration to conduct business	No special requirements, except possibly registration to conduct business	No special requirements, except possibly registration to conduct business	In states that do not recognize LLC, some uncertainty in legal ramifications; may subject members to partnership treatment and joint liability
Applicability of federal and state securities laws	No	Generally no for general partnerships; generally yes for the interests of limited partners in limited partnerships	Generally yes	Depends on developing law; some suggest no if any of the members exercise management rights
Limitations imposed on the corporate practice of medicine	No	No	Yes, varies by state; generally no for professional corporations	Possibly yes; varies by state

(Continued on next page)

TABLE 8-1. *(Continued)*

	Type of Organization			
Factor	*Solo or Private Practice*	*Partnership*	*Corporation*	*LLC*
Is income subject to tax at the entity level; double taxation factor	Yes; one level of federal income tax as the sole proprietor pays income tax on all income	Generally no, if the partnership lacks two of four tax characteristics of corporations; generally, one level of federal income tax at the ownership level	Yes, corporation pays federal income tax on income; but also two levels of federal income tax as shareholders must also pay income tax on dividends or cash distributions	Generally no, if formed pursuant to qualifying state act or unless operating agreement provisions disqualify this tax treatment of income
Predictability of federal tax status	Generally certain	Generally certain where partnership agreement structured to ensure organization lacks any two of four corporate characteristics	Yes, generally certain; S corporation requires election filing and must comply with strict limitations	Generally certain where operating agreement structured to ensure organization lacks any two of four corporate characteristics; there is some risk of reclassification causing taxation as corporation
Will dedication to entity of appreciated property be a taxable event?	Nontaxable	Generally nontaxable, unless the partner is relieved from debt obligations	Generally taxable, unless transferors comprise at least 80% of ownership and meet test of IRC Sec 351, except to extent of debt relief	Generally nontaxable, unless the member is relieved from debt obligations

Are losses atttributable to entity debt deductible?	Generally not	Yes, allocable share in loss to extent of tax basis in partnership interest is deductible	Yes, shareholder may deduct allocable share of losses to extent of tax basis *excluding* any portion of corporate debt	Yes, allocable share in loss to extent of tax basis in membership interest which *includes* allocable share in LLC debt
Passive activity tax limitations	All seven "material participation" tests apply	All seven "material participation" tests apply	Not applicable	Members can qualify under three of the "material participation" tests
Permissible fiscal year	Calendar year	Generally calendar year	No restrictions, except calendar year for S corporations	Generally calendar, matching the year of the majority of the members

(Continued on next page)

TABLE 8-1. *(Continued)*

	Type of Organization			
Factor	*Solo or Private Practice*	*Partnership*	*Corporation*	*LLC*
Use of cash method of accounting	Generally permitted	Generally permitted unless a C corporation is a partner	Not permissible for C corporation, except for personal service with gross receipts less than $5 million, but generally permitted for S corporation	Subject to some uncertainty; probably not permitted especially when C corporation is member or if more than 35% of the LLC losses are allocable to nonmanagerial members, except for personal service with gross receipts less than $5 million
Eligible for small business stock 14% capital gain treatment?	Not applicable	Not eligible	Stock eligible	Not eligible
How are cash distributions treated?	Not applicable	Nontaxable to the extent of a partner's tax basis in his or her partnership interest	For C corporation, taxable as dividend earnings, then nontaxable to extent of shareholder's tax basis; for S corporation, generally nontaxable to extent of shareholder's tax basis	Generally nontaxable to the extent of a member's basis in his or her LLC membership interest

What tax ramifications upon liquidation of entity?	Not applicable	Generally taxable, except nontaxable to extent of partner's tax basis	For C corporation, taxable to corporation and shareholder; for S corporation, nontaxable at the corporate level and taxable at the shareholder level	Nontaxable to extent of partner's tax basis
Marginal tax federal rate on income of the business	39.6%	39.6%	35.0%	39.6%
Section 1244 stock; treatment as ordinary loss upon sale or liquidation	No	No	Yes, if shareholders are original investors, they may qualify within limits	No

TABLE 8-2. Key Advantages and Disadvantages to a Sole Proprietorship

Advantages	*Disadvantages*
Simple to create and operate	Unlimited personal liability
Avoids double taxation of income	No continuity of existence
	Limited to single owner
	No transferability of ownership interest
	Limited to calendar fiscal year

the personal liability exposure of practicing as a sole proprietor, this type of business entity is becoming less common given the rapidly changing health care industry and the economic forces that mold the modern-day delivery of care. By definition, a sole proprietor is without some of the tools and advantages that a concentration of capital and labor can yield with a corporation, a professional corporation, or an LLC.

CORPORATION

A *corporation* is completely opposite from a sole proprietorship, with significant differences in formation, operation, and dissolution. The corporate form has certain key advantages and disadvantages, many of which derive from the characteristics that make it distinct from a partnership or other less formal forms of business organization. Two variations of the corporate theme discussed later in this section are the S corporation and the professional corporation.

General Characteristics of a Corporation

The key characteristics that distinguish a corporation from a sole proprietorship or a partnership are the required formalities in the entity's creation and operation, its continuity of existence, and the free transferability of ownership interest. A corporation is the creature of state law and exists at the pleasure of the state. Hence, it is an artificial or fictitious legal entity that has a separate legal existence from its incorporators and owners. It can make contracts, pay taxes, and be liable for debts. Generally, the corporation's owners or shareholders are not liable for its debts (although in cases where small corporations or thinly capitalized corporations engage in business with lending institutions, its business associates often will insist or require that the shareholders personally guarantee the corporate loans and debts). As the corporation's scale or size increases, its day-to-day management is usually vested in its executives and officers. Finally, the shareholders, as owners of the corporation, are entitled to any dividends the corporation pays and to all corporate assets (after any creditors or other priority debts are paid) in the event the corporation is liquidated.

The corporation's most important distinction remains the separateness and continuous nature of its legal existence. It is upon this separate existence that the protection of limited liability for shareholders rests. A corporation will continue as an entity despite the withdrawal or transfer of some or all of the ownership interests (the shares). The laws of most states provide many steps and burdens to obtain shareholder approval to dissolve a corporation.

An additional characteristic of a corporation is the free transferability of its ownership interest. That means, absent restrictions in the documents that formed the corporation (for example, the articles of incorporation, the bylaws, and restrictions contained in agreements by and among the shareholders), its shares can be freely transferred by one shareholder to a new shareholder without the approval of shareholders or the corporation.

Advantages to a Corporation

Clearly, there are substantial advantages to operating a physicians' practice in coordination with a health care entity as a corporation, not the least of which is the protection of the personal assets of the investors and shareholders from liabilities and the claims and creditors of the corporation. (See table 8-3.)

Another advantage is that the corporation has a long tradition. The laws of most states are fairly similar and uniform with respect to the formation and treatment of corporations. Thus, operation in more than one state or jurisdiction generally will not result in different or unintended consequences or treatment for the corporation. More important, because the corporation is a traditional and long-standing form of business entity for which a body of case law exists, legal, financial, and tax advisors can predict with some accuracy the consequences of various actions, agreements, and other decisions for the corporation. Thus, one of the organization's key advantages is its predictability and the general uniformity of state law.

Finally, because the corporation is a separate legal entity, it is taxed as such. Over the past several decades, federal and state laws have focused on more than simple revenue generation for government. Instead, there are incentives and disincentives built into the tax codes and regulations. Business organizations, including corporations, are no less susceptible to these incentives and disincentives than individuals.

TABLE 8-3. Key Advantages and Disadvantages to a Corporation

Advantages	*Disadvantages*
Limited liability for owners	Higher costs to create and operate
Long duration and continuity of existence	Requires formalities to protect personal liability shield
Ownership interest generally transferable without causing dissolution	Double taxation of income at corporate and shareholder level
No limits on number of owners	If a PC, limits owners to professionals
Except for S corporation and PC, multiple classes of owners permitted	Potential increased regulatory burden of securities laws, corporate practice of medicine
Fewer restrictions on fiscal year	
Fairly predictable federal tax status	
Reduced passive activity tax limitations	
Section 1244 tax treatment available	

Because in some circumstances the government wishes to encourage capital formation, there are certain opportunities and advantages for corporations. One important advantage corporations enjoy is that, although dividend interest on investments is taxable to the corporation, generally, 70 percent of those dividends are free of federal income tax. Additionally, retirement plans and deferred income implemented through the corporate structure are treated somewhat more favorably than similar plans that can be implemented by an individual. Finally, if shareholders are original investors, they may qualify, within limits, for section 1244 treatment of the stock, to allow ordinary losses upon sale or liquidation of the corporate entity.[3]

Disadvantages to a Corporation

The advantages to a corporation come at a cost, and there are some drawbacks to this form of business entity. (See table 8-3.) First, because the corporation requires the most formality in its establishment and operation, it carries with it the most significant transactional costs for both formation and operation. Second, corporations generally are required under federal law to pay unemployment taxes in connection with salaries paid to owners, which is a requirement not generally imposed on sole proprietors or partnerships.

Additionally, business profits are taxed to corporations at rates higher than those of some individuals (except for large corporations). Taxation at the corporate level, plus taxation of the individual shareholders on their income (in the form of dividends), is generally thought to be the most significant tax drawback to the corporate structure. This is often referred to as the *double-taxation issue.* Because the corporation and the individual are both legal entities that can be taxed, both pay taxes on the income of the corporate enterprise even if it is only truly earned once.

Finally, there are health care–specific and regulatory disadvantages and issues that need to be addressed in connection with the practice of medicine in a corporate structure. Although several states have recently passed so-called corporate practice of medicine reform bills indicating that this limitation or restriction on the corporation may be loosened, this regulatory restriction continues to be a concern for the corporate-structured entity. (This state-by-state issue is discussed in detail in chapter 10.)

S Corporation

The S corporation (formerly referred to as the *subchapter S corporation*) is a special subset of the ordinary corporation. The legal distinctions and differences between an ordinary corporation (for tax purposes, referred to as a *C corporation*) and an S corporation are insignificant. Thus, an S corporation is legally treated as a C corporation, except with respect to its tax treatment, as described below.

An *S corporation* is simply a regular corporation that meets certain federal tax code requirements and whose shareholders have elected to be treated somewhat like a partnership for federal income tax purposes. Therefore, its defining characteristics are generally regulated and controlled by federal income tax laws and regulations. The principal tax advantage of an S corporation is the avoidance of double taxation. An S corporation does not pay taxes on any of its income but, rather, passes through income or losses to the individual or shareholders in proportion to their stock ownership in the corporation. Thus, an S corporation is more like a partnership with respect to its tax attributes and the tax consequences of its business transactions.

Not all states recognize S corporations for state income tax purposes. Additionally, the federal income tax requirements for qualifying a corporation for "S" treatment are somewhat limiting and restrictive. For example:

- The corporation must be a domestic corporation, and no shareholder can be a nonresident alien.

- None of the shareholders of an S corporation may be corporations or partnerships; they must be individuals.
- S corporations cannot enjoy the same ownership flexibility as C corporations because there can be only one class of common stock and no preferred stock.
- There cannot be more than 35 shareholders.
- The S corporation cannot be a member of an affiliated group of corporations, or it may lose its ability to qualify as an S corporation.

Clearly, S corporations can have significant tax advantages, but those advantages come with some severe limitations and restrictions. More significant, the decision to elect conversion to an S corporation can have some substantial tax effects. Also, because of the complexities and nuances of federal tax law regarding S corporations, the transactional costs, legal and accounting fees, and expenses are generally higher.

Professional Corporation

The professional corporation (PC), though generally provided for by state law, is truly an entity driven by tax attributes and consequences. Its distinguishing legal characteristic is that all stock is generally held solely by licensed professionals. The principal tax benefit of organizing as a PC is that the corporation is taxed as a qualified personal service corporation (QPSC) and enjoys a 35 percent flat tax rate instead of the graduated tax rate (as income increases), which is applied to corporations. Additionally, the qualifications maintained in the federal tax law require that 95 percent of the stock be held by PC employees and that those employees perform services at least 95 percent of the time in a qualified professional field (including health).

Therefore, a PC carries with it all of the advantages, disadvantages, and attributes of an ordinary corporation, along with these additional restrictions in order to qualify for some advantageous tax treatment.

PARTNERSHIP

Like a corporation, a *partnership* is a collective of individuals contributing their capital and time to the business enterprise. It is a middle ground that enjoys some of the characteristics of a corporation and some of the characteristics of a sole proprietorship. And like a corporation, a general partnership is a long-standing and traditional form of business entity.

Defining Characteristics of a Partnership

Partnerships may either have a written agreement or simply be partnerships in fact (with no formal written agreement). The critical and defining characteristics of a partnership are that it possesses a potentially limited continuity of existence and its interests are not freely transferrable. Thus, in its basic characteristics and attributes, a partnership is less like a corporation than a sole proprietorship.

Of course, because the general partnership is a traditional form of business association and organization, creative attorneys and businesses have used adaptations of the partnership agreement to avoid the general characteristics of a partnership in order to make it behave and be managed more like a corporation.

Within certain limits, the written partnership agreement can provide that the partnership not dissolve simply upon the death or withdrawal of a single partner, thereby giving it more and longer continuity of existence. Likewise, although most state laws provide that an individual may not become a partner unless unanimously approved by the existing partners, generally this requirement can be ameliorated and overridden with a written partnership agreement.

Advantages to a Partnership

Besides the practical advantages of pooling capital and labor and sharing expenses (which are the common characteristics of a partnership), the informality and flexibility of partnership organizations offer other specific advantages. (See table 8-4.)

TABLE 8-4. Key Advantages and Disadvantages to a Partnership

Advantages	*Disadvantages*
Fairly simple to create and operate	Unlimited personal liability, except for LP and LLP forms
Avoids double taxation of income	No continuity of existence
If LLP or LP, lends some personal liability protection	No transferability of ownership interest
Any type of owner permitted	Exit of an owner generally causes dissolution, except where agreement provides otherwise
Losses are tax deductible to extent of basis in partnership	Fewer potential regulatory issues than corporation

These include:

- The income of the partnership is taxed to the partners at their individual tax rates, but partners, unlike shareholders in corporations, do not suffer the disadvantage of double taxation.
- Because the partnership is a traditional form of business organization, the laws of the various states generally provide for a fairly uniform approach to partnerships and the treatment of partnership businesses operating in multiple states. Thus, like corporations, partnerships enjoy the benefit of some substantial uniformity and predictability that the newer business organizations and forms do not always enjoy.
- Generally, a partnership can be organized more cost-effectively than a corporation because there are no filing fees, public filings, or formal organizational requirements.
- A partnership enjoys certain tax advantages that are not enjoyed by a corporation, including special tax allocations of income and loss (except to the extent that losses are restricted by passive loss-investment rules).
- Partnerships enjoy the avoidance of significant regulatory hurdles and costs that often can be required by federal or state securities laws in connection with the formation or marketing of ownership interests in corporations. Generally, a general partnership interest is not a security and is not regulated by state and federal "security" laws.

Disadvantages to a Partnership

One of the principal disadvantages to the partnership model is that each and every one of the partners is an agent of the partnership and can do anything necessary to operate the business and bind the partnership. The downside to such flexibility is that each and every partner is personally liable for all the debts, taxes, and other claims against the partnership. (See table 8-4.) Partners have unlimited liability to creditors of the partnership. In this respect, the partnership is like a sole proprietorship and unlike a corporation (or LP or LLP). An additional disadvantage to the partnership model is that it usually terminates when any partner dies or withdraws from the partnership, unless the written partnership provides otherwise. Likewise, under the laws of many states, bankruptcy of the partner or the partnership causes dissolution of the partnership regardless of any agreement.

Hence, although the partnership model can provide for the pooling of capital and labor, the business entity (partnership) often remains tied to its weakest link, and the partners remain personally liable to all creditors for any misstep or misjudgment made by any of its members.

Limited Partnership

Limited partnerships (LPs) (not to be confused with LLCs or LLPs) are a more recent development than corporations or partnerships. As might be expected, they have some characteristics of the partnership and some characteristics of the corporation. Most states have enacted an LP act that closely tracks the uniform act.[4] However, this business organizational form has generally been used primarily with real estate investments and similar business ventures. For the reasons described below, an LP generally is not a preferred approach for group medical practice or concentration and is used less frequently in the health care industry.

The distinguishing characteristics of an LP are that the types of partners are separated into two classes: a general partner, who exercises management discretion and decision-making power; and limited partner(s), whose rights and obligations are similar to those of a shareholder in a corporation. However, limited partners do not have the full right to participate in the LP's management. If a limited partner circumvents this obstacle by participating in management, he or she loses limited liability protection from the LP's creditors. Thus, general partners who exercise management subject themselves to unlimited liability, as would a partner in a general traditional partnership. Limited partners gain protection from the LP's claims and debts so that only their investment in the LP is at risk, but they must surrender the right to participate actively in management of the LP.

In most other respects, the LP is identical for legal and tax purposes to a general partnership. Thus, LPs are basically a variation on the partnership theme.

LIMITED LIABILITY PARTNERSHIP

Some states have enacted somewhat similar provisions permitting general partnerships to elect an LLP status, sometimes referred to as a *registered limited liability partnership*. LLPs (not to be confused with LLCs or LPs) are a more recent development than corporations, partnerships, or limited partnerships. The general partnership may elect limited liability status in such states by registration or filing notice of an election to be treated as a limited liability partnership. The limited liability protection gained by this election is not complete or absolute. Limited liability for a partnership in this context means that partners not participating in a particular activity are not personally liable to that particular creditor. However, the partnership assets and the active partners remain personally liable to such creditors. Thus, the scope of the protection provided by limited liability treatment is not as broad as the protection granted to shareholders of corporations or limited partners of LPs.

Although not globally adopted by the states, the significant advantage to an LLP is to provide to a general partnership some of the limited liability protection enjoyed by shareholders of corporations and limited partners of LPs. In all other respects, an LLP is identical to a general partnership.

LIMITED LIABILITY COMPANY

The LLC is the most recently developed type of business organization. The principal driving force behind the enactment of LLC statutes across the country (enacted by all but three states at last count) was the desire to provide a business entity that offers the limited liability protection and benefit of a corporation and the tax attributes and treatment of a partnership. By definition, therefore, the existence and benefits achieved by the LLC rely upon state laws creating the LLC option, as well as federal tax laws and regulation providing the favorable tax environment for the new entity. Whether this new partnership of state and federal regulations will survive depends on the unified action of both state and federal legislative bodies.

Unique Characteristics of a Limited Liability Company

The LLC is an unincorporated entity with many characteristics that are similar to a partnership, but with one very important characteristic of a corporation—insulation from personal liability (except to the extent of their investment in membership) afforded to the stockholders of the corporation. Simply stated, the LLC is treated as a partnership for tax purposes and as a corporation for liability purposes. If structured properly, it allows an entity to have the best of both worlds.

Advantages to a Limited Liability Company

Through use of a properly structured LLC, members can avoid the double taxation that occurs in the traditional corporation or professional corporation. Additionally, the LLC is a very flexible entity and can be formed with relative ease. (For a summary of advantages and disadvantages, see table 8-5.)

Tax Advantages of a Limited Liability Company In a traditional corporate form of business (assuming nonelection of "S" status), there exists the burden of double taxation: The corporation pays tax on its taxable income, and the shareholders pay tax on any income actually distributed

TABLE 8-5. Key Advantages and Disadvantages of a Limited Liability Company

Advantages	*Disadvantages*
Avoids double taxation of income, treated as partnership for tax purposes	Shorter track record than more traditional forms of business organization
Limits personal liability for LLC debt	Some negative consequences if operated in states recognizing differing LLC forms
Less formal than corporation	More favorable tax status dependent on federal tax law treatment
Will not lose personal liability protection if formalities not observed	
Very flexible management structure	
Losses are deductible to extent of owner's tax basis, including allocable portion of LLC debt	

to them in the form of dividends. Additionally, there is a taxable event upon distribution of corporate assets to shareholders. If there is a gain inherent in the distributed assets, the corporation must recognize such upon distribution. However, the reverse is not true if there is a loss in the same distribution, unless there is a liquidation distribution.

The Internal Revenue Service (IRS) very carefully scrutinizes avoidance of double taxation through payment by corporations of deductible salaries or the use of earnings to pay interest on debt owed to shareholders. Scrutiny is particularly intense in situations where there is very little service rendered to the corporate entity itself in return for the salary. When physicians are part of a corporate organization and their primary duty is that of patient care and not management, this issue can become problematic.

The above issues are minimized with the LLC organization because all income is taxed proportionately to the members regardless of their activities and based solely on their ownership. Generally, in most LLCs that involve physicians as members, the intent is to distribute all earnings, and, therefore, the physician member actually receives the income on which he or she is taxed once. In situations where all the income is not going to be distributed, "phantom income" may occur and members may actually be taxed on income not received (retained earnings or retained income).

Finally, as stated above, the LLC is flexible. This applies to tax treatment as well as other factors. Because the LLC is similar to a partnership, it may allocate income and loss among its members disproportionate to actual ownership based on the particular needs of the LLC and its members.

Other Advantages to the Limited Liability Company As stated above, the LLC is fairly easily formed, somewhat less formally and more cost-effectively than the corporation. The counterpart to the corporation's bylaws is the LLC's operating agreement, which can be structured much more loosely than corporate bylaws, allowing for greater flexibility in management and capital structure. In considering the different needs of physicians and other health care entities, such as hospitals, when the two are part of the same LLC, this flexibility can—and often does—make the difference in being able to put the groups together.

Disadvantages to the Limited Liability Company

Although the LLC has some major advantages, especially in flexibility, it also carries with it some disadvantages.

Tax Disadvantages Despite the fact that the LLC's tax advantages clearly outweigh its tax disadvantages, this form of business entity does have a few significant tax disadvantages. As mentioned above, there is the potential for phantom income and the resulting tax liability. In addition, there is the potential for "individual" members being subject to self-employment taxes (social security) on their distribution share of LLC income or loss. An LLC will probably need to have the calendar year as its fiscal year, as opposed to the noncalendar fiscal year used by corporations that allows for more favorable deferral of income in certain situations. Moreover, there are restrictions on certain nontaxable fringe benefits in an LLC that do not exist in a corporation. Finally, although the LLC is generally freely transferable, the transfer of more than 50 percent of the LLC's interest may be deemed by the IRS to be a liquidation under IRC §708, resulting in significantly adverse tax consequences.[5]

Other Disadvantages The one significant nontax disadvantage of the LLC is the fact that it is relatively new as compared to other forms of entities and, thus, there is some uncertainty associated with its use. This uncertainty will certainly dissipate as the LLC form becomes time tested.

FRAMEWORK FOR GOOD DECISION MAKING

The preceding does not purport to be a comprehensive review and analysis of these alternative business forms, but it does establish a framework for asking educated questions of persons with expert knowledge and experience. Furthermore, although there are some legal, practical, and tax differences among the various business organizational forms, in some instances, the collective pliability of state law, regulations, and tax laws permits modifications of the traditional form of each business organization that can blur the differences.

The final analysis should consider how the proposed entity, as structured and formed, will affect the organization's interests and accomplish its intended purposes. To this end, following are the top 10 crucial questions that should be asked concerning the proposed business form for any newly created physician practice group or organization:

1. To what extent will personal assets and capital investment be at risk with this type of business organization? Corollary: If this type of organization is otherwise the most suitable, what steps and measures can be taken to maximize protection of the investors' and shareholders' personal assets and capital investment?
2. To what extent will the physician be relinquishing control of the practice and business decisions to others with management decision-making power and discretion? Corollary: If this type of organization is otherwise the most suitable, what balancing steps and measures can be taken to retain certain strategic and important decision-making powers among the participants?
3. What threats, risks, or costs are associated with a particular form of business enterprise to continuity of existence if one or more of the participants elect to exit? Corollary: Can the dissolution that would be triggered by the exit of one or more participants be avoided by a written agreement or the formative documents?
4. What transactional and operational costs at the formative stage, and periodically thereafter, can be expected? Corollary: What steps and measures can be taken to minimize or reduce the transactional and operational costs? Corollary: What organization type can be selected to avoid the costs and expense of mandatory compliance with additional regulatory schemes (for example, state and federal securities laws)?
5. What specific tax advantages does the proposed business entity have over the alternatives? Corollary: Is this the best method to avoid double and excessive taxation (whether by income tax, employment taxes, social security taxes, or income taxes on investments)? Corollary: What are the advantages or disadvantages of the proposed entity with respect to tax advantages of deferral of income and retirement planning?
6. Are there any disadvantages or complications to this particular form of business entity due to federal or state laws and regulatory schemes (for example, constraints on the corporate practice of medicine, Stark I and II issues, and fraud and abuse compliance)? Corollary: Is there anything about the present relationship of a health care institution with the proposed

group practice form or with other health care providers that might present statutory compliance difficulties if you select a new proposed form of business organization?

7. What controls or rights will the participants in the proposed business entity possess to select, control, and limit the future participants, investors, and owners of the business? Corollary: Will ownership interests be freely transferable by the owners?
8. How flexible are the governance or formative documents of the proposed business organization in order to respond to a changing industry, developing regulatory environment, and so on? Corollary: What limitations, disadvantages, or negative tax consequences might transpire in the event of a subsequent merger or acquisition of the enterprise by a peer or larger enterprise? Corollary: What limitations, disadvantages, or negative tax consequences might occur in the event you chose to convert your present business enterprise to this new proposed type of business entity? Corollary: Does this form possess any characteristics that cause irreversible elections that are unattractive or disadvantageous in the event of possible significant changes in the practice of medicine or health care delivery over the proposed organization's expected lifetime?
9. Are there any specific concerns, limitations, or disadvantages to the proposed business organization in the context of a specific geographic practice area(s) or state(s)?
10. Are there any justified concerns about uncertainties implicit in the selection of a proposed business organization that is newly created or immature in comparison to more traditional business forms? Corollary: Do the advantages of a newer type of business entity outweigh the lack of a long track record, uncertainty in taxation issues and treatment, and some lack of predictability due to less historical legal guidance and case law?

CONCLUSION

Selection of the form of business organization for a new physician practice group, or conversion of an existing business to a jointly owned or coordinated physician's group, is not easy. The difficulty lies in the vast array of choices as well as in the fact that the decision has important ramifications in the present, where you expect the future of the practice and business to lead, and where the rapidly changing health care field may take the organizational structure. The decision is one that will require weighing each factor, cost, and advantages and disadvantages. More significant, the decision will be affected by size of the practice and group, geographic locale, and reach of the business. Clearly, no single organizational form will be best in all circumstances or in every situation. Understanding the most common forms of business entity, the general advantages and disadvantages to each, and the most important questions to ask will enable health care executives to choose a business form that will most benefit their organization.

References and Notes

1. The trends in the health care industry and the practice of medicine over the past 10 years, coupled with an accelerating rate of change, make selection of a business entity all the more important. With most community medical practice acquisitions and sales costing from $250,000 to $3 million, choosing the right organizational form and business planning becomes a necessity. Moreover, the trend toward group practice makes governance, control, and transferability of interests central topics of concern. Legislative initiatives and initiatives by group payers are expected to accelerate this trend toward a concentration of group practice, causing more group acquisitions as well as larger medical service organizations among alliances.

2. State laws govern the creation of partnerships, corporations, LLPs, PCs, and LLCs. With respect to the more traditional forms of business entities, state laws vary little in terms of the central characteristics of how an entity will be treated. Differences remain, but these usually can be predicted with some certainty so that counterbalancing measures and steps can be considered. Traditional approaches offer uniformity, predictability, and a track record; however, they also include actual or preceived inflexibility. There is little unformity among the states with respect to implementation of the new, more exotic business associations, including LLCs. Thus, if the practice reaches more than one state, more care and planning are mandated concerning how the proposed business organization will be treated in each state.

3. IRC Sec 1244 (26 USC §1244).

4. Uniform acts establish a matrix of partnership law compiled from various states, which serves to establish basic principles of law. Uniform acts are often compiled by legal commentators or authors with a goal of achieving uniformity among states in the enactment of laws. In the partnership context, the uniformity sought to be achieved by the Uniform Partnership Act is uniformity in the basic principles of partnership law to be supplied in the absence of a written agreement between partners.

5. IRC Sec 708 (26 USC §708).

9

Physician Services Management Issues

Kenneth M. Hekman

The market changes affecting medical practices are presenting new challenges to the way physicians define and deliver high-quality health care services. Professional autonomy and unquestioned medical judgment are giving way to elaborate systems designed to hold physicians accountable for optimal clinical outcomes at lower costs. The development of clinical and economic credentialing systems has become one of the most controversial issues in the evolution of the medical profession.

This chapter explores trends in defining and measuring the quality of care delivered by physicians in both group and solo settings. It also evaluates current systems for monitoring quality, identifying the strengths and weaknesses of those systems that are most prevalent. Finally, the chapter reviews the relationship between physician productivity and quality of care, and discusses options for managing the quality of physician services in the future.

TRENDS IN DEFINING THE QUALITY OF MEDICAL CARE

The past three decades have witnessed a significant shift in how the quality of medical care is to be defined and who is to define it. Consumer expectations of the quality of physician services are gradually gaining prominence over physician-defined quality of care standards. The historical understanding of physician peer review is being broadened to include critiques of physician services by patients, purchasers, and insurers.

Physician-Defined Quality of Care Standards

The historical wisdom was to assume that anyone who met the requirements for licensure as a physician was capable of providing high-quality care. Thus, quality of care was defined by medical academicians and state authorities charged with responsibility for issuing medical licenses. If the quality of care delivered by a practitioner was called into question, it became the responsibility of the licensing board, composed of physician peers, to ensure the restoration of quality in the profession through corrective action.

The goal of increasing medical quality led, in part, to development of extensive specialty residencies and certification requirements. In addition to licensure, board certification became a standard for ensuring that physicians achieve and maintain standards of proficiency that result in the delivery of high-quality medical care. The requirements for continuing medical education and periodic reexamination are designed to assure the public that physicians are well prepared to serve them.

Hospital medical staffs have affirmed and enforced the peer review efforts of the licensing and certification authorities. Physicians are subject to regular performance reviews of their surgical and medical care in hospital settings, and unusual incidents may trigger a special review at any time. Serious breaches of medical quality standards are frequently discovered at the hospital level first and then may be reported to licensing and certification authorities for review and corrective action.

Consumer Expectations of High-Quality Medical Care

Spiraling health care costs have caused consumers to question some of the most important assumptions about the health care system, including the assumption that physicians know best how to define and ensure the delivery of high-quality care. To this end, government and business purchasers of health care are demanding better value, described as better quality of care at lower cost, and are thus redefining expectations for physicians. Consumers are shopping more prudently and are selecting from among a growing set of options according to criteria of their own design. The rise in demand for alternative therapies is a demonstration of the breadth of the consumers' quest. Patients will go where they can find what they are looking for, regardless of the traditional physician-controlled definitions of quality of care.

Consumer expectations are mirrored in the offerings of managed care organizations (MCOs), and these organizations are playing a significant role in defining and measuring the quality of health care delivery. They also are leading the field in defining value in health care, and in so doing are drawing attention to the controversy over the cost-quality relationship.

The MCO focus is to improve clinical outcomes while reducing the total cost of health care services.

One of the most contemporary definitions of quality in health care comes from United HealthCare, an MCO based in Minneapolis:[1]

> "Quality" means health care service that:
> - Is appropriate—it's the right care for the patient at the right time and supported by current medical standards
> - Is performed well—that is, with the necessary level of skill and tools to optimize success
> - Achieves results—improves the health or functioning of the patient

These changes in the definition of quality of care have historical implications for physicians. The public has gradually shifted from a broad trust of physicians to a more cautious approach. The watchword now seems to be to "trust, but verify." Successful physicians will be those who submit themselves to regular monitoring and performance evaluation, by both professional peers and service-savvy consumers. Advances in information technology will hasten the depth and breadth of scrutiny, and significantly increase both the standards for quality of care and the accountability of physicians to meet them.

TRENDS IN MANAGING THE QUALITY OF CARE

Managing the quality of physician services is in the early stages of development. Currently, there are two primary approaches: internal peer review and the adoption of external standards. Each approach has many forms and adaptations within medical groups. The purposes here are to evaluate the conceptual approaches rather than each derivative and to set the stage for improving quality of care in physician services.

However, as explained below, most solo practitioners remain relatively isolated from peer review efforts and the impact of external standards, and medical groups are in the early phases of evaluating their options in advancing the quality of care. Thus, it is likely that widespread advances in systematizing quality of care will come from standards imposed by MCOs offering economic incentives to physicians that comply with quality assurance (QA) efforts.

Peer Review

Professional peer review takes on many forms for physicians. Beyond meeting and maintaining the requirements for licensure and specialty certification, physicians are held accountable for their medical performance by the medical staff bylaws and QA committees of the institutions they serve. Physicians in medical groups may face additional peer reviews by their colleagues in the group. In large multispecialty and academic groups, peer review usually is confined to colleagues within clinical departments.

Variances by Size of Practice The intensity and frequency of peer review varies widely by the size and character of the practice setting. In general, the larger the group, the more systematic the peer review process. Many solo practitioners are subject to only the most rudimentary levels of review, whereas most practitioners in large groups may be subject to rigorous oversight and monthly monitoring.

- *Solo practitioners:* Solo practitioners are the least likely to submit themselves to systematic peer review. Their most immediate need for anything resembling peer review may be their need to find peers with whom to share call responsibilities. The choice of peers for call sharing typically is based on a casual assessment of reputation and philosophy of care, but often is controlled by the more practical issues of availability and willingness to participate in a mutually beneficial and balanced call-sharing relationship.
- *Small groups:* Small groups may have no systematic method for dealing with physician medical quality issues other than to confront each other when a trust-threatening issue arises. Quality of care is managed essentially by exception, leaving the group vulnerable to challenge by competitors, discontented patients, and value-conscious insurers.
- *Medium-sized groups:* Medium-sized groups are more likely to appoint a physician as medical director to evaluate medical quality issues and to monitor compliance with loosely articulated expectations. The medical director role may be rotated annually among the group's physicians to maintain a degree of mutual accountability, or it may be given to a subgroup of physicians to ensure that judgments about medical quality reflect the collective wisdom of several peers. Medical QA activities may include annual performance reviews, chart reviews, in-depth studies of complaints and incidents, development of medical outcomes and performance standards, and training of both physicians and support staff in topics related to ensuring medical quality of care.
- *Large medical groups:* Large medical groups have some of the greatest opportunities to manage medical quality of care. Their extensive information systems enable physicians and executives to monitor service processes and clinical outcomes with greater refinement than might be found in smaller groups. Effective

management of the quality of care in larger medical groups may involve statistical analysis of physician performance on issues such as the following:

—Hospital lengths of stay
—Immunization rates
—Mammography screening rates
—Cesarean section rates
—Morbidity and mortality rates
—Surgical complication rates
—Recovery times for specific conditions
—Functional status of patients
—Patient satisfaction with treatment
—Return-to-work periods

Support Staff and Medical Quality Assurance As medical groups grow in size and complexity, the support staff plays a more prominent role in ensuring medical quality. Staff may be relied on to report incidents that demonstrate lapses in medical quality or patient discontent. The labor-intensive responsibility for monitoring charts may be assigned to specific staff trained in medical records management or QA methods, with the charge to report questionable practices to the medical director. Receptionists and nursing support staff also serve as significant links in the service delivery chain. Their interaction with patients can either enhance or endanger the quality of care delivered in the name of the physicians they represent. The risk of miscommunication or misinformation in the relationship between staff and patient directly reflects on the quality of care provided by the physician. When patients are unable to judge the quality of care they receive from their physician, they are prone to assess the quality of care on the basis of interactions they understand. For example, they may gauge the quality of physician services by the kindness and compassion they perceive from the support staff. Medical groups committed to providing the highest-quality care will thus make sure that physicians provide competent care and that the staff also offers supportive and compassionate interaction with each patient served by the practice.

The spread of managed care casts the support staff in a role of growing responsibility for medical quality assurance. As primary care physicians, in particular, seek to provide care to a growing patient base of capitated patients, they are likely to rely more consistently on triage systems to treat all but the most seriously ill patients with telephone nursing systems, physician assistants, and nurse practitioners, all performing under established protocols. The risks and opportunities for profitable service may rely heavily on the degree of successful delegation of care to lower-cost support teams. Management of the quality of information exchange between patients and support teams and the care-related judgments made before patients interact with physicians are likely to become the focal points for advancing quality of care in managed care environments.

Strengths of Peer Review Systems Peer review systems can be effective in modifying physician behavior under certain circumstances. For example, physicians generally accept feedback from peers more readily than from nonphysician administrators armed with data. Physician peers are able to discern the medical nuances of incidents based on their training and experience, and to weigh the seriousness of a physician's medical judgment fairly and equitably.

The effectiveness of peer review systems is enhanced when the following conditions can be found:

- *Physician peers are clearly identified as having authority to review physician performance and to apply corrective action to restore an acceptable level of quality of care.* Sociologists contend that conformity to social norms and expectations increases when peer pressure is applied from respected sources.
- *Peers are informed about the performance issues. Peer* ability to mold physician performance is strengthened when they have data to support their contention that the physician's experience is outside the range of mutually defined acceptable performance.
- *Meaningful sanctions can be applied.* Sanctions may include such actions as suspension of hospital admitting or operating privileges, suspension or reduction of bonus compensation that is contingent upon quality of care, or suspension of scheduled time off so that time may be devoted to meeting quality of care expectations such as bringing medical records up to date.

Weaknesses of Peer Review Systems Less effective peer review systems are found in groups where physicians find it dangerous to confront their peers. If the reviewers have limited authority to act or fear reprisals, peer review loses its ability to shape physician behavior and advance quality of care. Smaller groups may find peer review particularly uncomfortable because the trust that holds them together is deep and valuable. Their smallness diminishes the impartiality and autonomy of effective peer relationships. Their need to collaborate may weaken their drive to confront each other on quality of care issues. Small groups seem to adopt a culture of conflict avoidance, which can seriously weaken their opportunities for advancing their corporate quality of care.

Another potential weakness in peer review systems is that they typically focus on compliance with minimum standards rather than work toward advancing optimal patient care. For example, annual performance reviews are more likely to focus on experiences that failed to meet expectations than on challenging physicians to exemplary levels of quality of care. In smaller groups that do not consistently apply annual reviews, quality of care discussions are likely to arise only when they are stimulated by an adverse experience.

Peer review processes also may be insufficient for building market relevance, assuming that is one of the goals of improving quality of care. If physicians hold each other accountable for maintaining process standards, they may grow more collaborative but miss the mark in achieving better outcomes for patients at lower costs.

External Standards

Medical practices can accelerate their quality of care management efforts by seeking excellence through adoption of external standards. The derivation of external standards extends from regulatory agencies and legal precedents to researchers of best practices and health care think tanks. Physicians who aspire to positions of leadership in medical care delivery are driven to find fresh and inspirational methods for drawing out the best in their peers and establishing systems to maintain consistently high-quality care.

The search for national medical quality standards and measurement tools has drawn resources from both public and private sectors. Following are descriptions of some of the forerunners' efforts in measuring value at the level of physician services.

National Committee for Quality Assurance The Health Employer Data and Information Set (HEDIS) was developed by the National Committee for Quality Assurance (NCQA), a not-for-profit organization. NCQA's primary purpose was to evaluate and publicly report on the quality of managed care plans. Its accreditation program for HMOs is recognized as a symbol of integrity, and NCQA serves more than 330 plans nationwide with quality measurement services. The development of HEDIS was a natural step in determining the standards by which HMOs should be held accountable. Version 3.0 was released in July 1996, offering a mixture of more than 75 process and outcomes measurements in eight areas of interest, or "domains."[2] The two previous versions of HEDIS were criticized for their focus on process rather than outcomes. The latest version is an attempt to broaden the scope and includes an additional 30 "testing measurements" for future development.

Although positive HEDIS measurements have been the aspiration of MCOs, physicians are likely to find themselves increasingly challenged to comply with HEDIS expectations at the level of their own practice. Managed care plans that are composed of physicians who understand and achieve the performance standards of the plan's accrediting agency are more likely to win employer approval, thus ensuring a steady supply of patients for the member physicians. Compliance with HEDIS may become a marketing imperative for physicians, regardless of whether it actually improves the value of medical care delivery.

Foundation for Accountability The Foundation for Accountability (FACCT), a not-for-profit organization based in Portland, Oregon, was established in 1995 by several consumer organizations, government agencies, and private employers to ensure that consumers and purchasers have reliable information needed to make health care decisions. The members of its board of trustees include large consumer groups and purchasers (public and private) representing 80 million Americans. Trustees include representatives from groups as diverse as the American Association of Retired Persons, AT&T, and the Health Care Financing Administration. FACCT hopes a voluntary quality oversight effort based on the market clout of consumers and purchasers will promote accountability in the health care industry.

FACCT is devoted to developing innovative ways to measure the quality of health care and to further consumer education and research. Early efforts have focused on finding ways to measure the quality of care for people with specific conditions: asthma, breast cancer, diabetes, and depressive disorders. All measurements are built around three components. Quality care is assumed to result from the combination of appropriate steps to good care, high patient satisfaction, and good results. FACCT's approach to quality measurement reflects the interests of consumers and purchasers represented by the founding organizations.

FACCT is also working to find the best ways to present quality data to consumers so that, when information from its measures is made public, the information will be in a form consumers can easily use and understand.

Physicians have responded positively to FACCT's work thus far. Their feedback indicates that FACCT is measuring aspects of quality that physicians çonsider valid and significant.[3]

Stratis Health Stratis Health, based in Bloomington, Minnesota, is the result of a merger of the Health Outcomes Institute and the Foundation for Health Care Evaluation. The Health Outcomes Institute and its predecessor, InterStudy, have worked since the early 1970s to develop and distribute public domain outcomes instruments and protocols.

Several measurement instruments are offered including the popular Health Status Questionnaire, a 39-question survey for patients to complete in 5 to 10 minutes describing their current level of functional and emotional well-being. Other instruments include a patient satisfaction survey, condition-specific outcomes measurement tools, and *A Practical Guidebook for Implementing, Analyzing, and Reporting Outcomes Measurements*.[4] The approach of Stratis Health and its questionnaire is mildly outcomes oriented. It offers to patients a perspective on the effect of the health care system in their lives but ignores broader measures of process improvement, preventive measures, or service, over which physicians may have some degree of control. As such, it represents a complementary segment of information to help physicians and MCOs measure their effectiveness and demonstrate their value.

Accreditation Efforts Other organizations are working toward establishing quality standards for medical care delivery systems with less direct attention on clinical outcomes. One example is the Joint Commission on Accreditation of Healthcare Organizations, which publishes the *Ambulatory Health Care Standards Manual*.[5]

Strengths of External Standards Adoption of external standards for ensuring quality of care offers advantages over peer review systems in a variety of ways. The standards represent collective research and thought from leaders in the field of medical quality assurance, and can be helpful for groups with limited resources for developing extensive internal information systems. The expectations of the external standards are objective and less likely to be compromised by relational dynamics as may be the case with peer review systems.

Moreover, external standards are emerging as national standards, enabling comparison of groups on quality of care criteria. This characteristic may be an important precursor to the next generation of medical QA systems. As uniform definitions of expectations for physician performance grow, the medical community is likely to be subject to more widespread, and more public, monitoring.

Weaknesses of External Standards The current standards offered by the forerunners in the field are primarily focused on structural and process characteristics of medical care delivery. Until attention is turned fully toward development of expectations for outcomes, the effectiveness of adopting external standards will be limited. Advancing the quality of structures and processes may be valuable foundations for successful medical care delivery in managed care environments, but they are insufficient unless they lead to advances in delivering more cost-effective clinical results.

TRENDS IN MANAGING PHYSICIAN PRODUCTION

The adjustments physicians face in managing quality of care are affecting their production. Quality of care is taking a more prominent place in the determination of physician production and compensation. Under the fee-for-service (FFS) system, the physician incentive structure can be described as follows:

$$\text{Production} = \text{Volume}_{\text{encounters}} \times \text{Intensity}$$

Production is affected by other factors as well, such as selecting patients who are well insured, managing overhead costs, achieving billing and collections effectiveness, and developing a steady stream of new patients. However, the FFS formula is still easy to understand and follow. The highest rewards go to those who put through the greatest number of patients at the highest level of service. Throughput is measured by volume of units of service and current procedural technology (CPT) codes, or relative value units (RVUs).

Quality of care has played a minor role in the FFS environment. The assumption of quality is implied by the presence of a medical license. It also is verified by board certification and implied by the appearance of success. Physicians and patients typically assume that the busiest and most profitable physicians must be those who provide the most desirable quality of care. Patients, especially, may have relied on surrogate measures of quality because they had no other objective data to consider.

Formula for Success under Capitation

The definition of a successful physician under capitation can be particularly distressing to the FFS tactician. High volumes of intensive services may bankrupt physicians under capitation. Production under capitation is determined as follows:

$$\text{Production} = \text{Volume}_{\text{covered lives}} \times \left(\frac{\text{Quality}}{\text{Cost}}\right)$$

The formula for success under capitation is for physicians to take responsibility for as many patients as they can, providing care that is increasing in quality and decreasing in total cost. It calls for the measurement of quality of care and rewards physicians who increase the quality-to-cost ratio.

Increasing physician production in a capitated environment will require physicians and medical practice executives to manage the quality of care. Investments in quality improvement may be the most lucrative investments medical groups will make when they enter risk contracts. Cost containment efforts must extend from simply managing overhead infrastructure optimally to managing and controlling the costs of referrals, hospitalizations, and ancillary services, wherever they may be performed. Marketing efforts also will enhance production results by increasing the patient base. However, the greatest impact for boosting profits is projected to be in managing the quality of care.

Rewards and Benefits of Managing Quality of Care

Quality of care in the managed care environment brings both economic and medical rewards for effective physicians. Improving patient outcomes at lower total costs will benefit physicians who bear a portion of the financial risk for the health of their patients.

Moreover, improving quality of care in the managed care environment is likely to have benefits that extend beyond the short-term profitability of risk contracts. High-quality services attract patients and payers for long-term growth, thereby extending the profits for future benefits to the medical group. As the group's reputation for quality grows, its ability to recruit and retain high-quality physicians increases, the group captures the attention of other physicians in the community and fosters mutual benefits through referral relationships, and local institutions are more likely to honor their relationship with the physicians in the group.

The central role of quality management efforts for the medical practice engaged in risk contracts points to the opportunity for profitability in the emergence of the managed care environment. Physicians who measure and improve quality earliest and best stand to gain an early lead in the race for success under capitation. Their ability to adapt from the incentives under fee-for-service toward a quality-driven incentive will be rewarded with new production records.

DESIGN CRITERIA FOR QUALITY MANAGEMENT TOOLS

The next generation of systems and tools for measuring and advancing medical quality are likely to be considerably more demanding of physicians, to the extent that many physicians trained to rely on their professional autonomy and patient loyalty may find themselves displaced. Advances in technology and communication are blending with increasing medical competition, economic pressure, and educational advances to thrust physicians into dramatically new levels of public accountability. Patients and purchasers of health care are demanding greater standardization in the art of medicine. MCOs are transforming physician incentives and molding their performance to maximize the ratio of quality to cost. Consumers are weighing their choices among a growing list of alternative health care providers to select those most likely to meet their needs with the least consumption of resources. The market for medical care is coming of age, and the technological stage it is being played on is able to broadcast the results, physician by physician.

Few doubt that public report cards will be in the future of every physician in the United States. The form and distribution of those accountability instruments has yet to be determined, but the challenges for the medical community are already taking shape. The free flow of information may reward those who present leading scores without professional interpretation and ruin those who might provide valuable care that pales by comparison. Protecting the public interest without detracting from the important role of the medical profession will require clear thinking for the designers of the next generation of quality management tools. Following are some of the most important design criteria for physician services quality management tools.

Creation of Healthier Communities

The foundational work on quality assurance has focused on improving the structures and processes of delivering physician services. The next step will be to articulate how communities need to work together to improve the health of everyone. That goal will require a new focus on the outcomes not just of physicians' efforts, but also of educational systems in preventing unhealthy behaviors, of transportation systems in bringing people to the right health care resources at the right times, and of financial systems in producing the best combination of incentives to reward efforts at making the community a healthy place to live. In short, ensuring the quality of physician services needs to be viewed in the larger context of advancing the goal of designing healthier communities. Designers of healthier communities will need to work with each segment of the population, blending interests and incentives into a system that produces, by design, people who live longer, healthier, and more fulfilling lives.

Balance in the Physician-Patient Relationship

Advancing the quality of care will require a deepening understanding of how physicians fit into the equation of bringing health to people. Achieving better outcomes at lower costs will require physicians and patients to negotiate their individual responsibilities. Physicians cannot be held responsible for adverse outcomes and increased costs when patients remain committed to unhealthy lifestyles or fail to comply with treatment plans prepared in their interest. Likewise, patients should expect that physicians will refine their diagnostic and treatment tools to apply the least invasive, most effective resources at the right time to prevent illness, shorten recovery times, and reduce the total cost of care.

Striking an optimal balance in the physician-patient relationship may require an increased reliance on research-driven information systems. Physicians can advance their skill in achieving a prompt and accurate diagnosis if they know precisely which questions to ask and which tests to require with each patient. Developing consistency in managing the art of diagnosing illness may be enhanced by research on symptom detection and management. Maintaining a growing body of knowledge based on that research can lead to a rich resource to help physicians, and eventually patients, to understand the path of illness. As patients gain in managing responsibility for their care, using a research-driven information system may reduce their dependence on physicians for only the most difficult diagnostic and treatment services.

Wise Use of Technology

The free flow of information is clearly an essential requirement of a healthier community. As technological and communications capabilities increase, the health care delivery systems are likely to become more transparent. Patients will learn more about their physicians' training, history, and performance, and will exercise their choices on the basis of that information. Providers will be more accountable to their constituents, simply because more will be known about them. In a competitive economy, information provides power, and health care consumers will have more of both.

However, the widening availability of information also will present some challenges that communities need to prepare for. Performance information on physicians may be a powerful tool if it demonstrates complete truth in sufficient clarity to enlighten those who use it. But if the information represents only a part of the story, or if it is subject to broad interpretation, the results of its misuse may be devastating not just to the subject physician, but to the medical profession as a whole. If abuse of information results in unfair perspectives of individuals, the community may discover that it will have greater difficulty attracting talented practitioners to meet its needs. Wisdom of use and balance of interests will be important design criteria for quality of care monitoring systems.

CHALLENGES TO MANAGING QUALITY OF CARE

Advancing the state of the art in managing the quality of care will require new tools prepared according to thoughtful design criteria, but it also will require a fresh way of thinking about the barriers that inhibit the delivery of high-quality health care. For example:

- *The assumption that the quality of physician services is directly related to the time spent in cognitive care will need to be reconsidered.* Those who argue for physician autonomy frequently press the claim that managed care causes physicians to rush with their patients and therefore to either risk not gathering critical information or ignore patients' needs for additional information. Managed care advocates counter that managing care is managing information, and the tools for success are not necessarily bound by time.
- *Defining quality will take a collaborative effort by physicians, purchasers, public policy makers, executives, and patients.* Historically, physicians have been the champions of medical excellence and protective of their autonomous role in self-regulation. However, purchasers of health care services now are demanding a reexamination of the cost-to-quality ratio and claiming a role in defining the quality and outcomes of the care the community finds affordable. The conclusion is likely to be the result of a protracted negotiation between physicians and their constituents.
- *Physicians and their collaborators will need to become comfortable with information technology.* Those who remain fearful of such technology will be less able to participate in its design and implementation, whereas those who embrace it and become early adopters of advances in the art and science of managing quality of care are likely to lead the field and have the strongest influence on its effectiveness.
- *Medical practices will need to become learning organizations committed to continual renewal of their information, tools, assumptions, and beliefs about how to care for people in their responsibility.* They will need to readily critique their structures and processes, with the clear goal of improving outcomes. Additionally, they will have to abandon ideas that are no longer functional and experiment with fresh concepts to refine their effectiveness. Maintaining their awareness of changing market expectations and converting that knowledge into responsive action to deliver higher-quality care at lower cost will drive medical practices to new levels of performance, set higher standards for quality of care, and create models for healthier communities worldwide.

CONCLUSION

Among the challenges facing today's physicians is the growing demand to better manage the quality of patient care. In large part, that demand has come from those who pay for the care provided—patients, purchasers, and insurers. These groups now expect to play a key role not only in defining quality of care, but also in managing it.

Currently, there are two approaches to managing quality of care: peer review and external standards. Although both approaches can be effective under certain circumstances, both still tend to focus more on improving care structures and processes than on providing better outcomes at lower cost. In all likelihood, this latter aspect of care management will be enforced by managed care organizations and will assume a significant role in determining physician production and compensation.

Various factors, including advances in technology and communication, are exposing physicians to increased public scrutiny and accountability, and thus are driving the need for a new generation of quality management tools. To a large extent, the trends for the future reflect a greater collaboration among physicians, patients, and communities in determining what constitutes quality of care and in ensuring that it is attainable at reasonable cost.

References

1. J. Burns, "Measuring Health Care Quality: Employers Shop for Value," *Medical Benefits Special Report,* no. 2 (Apr. 1996): 1–11.

2. HEDIS, version 3.0, July 1996, National Committee for Quality Assurance web site, http://www.ncqa.org.

3. D. Lansky, "Foundation for Accountability (FACCT): A Consumer Voice on Health Care Quality," *Journal of Clinical Outcomes Management* 3, no. 6 (Nov./Dec. 1996): 54–58.

4. Health Outcomes Institute, 2901 Metro Drive, Suite 400, Bloomington, MN 55425, 612/858-9188.

5. Joint Commission on Accreditation of Healthcare Organizations, *Ambulatory Health Care Standards Manual* (Oakbrook Terrace, IL: Joint Commission, 1995.)

Bibliography

Gray, B., "Measure for Measure," *LACMA Physician* 126, no. 3 (Feb. 1996): 24–27.

Miller, J., "Is 'Value' the New Frontier?" *Integrated Healthcare Report* 4, no. 2 (Feb. 1996): 1–11.

Murray, C. J. L. and A. D. Lopez, *Global Comparative Assessments in the Health Sector* (Geneva: World Health Organization, 1994).

"Plans, Providers Brace for HEDIS Headache Next Year," *Public Sector Contracting Report* 2, no. 10 (Oct. 1996): 145–49.

Pope, C., "Outcomes Studies Help Empower Patients," *Medical Group Management Update* 35, no. 2 (Feb. 1996): 11.

Rosenstein, A., "Provider Profiling: Improving Outcomes of Care," *Journal of Outcomes Management* 3, no. 2 (Aug. 1996): 10–17.

Rulon, V., "Measurement Systems beyond HEDIS: The Evolution of Healthcare Data Analysis in Managed Care," *Journal of AHIMA* 67, no. 2 (Feb. 1996): 48, 50–52.

Wennberg, J., and others, *Dartmouth Atlas of Health Care* (Chicago: American Hospital Publishing, 1996).

World Health Organization, *World Health Statistics Annual* (Geneva: WHO, 1995).

10

The Corporate Practice of Medicine Doctrine

Jeffrey F. Chase-Lubitz, JD

In a world of management services organizations (MSOs), physician practice management companies (PPMCs), and integrated delivery systems (IDSs), the corporate practice of medicine doctrine continues to be a potentially serious obstacle to integrating new forms of health care delivery. Although considered anachronistic by many, the doctrine must be addressed by developers of any health care delivery entity that includes a physician practice component.

This chapter traces the development of the corporate practice of medicine doctrine and categorizes, by state, how it is currently applied. It also details recent cases in Texas and California where application of the doctrine is most strident and discusses recent efforts in those jurisdictions to soften the doctrine's impact.

EVOLUTION OF THE CORPORATE PRACTICE OF MEDICINE DOCTRINE

The doctrine against the corporate practice of medicine developed out of the medical profession's poor standing in the mid-1800s. At that time, many people considered the practice of medicine an inferior occupation, offering little security and no guarantee of increased social standing. Physicians competed for patients with the so-called irregulars, a group including quacks and healing sectarians. In an effort to distinguish themselves from the "irregulars," the physicians, referred to as the "regulars," established the American Medical Association (AMA) in the 1840s. Over the next 50 years, the AMA successfully established a code of ethics, developed licensure requirements in a vast majority of the states, and reformed medical education to require significantly higher standards. In time, competition became limited to that among formally trained physicians, and the quality of care increased. By the early 1900s, the AMA's efforts had dramatically increased public respect for the profession, and medical practitioners began to reap financial rewards. Equally important, organized medicine had gained control over the provision of medical care.

Growing Corporate Involvement in the Practice of Medicine

In the early 1900s, corporate involvement in medical care threatened the professional autonomy the AMA had struggled to obtain. Business corporations became involved in medicine by employing physicians to serve the medical needs of their own employees—a form of contract practice—and by employing physicians and marketing their services to the public—a form known as *corporate practice.* Contract and corporate practice raised a variety of concerns within the medical community, including the following:

- The quality of patient care would decrease because physicians would be required to undertake too high a patient load.
- The typical fee-for-service arrangement that allowed physicians to set a value for their services would be replaced by fixed salaries and fees.
- Contract and corporate practice would result in physicians competing against each other for specific contracts, which in turn would result in lower reimbursement.
- Such arrangements would permit laypersons to oversee the professional judgments of physicians, as well as to dictate to physicians the patients they could see and the resources they could spend.

Needless to say, the AMA fought back with a series of pronouncements and ethical provisions published between 1912 and 1934, confronting contract and corporate practice with several compelling arguments. First, the AMA argued that the corporate practice schemes would result in the unacceptable commercialism of the medical profession. Allowing lay entities to profit from physician services would cause the profession to suffer a loss of dignity and become subject to unfair competition. Additionally, it was believed that commercialism would lead to lay involvement in physician decision making, interfering with the doctor-patient relationship. The specific characteristics of corporate and contract arrangements the AMA deemed undesirable included new pressures to solicit patients, competitive bidding to obtain contracts, and conditions of employment that prevented physicians from rendering adequate medical care. Conversely, the AMA called for requirements that patients be free to choose their physicians.

Legal Prohibition of Corporate Practice

The AMA successfully laid the public policy foundation for the legal prohibition of corporate practice, as generally recognized in most state jurisdictions. Indeed, a review of state court holdings on corporate practice issues shows that most courts relied on the state's medical practice act. In doing so, the states concluded, whether rationally or not, that a corporate entity cannot be licensed to practice medicine because it is not an individual and thus cannot possess the qualifications needed for licensure. Closer examination of these cases reveals that corporate practice prohibition is not based on the medical practice acts but, rather, on the same public policy themes articulated by the AMA through the 1930s. It is these policy considerations that are truly at issue in the corporate practice debate: fidelity of the physician-patient relationship, the potential for commercial exploitation of medical practice, and the problem of lay control over the physician's professional judgment. Although one commentator argues that much of the public policy basis for the doctrine is no longer relevant, most would agree that these three principles are still worthy of protection.[1]

Fidelity of Physician-Patient Relationship The notion that a special relationship between physician and patient is necessary for appropriate medical treatment is a basic tenet of medicine. Few would argue against the assertion that a patient is better served by a physician who is entrusted with the patient's confidences. Also, a physician is likely to provide better care if his or her loyalty to the patient is paramount. Imposition of the third party, especially one that oversees the physician's compensation, is thought to breach fidelity between physician and patient. The concern is that the physician will be required to put the interest of his or her employer above that of the patient.

Commercial Exploitation of the Medical Profession Courts frequently have pointed to commercial exploitation of the medical profession as a rationale for limiting corporate involvement. It is argued that permitting a corporation, controlled by laypersons, to provide medical services allows persons not bound to the physician's ethical code to solicit patients and advertise competitively. Courts have stated that outside investors would pressure the medical services corporation to promote the sale of professional services in order to maximize profits. The obvious concern is that the corporation's financial interests will supersede those of providing high-quality care to patients.

Lay Control over Physicians Lay control over physicians has been fundamental to the corporate practice prohibition. It is widely accepted that licensed entities, regardless of their form, are unqualified to oversee the judgment of professionals who have been trained and qualified in their profession. The reason that states adopted medical practice acts was to ensure that medical treatment would be provided only by those who met specific educational training standards. To allow the professional judgment of these licensed individuals to be overruled by others without such training cannot be justified.

CURRENT APPLICATION OF THE DOCTRINE

Application of the corporate practice of medicine doctrine is as diverse as the jurisdictions in which it has been addressed. A survey presenting how each state applies the doctrine is outside the scope of this chapter. Rather, this chapter relies on an earlier survey by Wiorek, who cataloged the states into three groups corresponding to their application of the doctrine.[2] The first group comprises those states that prohibit employment of physicians by nonmedical corporations; recent case law and attorney general opinions evidence their position. The second group includes those states that applied the prohibition at one time but currently do so on an inconsistent basis. And the third group includes those states where the doctrine has either been ignored or overturned.

Group I Jurisdictions

Only five states indicate recent and unambiguous activity in their application of the corporate practice of medicine doctrine. These are Texas, California, Kansas, Illinois, and Iowa. The following subsections discuss a sampling of cases from these states.

Cases in Texas The 1974 case of *Garcia v. Texas State Board of Medical Examiner* states the reasoning behind Texas's general rule of prohibition against corporate practice.[3] In *Garcia,* the U.S. District Court for the Western District of Texas upheld provisions of the Texas Medical Practice Act against the challenge that the act denied plaintiffs certain constitutional rights. Plaintiffs in *Garcia* wished to incorporate a lay-controlled, nonprofit organization that would provide medical services to low-income persons through salaried physicians. The Texas secretary of state refused to issue a corporate charter because the incorporators were not licensed to practice medicine as required by the state's medical practice act.

In affirming the secretary's denial of a corporate charter, the court relied on earlier state cases, which found corporations to be engaged unlawfully in the practice of medicine when the corporation employed physicians to treat patients but required patients to pay medical fees directly to the corporation. The court noted that the medical profession is a "complex, esoteric discipline," the "administration of which by the ignorant or untrained, historically and inevitably leads to the exploitation of a naive public." It held that the state medical practice act was rationally related to the state's legitimate interest in preserving "the vitally important doctor-patient relationship, and preventing possible abuses resulting from layperson control of a corporation employing licensed physicians on a salaried basis." In its opinion, the court expressed concern about interference with the doctor-patient relationship, emphasis on budget considerations rather than patient care, and lay supervision over medical procedures.

In 1987, a Texas appeals court enforced the corporate practice doctrine in *Flynn Brothers, Inc. v. First Medical Associates,* a case involving a nonprofessional corporation's contractual arrangement with physicians.[4] Following the holding in *Garcia,* the court declined to enforce a management contract between First Medical Associates, a medical services contractor, and Flynn Brothers, its managing corporation, which was not authorized to practice medicine. Flynn Brothers, along with a physician, initially wished to form a company to bid on a hospital's contract to staff its emergency department. Because Flynn Brothers was a corporation not licensed to practice medicine, the physician formed First Medical Associates to act as the contractor to meet the stricture of the Texas Medical Practice Act and contracted with Flynn Brothers to provide it with management services. The management contract provided that Flynn Brothers receive 66.67 percent of First Medical's net profits for its management services. In addition, Flynn Brothers would solicit contracts with other hospitals on First Medical's behalf.

The court held that the contract was invalid and unenforceable because it constituted the practice of medicine by Flynn Brothers. Although the physician who established First Medical was not employed by Flynn Brothers, the court found that the agreement to share the majority of the physician's net profits had essentially the same effect as employment. Further, the court held that Flynn Brothers' use of the physician's license to obtain contracts with hospitals was an indirect practice of medicine without a license.

Cases in California In 1980, the California attorney general noted that California courts were repeatedly holding that the practice of commercial entities engaging physicians to provide medical services to parties contracting with the entity constituted practicing medicine without a license.[5] The attorney general gave two reasons for preventing commercial entities from practicing medicine through physicians: the limitation of licensing to individuals and the corporation's interference with the physician-patient relationship.

In 1982, the attorney general's office was asked to give an opinion on the legality of a general business corporation that contracted with another entity to provide physicians to treat that entity's employees.[6] These general business corporations, known as *industrial medical corporations,* are lay-controlled entities that contract with physicians to perform preemployment examinations and to treat employment-related injuries sustained by employees of large corporations and the government. The physicians are not employees of the medical corporation but, rather, are independent contractors paid on a fixed-fee basis.

Relying on the early corporate practice cases, the attorney general ruled the arrangement unlawful and reiterated the rationale finding a corporation's presence "incongruous in the workings of a professional regulatory licensing scheme which is based on personal qualification, responsibility and sanction." Further, the attorney general questioned the damage to the physician-patient relationship caused by corporate involvement, noting that a corporation's participation "would give rise to divided loyalties on the part of the professional and would destroy the professional relationship into which it was cast." The attorney general reached this conclusion despite the physicians' independent contractor status.

Commentators have argued that the corporate practice prohibition should not apply to a physician's independent contractor arrangement with a corporation because such arrangements do not involve the corporation's control over the physician's relationship with a patient. As a matter of course, most hospitals engage physicians as independent contractors. California, however, still relies on a pair of 50-year-old cases holding that evils of corporate involvement are present whether physicians are employees or independent contractors of a corporation that provides medical care to the general public.[7]

As recently as 1983, a California court of appeals faced the corporate practice doctrine in a context analogous to medical practice. In *California Association of Dispensing Opticians v. Pearle Vision Center, Inc.*, the court affirmed a trial court's preliminary injunction to prevent Pearle from operating retail ophthalmic dispensing outlets, noting the state's historic policy against lay interference with health professionals' treatment decisions.[8] The court examined Pearle's franchise agreement and found it to exercise extensive control over the franchisee's/optometrist's practice, both its treatment decisions and its financial operations. This evidence of control established to the court's satisfaction that Pearle intended to practice optometry. In upholding the lower court's injunction, the appeals court pointed to the destructive effect of corporate practice on the fidelity of the physician-patient relationship and noted the potential for commercial exploitation.

Without eradicating its prohibitions against the corporate practice of medicine, California has allowed corporate involvement under the medical care service plan model. Similar to an HMO, a medical care service plan "means any person [firm, association, or corporation] who undertakes to arrange for the provision of health care services to subscribers or enrollees . . . in return for a prepaid or periodic charge paid by . . . subscribers or enrollees."[9] The plan may employ or contract with any professional to deliver professional services. Such employment of professionals or physicians does not constitute the practice of medicine by the plan. Furthermore, a 1975 attorney general's opinion held that compliance with the Federal Health Maintenance Organization Act of 1973 supersedes California's medical practice act's prohibitions on the employment of physicians by nonprofessional or lay corporations.[10]

Group II Jurisdictions

The second group of states cataloged by Wiorek are those that apply the corporate practice of medicine doctrine on an inconsistent basis. These states include Alabama, Arizona, Arkansas, Colorado, Connecticut, Florida, Georgia, Indiana, Kentucky, Louisiana, Maryland, Massachusetts, Michigan, Minnesota, Missouri, New Jersey, New York, Oklahoma, Oregon, Pennsylvania, South Carolina, South Dakota, Tennessee, Virginia, Washington, and West Virginia, as well as the District of Columbia.

Cases in Colorado Inconsistent application is exemplified in Colorado, where the 1930s saw a series of cases in which the Colorado Supreme Court held that a corporate entity could not practice dentistry or employ licensed dentists to provide services on behalf of the corporation.[11] Later in 1944[12] and 1962,[13] Colorado courts relied on the corporate practice of medicine doctrine to hold that hospitals were not liable for the negligence of surgeons they employed, rationalizing that if the hospital corporation could not practice medicine, it could not be liable for the activities of its professional employees. In 1969, the Colorado Supreme Court reversed a trial court finding that permitted optical retailers to sublease adjacent space to optometrists.[14] The high court remanded the case for determination as to whether the optical corporation was directing or controlling the optometrist. Finally in 1972, the Supreme Court held that the State Board of Optometric Examiners could not prohibit optometrists from conducting their profession on the premises of an optical retailer.[15] In three years' time, the court had reversed its position without even referencing its earlier holding.

Cases in Louisiana Unfortunately, in those jurisdictions with inconsistent holdings, legal planning around the corporate practice issue is guesswork at best. Some states in the second category have focused recently on the functional relationship between the corporate entity and the professional provider, rather than simply the form of the arrangement. In a 1992 opinion, the Louisiana State Board of Medical Examiners addressed two issues:[16]

- Whether a nonprofessional corporation can legally employ a physician
- What the appropriate limitations are in relationships between a nonprofessional corporation and its physician employees

The board determined that employment by a business corporation may, but does not necessarily, lead to improper influence over the physician's professional judgment. Thus, it found that the employment of physicians is not illegal per se. Further, the board offered the following eight guidelines for business corporation employers and their physician employees to avoid the so-called evils of the corporate practice of medicine:

1. Employment should be structured so as to respect the physician-patient relationship.
2. Employment should be structured to permit the physician to exercise independent medical judgment without corporate intrusion.
3. Employment termination should provide for continuity of patient care.
4. Ownership of, and access to, medical records should be addressed in a way that provides for continuity of patient care.
5. The agreement should ensure patient freedom of choice.
6. The agreement should provide for patient confidentiality.
7. The agreement should provide for personal professional accountability.
8. The physician should retain both responsibility and authority to determine the fees charged for professional services to patients and third-party payers (governmental and private).

Attorney General Opinions in Iowa and Virginia This type of facts-and-circumstances analysis may become more prevalent, as evidenced by some recent attorney general opinions. In 1991, the Iowa attorney general stated that "a determination whether a particular relationship between a corporation and a physician gives rise to the unauthorized practice of medicine by the corporation must be resolved on a case-by-case basis."[17] The Iowa attorney general found that corporate practice should only be prohibited where the corporate entity exercises improper dominion and control of the medical practice. In 1994, the Virginia attorney general determined that a hospital could employ a full-time orthopedic surgeon as long as the relationship met certain conditions. The attorney general stated that the agreement would be acceptable if it "authorizes the physician to exercise control over the diagnosis and treatment of the patient, the physician's professional judgment is not improperly influenced by commercial or lay concerns and the physician-patient relationship is not altered."[18]

Group III Jurisdictions

The last general category includes those states in which the corporate practice doctrine has effectively been repudiated. The states included in this category are Alaska, Delaware, Hawaii, Idaho, Maine, Mississippi, Montana, Nebraska, Nevada, New Hampshire, New Mexico, North Carolina, North Dakota, Ohio, Rhode Island, Utah, Vermont, Wisconsin, and Wyoming.

Some of the states in this group never accepted one of the most common rationales for the corporate practice doctrine. The courts in these states held that statutes prohibiting the unlicensed practice of medicine did not apply to a corporation. They determined that impersonal entities were not meant to be covered by the medical practice acts.[19] Further, other courts have not found any difficulty in distinguishing the business side of medicine from its professional activities. Thus, employment of a physician in a nonprofessional corporation was not deemed to be prohibited.

SEARCH FOR LOGICAL APPROACHES

It is no accident that the two states most famous for enforcing a corporate practice prohibition—Texas and California—are the jurisdictions that most recently have articulated more workable and logical approaches to the corporate practice issue. Market forces are requiring Texas and California to find better solutions to the corporate practice conundrum.

Efforts in Texas

Because of the recent growth in the formation of not-for-profit health corporations with nonphysician members (for example, health care entities established by medical schools or hospitals that include administrators and other nonphysicians as corporate members but maintain a board of directors of physicians only), the Texas State Board of Medical Examiners is working to clarify the existing rules that regulate such entities.[20] The purpose of the rules is to protect the medical treatment decisions of physician employees from the improper influence of nonphysicians. The proposed rules identify those decisions that ought to be made exclusively by physicians and exclusively prohibit input from nonphysicians. The rules are as follows:

- A nonphysician member of the corporation may not appoint or elect any director without the approval of at least a majority of the board of directors, nor may the member unilaterally remove a director for any reason relating to credentialing, utilization review, or peer review.
- All credentialing, quality assurance, utilization review, and peer review policies shall be made exclusively by the physician board of directors.
- Any decision of the nonprofit organization to terminate the contract of any physician employed by, or otherwise under contract to, the corporation to provide medical services must be made exclusively by the physician board of directors.

The rules allow nonphysician members of the corporation to approve financial decisions including approval of capital and operating budgets and managed care contracts. Although these rules constitute significant movement away from Texas's blanket prohibition on corporate practice, they are limited only to not-for-profit health corporations. Thus, the rule changes made by the Texas board are likely to help in IDS development and managed care contracting for not-for-profit hospital organizations and medical schools—the entities most likely to organize a not-for-profit health corporation. However, the benefit of the rules is unlikely to spread, in Texas at least, to the for-profit sector.

Efforts in California

The California Medical Association (CMA) recently called for a more rational approach to applying the corporate practice prohibition in California. As a prime supporter of the prohibition in a state where it is applied so consistently and severely, the CMA is sending a clear message that current application of the corporate practice prohibition is no longer practical in the state. The CMA recognized that with the advent of IDSs, physician practice affiliations, and new models of physician practice, the focus of the corporate practice prohibition needed to be shifted to an examination of the types of decision making that take place in the medical practice context. According to its policy statement, members of the CMA's Technical Advisory Committee (TAC) agree that although certain elements of medical practice require exclusive physician control, other aspects appropriately fall within the shared control of physicians and lay administrators.[21] Still other aspects are deemed not to require any physician involvement. As such, the TAC identified what it believed to be the principal administrative and professional decisions being made by medical practices in the managed care environment and determined whether those decisions should be made by physicians, the administrative entity, or both. In addition, the TAC assigned each decision a level of decision-making authority to be exercised by the physician group or the lay entity—that is, exclusive, consultative, shared, or joint. (See figure 10-1 for the TAC's decision-making matrix.)

Although parties may disagree as to whether the TAC appropriately categorized the different decisions, all must acknowledge that its approach (if actually implemented) is far more rational than the current scenario in California, where the corporate practice prohibition is applied blindly. The TAC's matrix is one of the first attempts to deal practically with the corporate practice prohibition as it relates to the administrative and clinical aspects of medical practice.

CONCLUSION

The conflict between the corporate practice of medicine doctrine and the new models of physician practice is self-evident. The doctrine arose out of concerns that apply no less to the MSOs, PPMCs, and IDSs of the present than to corporate employers in the 1800s. Clearly, if certain jurisdictions hold to the principles behind the practice prohibition, it will continue to be an obstacle in the formation of these new entities.

Although counsels to MSOs and PPMCs must examine the corporate practice precedent in each state where their clients plan to operate, they need to advise their clients generally regarding lay involvement in physician decision making. Perhaps the safest course for these entities is to abide by particular rules maintaining professional autonomy, rather than trying to interpret and fit into some archaic court holdings with little application to the present time. The decision-making matrix generated by the CMA serves as a useful tool for analyzing the role of lay administrators in medical practice. Although it carries no legal authority, it may provide a foundation for courts to use when analyzing corporate practice issues in the future.

FIGURE 10-1. Decision-Making Matrix

Practicing Physicians Make Ultimate Decision		
No Duty to Consult *Exclusive*	*Informal Advice* *Consultative*	*Formal Recommendation* *Shared*
Setting purely medical practice policies	Practice parameters	Approving annual budget
What conditions can be referred to another physician specialist	Making treatment decisions that involve bioethical issues	Establishing bioethics policies
What diagnostic tests are appropriate for a particular condition	Credentialing for specific procedure, establishing general standards and as applied to individuals	Types of technology, new or old, that should be employed
What gets included in a particular patient's medical records	Scheduling on-call coverage	To whom a physician can refer
Whether a particular patient visit requires a particular billing code	Handling impaired physicians	Credentialing; establishing the standards for admission to the group
Communication of a purely clinical nature with patients	Which continuing medical education courses should be taken	Credentialing; an individual application for admission to the group
Determination as to whether an emergency medical condition exists	Terminating physicians from practice arrangements on discretionary grounds, i.e., quality of care and business concerns, failure to comply with UR procedures "without cause"	Developing a UR/QA plan
		Implementing a UR/QA plan
		Enforcing the UR/QA plan (except terminations from groups)
		Whether and when to utilize limited license practitioners
		Determining whether to consider an application for admission
		Selecting independent limited license practitioners and "physician extenders"
		Developing drug formularies
		Selecting key administrative-medical officers
		How many patients a physician should see
		Controlling medical data
		Terminating physicians from practice on nondiscretionary grounds
		Selecting, disciplining, and discharging nonphysician-dependent practitioners only

FIGURE 10-1. *(Continued)*

Neither Party May Solely Make Ultimate Decision

Formal Consultation and Agreement

Joint
How many hours a physician should work
Nonclinical decisions concerning medical records
Contractual relationships with third-party payers
Level and scope of malpractice coverage
How much the physician group (including cost of all benefits) should be compensated
Settling cases for all parties named
Marketing
Setting the global budget for limited-license practitioner compensation
Mergers, acquisitions, conversions, and affiliations
Ownership and scope of ancillary ventures
Establishing grievance policies
Making a decision to transfer a stable patient
Level of indigent care provided
Employment matters
How much the lay entity, including the entity's executive management, should be compensated

Lay Entity Makes Ultimate Decision

Formal Recommendation *Shared*	*Informal Advice* *Consultative*	*No Duty to Consult* *Exclusive*
Selecting key administrative positions	Coding and billing procedures	Compensation for allied health and lay staff
Purchasing, replacing, and repairing equipment	Controlling administrative data	Selecting purely administrative staff who do not hold key positions
How much patients should pay		

Source: Technical Advisory Committee, California Medical Association, Sacramento.

References

1. John Wiorek, "The Corporate Practice of Medicine Doctrine: an Outmoded Theory in Need of Modification," *Journal of Legal Medicine* 8, no. 465 (1987): 486–88.

2. Wiorek, p. 470.

3. 384 F. Supp. 434(1974), aff'd, 421 U.S.995(1975).

4. 715 S.W. 2d 782 (Tex. App.1986).

5. 63 Op. Cal. Att'y Gen. 723(1980).

6. See 65 Op. Cal. Att'y Gen. 223(1982).

7. Id. at n.4.

8. 143 Cal. App. 3d 419, 191 Cal. Rpt. 762(1983).

9. Cal. Health & Safety Code s1346(f) & (i) (West Supp. 1993).

10. 58 Op. Cal. Att'y Gen. 571(1975).

11. See *People v. Painless Parker Dentist,* 85 Colo. 304, 275 P. 928 (1929); *State Bd. of Dental Examiners v. Savelle,* 90 Colo. 177, 8 P.2d 693 (1932); *State Bd. of Dental Examiners v. Heitler,* 90 Colo. 191, 8 P.2d 698 (1932); *State Bd. of Dental Examiners v. Miller,* 90 Colo. 193, 8 P.2d 699 (1932); *State Bd. of Dental Examiners v. Patch,* 90 Colo. 207, 8 P.2d 704 (1932); *State Bd. of Dental Examiners v. Walsh,* 90 Colo. 208, 8 P.2d 704 (1932).

12. *Rosane v. Senger,* 112 Colo. 363, 149 P.2d 372 (1944).

13. *Moon v. Mercy Hospital,* 150 Colo. 430, 373 P.2d 944 (1962).

14. *People ex rel. Dunbar v. Lee Optical Co.,* 952 P.2d 21 (1969).

15. *Dixon v. Zick,* 179 Colo. 278, 500 P.2d 130 (1972).

16. Louisiana State Board of Medical Examiners, Sept. 24, 1992.

17. Op. Iowa Att'y Gen. No. 91-7-1 (1991).

18. 1992 Va. Ag. LEXIS 66.

19. See *State Electro-Medical Institute v. State,* 74 Neb. 40, 103 N.W. 1078 (1905).

20. Forum on Health Law of the American Bar Association, *Health Care Mergers and Acquisitions* (Chicago: American Bar Association, 1995), p. 173.

21. California Medical Association, *The Corporate Practice of Medicine Bar: Decision-Making Authority for Integrated Entities Criteria*

PART IV

The Valuation and Sale of Physician Practices

In the current health care environment, many physician practices are being bought and sold. Prior to the purchase or sale of a physician practice, a detailed study is usually performed to establish the value of the practice. Part IV consists of two chapters. Chapter 11, "The Valuation of Physician Practices," provides a step-by-step overview of the methods involved in determining the market value of a physician practice. Chapter 12, "Physician Practice Acquisition/Divestiture: A Case Study," describes the process of buying and selling a physician practice from the perspectives of both buyer and seller.

11

The Valuation of Physician Practices

Patrick M. Hurst

The 1990s is an era of consolidation in the practice of medicine, characterized by a frenzy of mergers and acquisitions involving physician practice organizations. A great deal of this activity has taken place in areas with a high degree of HMO penetration, which supports the notion that managed care plans are a major driving force behind physician practice integration. The reconfiguration of health care providers from solo practitioners to group practitioners has taken many forms, ranging from loose affiliations of physicians to fully integrated delivery systems providing a complete continuum of care. The extent to which physicians affiliate with other physicians or other health care entities depends on their objectives and the perceived importance of the trade-offs accompanying each integration model. For physician practice integration to occur, each practice must be properly valued prior to merger or acquisition.

This chapter defines physician integration and discusses the standard methods for valuing physician practices. It also describes how a financial analysis might be performed for a hypothetical multispecialty group practice.

PHYSICIAN INTEGRATION

The integration of physician practices is generally classified as either horizontal or vertical. *Horizontal integration* entails a collaboration or affiliation among independent physicians and medical groups whereas *vertical integration* entails an affiliation between physicians and other types of health care providers, such as hospitals or HMOs.

Horizontal Integration

Often the pursuit of horizontal integration has three objectives: to create cost efficiency, to expand the services provided, and to develop negotiating power in contractual relationships with health alliances or HMOs. The benefits of horizontal affiliation for the physician include the ability to access managed care contracts to stem the decline in fee-for-service (FFS) revenue. Physicians who merge their practice into a larger group also benefit from a reduction in time and resources devoted to administrative overhead, leaving more time for patient care. A medical group can operate more profitably than a sole practitioner given the economies of scale in administration and information management services.

Other benefits of a medical group include lower financial risk for the physician and greater access to financing for expansion and capital expenditures. The principal disadvantage of any form of affiliation or integration is the physician's loss of autonomy.

Vertical Integration

Vertical integration is most commonly accomplished through acquisition of a physician practice by a hospital. Integration allows providers to offer a broader range of services while enjoying the efficiency and cost savings attributable to centralized administrative functions. By forming a vertically integrated system, hospitals also are able to provide coordinated case management, which can reduce utilization and, in turn, control health care costs. Hospitals in an integrated system are able to provide more diversified care alternatives and thus a broader-based revenue stream. Moreover, the wider range of services offered by vertically integrated hospitals will be attractive to employer groups and managed care organizations (MCOs). A vertically integrated health care provider is in a better position to enter into global capitation contracts.

PHYSICIAN PRACTICE MANAGEMENT COMPANIES

One of the most active sectors in the health care industry involves physician practice management companies (PPMCs). These firms usually provide capital and other management services in connection with physician practices. Transaction activity in this section has been heavy, including one of the largest-ever mergers of two PPMCs with MedPartners' $412 million acquisition of Mullikin Medical Enterprises L.P. and the subsequent $332 million purchase of Pacific Physician Services, Inc., by the resulting entity, MedPartners/Mullikin. Other large PPMC transactions include Caremark International's purchase of the assets of CIGNA Medical Group and Friendly Hills HealthCare Network. Consolidation of the estimated $200 billion physician practice management industry is expected to continue, particularly because the industry is still relatively fragmented.

Much of the consolidation of the physician practice management industry is being driven by the need for management services by physician groups, created by the increase in managed care penetration in these markets. In addition to offering these provider groups much-needed expertise in negotiating with payer groups, PPMCs also can provide the capital required to develop the critical mass needed for these negotiations. In addition, large medical groups can provide an entry point for PPMCs into untapped markets.

MEDICAL PRACTICE VALUATION

In the current environment, the transactions necessary to form integrated health care delivery systems require sophisticated financial and valuation analyses. In addition to serving in the capacity of a financial advisor familiar with a wide variety of transaction structures, today's valuation expert must have an appreciation for the trends in the health care industry, including the numerous regulations affecting the delivery of health care and the impact of managed care and legislated health care reform. A thorough understanding of the industry and the factors influencing its future are essential to the effective valuation of a medical practice under a variety of models and structures.

Historically, medical practice valuations were performed for the purpose of practice buy-sell agreements, marital dissolution litigation, and estate planning. The medical practice being valued usually consisted of a few physicians and often was valued using industry rules of thumb. Today, however, medical practices are larger and more complex. In addition, the evolution of managed care and the related shift to capitated revenue have had a profound impact on medical practices' operational and financial characteristics. The purpose of medical practice valuation in the current environment ranges from strategic affiliations to mergers and acquisitions by nonphysician entities. The appraiser now must conduct more sophisticated valuations requiring a more rigorous analysis of the subject practice, giving due consideration to the current trends and regulatory environment in the health care industry. Some of these major trends are discussed in the following subsections.

Reimbursement Trends and Managed Care

The reimbursement system has been going through a great deal of change since 1992 when Medicare began phasing in a resource-based relative value scale (RBRVS). (See chapter 6.) The RBRVS assigns relative values to thousands of medical procedures based on the amount of relative work, overhead, and malpractice premiums involved. Based on this scale, physicians are paid a fixed fee for services provided to Medicare patients. The RBRVS is designed to reduce payment imbalances between specialty physicians and primary care physicians (PCPs) and between urban and rural physicians.

Private payer reimbursement is provided through HMOs, preferred provider organizations (PPOs), and indemnity insurance plans. Traditionally, these plans reimbursed health care providers on an FFS basis. Because of their failure to contain costs and control the provision of unnecessary procedures, open-access FFS plans are being replaced with restricted-panel, discounted FFS plans and capitated or prepaid, fixed-fee contracts.

Plans established by MCOs are becoming more popular among health care payers because of their ability to control costs. Capitated plans pay health care providers a fixed monthly fee, called a *capitated payment,* for each member of the plan receiving health services by the provider. (See chapter 5.) HMO agreements have most often been implemented with PCPs. In many plans, the PCPs serve as gatekeepers to the system and have a high degree of control over patient care decisions and thus the cost of health care. Increasingly, capitated payment arrangements are being extended to specialty practices. The changes in the form and uncertainty surrounding reimbursement have a significant effect on the projected revenue and profitability of a medical practice or group, which must be considered in any valuation.

Regulation

Any valuation must consider the regulatory context in which it is being performed. Certain regulations dictate the most appropriate premise and standard of value. The greater level of sophistication is necessitated by the increased scrutiny applied by the Internal Revenue Service (IRS) and various regulatory bodies. The increased scrutiny by regulators in practice acquisitions demands an understanding of these regulations and their impact on the determination of value, as well as greater care in the documentation of the rationale and support underlying the value conclusions. The following are the major regulations affecting medical practice valuation:

- *Medicare/Medicaid anti-fraud and abuse laws:* Medicare anti-fraud and abuse legislation was issued to prevent physicians from receiving public reimbursement for false, unnecessary, or overpriced medical tests and procedures. The anti-kickback provision of the Medicare and Medicaid Patient and Program Protection Act of 1987 stipulates criminal penalties for individuals or entities that knowingly and willfully solicit, receive, offer, or pay remuneration to induce business that is reimbursable under Medicare or state health care programs.[1] These regulations can affect a hospital's ability to pay for the intangible assets of a physician practice if regulators consider the payment as an inducement for referrals.
- *Internal Revenue Code 501(c)(3):* This section of the Internal Revenue Code provides an exemption from federal income tax for qualifying not-for-profit entities.[2] A merged integrated delivery system (IDS) may qualify for tax-exempt status if it meets the fundamental requirements for tax exemption, which were traditionally applied to stand-alone hospitals. In reviewing applications for tax-exempt status, the IRS considers, among other things, three issues: the community benefit standard; prohibitions under Section 501(c)(3) against private inurement and private benefit; and the provisions of the Medicare anti-fraud and abuse statutes previously discussed. Private inurement and private benefit restrictions prohibit payment in excess of fair market value by an exempt organization for goods, services, facilities, or financing. Likewise, providing goods, services, facilities, or financing by an exempt organization for an amount less than fair market value also is prohibited. Inurement restrictions were put in place to prevent the channeling of profits through a tax-exempt organization to the benefit of an individual.
- *Antitrust laws:* Federal and state antitrust laws are aimed at controlling anticompetitive practices through the promotion of competition and the prevention of unfair trade practices. In the case of horizontal integration, an affiliation of health care providers cannot operate so as to exclude other physician groups from entering a geographic market for medical services. For example, if an independent practice association (IPA) became the exclusive provider of physician services to all the health alliances in a given region, it may be subject to antitrust enforcement. The degree of economic integration among the participating physicians

is a determinant in deciding whether an IPA is a legitimate economic entity or a price-fixing association. In the context of vertical integration, a physician-hospital organization (PHO) that deliberately drives out competing physician practices and hospitals in a regional market also could be subject to antitrust enforcement. Antitrust enforcement against IDSs will most likely be analyzed under the rule of reason, in which the societal benefits of the integration are weighed against its actual or potential anticompetitive effects.

- *State corporate practice of medicine laws:* Many states prohibit the practice of medicine by individuals or entities (including corporations) that are unlicensed to practice medicine. The rationale for such laws is the concern that providers of care cannot have their loyalties divided between the patient's care and the corporation's interests. Given these restrictions, integrated models in certain states must be structured carefully to avoid the perception that the corporation is determining the course of treatment. This typically involves establishing a management services organization (MSO), owned and controlled by the buyer, to acquire the clinic's tangible and intangible assets. The clinic professional corporation employs, and is governed by, the physicians and enters into a long-term management service agreement with the MSO.
- *Anti-self-referral legislation (Stark I and II):* The Ethics in Patient Referrals Act, commonly referred to as the Stark Law after its sponsor, U.S. Representative Fortney "Pete" Stark, enacted certain prohibitions against a physician's referring patients to an entity in which he or she shares a financial interest.[3] With certain exceptions, the Stark Law prohibits a referring physician who has a financial relationship with an entity from making a referral to that entity for the furnishing of designated health services reimbursable under Medicare or Medicaid. In addition, the entity may not present, or cause to be presented, a Medicare claim or bill to any individual, third party, or other entity for designated health services furnished pursuant to a prohibited referral.

VALUATION PRINCIPLES

The fundamental premise on which all investment decisions are based is that value to a potential investor is equal to the present worth of future benefits. This basic concept should be applied to the valuation of a medical practice, as well as to particular securities that form the capital structure of such a practice. In each instance, it is a matter of identifying the future returns the practice can be reasonably expected to generate and determining their present value within the context of the uncertainty associated with realizing these returns.

Fair Market Value

Many buyers of a medical practice are restricted from paying more than its fair market value on a stand-alone basis. *Fair market value,* in a definition modified from *Black's Law Dictionary,* is the price at which an asset would change hands between a willing buyer and willing seller when the former is not under any compulsion to buy and the latter is not under any compulsion to sell and both parties are able, as well as willing, to trade and are well-informed about the asset and the market for that asset.[4]

This definition is applicable to a valuation if the funds for an acquisition are provided by either a tax-exempt organization or a provider in a position to receive referrals. No consideration can be given to increased earnings that may arise due to synergy or economies of scale resulting *specifically* from the combination of the two entities. The concept of fair market value does not assume any specific buyer. In contrast, the determination of *investment value,* which is the specific value of an asset to a particular investor (or class of investors) for individual investment reasons, allows for the incorporation of factors that may be unique to a specific buyer. However, an argument has been made that the cost savings a practice could realize, either on its own or through consolidation with other practices, can be considered in the valuation.

Relative Levels of Value

The size of the block and the liquidity of the stock being appraised are important factors to be considered in any valuation. If a specific block allows the owner, or a purchaser, to control a practice, a higher value (relative to a minority position) is justified. Just as a controlling interest is worth more on a per-share basis than a minority interest, a marketable minority interest is worth more than a unmarketable minority interest. Thus, three relative levels of value exist in the context of valuing a stock interest: control, marketable minority, and unmarketable minority.

VALUATION METHODS

There are four generally accepted approaches used to determine the value of a medical practice or its underlying assets: the income approach, the market approach, the cost approach, and the excess earnings approach.

The income and market approaches can be applied on either a leveraged or unleveraged (debt-free) basis. As discussed in the following subsections, the discounted cash flow (DCF) approach (income approach) uses discount rates and the market approach uses capitalization rates (or multiples). The types of discount and capitalization rates used must be consistent with the specific cash flows being discounted. If the projected cash flows contain no deduction for debt expense, an *unleveraged* capitalization rate and a weighted-average cost of capital (WACC) as a discount rate are the appropriate rates to use. Using unleveraged cash flows results in the determination of the total invested capital (TIC), which includes both debt and equity. Therefore, the market value of any interest-bearing debt must be subtracted from the TIC to arrive at the market value of equity. However, if the projected cash flows include a deduction for debt expense, a *leveraged* capitalization rate and a cost of equity (K_e) as the discount rate are the appropriate rates to use. Using leveraged approaches results in the determination of the practice's equity. To arrive at the TIC, the market value of the interest-bearing debt must be added to the market value of equity calculated.

Income Approach

The income approach estimates value by determining the present worth of the anticipated future cash flows. The most commonly used methodology under this approach is DCF.

DCF can be used to determine the value of the complete ownership of the entire medical practice. The procedure entails estimating the present worth of the cash flow to be generated from ownership of the medical practice and theoretically available, although not necessarily paid, to the owners as dividends for a particular period. Provisions also are made for the value of the enterprise at termination of the forecast period, referred to as the *terminal value*. The resulting cash flow and its terminal value, discounted at an appropriate risk rate, yield an indication of the amount justified for complete ownership of the practice. Thus, DCF incorporates the following major components:

- Projected future cash flow
- Terminal value
- Discount rate

Projected Future Cash Flow *Projected future cash flow* represents the difference between estimated operating cash inflows and outflows. These cash flows are relevant for determining the fair market value of the capital structure because they represent the cash available to both debt holders and shareholders. *Available cash flow* is the amount that could be paid to the equity and debt investors without impairment of the medical practice's business operations. It is important to identify and separate the return to a physician for services performed (compensation) and return on investment in the practice (investment return). A potential buyer is only interested in determining and valuing the potential investment return of a medical practice. (See figure 11-1 for a calculation of available cash flow.) Because there is no deduction for interest expense, this would be an unleveraged, or debt-free, cash flow.

After-tax operating profit is based on a projected income statement and balance sheet over a specific forecast period, usually five years. Because depreciation and amortization are included as operating expenses but involve no cash outlay, they are added back to after-tax operating income. Although not part of operating expenses, capital expenditures represent cash outlays for new and replacement equipment. Because capital expenditures are an integral part of the practice's normal operations, they are subtracted from available cash flow. Incremental working capital requirements (the increase in total current assets minus the increase in total current liabilities) are part of the practice's production requirements and also are subtracted from available cash flow. The current portion of long-term debt and notes payable represent sources of financing rather than a direct investment in working capital to support operations. Excluding interest-bearing debt from working capital allows an evaluation independent of financing decisions.

Terminal Value The terminal value used in the DCF approach is essentially an estimate of the value of the practice at the end of the forecast period. This value must be computed if the medical group is to remain a viable, going concern beyond the final projection period. There are two basic methods of computing terminal value for a going concern, the multiple method and the perpetuity method.

FIGURE 11-1. Calculation of Available Debt-Free Cash Flow

After-tax operating income

plus (+)

Depreciation and amortization

minus (−)

Capital expenditures

minus (−)

Incremental working capital requirements

equals (=)

Debt-free cash flow

The *multiple method* uses a projected market multiple, as in the market capitalization approach (discussed later), applied to an earnings level to calculate the terminal value. Typically, the operating income for the final projection period is adjusted to arrive at a "normalized" level and then capitalized at a reasonable multiple to yield an indication of value for the medical group's TIC. The *perpetuity method* uses the projected free cash flow as its basis, rather than operating income. The free cash flow projected in the final period is adjusted to arrive at a level of cash flow for the first year beyond the projection period, which is representative of the medical group's future cash-generating capability. This "normalized" cash flow figure incorporates expectations of the level of investment required to maintain the business into the future, as well as the investment return the business can be expected to sustain. The normalized cash flow figure is then capitalized as a perpetuity by the determined discount rate, adjusted for some level of growth that can be expected into perpetuity.

Discounting both the projected future cash flows during the forecast period and the terminal value back to the present, using the discount rate as determined below, and summing the results yields an indication of value for the entire medical practice.

Discount Rate In the valuation of a medical practice, it is necessary to select a discount rate that can be reasonably applied to calculate the present value of future cash flows and the terminal value. Discount rates are selected on the basis of the overall risks of medical practice ownership and the inherent risks in realizing the projected income stream. They are the rate of return that would be required by providers of capital (buyers) to the medical practice to compensate them for the time value of their money, as well as the risk inherent in the particular investment. Unless the purchasers could expect to earn this required rate of return, it would not be in their interest to invest. Thus, the required rate of return is the *opportunity cost of capital.*

As mentioned earlier, it is important that the type of discount rate used be consistent with the specific cash flows being discounted. If the projected cash flows include a deduction for debt expense, the cost of equity (K_e) is the appropriate discount rate to use. However, if the projected cash flows contain no deduction for debt expense, a weighted-average cost of capital is the appropriate discount rate. These discount rates are defined as follows:

- *Cost of equity:* Unlike fixed-income instruments, common stock does not provide investors with a predictable stream of future payments. As a result, it is impossible to know exactly what returns they can expect from their investments in common stock. The most widely used method of estimating the cost of common equity is the capital asset pricing model (CAPM). The

CAPM is an expectational model that attempts to relate the risk inherent in an investment with the returns expected by investors. In short, the price paid for an asset must yield an expected return sufficient to compensate the investor for the risk that the asset's expected future value will not be realized. However, expected return estimates generated by the CAPM will not compensate the investor for elements of risk that can be easily reduced through diversification in a portfolio of investments. The representation of the CAPM in figure 11-2 can be used to determine the cost of common equity for a medical group. This application of the CAPM is based on the theory that the expected return on a common stock investment can be explained by four factors: risk-free rate of return, equity risk premium, small stock premium, and beta. The risk-free rate of return represents the market consensus expected return on a security with no risk of default. Hence, it compensates the investor for the time value of his or her money.

- *WACC:* WACC is an average of the costs of all sources of capital (debt and equity) for the medical group, with each source weighted by its respective percentage share in the group's capital structure. The representation of the WACC in figure 11-3 can be used in the analysis of medical groups. The costs of capital used in the WACC are estimates of appropriate expected returns for the various providers of capital to the subject medical group. The best method of estimating these variables is to examine similar investment opportunities and attempt to determine the market consensus-expected returns for these investments. These figures then can be used as a basis for selecting appropriate expected returns for the subject practice.
- *Cost of debt:* In the calculation of weighted average cost of capital, both the cost of capital and the cost of debt appear in the formula. Cost-of-debt capital is defined as the yield to maturity on comparable debt instruments traded in the public market, as adjusted for specific risk factors related to the subject practice. In general, the yield to maturity represents the market consensus on what percentage of return is appropriate for the particular security. It is an estimate of expected return as of a particular point in time, and is easy to compute given that the amount and timing of future payments from a fixed-income security (interest or dividends) are contractually fixed.

Market Approach

The market approach involves determining a level of earnings or operating characteristics that is considered to be representative of the

FIGURE 11-2. Capital Asset Pricing Model (CAPM)

$$K_e = R_f + (\beta \times R_p)$$

Where:

K_e = Cost of common equity capital
R_f = Risk-free rate of return
β = Beta
R_p = Equity risk premium

FIGURE 11-3. Weighted-Average Cost of Capital (WACC)

$$WACC = K_d\,(1 - t)(D/TIC) + K_e(E/TIC)$$

Where:

WACC = Weighted-average cost of capital
K_d = Cost of debt capital (pretax)
K_e = Cost of common equity capital
D = Debt capital (market value)
E = Common equity capital (market value)
TIC = Total invested capital (market value)
t = Marginal corporate tax rate

practice's future performance and capitalizing this figure by an appropriate risk-adjusted rate. It provides an indication of value for the practice that corresponds to the particular earnings or operating characteristic being capitalized. The *capitalization rate* is an expression of what investors believe to be a fair and reasonable rate of return for the particular security given the inherent risk of ownership. It incorporates expectations of growth and is based on the implicit assumption that some level of earnings will be generated by the enterprise into perpetuity.

The market approach can take two forms: the market comparison method and the comparative transaction method. The following subsections describe these two methods and the steps involved in applying either method to medical practice valuation.

Market Comparison Method In the market comparison method, a practice's value is based on the market prices of publicly traded practices found to be similar to the subject practice. This implicitly takes into account the consensus of what investors are willing to pay for the stock of comparable public companies, adjusted for the specific circumstances of the subject practice. The prices paid in relation to the practice's earnings and cash flows result in capitalization rates that are an expression of what investors believe to be fair and reasonable rates of return for these securities given the risk inherent in those businesses. This method requires a search in the market for publicly traded practices that are similar to the subject practice in terms of medical services, markets, size, operations, growth, and stability.

Unfortunately, no physician practices are publicly traded. However, PPMCs are publicly traded. Most PPMCs have concentrated on primary care areas, but recent independent practice organizations (IPOs) tend to focus on such medical specialties as cardiology, radiology, oncology, and mental health. These companies have been extremely aggressive in acquiring medical practices. The market capitalization rates for these PPMCs reflect growth expectations that cannot be duplicated by a single medical practice. Therefore, comparisons of these publicly traded companies to most medical practices are not meaningful.

Comparative Transaction Method The comparative transaction method determines the capitalization rate of the subject practice by analyzing similar practices that have been recently acquired. For this method, access to reliable information pertaining to medical practice acquisitions is required. The terms of the transaction must be analyzed carefully to determine the appropriate implied capitalization rates. The subject practice's business growth and risk attributes are compared to each acquired practice. The ratio of the purchase price to the acquired practice's earnings or cash flow suggests how much investors will pay for the subject practice's earnings or cash flow. In addition to the capitalization rates previously described, medical practices sometimes are sold based on such operating characteristics as full-time equivalent physicians and number of enrollees. Because these multiples are derived from transactions involving entire practices (that is, a controlling interest), a control premium is implicit in the multiples. As above, the terms of the transaction must be analyzed carefully to determine the appropriate capitalization rates of the sold practices. Of particular importance is the level of compensation paid to the physician going forward. Lack of knowledge of the compensation and other information can lead to drastically distorted capitalization rates.

Application of the Market Comparison and Comparative Transaction Methods Four steps are involved in applying either the market comparison or the comparative transaction method to the valuation of a medical practice:

1. Determine the representational earnings and cash flow levels for the subject practice.
2. Select comparable practices recently sold or publicly traded.
3. Based on a relative risk analysis of the subject practice and the comparable practices, select appropriate capitalization rates.
4. Determine the fair market value of the subject practice.

The noteworthy difference between the market comparison and the comparative transaction methods is the source of comparable practices. Representative earnings, risk analysis, and capitalization rates are discussed below, followed by discussion of the selection of comparable practices under each approach.

Representative earnings: The subject practice's respective earnings and cash flow levels must be based on its normal operations. Thus, the effects of one-time, or nonrecurring, charges should not be reflected in the subject practice's representative levels. An income or expense item is considered to be *nonrecurring* if it is not expected to occur on an ongoing basis. Examples of nonrecurring items include unusual legal and professional fees, start-up costs associated with new ventures, temporary declines in operating margins, and gains or losses on the sales of assets. Adjustments also are made for income and expenses relating to nonoperating assets or liabilities because these should be valued separately. Most practices need to be converted from a cash basis to an accrual basis for purposes of performing the valuation. Earnings and cash flows are calculated on both a leveraged and unleveraged basis (discussed earlier).

Risk analysis: A relative risk analysis is performed to compare the subject practice with comparable practices. The comparison is done on the basis of both quantitative (size, revenue composition, payer concentration, leverage, profitability, growth, and so on) and qualitative (age and working relationships of the physicians, for example) factors. Of particular importance is the physician's motivation post-transaction given the governance of the new entity. The comparison is done to determine the overall investment risk of the subject practice relative to that of the selected comparable practices. Through these comparisons, a representative capitalization rate for the subject practice's earnings and cash flow is determined.

Selection of capitalization rates: As stated earlier, both market approaches rely on the determination of a market multiple, or capitalization rate, which is applied to the subject practice's representative earnings or cash flow levels. Typically, in determining unleveraged capitalization rates, the aggregate market value of the comparable practice's debt and equity is divided by the subject practice's debt-free earnings and cash flow. Use of a practice's earnings and cash flow on a debt-free basis is useful when comparing medical practices that have substantially different levels of debt in their capital structures. Although traditional medical practices do not have a great deal of debt, this approach reduces any distortions in price/earnings (P/E) or price/cash flow (P/CF) ratios that might be present because of various degrees of debt in each practice's capital structure. There are several commonly used unleveraged, or debt-free, earnings and cash flow levels: revenue; earnings before interest and taxes (EBIT); earnings before depreciation, interest, and taxes (EBDIT); debt-free earnings (DFE); and debt-free cash flow (DFCF).

Cost Approach

The cost approach determines value based on the replacement value of the company's assets. It measures value by estimating the cost of replicating the subject practice. This approach is helpful in analyzing a "make-versus-buy" decision. However, the cost approach has limited usefulness in the valuation of medical practices on a going-concern basis.

The cost approach most often used is referred to as the *adjusted book value approach*. Applicability of this approach is generally limited to specific situations in which the market capitalization and DCF approaches are less suitable. The adjusted book value approach differs from the market capitalization and DCF approaches in two important ways. First, it focuses on individual asset and liability values from the practice's balance sheet, which are adjusted to fair market value. In contrast, the market capitalization and DCF approaches focus on the aggregate returns generated by all the practice's assets. Second, the adjusted book value approach can be applied in situations where liquidation is imminent. The market capitalization and DCF approaches have very limited applicability in a liquidation scenario.

Excess Earnings Approach

The excess earnings methodology is a hybrid of the cost and income approaches, in which the value of the practice is based on tangible assets plus intangible assets to the extent that the practice's earnings support a value. Based on the practice's earnings, this approach estimates the value of its intangible assets, including goodwill (discussed later). To determine the value of the practice's intangible assets, the earnings in excess of appropriate returns for the tangible assets are multiplied by a capitalization multiple (the inverse of the capitalization rate). The fair market value of the tangible assets is added to the fair market value of the intangible assets, including goodwill, to yield the practice's fair market value. The basic steps of the excess earnings method are as follows:

1. Normalize historical earnings and project next year's expected earnings before depreciation, interest, and taxes (normalized EBDIT).

2. Estimate the value of tangible assets in the form of net working capital and fixed assets, and calculate the annual cost to replace fixed assets.
3. Estimate normal returns for investments in both working capital and fixed assets (normal returns on the investments).
4. Estimate excess earnings (normalized EBDIT less both the annual cost to replace fixed assets and the normal investment return), and subtract applicable federal and state income taxes
5. Estimate a capitalization rate to apply to the excess earnings amount.
6. Calculate the value of the intangible assets (excess earnings less taxes, divided by the capitalization rate).
7. Estimate the total business enterprise value by adding the tangible asset values to the value of the intangibles.

Since the core of this method involves estimation of excess earnings and capitalization rates, both of these concepts are defined next.

Estimate Excess Earnings *Excess earnings* is defined as the earnings above and beyond a normal return for use of the medical group's tangible assets. Normalized earnings represent the group's expected earning power before depreciation, interest, and taxes. *Expected earning power* is defined as the typical earnings that may be generated. If the group is to be valued without regard to the synergy of a combination, the normalized earnings should reflect the group's current position without regard to changes or investments the purchaser intends to make in the future. Expected normalized earnings also should be net of the required physician base and incentive compensation.

The annual cost to replace fixed assets is a substitute for depreciation and is calculated by dividing the estimated fair market value by the estimated remaining economic life of the various fixed assets. It is based on the fair market value rather than the historical cost of the fixed assets. The normal investment return on tangible assets is based on the fair market value of both the fixed assets and the working capital (current assets less non-interest-bearing current liabilities). The normal return on tangible assets is calculated by multiplying their value by the rate of return appropriate for each type of asset.

The *rate of return* is the annual opportunity cost of owning the medical practice's tangible assets. Rates differ for each type of asset, depending on its riskiness. For example, land has relatively little risk compared to high-technology equipment. Therefore, the rate for land should be lower than the rate for equipment.

Estimate Capitalization Rates The next step in the excess earnings approach is to estimate a capitalization rate that is to be applied to the excess earnings. Capitalization rates are determined by market factors and are expressed as a percentage return on an expected stream of income. The stream of income to be capitalized is the excess earnings previously determined. Capitalization rates vary depending on perceived risks, stability, and other factors inherent in the practice. As in the calculation of the discount rate in the DCF approach, the investment that is generally considered most risk free is a U.S. Treasury Bond. Venture capitalists, on the other hand, require 35 to 50 percent compounded annual rates of return on equity investments in new and riskier ventures. Selection of the appropriate capitalization rate is based on a detailed analysis of the medical group. Revenue Ruling 68-609 suggests that capitalization rates of 15 to 20 percent may be appropriate for intangible assets.[5] However, these guidelines should be used only as an indication of, and not as a substitute for, independent analysis.

Determination of the capitalization rate may be analyzed by separating risk characteristics of a medical practice into 10 categories:

1. Practice type (sole practitioner, single group, multispecialty group)
2. Specialty type (including consideration of average term of the patient-physician relationship and average volume of encounters per patient)
3. Facilities (including location, length of time, surrounding demographics)
4. Historical profitability
5. Current physician utilization
6. Payment mix
7. Physician age and health
8. Physician reputation
9. Quality of management and staff
10. Competition

These factors try to encapsulate the basic values the market may place on the quality of a particular physician practice's earnings. Each is subjectively assigned a value by the appraiser ranging from 1 to 5 percent, where 1 percent represents a low level of risk and 5 percent represents the highest level of risk for the practice. The summation results in a subjectively reasonable capitalization rate to be used in the excess earnings approach. The value of the intangible assets derived from dividing the excess earnings by the capitalization rate is added to the value of the tangible assets to arrive at an indication of the practice's TIC.

INTANGIBLE ASSETS

Intangible assets may or may not be reflected on a company's balance sheet depending on certain accounting rules. Either way, the true value of a company's intangible assets is likely to be reflected in its earnings. Intangible assets for a medical practice may include noncompetition agreements, patient charts and records, assembled workforce, computer software, managed care contracts, trade names, and below-market leases.

The *1995 Continuing Professional Education Guide,* authored by IRS-exempt organization specialists, mentions the difficulty of valuing intangible assets and states, "it is with respect to valuation of intangibles that inflation of value is most likely to occur. Valuation of intangibles is made even more complicated by the fact . . . that valuation analysts are constrained from assigning value to the anticipated indirect revenue from referrals. Often, the same value is assigned to other intangible assets."[6]

Valuation of Intangible Assets

Intangible assets are typically valued using the income or cost approach. The *income approach* values the intangible assets by valuing the incremental stream of income or cost savings attributable to the asset. For instance, a below-market lease generates cost savings for the buyer for a contracted period of time. The *cost approach* estimates value based on the cost of recreating the asset. For example, patient charts and records can be valued by estimating the cost of the staff time and materials necessary to replicate this important information. If the buyer did not buy this particular asset, it would have to incur these expenditures to generate the projected revenue and earnings stream.

It is important to remember that individual assets should be valued as support for, rather than determination of, the medical practice's overall value. Therefore, the aggregate value of the individual assets should equal the value of the practice determined using the income and market approaches. Valuing a practice using a buildup of individual asset values ignores the importance of earnings, which are largely determined by the level of compensation expected to be paid to the physicians.

Goodwill One of the biggest issues in medical practice valuation is the treatment of goodwill. The *goodwill* of a business is typically a fragile asset that, but for constant nurturing, would quickly disappear. It also is an asset that has no value separate from the enterprise of which it is a part. A thorough definition of goodwill has been set forth: "The advantage, or benefit, which is acquired by an establishment beyond the mere value of the capital, stock, funds, or property employed therein, in consequence of the general public patronage and encouragement which it receives from constant or habitual customers, on account of its local position, or common celebrity, or reputation for skill or affluence, or punctuality, or from other accidental circumstances or necessity, or even from ancient partialities or prejudices."[7] Goodwill exists where there is an "expectancy of both continuing excess earning capacity and also of competitive advantage or continued patronage."[8]

Goodwill in a medical practice can be classified as either practice goodwill or professional goodwill. *Practice goodwill* is attributed to a medical group whereas *professional goodwill* is attributed to the individual physicians. The more integrated the practice, the greater the ability to "carve out" identifiable intangible assets and practice goodwill. This is an important distinction with regard to fraud and abuse laws. An acquiring hospital payment for professional goodwill could easily be construed as an inducement for referrals. However, payment for practice goodwill may be seen as a more legitimate acquisition.

Managed care plans will dramatically reduce the availability of referrals for freestanding, noncapitated specialty practices because the referrals of a managed health care network will be made internally whenever possible. Because the value of goodwill depends on the magnitude and predictability of earnings, its value in an FFS specialty practice diminishes in proportion to the decline in the expectancy of continued patient patronage.

In a managed care environment, provider agreements executed between HMOs and health care networks dictate the flow of capitated revenue. The goodwill value of a capitated practice increases directly with the number of covered lives under the agreement. The relationship between patient and doctor becomes less important whereas the relationship between the practice and the HMO or PPO becomes a major determinant of value. Patients and physicians may come and go, but the HMO or PPO and its pool of covered lives remain.

The *Goodwill Registry*, published by the Health Care Group of Plymouth Meeting, Pennsylvania, provides the average goodwill value of physician practices as a percentage of annual gross income.[9] Average goodwill values are broken down by specialty. The analysis entails simply adding the calculated goodwill value to the estimated value of the practice's tangible assets. The concern with using the *Goodwill Registry* is the lack of information available on the transactions that comprised the sample. Additionally, the figures provided are mean values, rather than median values, and can be heavily influenced by outliers. Finally, reliability of the data is an issue because it is impossible to verify the completeness or accuracy of the data provided by the respondents.

ANALYSIS OF MEDICAL PRACTICES

In performing an appraisal of a medical practice, factors described in IRS Revenue Rulings 59-60, 1959-1, and C.B. 237, should be considered.[10] These factors include the following:

- Nature and history of the practice
- Economic outlook and condition of the industry
- Book value of the stock and financial condition of the practice
- Earnings capacity of the practice
- Dividend-paying capacity
- Goodwill and other intangibles
- Prior sales and size of the block to be valued
- Market price of similar stocks actively traded in open markets

Specific Considerations

Any analysis of a medical practice should specifically consider the 10 risk-characteristic categories mentioned earlier in determining capitalization rates, plus physician compensation. These factors encapsulate the basic values the market may place on the quality of earnings of a particular medical practice.

Revenue Mix of the Medical Practice

An analysis of a medical group should consider its revenue mix. Revenue for a medical group is composed of FFS revenue and capitated revenue, in addition to ancillary service revenue. *FFS revenue* is a function of the number of patients regularly coming to the practice, the number of visits per patient, the gross fee charged per patient visit, and the ratio of realizable fees to total gross fees. It includes reimbursement from traditional indemnity insurers, Medicare, Medicaid, and PPOs. *Capitated revenue,* on the other hand, is simply a function of the number of enrollees assigned to the medical group and the capitated fee per enrollee. Enrollees for a medical group are the members of HMOs who have designated the group as their primary care provider. The capitated fees paid by the HMO are outlined in the provider agreement, and vary by copayment requirements as well as age and sex, based on the expected cost of providing designated health care services to individuals in each demographic segment.

As discussed earlier, a general trend in the revenue mix of medical groups is the shift from predominantly FFS revenue to capitated revenue, although FFS still constitutes the largest percentage of the typical group's revenues. For practices with capitated revenue, the analysis also should focus on the contracts and provider agreements with managed care payers.

Information on volume of patient visits and utilization of practice resources also must be addressed. Specifically, the valuation requires an estimate of the projected growth in capitated rates, enrollment, and the incremental expenditures required to handle growth.

Compensation Paid to Practice Physicians

One of the most important considerations in a physician practice valuation is the level and nature of compensation paid to the physician going forward in the compensation agreement. Physician practices are unique in that physician compensation typically is their largest expense, possibly equal to 35 to 70 percent of collections. If the physicians demand a high level of compensation, the expected return remaining for an investor is reduced; thus, the value (or front-end payment) of the practice is reduced. If the physicians are willing to accept lower salaries, the expected return for an investor is higher, which increases the practice's value, or front-end payment. If the physicians are willing to accept some downside risk in terms of compensation, the variability of the future cash flow is reduced and the expected return on investment is worth more.

Medical Practice Operating Expenses

When projecting the medical practice's operating expenses, it is important to determine whether the particular expense category is fixed, semifixed, or variable. *Fixed expenses* typically grow at a rate that approximates inflation, whereas *variable expenses* are more closely related to revenue production or a component of revenues, such as visits. *Semifixed expenses* may have a component tied to some level of production such as visits and a fixed component that grows at the rate of inflation. As a checkpoint, if aggressive growth assumptions have been made, the variable component of operating expenses must increase accordingly.

Medical Practice Assets and Liabilities

For the valuation of a going concern, the practice's earnings potential is the primary focus and individual assets are only a secondary concern. However, the financial appraiser must consider the assets that drive a practice's earnings potential. These can be divided into tangible and intangible assets. *Tangible assets* include such financial assets as cash, accounts receivable, supplies, and prepaid expenses; and such fixed assets as land, buildings, leasehold improvements, medical equipment, and office furniture. As discussed earlier, *intangible assets,* usually include trade names, provider contracts, patient records, employment contracts, covenants not to compete, favorable lease agreements, and unidentifiable intangible assets. Unidentifiable intangible assets account for a medical practice's ability to earn income in excess of a fair return on the aforementioned tangible and intangible assets, and are referred to as *goodwill* (discussed earlier). It is important to examine all the liabilities of the practice, including current, interest bearing, and contingent.

EXAMPLE OF A PRACTICE VALUATION

The determination of fair market value of a closely held medical group requires a thorough financial analysis of the subject group, including a review of historical operating results and an estimate of the group's representative and sustainable earnings capacity. The following analysis involves a hypothetical 30-physician, multispecialty medical group. The historical income statement, common-size income statement, and balance sheet are presented and analyzed for the past three fiscal years. Also, a five-year projected income statement and debt-free cash flow calculation is provided. Typically, five years is the minimum period that should be used for projections. In this example, the financial statements and related assumptions have been condensed and simplified for ease of presentation. Usually, the model is much more detailed in terms of assumptions and value drivers.

In addition to a review of financial statements, analysis of any medical group must include a review of all other pertinent information bearing on its future operating results and financial condition. This includes an analysis of the practice's qualitative factors, such as physician backgrounds, credentials, employment horizons, and so on. In addition, the analysis must consider a thorough understanding of the local market, including competition, market share, and managed care penetration. It is important not to underestimate the importance of how the qualitative factors affect value.

Historical Financial Analysis

Tables 11-1 and 11-2 present the historical comparative income statement and common-size income statement, respectively, for the sample medical group. As table 11-1 shows, revenue generated by the group increased at a compound annual rate of 5 percent, from $11,156,000 in 1994 to $12,300,000 in 1996.

Total operating expenses increased at a compound annual growth rate of 3.7 percent, from $4,838,000 in 1994 to $5,200,000 in 1996. Most

TABLE 11-1. Historical Comparative Income Statement

($000,000s omitted)

	1994	1995	1996
Total net revenues	$11.156	$11.714	$12.300
Operating Expenses:			
Direct nonphysician expenses	3.328	3.462	3.600
Other expenses	0.680	0.707	0.735
General & administrative	0.569	0.591	0.615
Depreciation	0.262	0.256	0.250
Total operating expenses	$4.838	$5.015	$5.200
Operating income before physician compensation	6.318	6.699	7.100
Physician compensation	6.195	6.442	6.700
Operating income	$0.124	$0.257	$0.400

TABLE 11-2. Historical Common-Size Income Statement

	1994	1995	1996
Total net revenues	100.0%	100.0%	100.0%
Operating Expenses:			
Direct nonphysician expenses	29.8	29.5	29.3
Other expenses	6.1	6.0	6.0
General & administrative	5.1	5.0	5.0
Depreciation	2.3	2.2	2.0
Total operating expenses	43.4%	42.8%	42.3%
Operating income before physician compensation	56.6	57.2	57.7
Physician compensation	55.5	55.0	54.5
Operating income	1.1%	2.2%	3.3%

of this increase is the result of the increase in direct nonphysician expenses, from $3,328,000 in 1994 to $3,600,000 in 1996, which is composed primarily of medical support salaries. Physician compensation increased at a compound annual growth rate of 4 percent, from $6,195,000 in 1994 to $6,700,000 in 1996. As a percent of revenue, physician compensation decreased from 55.5 percent in 1994 to 54.5 percent in 1996. The medical group's operating income increased from $124,000 in 1994 to $400,000 in 1996, representing a compound annual growth rate of 79.6 percent. Operating margin increased from 1.1 percent of net revenues to 3.3 percent.

Table 11-3 presents the medical group's historical balance sheet for the years ended 1994 through 1996. Current assets increased from $957,000 as of the year ended 1994 to $1,225,000 as of the year ended 1996. The largest component of current assets was accounts receivable, which increased from $816,000 as of the year ended 1994 to $900,000 as of the year ended 1996.

As discussed earlier in the section on the market approach, it is important to determine a level of earnings that is representative of the future performance of the practice, for at least the last historical period analyzed. Historical results are adjusted for the effects of one-time or nonrecurring charges to arrive at a practice's representative level of earnings. In the example, a group of physicians owns the real estate in which the medical group operates. An independent analysis of the rent charged to the medical group indicated that it was below fair market value; therefore, occupancy expense was adjusted to reflect increased rental expense. Other nonrecurring expenses can include one-time legal expenses and expenses related to a move or expansion. In determining the representative levels for the medical group, primary focus was given to the results of the most recent period in which nonrecurring expenses were removed. In table 11-4, the projected income statement for 1997 reflects the representative levels of earnings for the medical group.

Financial projections are an important part of the valuation analysis because, regardless of the medical practice's previous performance, a prospective buyer will participate only in its future earnings and cash flow. Management-prepared projections and their underlying assumptions must be checked for reasonableness when analyzing a practice. A projected income statement and a common-size income statement for the example medical group are provided in tables 11-4 and 11-5, respectively.

Future Revenues

The analysis of a medical group should include management-provided estimates of future revenues. The analyst should review these estimates of future operating performance for reasonableness after analyzing historical revenue and expense patterns, and prospective changes in reimbursement practices and capitated enrollment. As shown in table 11-4, total net revenues increased from $12,915,000 in 1997 to $15,698,000 in 2001, representing a compound annual growth rate of 5 percent. The medical group's payer mix, as measured by revenue, consists of 50 percent indemnity insurance, 20 percent managed care, 15 percent capitated HMO, and 15 percent Medicare/Medicaid. A detailed physician practice valuation will consider different revenue assumptions based on each type of revenue. However, in this example, only net revenues have been shown for ease of presentation.

TABLE 11-3. Historical Comparative Balance Sheet, 1994–1996

($000,000s omitted)	1994	1995	1996
Assets			
Current assets:			
Cash	$0.073	$0.123	$0.250
Accounts receivable	0.816	0.857	0.900
Other current assets	0.068	0.071	0.075
Total current assets	0.957	1.052	1.225
Net fixed assets	2.356	2.300	2.250
Other assets	0.050	0.050	0.050
Total assets	$3.363	$3.402	$3.525
Liability & equity			
Current liabilities:			
Accounts payable	0.465	0.482	0.500
Accrued expense	0.419	0.434	0.450
Other current liabilities	0.068	0.071	0.075
Current liabilities	0.952	0.988	1.250
Notes payable	1.411	1.335	1.250
Total liabilities	2.363	2.322	2.275
Total stockholders' equity	1.000	1.080	1.250
Total liabilities & equity	$3.363	$3.402	$3.525

TABLE 11-4. Projected Income Statement, 1997–2001

($000,000s omitted)	1997	1998	1999	2000	2001
Total net revenues	$12.915	$13.561	$14.239	$14.951	$15.698
Operating expenses:					
Direct nonphysician expenses	3.744	3.894	4.050	4.211	4.380
Other expenses	0.764	0.795	0.827	0.860	0.894
General & administrative	0.640	0.665	0.692	0.719	0.748
Depreciation	0.245	0.265	0.285	0.305	0.325
Total operating expenses	$5.393	$5.619	$5.853	$6.096	$6.347
Operating income before physician compensation	7.522	7.942	8.386	8.855	9.351
Physician compensation	6.968	7.247	7.537	7.838	8.152
Operating income	$0.554	$0.695	$0.849	$1.017	$1.199

TABLE 11-5. Projected Common-Size Income Statement, 1997–2001

	1997	1998	1999	2000	2001
Total net revenues	100.0%	100.0%	100.0%	100.0%	100.0%
Operating expenses:					
Direct nonphysician expenses	29.0	28.7	28.4	28.2	27.9
Other expenses	5.9	5.9	5.8	5.8	5.7
General & administrative	5.0	4.9	4.9	4.8	4.8
Depreciation	1.9	2.0	2.0	2.0	2.1
Total operating expenses	41.8%	41.4%	41.1%	40.8%	40.4%
Operating income before physician compensation	58.2	58.6	58.9	59.2	59.6
Physician compensation	54.0	53.4	52.9	52.4	51.9
Operating income	4.3%	5.1%	6.0%	6.8%	7.6%

Total Operating Expenses

As shown in table 11-4, the total operating expenses of the medical group are projected to increase at a 4.2 percent compound annual growth rate. Following is a breakdown:

- *Direct nonphysician expenses:* These consist of medical support compensation, medical supplies, and ancillary service expenses. Medical support compensation will typically be a fixed expense that grows at a level approximating inflation. However, to the extent that the valuation of the medical group assumes the recruitment or acquisition of additional physicians, medical staff will need to be added. Medical supplies typically are a variable expense based on some unit of production, such as visits. Additionally, the cost per visit should grow at a rate that approximates inflation. Likewise, ancillary service expense is growing at a production-based level of increase and incorporates an inflationary-based component. Direct nonphysician expenses are projected to increase at a compound annual growth rate of 4 percent.
- *Other expenses:* These consist of occupancy expense, outside professional services, and insurance. Occupancy expense and insurance expense normally are fixed expenses that will grow at a rate approximating inflation. A model contemplating aggressive growth assumptions will need to have adjusted occupancy expense if additional space is required for new physicians and

higher insurance expense due to the greater amount of malpractice insurance required with more physicians. In this example, operating expenses increased at a compound annual growth rate of 4 percent.

- *General and administrative expenses and depreciation:* General and administrative expenses are projected to increase at a 4 percent compound annual growth rate. Depreciation is expected to increase from $245,000 in 1997 to $325,000 in the year ended 2001. Projected depreciation was based on the tax life of existing and new fixed assets, and was calculated using an average total useful life of the equipment of approximately 10 years.

Physician Compensation

As mentioned earlier, a medical group's largest expense is typically physician compensation, which includes both salaries and benefits. In a valuation analysis, all expected payments to the physician must be incorporated into the projected income statement. As discussed earlier, for a reasonable investor to justify payment for a stand-alone medical group, some level of earnings must be available after paying operating expenses and physician compensation. This assumes that a structure contemplating a management fee is not being modeled. The level of earnings "left over," or operating income, drives the value of the practice.

The physician employee expense in table 11-4 increases from $6,968,000 in 1997 ($232,000 per physician) to $8,152,000 in 2001, representing a compound annual growth rate of 4 percent. As a percentage of revenue, physician employee expense decreases from 54.0 percent in 1997 to 51.9 percent in 2001. In this example, compensation included a base salary and benefits lower than historical levels, plus an incentive component.

Operating Income

The medical group's operating income as a percentage of revenue increases from 4.3 percent in 1997 to 7.6 percent in 2001. This increase in margin is due to the slightly higher growth in revenues than in operating expenses and physician employee expense.

Balance Sheet

The projected balance sheet for the medical group is provided in table 11-6. Total current assets are projected to increase from $1,519,000 in

TABLE 11-6. Projected Balance Sheet, 1997–2001

($000,000s omitted)

	1997	1998	1999	2000	2001
Assets					
Current assets:					
Cash	$0.485	$0.802	$1.226	$1.767	$2.419
Accounts receivable	0.955	1.003	1.053	1.106	1.161
Other current assets	0.079	0.083	0.087	0.091	0.096
Total current assets	1.519	1.888	2.367	2.964	3.676
Net fixed assets	2.205	2.140	2.055	1.950	1.825
Other assets	0.050	0.050	0.050	0.050	0.050
Total assets	$3.774	$4.078	$4.472	$4.964	$5.551
Liabilities & equity					
Current liabilities:					
Accounts payable	0.532	0.554	0.577	0.601	0.626
Accrued expense	0.488	0.508	0.529	0.551	0.574
Other current liabilities	0.079	0.083	0.087	0.091	0.096
Current liabilities	1.098	1.145	1.193	1.244	1.296
Notes payable	1.158	1.058	0.948	0.828	0.666
Total liabilities	2.257	2.203	2.142	2.072	1.961
Total stockholders' equity	1.517	1.875	2.330	2.892	3.589
Total liabilities & equity	$3.774	$4.078	$4.472	$4.964	$5.551

1997 to $3,676,000 in 2001. Total current liabilities increase from $1,098,000 in 1997 to $1,296,000 in 2001. When analyzing a medical group, an estimate must be made for a reasonable level of working capital necessary to operate the group. Any growth in the practice typically requires increased working capital requirements.

Discounted Cash Flow Analysis

As described earlier, the DCF method is used to determine the value of a medical practice, based on projected operating and financial performance. The four basic steps described are the following:

1. Determine the appropriate cash flows to discount, based on projected income statements for the subject practice.
2. Select an appropriate discount rate for the subject practice projections, based on an analysis of alternative investments.
3. Determine a terminal value for the subject practice, as of the end of the last period for which projections are available.
4. Determine value for the subject practice's TIC.

Determine Free Cash Flows

The cash flow figure used in the DCF approach represents more accurately the true cash flow being generated by the practice's operations. Often referred to as *free cash flow,* this figure is the cash available to all the capital providers of the medical group, regardless of the particular capital structure selected. Thus, the present value of a stream of these cash flows provides an indication of value for the group's TIC. Any assumptions regarding the medical group's capital structure must be incorporated into the discount rate applied to the projected cash flows.

The adjustments to projected operating income (EBIT), which were required to develop free cash flows, are shown in table 11-7. In general, free cash flow is equal to the earnings that would be available to common and preferred stockholders assuming no debt existed in the capital structure, plus the add-back of depreciation and other noncash expenses, and net of other projected expenditures, such as additions to working capital and property, plant, and equipment.

Table 11-7 reflects the projected change in working capital requirements of the medical group. The working capital requirements are relatively small, as this example reflects a relatively small amount of growth. The projected capital requirements are slightly less than the amount necessary to replace the existing owned assets over a 10-year period. Net fixed assets decrease from $2,205,000 in 1997 to $1,825,000 in 2001. (See table 11-6.) The estimated levels of capital expenditures are in line with historical levels. When valuing a medical group with aggressive growth assumptions, capital expenditure requirements must be analyzed for reasonableness, particularly if new physicians are assumed and additional space and equipment are required.

Determination of Discount Rate

After analyzing the risk characteristics of a particular medical group, a discount rate is selected. For instance, the extent to which the employed physicians are willing to accept an incentive compensation package in lieu of salary determines how much risk will be borne by the physicians versus the purchaser. As part of the transaction, the incentive package has been structured whereby compensation will be tied to performance. If revenue falls short of targeted levels, the medical group's physician compensation payments will be reduced. Thus, the distribution of possible outcomes for the group's earnings has a lower variance.

The discount rate reflects market conditions for medical groups, both locally and nationally, and the required rate of return for investments made by taxable, for-profit enterprises in entities with similar risk attributes. Consideration also is given to the caliber of physicians in the group as recognized leaders in the market, the group's market share in its service area, and its ability to attract and effectively perform under managed care contracts. For purposes of illustration, this analysis yields an estimated WACC for the medical group of between 16 and 19 percent.

Discounted Cash Flow Summary

As mentioned earlier, the discounted free cash flow calculations are provided in table 11-7. Based on the foregoing, the value indications using

TABLE 11-7. Discounted Cash Flow Analysis

($000,000s omitted)

Projected Debt-Free Cash Flow Calculation

	1997	*1998*	*1999*	*2000*	*2001*
Operating income	$0.554	$0.695	$0.849	$1.017	$1.199
less taxes @ 40.0%	0.222	0.278	0.340	0.407	0.480
Debt-free earnings	0.332	0.417	0.509	0.610	0.720
Plus: Depreciation	0.245	0.265	0.285	0.305	0.325
Less: Capital expenditures	(0.200)	(0.200)	(0.200)	(0.200)	(0.200)
Change in working capital requirement	0.014	(0.005)	(0.006)	(0.007)	(0.008)
Debt-free cash flow	$0.392	$0.477	$0.589	$0.708	$0.837

Total Invested Capital Calculation

		Year					
	WACC	*1997*	*1998*	*1999*	*2000*	*2001*	*Total*
Identifiable cash flows	16.0%	$0.364	$0.382	$0.406	$0.421	$0.429	$2.002
	17.0%	$0.362	$0.377	$0.398	$0.409	$0.413	$1.958
	18.0%	$0.360	$0.372	$0.389	$0.397	$0.397	$1.916
	19.0%	$0.359	$0.367	$0.381	$0.385	$0.383	$1.875

		Growth Rate				
	WACC	*1.0%*	*2.0%*	*3.0%*	*4.0%*	*5.0%*
Terminal value (perpetuity)	16.0%	2.458	2.659	2.892	3.163	3.484
	17.0%	2.217	2.388	2.584	2.809	3.073
	18.0%	2.008	2.155	2.321	2.511	2.730
	19.0%	1.826	1.952	2.095	2.256	2.440

		Growth Rate				
	WACC	*1.0%*	*2.0%*	*3.0%*	*4.0%*	*5.0%*
Total invested capital (perpetuity)	16.0%	4.460	4.661	4.894	5.165	5.486
	17.0%	4.175	4.346	4.542	4.768	5.031
	18.0%	3.924	4.071	4.237	4.427	4.646
	19.0%	3.701	3.828	3.970	4.131	4.316

the DCF approach yield an indication of total invested capital for the medical group ranging from $3,701,000 to $5,486,000, based on discount rates ranging from 16 to 19 percent and terminal growth rates ranging from 1 to 5 percent. For instance, the value of $3,701,000 is determined by adding the identifiable cash flows of $1,875,000 with the terminal value of $1,826,000, assuming a WACC of 19 percent and terminal growth rate of 1 percent. The next step is to allocate the value of the medical group to its various assets, including tangible and intangible assets. As discussed earlier, this step is used only to lend support to the valuation as determined from the income and market approaches. To arrive at the market value equity, the interest-bearing debt of the practice must be subtracted from its TIC.

As discussed, physician compensation agreements have a significant impact on value. The actual agreements accepted must be incorporated in the projections used to calculate value. In table 11-8, the figures on the left show how the indicated value decreases with an increase in the discount rate, holding all other factors, including physician compensation, at the previous levels projected. The figures on the right hold the discount rate constant at 16 percent and allow physician compensation to increase to the amounts indicated in 1997. As indicated, an increase in physician compensation from $6,968,000 in 1997 to $7,900,000 decreased the value of the practice from $4,894,000 to $124,000, assuming a 16 percent discount rate and 3 percent terminal growth.

Relative Risk Analysis

As mentioned earlier, in a comparative transaction method under the market approach, a relative risk analysis would be performed to compare the subject group with comparable groups. Through such comparisons, representative capitalization rates for the subject group's operating characteristics

TABLE 11-8. Effect of Discount Rate/Physician Compensation on DCF Value Indicators

Constant Projections[a]		*Constant Discount Rate*[b]	
Discount Rate	*Value*	*Compensation*	*Value*
16.0%	$4,894,000	$6,968,000	$4,894,000
17.0%	$4,542,000	$7,300,000	$3,195,000
18.0%	$4,237,000	$7,600,000	$1,660,000
19.0%	$3,970,000	$7,900,000	$124,000

[a]Assumes total physician compensation is $6,968,000 in 1997, and 3% terminal growth.

[b]Assumes discount rate of 16.0%.

TABLE 11-9. Multiple Summary

Indicated TIC Value	TIC/Physician[a]	TIC/Revenue[b]	TIC/EBIT[c]
$3,700,000	$123,000	.30	6.7
$5,500,000	$183,000	.45	10.0

[a]30 FTE physicians.

[b]Medical group stabilized revenue of $12,300,000.

[c]EBIT of $550,000.

are determined. A set of comparative transactions is selected from a proprietary database of medical practice transactions as well as from disclosures of public companies that have acquired physician practices. Capitalization rates are calculated from these comparable practices. Three multiples are used: TIC/physician, TIC/revenue, and TIC/EBIT. Based on an independent risk analysis comparing the comparable company transactions to the medical group, capitalization rates are established for the group.

In this example, based on a range of values for TIC of between $3,700,000 and $5,500,000, the implied range of TIC/physician multiples is from $123,000 to $183,000 per physician. The range of price-to-revenue multiples is from 0.30 to 0.45 times revenue. (See table 11-9.) The price to EBIT multiples ranged from 6.7 to 10.0. This range was selected to coincide, for illustrative purposes, with the range indicated from the DCF analysis.

The revenue generated by a single-specialty primary care practice per physician generally is less than revenue per physician for a multispecialty group. Based on this, the appropriate price-to-revenue multiple should be higher than the median price-to-revenue multiple given that single-specialty primary care medical groups command greater multiples.

CONCLUSION

The integration of physician practices is an ever growing phenomenon in the health care industry, brought on in large part by managed care. Prior to the purchase or sale of the practice, and before any type of integration takes place, a valuation of the practice must be performed.

Generally, physician practice integration is of two types: horizontal, affiliation among physicians and medical groups; and vertical, affiliation between physicians and hospitals or HMOs. In recent years, affiliation with a PPMC has become a very important integrating structure.

The valuation of physician practices first involves an analysis of the external environment, including reimbursement trends and managed care penetration, and an examination of the regulatory context in which the valuation is being performed. Generally, there are four types of methods used in a valuation: the income approach; the market approach; the cost approach; and the excess earnings approach, a hybrid of the cost and income approaches. In addition to certain specific considerations such as type of practice, payment mix, market and competition, and so on, analysis of a medical practice must include a look at the practice's revenue mix, physician compensation, operating expenses, and assets and liabilities.

References

1. Medicare and Medicaid Patient and Program Protection Act of 1987 (Washington, DC: U.S. Government Printing Office, 1987).

2. Internal Revenue Code Section 501(c)(3).1, Internal Revenue Code (Washington, DC: U.S. Department of the Treasury, 1990).

3. P.L. 101-239 and P.L. 103-66. U.S. Statutes at large. 101st Congress and 103d Congress (Washington, DC: U.S. Government Printing Office, 1993 and 1995).

4. Black, Henry Campbell, *Black's Law Dictionary,* 5th ed. (St. Paul, MN: West Publishing Co., 1979), p. 537.

5. Internal Revenue Service, Revenue ruling 68-609. *Internal Revenue Bulletin, Cumulative Bulletin, 1968-2* (Washington, DC: U.S. Government Printing Office, 1969).

6. C. Kaiser, P. Haney, and T. J. Sullivan, 1995 Continuing Professional Education Guide (1996).

7. *Metropolitan Bank v. St. Louis Dispatch Co.*, 149 U.S. 436, 446 (1893). *United States Reports. Cases Judged in the Supreme Court* (Washington, DC: U.S. Government Printing Office, 1893).

8. *Wilmont Fleming Engineering Co. v. Commissioner* (Dec.33,634), 65 T.C. 847, 861 (1976). *U.S. Tax Cases* (Chicago: Commerce Clearinghouse, 1976).

9. Health Care Group, *The Goodwill Registry* (Plymouth Meeting, PA: Health Care Group, 1996).

10. IRS revenue ruling 59-60, *Internal Revenue Bulletin, Cumulative Bulletin, 1959-1* (Washington, DC: U.S. Government Printing Office, 1959); IRS revenue ruling 1959-1, *Internal Revenue Bulletin, Cumulative Bulletin, 1959-1* (Washington, DC: U.S. Government Printing Office, 1959); and IRS revenue ruling 59-237, *Internal Revenue Bulletin, Cumulative Bulletin, 1959-2* (Washington, DC: U.S. Government Printing Office, 1960).

12

Physician Practice Acquisition/Divestiture: A Case Study

Patrick M. Hurst

According to a report published in November 1995 by Moody's Investor Service, most hospitals are not making money on physician practice acquisitions due to lower-than-expected revenue or higher-than-expected costs.[1] Certain issues cannot be avoided in hospital acquisitions of medical practices. For example, a number of up-front costs are related to the transaction, such as engaging the necessary legal and financial advisors. Integration of the medical practice into a larger organization also creates additional costs. For instance, many small physician practices offer minimal health and other benefits to their nonphysician staff. To avoid benefits discrimination, the buyer typically must provide the employees who remain with the practice after the transaction with benefits consistent with the buyer's existing employees. This may increase the practice's overhead. It is anticipated that these increased costs would be offset by the many benefits to physician integration, including administrative synergy, economies of scale, and concentration of negotiating power.

Many of the events that lead to disappointing financial results from practice integration can be avoided. Some of the greatest pitfalls are overpaying for the practice, structuring the transaction with poor incentives, and improperly integrating the practice after acquisition. The intent of this chapter is to provide a specific plan that can be used for buying or selling a medical practice so that many of these mistakes can be avoided.

This chapter describes the process involved in buying or selling physician practices, from both the buyer and seller perspective. From a buyer's perspective, many of the issues discussed apply equally to hospitals, HMOs, physician practice management companies (PPMCs), and other medical practices and groups. However, certain of the issues are highlighted from a hospital's perspective, given its regulatory constraints. Further, the chapter offers case studies of practice integration transactions involving a sole practitioner and a multispecialty medical group.

ACQUISITION PROCESS

The acquisition process involves a number of steps, including the following:

1. Develop a strategy
2. Prepare for the acquisition or sale process
3. Gather market information
4. Establish a dialogue
5. Perform a valuation
6. Present a letter of intent
7. Conduct due diligence

Step 1. Develop a Strategy

The first step in pursuing physician integration is to develop an overall strategy defining the objectives to be met and determining how integration meets them. For the buyer, the objectives behind an integration strategy include establishing and enhancing market share in physician services and participating on the front end of managed care contracting. The seller's physician integration objectives generally include protecting or enhancing compensation through synergy, eliminating administrative responsibilities, and attaining liquidity for the owners. Both buyer and seller also may be interested in entering into global capitation arrangements through physician-hospital integration.

If it is determined that physician integration will satisfy the organization's objectives, an appropriate structure must be selected. The alternatives range from an independent practice association (IPA), where physicians maintain their own practices and a fair degree of autonomy, to a staff model integrated delivery system (IDS), where the physicians sell their practices and enter into an employment agreement with the buyer.

The arrangements with physicians can range from contractual relationships through physician-hospital organizations (PHOs) or IPAs to acquisition and employment relationships or, alternatively, a foundation model where the physicians donate their practices to a 501(c)(3) tax-exempt entity controlled by an independent board and operated for the benefit of the community. The type of structure will be based on the buyer's strategic objectives but also will depend largely on state laws and Internal Revenue Service (IRS) regulations for tax-exempt organizations. (See chapters 13 through 17 for discussions of the various structural models.)

Step 2. Prepare for the Acquisition or Sale Process

Preparing for the acquisition or sale process includes deciding on advisors (both financial and legal), establishing process parameters, and dealing with postacquisition integration.

Deciding Whether to Engage a Financial Advisor The buyer/seller must decide whether a financial advisor will be engaged to facilitate the transaction. The advantages of engaging a financial advisor, for both buyer and seller, include identification of candidates, objective analysis, and assistance in negotiations. One of the most important advantages of a third-party representative is that it protects the buyer-seller relationship, regardless of whether the deal goes through. The most important asset in a medical practice acquisition, like many service organizations, is the relationship between providers and their clients. The relationship between buyer and seller after the transaction is critical to preserving the value of the practice following the transaction. The buyer wants the newly employed physician to remain highly motivated and the patients and managed care organizations (MCOs) to continue their patronage. If direct negotiations between buyer and seller become acrimonious, the relationship may suffer irreparable damage. Another element is added when the selling physicians are represented by the practice administrator, who is in the uncomfortable position of negotiating the terms of the transaction with his or her potential future managers. Most important, a financial advisor can contact a number of buyers and, to the extent the practice is interested, conduct an auction process to maximize price.

Deciding Whether to Engage a Legal Advisor Another decision to be made early in the process is the engagement of a legal advisor. Myriad regulations exist that govern the relationships among patients, payers, physicians, and employers. The regulations surrounding medical practice acquisitions can be divided into several areas: Medicare/Medicaid antifraud and abuse,[2] Internal Revenue Code 501(c)(3),[3] Stark I and II,[4] antitrust laws; and corporate practice of medicine laws. The enforcement agencies can include the IRS, the Department of Health and Human Services (DHHS), the Health Care Financing Administration (HCFA), the Federal Trade Commission (FTC), and the states in which the physician practices. These regulatory issues need to be addressed early in the process because they will have a significant impact on the structure of the transaction. The many risks inherent in a medical practice acquisition and employment arrangement, for both buyers and sellers, necessitate qualified legal assistance.

Establishing Process Parameters An important decision for the seller to consider is whether to negotiate exclusively with one party or initiate an auction process. If the physician group has a strong relationship with a potential buyer, the benefits of exclusive negotiations include speed and confidentiality. Additionally, the physicians may feel more comfortable entering into such an extensive relationship with a familiar party. However, there is less assurance in a negotiated sale that the medical group is getting the highest price available. An auction process, where a financial advisor conducts a continuous process of soliciting competitive bids from a number of prospective buyers, generally will result in a higher price. The downside is that the process may take longer and the medical group is subject to a greater degree of due diligence from one or more outside parties.

Dealing with Postacquisition Integration Throughout the entire acquisition process, buyer and seller should prepare for one of the most important steps: postacquisition integration. The most critical step toward integration, particularly for a publicly traded practice management company, is that of integrating financial reporting and budgeting. A number of PPMCs have seen their stock prices drop substantially due to inadequate financial and management information system (MIS) integration. Integration of the physician group into the IDS requires not just an understanding of how it will fit into the existing structure, but also how the different physicians will work together and how prepared they are for managed care contracting.

Step 3. Gather Market Information

Both buyers and sellers should gather information on the current marketplace for medical practices. That includes investigating prices paid in comparable medical practice acquisitions, identifying the universe of potential buyers and sellers, and understanding a potential candidate's alternatives to the transaction. However, it should be noted that information on acquisitions of comparable medical practices provides only one measure of value and that, generally, it is very difficult to know all the relevant terms and conditions of the transaction, particularly the nature and level of compensation received. This information is usually misleading and leads to unrealistic expectations, which often negatively affect transactions.

Identifying information on the universe of buyers and sellers helps determine how aggressively the buyer needs to pursue a particular practice. In a midsize community, for example, there may be only a handful of potential buyers and only one or two that are actually competing to acquire medical practices—although it should be kept in mind that efforts to acquire a practice may trigger an aggressive response from competitors.

A list of integration candidates in the market area should be developed. The buyer's acquisition criteria will include service area; the nature and type of practice; performance or activity requirements; and experience with, and openness toward, managed care contracting. The candidates should be evaluated and prioritized in terms of performance and desirability. Next, an assessment should be made of how well the physicians' personality and style fit into the buyer's organization. Finally, the physicians' willingness to relinquish control over much of the practice should be determined.

Knowledge of prospective buyers and sellers will assist both the buyer and the selling practice in evaluating the current market for the practice. The universe of potential medical practice buyers includes other medical practices that may wish to pool their strength and create a larger clinic, as well as hospitals, PPMCs, MCOs, and insurance companies. The market information will help both buyers and sellers determine the benefits of integration versus the costs and benefits of alternative courses of action.

Step 4. Establish a Dialogue

Once the candidates have been identified and screened, the next step is to establish a dialogue with the prospective partner. The buyer should attempt to outline its strategy to acquisition candidates and explain how the practice fits into the buyer's strategy. The physicians should be encouraged to express concerns about integration. This is an important first step toward preparing for postacquisition integration. An up-front approach with physicians will set the tone for good-faith negotiations.

Managing Physician Expectations If the buyer intends to reduce the selling physician's compensation through a management fee, the buyer should be prepared to demonstrate how increased revenue, synergy, and economies of scale will increase physician compensation. Managing expectations will prove to be extremely important. The "rumor mill" will generate a wide variety of stories about prices paid for medical practices. Although the accuracy of rumors is extremely unreliable, physicians are nonetheless influenced by their existence. Managing physician expectations is a concern for both buyer and seller. For buyers, inflated expectations of purchase price and compensation terms may get the physicians' attention. However, they also may do irreparable harm to the prospects of a transaction. If a physician who always believed that $100,000 was an appropriate value for his or her practice hears that an offer may exceed $200,000, the physician will quickly adjust his or her assessment of what is a reasonable offer. If an offer is extended at $150,000, the physician will likely be disappointed, even though it is 50 percent above his or her initial expectation. Getting the physician to accept the $150,000 offer now will prove to be very difficult.

Every effort should be made to control the type and amount of information being released to the sellers, especially if the acquisition team is fairly large. The same holds true for medical groups given how difficult it is to satisfy a large majority of shareholders. Usually, a control group is established with a lead person identified to control the flow and nature of information. This is extremely useful in preventing a buyer from trying to splinter a group by negotiating separately with different physicians in the same group.

Obtaining a Majority of Affirmative Votes Although acquisitions of many companies require simple majority shareholder votes, buyers of physician groups often are interested in affirmative votes for an acquisition in excess of 80 percent of shareholders. This desire for a strong vote in favor of the transaction is based, of course, on the importance of the physicians' working relationship with the buyer after the transaction. If 20 percent of the physicians are not satisfied and feel coerced into the transaction, the acquisition may be a failure. Securing a favorable vote of more than 80 percent can be difficult, especially for practices with a certain age and specialty mix.

The constituents of a medical group can be divided into three age groups with very different interests and motivations: older physicians, who are nearing retirement and have experienced turbulent change in recent years; middle-aged physicians, who also have seen tremendous change but still have 15 to 20 years left to practice; and younger physicians, who already may have adjusted to the new environment and have their entire careers ahead of them. If a compensation reduction is required to generate a certain purchase price, it may be relatively easier to encourage the older physicians to support the deal. However, persuading the younger shareholders is a different matter. The different interests of specialists versus primary care physicians complicate this matter further. Communicating the various benefits of integration to each of these groups is necessary to generate affirmative votes.

Engaging an Advisor A medical group initiating an auction process generally will engage a financial advisor to establish a dialogue. He or she will prepare descriptive material related to the group, identify potential buyers, and assist in analyzing, structuring, and negotiating the terms of the transaction. The dialogue between prospective buyers and the group should take place primarily through the financial advisor. This will prevent the disclosure of information that may compromise the group's bargaining position. Prior to giving information to prospective buyers, a confidentiality agreement must be executed. Often prospective buyers are also primary competitors, and the information provided to them may harm the group.

Physician groups pursuing exclusive negotiations with one particular party can still benefit from hiring an advisor. An advisor may be engaged to control the dialogue as well as assist in analyzing, structuring, and negotiating the terms of the transaction. Control of the dialogue between the practice and a buyer is even more important where a relationship already exists between a medical group and the buyer. Often hospital buyers will casually "lobby" with physicians in hospital hallways to persuade them or to gain valuable information on the practice's bargaining position.

Step 5. Perform a Valuation

Both buyer and seller need an estimate of the value of the practice. (See chapter 11.) A valuation can range from an informal preliminary valuation to a formal one. Its results will provide information the buyer needs to formulate a bid. A valuation helps the seller establish realistic expectations and provides a framework the seller can use to evaluate bids.

From a valuation standpoint, some of the most important elements of an acquisition strategy are consistency, thoroughness, and reasonableness. Although all these elements are obviously important from a regulatory standpoint, it is the consistency of the valuation approach that is important from a physician integration standpoint. Because physicians will compare offers, differences in price that cannot be explained by differences in performance characteristics could lead to difficulties in negotiating with a practice and integrating it, once acquired.

Despite all the discussion in recent years about physician integration, most markets are still very fragmented and dominated by small practices. Given a fragmented market, most hospitals acquiring physician practices will be evaluating a high volume of practices. For example, if the goal is to develop an IDS that will, in a fully capitated environment, keep a 300-bed hospital operating at 70 percent capacity where days per thousand (commercial and senior) are 350, the hospital will require a patient base of more than 215,000. Assuming the average primary care physician can serve as gatekeeper for 2,000 patients, the size of the primary care physician network needs to be more than 100. Thus, it will be critical to develop a systematic approach to handle the volume of practices analyzed.

Fair Market Value Many buyers of medical practices are restricted from paying more than the fair market value of the practice on a stand-alone basis. This is true if the funds for an acquisition are provided by either a tax-exempt organization or a provider in a position to receive referrals. No consideration can be given to increased earnings that may arise due to synergy or economies of scale resulting *specifically* from a combination of the two entities. One commonly used definition of *fair market value* is: "The price at which an asset would change hands between a willing buyer and willing seller when the former is not under any compulsion to buy and the latter is not under any compulsion to sell and both parties are able, as well as willing, to trade and are well-informed about the asset and the market for that asset."[5]

Fair market value does not assume any specific buyer. In contrast, the determination of *investment value,* which is the specific value of an asset to a particular investor (or class of investors) for individual investment reasons, allows for the incorporation of factors that may be unique to a specific buyer. However, an argument has been made that the cost savings a practice could realize, either on its own or through consolidation with other practices, can be considered in the valuation. Certain buyers of medical practices such as PPMCs and MCOs are not precluded from paying above fair market value for a medical practice.

Buyer and seller should understand the factors that influence value. The factors that influence the value of any business are outlined in various guidelines used by appraisers, including IRS rulings 59-60, 1959-7, and C.B. 237.[6] A medical practice analysis should specifically address the following factors:

1. The practice's geographical service area
2. Demographics of the patient population
3. Principal competitors
4. Historical and projected financial performance
5. Future capital spending requirements
6. Payer mix
7. Age, health, and reputation of physicians
8. Experience with managed care
9. Possible contingent liabilities
10. The assets to be involved in the transaction, which may or may not include buildings, automobiles (typically excluded), accounts receivable, and ancillary service facilities or equipment

The valuation must consider all forms of physician compensation (base, incentive, deferred, and so on) in the determination of available cash flows. And finally, it must assume that state and federal taxes are paid even if the buyer is tax exempt. To do otherwise would confer benefits of the buyer's tax-exempt status to the seller.

Approaches to Valuing Medical Practices All the various methods used to value medical practices are derivatives of three basic approaches: income, market, and cost. (See chapter 11.) The most appropriate approach depends on the circumstances of each transaction. As discussed in chapter 11, the income approach, particularly the discounted cash flow (DCF) approach, is the most useful to medical practice valuation. The DCF approach allows for a number of interdependent factors to be modeled.

The DCF method relies heavily on projections of future performance. When constructing the projections, the practice should provide evidence supporting such growth prospects as area population growth, increases in the practice's market share at the expense of competitors, or negotiations for new managed care contracts. Also, there should be discussion on how growth in patients and visits will impact expenses. The analysis also should determine whether new physician or medical support staff will need to be hired or whether additional space and equipment will be needed.

A DCF model can be used to illustrate the trade-offs between the upfront payment for the practice and compensation commitments to the physicians. The valuation model also will allow the buyer to demonstrate operational and market synergy that will enhance future physician compensation. Demonstrating these benefits is crucial to satisfying the concerns of younger physician shareholders for whom a reduction in compensation may outweigh the value of their portion of the purchase price.

The income and market approaches should be used to determine the practice's total invested capital (TIC). (See chapter 11.) The TIC encompasses the value of all the assets necessary to operate the practice and generate the projected earnings, including the practice's fixed assets, accounts receivable, and intangible assets. Often accounts receivable are not included in the transaction and remain the property of the seller. The receivables are a necessary component of the practice because they provide liquidity following the transaction and satisfy the patient and payer desire for credit terms. If they are not acquired, the practice must forego cash until they are built up to an appropriate level. If the accounts receivable are not being acquired in the transaction, the value of the practice must be adjusted accordingly to reflect this fact. Also, it is extremely important from the outset to state explicitly whether the valuation includes the practice's cash and liabilities.

Once the TIC is determined, an allocation of the value to the component assets may be conducted. This allocation will determine the reasonableness of the practice valuation as well as assure a tax-exempt buyer that the entire purchase price can be specifically allocated. Often the concern is that if cash were paid but the assets cannot be reasonably identified (for instance, goodwill), the payment was made as an inducement for future referrals rather than a particular asset.

Step 6. Present a Letter of Intent

Once a purchase price and major terms are agreed to, the buyer should present a letter of intent. The letter is generally nonbinding and, if acceptable to both parties, opens up the process to more extensive due diligence and negotiation of detailed aspects of the transaction. However, both buyer and seller need to recognize that, although the letter of intent is an important step in the process, the deal is far from closed.

Step 7. Conduct Due Diligence

The due diligence process allows the prospective buyer to conduct a detailed investigation into the practice's financial, accounting, contractual, and operational activities. The procedure covers such areas as the following:

1. Corporate matters (articles of incorporation, bylaws, and so on)
2. Employment matters (agreements with physicians and key management members, personnel policies and procedures, and retirement plans)
3. Tax matters (federal and state returns, and tax bases of stock and assets)
4. Financial matters (income statement items, balance sheet items, accounts receivable, pricing issues, payer mix, and so on)
5. Contracts (managed care, management, billing and administration, noncompetition, physician service agreements)
6. Insurance
7. Regulatory matters
8. Litigation

TERMS OF THE TRANSACTION

The terms of the transaction are outlined in a purchase agreement and an employment agreement.

Purchase Agreement

The purchase agreement indicates the purchase price, whether the transaction is an acquisition of stock or assets, and what assets are being acquired. As mentioned earlier, if the accounts receivable are not included in the asset purchase, the practice valuation needs to reflect that. The payout of the purchase price may be immediate; however, the buyer may propose an installment sale or an earn-out. In an installment sale, the future payments to the seller generally are not at risk, whereas earn-out payments are contingent on physician or practice performance. There are important tax implications to the structure of the purchase agreement and the payout of the purchase price.

Employment Agreement

The employment agreement indicates base salary and benefits, compensation structure, incentive compensation, deferred compensation, duration of employment, and other agreements including service and lease agreements (if physician-owned assets are being used in the future operations of the practice) and restrictions on competition. Although the purchase price of the medical practice is clearly important, it should not receive a disproportionate amount of attention during the negotiations because the compensation a physician receives in an employment agreement can be greater than the purchase price, depending on the agreement's duration. The compensation structure may be straight salary, salary plus incentive, percent of professional collections, or percent of collections net of certain expenses. The employment agreement also may provide for deferred compensation. Under most interpretations of Stark I and Stark II legislation, a physician who provides services reimbursed by Medicare cannot be provided a direct incentive based on the amount of ancillary revenue (designated services) produced by that physician.

Compensation arrangements where a simple base salary is being paid may make sense for a retiring physician where the buyer is encouraging the physician to "transition" his or her patient base to a new physician. However, outside this specific circumstance, compensation structures without productivity incentives can often lead to disappointing performance. A base salary coupled with an incentive compensation structure gives physicians some level of comfort on the downside while keeping them motivated to maintain productivity and cost-efficiency. Compensation arrangements based on percent of professional collections are effective in maintaining productivity, but the physician has little incentive to control costs. A popular arrangement used by PPMCs acquiring medical groups is to compensate physicians based on a percent of professional collections after operating expenses have been paid. This keeps the involved parties interested in both productivity and cost containment. In many PPMC transactions, physicians accept a reduction in compensation of perhaps 10 to 20 percent in exchange for a larger purchase price. The expectation is that synergy and economies of scale generated by the combination of the two entities will increase collections after operating expenses sufficiently to compensate for the reduction in salary and benefits.

The duration of employment agreements vary, generally between 1 and 10 years; however, salary terms are rarely guaranteed for more than five years. Management service agreements between a clinic and a management services organization (MSO) that has acquired the clinic's assets can range from 10 to 40 years. Finally, restrictions on competition usually are structured so as to become effective after a physician voluntarily leaves the practice. The duration and service area or patient relationships they cover vary depending on state laws, the type of community, and the nature of patient relationships. In some settings, a one-year, five-mile noncompetiton restriction can be devastating, whereas in other settings, the impact of this same restriction to a departing physician may be nominal.

As the details of the purchase and employment agreements are being negotiated, the parties to the transaction must assess the importance of each issue to both themselves and each other. Many elements that have little to do with money may be equally important to the two parties. These may include the following:

- Governance of practice entity
- Degree of independence
- Community outreach programs
- Commonality of goals

COMPARISON OF A SMALL PRACTICE TO A LARGE GROUP TRANSACTION

Transactions involving small medical practices generally are very different from those involving large groups. For example, employment terms in a small medical practice acquisition often are much more important than those in the purchase agreement. Following are a discussion of the characteristics of small and large practice transactions, and two case studies.

Transactions involving a small practice (from a sole practitioner up to a three-physician group) tend to be negotiated exclusively with one or two buyers that already have a relationship with the seller. The significant amount of effort required of outside buyers to evaluate a practice sometimes precludes them from pursuing small practices. Thus, the seller usually is facing a more limited market. The market for large medical groups includes a number of health care buyers and occasionally (although rarely) includes financial buyers. Many buyers of large groups use the acquisition as a means of entry into the group's markets.

The purchase price for a small practice will likely not include significant intangibles. Most of the intangible assets of a small practice are tied directly to the individual physicians. This intangible asset is often referred to as *professional goodwill.* (Goodwill is discussed in chapter 11.) It is very difficult to transfer professional goodwill to the buyer in a practice transaction. In a sense, the buyer tends to "rent" the physician's professional goodwill by providing competitive compensation. *Practice goodwill,* on the other hand, refers to going-concern value, economies of scale, and trade name recognition, which *can* be transferred to a buyer. Larger groups may contain a substantial amount of practice goodwill value.

The difference between professional and practice goodwill can be illustrated by estimating the impact on the practice of a physician's departure. If the practice operates in a competitive environment with fee-for-service (FFS) patients, there may be very little reason for the patients to continue to patronize the practice after the physician leaves. This would indicate that most of the intangible value is professional goodwill. However, if many of the patients are tied into managed care contracts, are familiar with other physicians in the practice, or are drawn to the practice because of its trade name or unique attributes, the loss of patients following the physician's departure may be limited. This would support a greater degree of practice goodwill.

Sole Practitioner Case Study

General Hospital is a 300-bed facility located in Suburbia, a suburb of 50,000 people just outside Anywhere, a city with one million inhabitants. For the past 12 months, General has been developing a physician network and has five physicians employed, with another three close to signing. The hospital anticipates operating a network with at least 50 primary care physicians.

Dr. Smith is a 48-year-old family practice physician who has been in private practice in Suburbia for 18 years. Approximately 80 percent of his patients reside within a five-mile radius of his practice and the remaining 20 percent are located throughout the Anywhere metropolitan area. Dr. Smith's practice moved six years ago to its current location from a smaller office two miles away. He estimated that he lost 10 percent of his patients due to the move but quickly recovered the lost volume through new patients. Dr. Smith owns the building in which the practice operates through another entity that has been charging the practice rent of \$25,000 (\$16.67/sq. ft.). The practice's payer mix, measured by revenue, is as follows: indemnity insurance, 50 percent; managed care, 30 percent;

capitated HMO, 15 percent; and Medicare/Medicaid, 5 percent. Dr. Smith maintains privileges at General Hospital and St. Mary but mainly uses General Hospital. He completed his residency at General Hospital and has a good relationship with the staff.

For the past few years, Dr. Smith has been considering integration strategies. Although his income has been growing steadily, he feels he is working much harder to balance the practice's managerial, administrative, and clinical requirements. As more of his patients shift from indemnity to discounted FFS, he is forced to accept lower realization of his charges. His capitated revenue has been increasing, and he believes these accounts are profitable but does not have the systems in place to determine profitability.

General Hospital approached Dr. Smith about joining its physician organization by selling his practice and entering into an employment arrangement. Soon after General expressed an interest in a transaction, St. Mary also indicated that it was starting a physician network and was interested in acquiring Dr. Smith's practice. St. Mary is a member of a five-hospital network that covers the Anywhere metropolitan area. Due to the development of the hospital network, St. Mary's practice development plans were put on hold. General Hospital, on the other hand, already had a team assembled with financial and legal advisors. They also had conducted an analysis of the primary care physicians' market in Suburbia.

After hearing brief presentations from both hospitals about the strategy behind their practice development and the level of progress, Dr. Smith decided to enter into serious discussions with General. The two primary reasons for the decision were his relationship with General's administration and his concern that, because St. Mary's had only recently initiated practice development efforts, he would be one of the first physicians in the organization. Dr. Smith decided that if General were able to put a fair deal on the table, he would not "shop" the practice to competing buyers.

General Hospital submitted an information request to Dr. Smith and, after receiving historical financial statements, began the valuation analysis. During the interview, Dr. Smith indicated that he had been amortizing a noncompetiton agreement related to a practice he acquired three years ago. The last payment was made in 1995, and the restrictions were lifted. He indicated that the selling physician did not pose a competitive threat to the buyer even though the agreement had expired. The interview with Dr. Smith uncovered the fact that rent paid by the practice is above market. After consulting with a real estate agent, General Hospital determined that the normalized rent would be $12/sq. ft., or $18,000.

Adjustments were made to the most recent financials to reflect the rent, lower amortization expense, and the agreed-upon level of physician compensation. The practice's comparative income statement and the adjustments for representative earnings and balance sheet are presented in tables 12-1 and 12-2, respectively.

Dr. Smith discussed his expectations for future growth at the practice, indicating modest increases in FFS rates and capitated rates. Certain expenses, such as staff salaries, rent, and general and administration costs were expected to increase at the rate of inflation, whereas variable

TABLE 12-1. Dr. Smith's Comparative Income Statement

	1994	*1995*	*1996*	*Representative Fiscal 1996*
Net revenue	$255,800	$268,800	$285,600	$285,600
Direct expenses	49,500	52,700	56,700	56,700
Overhead expenses	68,100	71,000	75,350	63,350
Total operating expenses	117,600	123,700	132,050	120,050
Operating income before physician expenses	138,200	145,100	153,550	165,550
Physician compensation	134,610	140,900	148,700	159,000
Pretax earnings	$ 3,590	$ 4,200	$ 4,850	$ 6,550

TABLE 12-2. Dr. Smith's Comparative Balance Sheet

	1994	*1995*	*1996*	*Representative Fiscal 1996*
Cash	$10,000	$11,000	$11,000	$11,000
Receivables	0	0	0	36,000
Other current assets	2,000	2,500	2,500	3,500
Current assets	12,000	13,500	13,500	50,500
Net fixed assets	30,000	28,000	27,000	27,000
Covenant not to compete	10,000	5,000	0	0
Total assets	$52,000	$46,500	$40,500	$77,500
Accounts payable	0	0	0	10,000
Accrued expenses	3,000	2,500	2,500	2,500
Current portion of long-term debt	1,000	1,000	1,000	1,000
Current liabilities	4,000	3,500	3,500	13,500
Deferred taxes	0	0	0	10,400
Long-term debt	15,000	9,000	3,000	3,000
Shareholder equity	33,000	34,000	34,000	50,600
Total liabilities and shareholder equity	$52,000	$46,500	$40,500	$77,500

expenses, such as medical supplies and ancillary expenses, were expected to increase based on both inflation and the volume of visits.

General Hospital performed a discounted cash flow (DCF) analysis based on the information Dr. Smith provided. The projected available debt-free cash flow is shown in table 12-3, and a summary of the assumptions underlying the projections follows.

The projections assume that physician compensation includes a base of $150,000 and benefits of $10,000. Dr. Smith also would receive incentive compensation of 50 percent of professional collection in excess of a hurdle, which is $250,000 in 1997. The incentive is structured so that Dr. Smith will not receive any increase in compensation unless professional collections increase. On the downside, the base salary is predicated on a minimum number of professional encounters. If encounters decrease, his base salary may be decreased proportionately. Given that the practice is still FFS, the incentive structure is based on professional production. The employment agreement leaves open the provision that, if capitated revenue is generated, the incentive would be restructured.

TABLE 12-3. Dr. Smith's Projected Available Debt-Free Cash Flow

	1997	*1998*	*1999*	*2000*	*2001*
Projected Income Statement					
Net revenue	$316,700	$344,700	$360,400	$374,800	$389,900
Direct expenses	59,524	62,375	64,921	67,488	70,136
Overhead expenses	65,253	67,748	70,338	73,029	75,822
Total operating expenses	124,777	130,122	135,259	140,516	145,958
Operating income before physician expense	191,923	214,578	225,141	234,361	243,942
Physician compensation	177,740	192,515	201,213	209,261	217,632
Earnings before interest and taxes	$ 14,183	$ 22,063	$ 23,928	$ 25,023	$ 26,310
Calculation of Available Cash Flows					
Earnings before interest and taxes	$ 14,183	$ 22,063	$ 23,928	$ 25,023	$ 26,310
Less income taxes	(5,389)	(8,384)	(9,093)	(9,509)	(9,998)
After-tax earnings	8,794	13,679	14,835	15,514	16,312
Add depreciation	4,399	4,553	4,712	4,877	5,048
Less capital expenditures	(5,175)	(5,356)	(5,544)	(5,738)	(5,048)
Less increase in working capital	(1,657)	(1,546)	(1,608)	(1,672)	(1,739)
Available debt-free cash flow	$ 6,361	$ 11,330	$ 12,395	$ 12,981	$ 14,573

The DCF approach, along with the comparable transaction and excess earnings approaches, supported a range of values of between $95,000 and $105,000. Of this amount, $35,000 was the value of the fixed assets (estimated by a machinery and equipment appraisal), $40,000 was the value of the working capital, and the remaining $25,000 represented the intangible assets. This amount was further allocated to medical charts and records ($10,000) and a noncompetiton agreement ($15,000).

Once Dr. Smith accepted the valuation model as reasonable, a letter of intent was executed that proposed a purchase price of $100,000 for the practice's assets. The buyer would assume reasonable accruals and accounts payable, but the seller was responsible for eliminating the practice's interest-bearing debt from the proceeds. After many discussions regarding governance, tax issues, continuity for employees, and compensation issues, the offer was accepted and agreed to.

Multispecialty Medical Group Case Study

ABC Medical Group is a 30-physician multispeciality medical group with three practice sites in and around Anywhere. It was established in 1962 by five specialists. During the early 1980s, the practice recognized the need for a more secure base of referral sources and began recruiting and acquiring primary care physicians. In the early 1990s, the group was able to enter into full-capitation contracts, where it is responsible for all professional and ancillary services in an ambulatory setting.

ABC Medical decided to explore strategic affiliation with other health care organizations to increase its market strength, access capital for growth, attain shareholder liquidity, and improve medical management techniques. The comparative income statement and the comparative balance sheet are presented in tables 12-4 and 12-5, respectively.

ABC Medical engaged an investment bank to estimate the value of the practice, identify prospective buyers, prepare descriptive material, and negotiate and close a sale transaction. The descriptive memorandum prepared included information on the practice's history, current operations, range of services, facilities, payer mix, competition, patient demographics, utilization management, and malpractice coverage.

The initial list of potential buyers included other groups, hospitals, PPMCs, MCOs, and insurance companies but was narrowed down following a discussion with the group's management. The companies on the revised list all were contacted by the investment banker on a confidential basis to gauge their level of interest. Those that expressed interest were sent a memorandum following execution of a confidentiality agreement.

After a month, initial bids were received from four of the prospective buyers in the form of nonbinding "letters of interest." The next two

TABLE 12-4. ABC Medical Group's Comparative Income Statement

	1994	1995	1996
Net revenue	$20,372,000	$21,188,000	$22,164,000
Direct expenses	7,150,000	7,460,000	7,850,000
Overhead expenses	4,910,000	5,275,000	5,745,000
Total operating expenses	$12,060,000	$12,735,000	$13,595,000
Operating income before physician expense	8,312,000	8,453,000	8,569,000
Physician compensation	8,029,392	8,185,632	8,269,085
Pretax earnings	$ 282,608	$ 267,368	$ 299,915

TABLE 12-5. ABC Medical Group's Comparative Balance Sheet

	1994	1995	1996
Cash	$350,000	$375,000	$400,000
Receivables	2,600,000	2,650,000	2,700,000
Other current assets	200,000	250,000	250,000
Current assets	3,150,000	3,275,000	3,350,000
Net fixed assets	2,000,000	2,200,000	2,500,000
Other noncurrent assets	250,000	275,000	310,000
Total assets	$5,400,000	$5,750,000	$6,160,000
Accounts payable	$1,000,000	$1,050,000	$1,100,000
Accrued expenses	3,000,000	3,100,000	3,300,000
Current portion of long-term debt	100,000	100,000	100,000
Current liabilities	4,100,000	4,250,000	4,500,000
Long-term debt	400,000	400,000	400,000
Shareholder equity	900,000	1,100,000	1,260,000
Total liabilities and shareholder equity	$5,400,000	$5,750,000	$6,160,000

months involved an exchange of additional information from the seller and more detailed proposals from the buyers. The proposals addressed purchase price, compensation structure, governance issues, synergy that could enhance compensation, and advantages of affiliating with each particular buyer. Given corporate practice of medicine restrictions in this state, each of the proposals contemplated the creation of an MSO that would hold the clinic assets and a professional corporation that would employ the physicians.

Finally, the bidding process was narrowed down to two buyers that were asked to submit their final and best offers prior to entering into exclusive negotiations. The investment banker and the group management reviewed these final bids in detail. The purchase price was offset by reductions in physician compensation related to the buyer's management fee of 15 percent. The management fee, however, was offset by administrative and marketing synergy that would increase physician compensation. The group management compiled projections for the buyers that recognized certain synergy that reasonably could be attained. The investment bank created a model to evaluate the trade-off between purchase price and compensation, as well as the prospective benefits of the synergy. This model was utilized to assess various alternatives, including variations to management fees, in terms of rates and method of calculation; physician compensation, including base and incentives; and a front-end payment. (See table 12-6 for a summary of the model.)

On a representative basis, average compensation per physician with the buyer's 15 percent management fee decreased by more than 10 percent. In the absence of growth or synergy, the reduction was projected to worsen as fixed costs increased and revenue was squeezed. Historically, fixed assets were kept low and were projected to increase. The group was reminded, though, that, in the absence of a transaction, physician compensation was at risk of being reduced. One of the more difficult aspects of any physician practice transaction is making the physicians comfortable with a reasonable base case that recognizes the challenges of remaining independent. Agreement on the parameters of the base case form a point of departure from which any proposed final agreement can be measured.

Under the scenario presented above, the reduction in compensation was offset by growth in capitation as well as expected reductions in outside medical services and administrative staff. Physician compensation in 1997 was projected to approximate the 1996 level, with upside potential if projected levels were surpassed. Given the management fee and compensation parameter, a front-end payment acceptable to both parties was reached. Once the physicians were comfortable with the prospective synergy and the proposed purchase price, they agreed to enter into exclusive negotiations with the buyer. The two parties closed a transaction six months later.

CONCLUSION

Buying or selling a physician practice is a complex transaction with many pitfalls that can lead to failure. However, there is a method for negotiating

TABLE 12-6. ABC Medical Group's Projected Available Debt-Free Cash Flow

	1997	*1998*	*1999*	*2000*	*2001*
Projected income statements					
Net revenue	$23,589,696	$24,841,670	$26,003,715	$27,043,864	$28,125,618
Direct expenses	8,006,154	8,194,904	8,480,954	8,770,865	9,073,547
Overhead expenses	5,878,400	6,105,256	6,340,896	6,585,663	6,839,909
Total operating expenses	13,884,554	14,300,160	14,821,850	15,356,528	15,913,455
Operating income before physician expense/ management fee	9,705,142	10,541,510	11,181,865	11,687,336	12,212,163
Management fee	1,455,771	1,581,226	1,677,280	1,753,100	1,831,824
Physician compensation	$8,249,371	$8,960,283	$9,504,585	$9,934,235	$10,380,338
Calculation of Available Cash Flow					
Management fee	$1,455,771	$1,581,226	$1,677,280	$1,753,100	$1,183,824
Less income taxes	(553,193)	(600,866)	(637,366)	(666,178)	(696,093)
After-tax earnings	902,578	980,360	1,039,913	1,086,922	1,135,731
Add depreciation	439,875	455,271	471,205	487,697	504,767
Less capital expenditures	(517,500)	(535,613)	(554,359)	(573,762)	(504,767)
Less increase in working capital	121,620	(105,955)	(110,193)	(114,601)	(119,185)
Available debt-free cash flow	$946,573	$794,063	$846,566	$886,257	$1,016,546

the acquisition process that will minimize the dangers and bring the venture to a satisfactory conclusion.

The acquisition process involves several steps, the first of which is to develop an overall strategy for the future of the practice. The second step, preparing for the acquisition or sale, includes deciding what kinds of advisors to use, establishing process parameters, and dealing with such postacquisition issues as integrating financial reporting and budgeting. These steps are followed by looking at the current marketplace for physician practices, establishing a dialogue between buyer and potential sellers, performing a practice valuation, presenting a letter of intent, and finally, conducting a due diligence process, which enables the prospective buyer to look at the practice's operations in depth.

As a final step, the buyer presents a purchase agreement and an employment agreement. Together, these agreements outline what is being purchased and give the details of the employment arrangement, including the physician compensation structure, duration of employment, and restrictions on competition.

The purpose of the acquisition process is to bring as much information to the table as possible so that buyer and seller can make an informed decision. It is only through a thorough and systematic process such as this that both can reap benefits from the transaction.

References

1. Moody's Investor Service, *Credit/Survey Moody's Investor Service*. New York, Nov. 1995.

2. Medicare and Medicaid Patient and Program Protection Act of 1987 (Washington, DC: U.S. Government Printing Office, 1987).

3. Internal Revenue Code Section 501(c)(3).1, *Internal Revenue Code* (Washington, DC: U.S. Department of the Treasury, 1990).

4. P.L. 101-239 and P.L. 103-66. U.S. Statutes at large. 101st Congress and 103d Congress (Washington, DC: U.S. Government Printing Office, 1993 and 1995).

5. Black, Henry Campbell, *Black's Law Dictionary,* 5th ed. (St. Paul, MN: West Publishing Co., 1979), p. 537.

6. IRS revenue ruling 59-60, *Internal Revenue Bulletin, Cumulative Bulletin, 1959-1* (Washington, DC: U.S. Government Printing Office, 1959); IRS revenue ruling 1959-7, *Internal Revenue Bulletin, Cumulative Bulletin, 1959-1* (Washington, DC: U.S. Government Printing Office, 1959); and IRS revenue ruling 59-237, *Internal Revenue Bulletin, Cumulative Bulletin, 1959-2* (Washington, DC: U.S. Government Printing Office, 1959).

PART V

Evolving Physician Practice Organizational Models

Part V consists of five chapters focusing on various methods for organizing the delivery of physician services. Chapter 13, "Integrated Delivery Systems," introduces this section with a discussion of the forces in today's health care environment that are causing physician integration and group practice formation. Chapter 14, "Independent Practice Associations," focuses on an organizational practice strategy developed for the purpose of contracting with managed care companies. Chapter 15, "Group Practice Affiliation Structures," discusses three categories of physician group structures: partially integrated physician organizations (with special emphasis on group practices without walls), fully integrated medical organizations, and "supergroups."

Chapter 16, "Physician-Hospital Organizations," and chapter 17, "Physician-Hospital Organizations: Strategy, Structure, and Conduct," explore the potential of this vertically integrated model for delivering cost-effective health care. Both chapters use case studies to illustrate physician-hospital organization success as an important link in the restructuring of the American health care industry.

13

Integrated Delivery Systems

Allan Fine

The current health care market is forcing physicians to become more aggressive in managing the business operations of their practices and in examining the potential of collaborating with their hospital partners or, in some instances, other physician groups. These factors have contributed to the rise of integrated delivery systems (IDSs) and managed care organizations (MCOs), two types of structures with which physician groups traditionally have not had close, collaborative relationships.

This chapter provides an overview of the conditions and circumstances in the current health care environment that are leading to physician integration and group practice formation. It also introduces four principal types of integration that are discussed in detail in subsequent chapters.

PHYSICIAN GROUP PRACTICE FORMATION

An integrated delivery system is an organized system of health care providers designed to span a broad range of health care services. Objectives of an IDS include:

- Creating and managing an entire continuum of care
- Accessing the market on a broader basis
- Optimizing cost and value and clinical outcomes
- Accepting and managing a full range of financial arrangements
- Accepting responsibility for arranging and/or providing a set of benefits to a defined population

- Financing projects of strategic and clinical value
- Aligning financial incentives among participants
- Operating under a cohesive management structure so that where or from whom a patient receives care in the system becomes financially immaterial

Factors Contributing to Physician Group Practice Formation

A number of significant changes have been occurring in the American health care delivery system that are, and will continue to be, contributing factors to the demise of solo practice (discussed in chapter 3) and the advent of physician aggregation, or group practice formation. These changes include, but are not limited to, the following:

- Continued decline in inpatient utilization
- Shift in reimbursement
- Impact of medical management
- Decline in specialist income, in addition to an oversupply of specialists
- Increased demand for primary care physicians (PCPs)
- Economic credentialing
- Purchaser willingness to create "steerage" or channeling mechanisms for directing employees to preferred providers
- Realization of a single payment to be shared by multiple providers
- Interdependence on physician colleagues for overall performance, particularly under a capitated system
- Risk of being excluded from a managed care contracting opportunity
- Difficulty for solo practitioners to respond to evolving purchasers' demands (for example, outcomes information, patient satisfaction, and so on)
- Risk of existing patient base being lost to other physician groups selected by purchasers and payers

To adjust for these changes, physician groups will increasingly need to focus on the following:

- Persuading their colleagues to modify their practice styles and educating them on how this can be done
- Managing physician resistance to change
- Anticipating change and developing a vision and process for successful implementation

- Learning how to practice and articulate the values critical to managed care (high quality and low cost)
- Becoming more receptive to the use of midlevel providers (such as nurse practitioners, physician assistants, nurse anesthetists, and so on) as well as to the changing roles of PCPs and specialists
- Adapting to changes in compensation programs
- Establishing service standards and acknowledging that part of their performance will be measured by their ranking
- Being open to challenging each other in terms of identifying optimal modalities, treatment protocols, and diagnostic methods and to importing new knowledge from outside the organization
- Balancing the mix of fee-for-service (FFS) and capitation reimbursement

Impact of Capitation on Physician Group Formation

Physician groups will need to establish financial systems enabling them to more effectively negotiate contracts based on capitation. (See chapter 5 for a discussion of capitation arrangements.) In many instances, becoming part of a provider network enhances their ability to gain leverage when negotiating with MCOs and payers. Physicians will have to apply case management principles to practicing under a capitated environment.

The goal of capitation risk sharing will be to provide an incentive for hospitals and physicians to be cognizant of the cost of services provided. Capitation offers a myriad of benefits to both physicians and hospitals. Physicians are able to lock in market share, more accurately predict cash flow, have a greater degree of physician-hospital interdependence, better align incentives, and realize greater performance rewards. Hospitals are able to share risk with the physicians, more accurately predict medical costs, and see added incentives for physicians to be cost-effective.

As physicians prepare for accepting capitation, they can anticipate that the following events will likely transpire:

- Changes in physician practice patterns
- Declines in office visits, admissions, and length of stays
- Additional payment denials and days in accounts receivable
- Increased administrative requirements

Capitation requires enormous shifts in physician priorities. New physician priorities will focus primarily on decreasing cost through:

- Emphasis on prevention
- Administration of fewer tests

- Use of fewer specialists (for example, physicians themselves must channel enrollees to a decreasing panel of specialists in order to obtain the required incentives)
- Lower hospital utilization
- Increased reliance on information and data

Physician groups will need to gain experience in managing the transition to capitation. Some of the patient issues they will need to consider include:

- *Making capital allocation decisions:* Determining and allocating levels of capital required to develop and implement a system will effectively allow physician groups to administer capitation contracts.
- *Assessing information system needs:* Capital will be required to develop the system's capability to monitor physician performance, lengths of stays, and practice patterns related to modalities.
- *Measuring and reporting quality and outcomes:* This information will need to be disseminated both internally (to other physicians withing the group) as a mechanism to encourage change in practice styles and to serve as a barometer of acceptable standards, and externally (to managed care organizations, payers, and employers) as evidence of the group's superior outcomes and their adherence to quality standards.
- *Aligning incentives:* This will ensure that the economic and clinical targets are compatible and that physician performance is rewarded by meeting these goals.

EXPECTATIONS OF THE INTEGRATED DELIVERY SYSTEM IN A PAYER-DRIVEN ENVIRONMENT

In today's health care environment, decision making is passing from providers to payers. The payment environment is changing from an FFS to a capitated system where an IDS will serve all the medical needs of a defined population. Although competition will continue to be fierce, there will likely be greater value placed on collaborating with other health care organizations in order to deliver cost-effective health care services.

In this environment, a number of expectations have been placed on IDSs. They will be expected to contribute to all of the following:

- Delivering more cost-effective health care services
- Improving their ability to position for changes in their local markets
- Producing physician leaders

- Enhancing the quality of the administrative management of health care organizations
- Decreasing duplication of ancillary services, facilities, and equipment

However, the challenge for IDSs will be to document and prove that their existence decreases cost and increases quality and access. Physician leadership and commitment will be vital ingredients for success.

DEVELOPMENT OF PARTNERSHIPS

As IDSs evolve, "partnerships" will emerge between provider, payer, and patient. At a minimum, strong partnerships should be based on certain tenets, including the following:

- Each party treats the other fairly and with respect.
- Each party communicates with the other.
- In the end, all parties are content with the partnership that creates mutual benefits.

Further, IDSs should expect that MCOs and payers will attempt to align incentives enabling provider and payer to share equally in risk and reward. Moreover, the IDS must take the initiative to ensure that this alignment occurs. It must be achieved with an exchange of information, which, at a minimum, includes routine updates on performance, making the transition to electronic data interchange and adhering to requirements of HEDIS (Health Plan Employer Data and Information Set) and the NCQA (National Committee for Quality Assurance). (See chapter 9.) The impact on physicians will be in the creation of physician incentive fund models that take into account quality measures, patient satisfaction, and other indicators besides simply claims paid.

IDSs will be challenged to focus not only on service but also on clinical improvement and education. Some IDSs will internalize those functions and conduct the activities themselves. Other IDSs will outsource those activities and rely on organizations that have considerable experience in offering them. The expectation is that the IDS does not have to make considerable up-front investments in developing an infrastructure to support these functions, but rather capitalizes on the "economies" and experience of outside vendors.

Further, physicians should anticipate that their payer and MCO partners will expect them to demonstrate a concern with patient wellness and with managing the health care needs of individuals, never placing patients in the middle of a dispute. Physicians also will be expected to show a willingness to work with the plan on medical management and member service issues and to accept payment in accordance with market reimbursement. Member service issues may include explaining the physician referral process to patients (for example, the gatekeeper model) and/or referring patients to physicians within the panel and clarifying authorization protocols. Finally, physicians will be expected to submit encounter data—patient utilization information that is used to evaluate clinical efficacy and cost efficiency related to physician performance.

REEVALUATION OF PHYSICIAN GROUP STAKEHOLDERS

Although IDSs, MCOs, the government, and employers are viewed as the principal change agents in the health care delivery system confronting physician group practices, it should not be assumed that physicians and patients have no power in IDS and MCO arrangements. In fact, they will continue to be key stakeholders, although individual patients will become less important from a business point of view. In contrast, the influence of government on physician groups will grow, particularly due to proposed changes in Medicare and Medicaid, which are increasingly requesting larger shares of physician groups' patient mix.

Employers also will exercise substantial power over physician groups. Employers have come to recognize that the cost of health benefits are rising rapidly relative to other operational and benefit expenses. Thus, increasingly, they are forming coalitions and purchasing alliances for the purposes of selecting and negotiating health care services from specific providers.

In addition, system hospitals are expected to have greater power over physician groups than independent hospitals do. Indeed, to be viable in the future, most hospitals are realizing they probably will have to become part of a health care system. As IDS prevalence grows, physicians will have to align themselves and become increasingly more committed to this structure. The proverbial system of referrals will diminish, thereby affecting the independent hospital's ability to operate.

Physician groups will have to attribute a greater level of importance to service and quality when considering patient satisfaction. Purchasers and payers of health care services are demanding positive patient outcomes, which can only be enhanced through a strong physician-patient relationship. Physician groups will be under increasing pressure from their stakeholders to demonstrate high levels of performance in the areas of cost, quality, and access. Those groups unable to do so will risk their relationships to their IDS stakeholders.

MODELS OF INTEGRATED DELIVERY SYSTEMS

IDSs can incorporate physician practice groups in a number of ways. They can acquire the practice and employ its physicians, acquire the assets of the practice and manage it, provide full or partial management, or offer managed care support. Federal and applicable state law will strongly influence selection of the final structure. Currently, the most common IDS system models are independent practice associations (IPAs), group practices without walls (GPWWs), physician-hospital organizations (PHOs), and management services organizations (MSOs). An emerging form of physician integration is the physician organization (PO). In addition, hospitals and physicians are pursuing other integration models that might better suit their needs and specific situations.

Independent Practice Associations

IPAs are legal organizations of independent physicians who have joined together for the purpose of organized group contracting with MCOs. IPA physicians typically work in their own offices. Some IPAs use the services of a management company to assist in administering their contracts and helping them with administrative activities such as claims processing, membership, utilization management, and quality assurance. Generally, IPA physicians treat both managed care and private patients.

The IPA contracts with MCOs at a capitated rate that includes all physician services. It does not necessarily use capitation to reimburse member physicians.

The following are some advantages of IPAs:

- Start of contracting
- Start of risk sharing
- Maintenance of physician control
- Maintenance of private practice
- Minimal amount of capital
- Short lead time for development

The advantages of IPAs include a greater ability to share risk and obtain managed care contracts compared to other models (PHOs, for example) by offering more convenient geographic access, limiting specialist membership, and proving success in bearing risk. By contrast to a staff model HMO, an IPA requires less capital to start up and operate and appears to have physicians who are better motivated than are salaried staff.

The disadvantages of IPAs include the following:

- Low access to capital
- Low probability of centralized utilization management

- Unlikelihood of management information system coordination
- Lack of overhead consolidation
- Open-access problems
- Loose-knit organization
- Tenuous commitment from physicians
- Physician ability to be in multiple IPAs

IPAs typically comprise a large number of independent physicians, which limits their ablity to leverage resources, achieve economies of scale, and modify physician behavior.

IPAs are discussed in greater detail in chapter 14.

Group Practices without Walls

The legal structure of an IPA can vary and includes models in which the entity is a general partnership and those in which it is a professional limited liability company (LLC). Often the initial step taken by physicians considering integration, the GPWW model can evolve into a fully integrated group model. Typical services offered by the GPWW include the following:

- Billing
- Scheduling
- Group purchasing
- Data management
- Nonphysician staffing
- Merged revenues

GPWWs are generally formed by private practice physicians who aggregate their practices into a single legal entity but continue to practice medicine in independent locations. The entity consists of a legal merging of all assets of the physician practices rather than acquisition of only the tangible assets. GPWWs are owned solely by member physicians.

The advantages of GPWWs include:

- Less capital investment is required of physician members.
- Physicians have a greater degree of autonomy.
- There is potential for cost savings through economies of scale.

Under a GPWW arrangement, there is some alignment of incentives because physicians' personal incomes are affected by the performance of the group as a whole. Its legal structure enables the GPWW to negotiate and contract with MCOs on behalf of all members of the group.

The disadvantages of GPWWs include the following:

- They may create liability exposure for certain physician partners, depending on the selected structure (for example, general partnership).
- They may not be conducive to expedient decision making.
- They offer little integration between the hospital and its physicians.
- There is little overhead consolidation.
- Risk sharing is difficult.

In this model, physicians generally remain independent and typically continue to practice in the style to which they have become accustomed, which in essence limits the ability of the GPWW to achieve efficiencies.

GPWWs are discussed in greater detail in chapter 15.

Physician-Hospital Organizations

PHOs are legal organizations composed of physicians and a hospital(s). They may be joint ventures between IPAs and a hospital seeking to become a single-point contracting source with MCOs. In some instances, the PHO accepts full risk for all physician and hospital services; in other cases, it negotiates as an agent for the IPA and hospital. PHOs typically provide administrative services, and PHO physicians generally work in their own offices. Like IPA physicians, PHO physicians treat both managed care and private patients.

Often PHOs are the initial attempt by hospitals and physicians to develop an economic relationship for delivering and financing health care services. Different structures have been used for PHOs, including not-for-profit corporations (both taxable and tax-exempt), for-profit corporations, and LLCs. In some instances, a physician organization (PO) is formed initially, in which all participating physicians are members/shareholders, and in turn the PO and the hospital each holds more than half of the PHO's stock or voting interest.

The advantages of PHOs include the following:

- They serve as a solid first step in developing a significant physician-hospital relationship (that is, they engender dialogue and cooperation).
- They serve as a vehicle for physicians and the hospital to accept global capitated payment (in states where such activities are permitted).
- They provide a vehicle for physicians and the hospital to share in incentive/risk pools (again, in those states where it is legal).
- Potentially, they can address corporate practice of medicine issues (discussed in chapter 10) in states that preclude greater forms of integration.

- Less capital investment is required in comparison to other integrated models.
- They spread overhead.

The disadvantages of PHOs include the following:

- They present some antitrust risks if competing hospitals and physicians participate on their board and committees.
- Depending on governance and control issues, the potential exists for voting impasses.

PHOs frequently fail to enhance contracting ability because they are perceived as offering marginal value over existing MCO contracts with providers. Open PHOs (open to any medical staff member who meets minimum credentialing requirements) compared to closed PHOs (that limit physician membership by specialty and/or practice profiling) tend to be unattractice to MCOs because of specialist domination. There are political sensitivities to establishing closed PHOs because high-admitting specialists generally do not want to be excluded from participation.

Many provider networks are evaluating the potential of creating super PHOs. Common roles for the super PHO include:

- Negotiate managed care contracting with joint risk sharing
- Establish standards of care
- Monitor delivery of cost-effective care
- Compile, analyze, and disseminate clinical performance and financial information
- Oversee primary care development

If the super PHO is to be successful, it must have authority to contract exclusively on behalf of its members. The advantages of super PHOs include:

- They enable provider networks to respond to payer demands for geographic accessibility and high-quality, cost-effective care.
- They provide vehicles for joint program development and joint ventures.
- They can address common "nemeses" or competitors.

The disadvantages of super PHOs include:

- They do not represent a stable, long-term structure for an IDS.
- There are potential legal risks.
- They fail to reduce capacity or eliminate duplication of services.

- They have limited ability to raise capital.
- They present problems resulting from dissimilarity of components of different PHOs.

A super PHO will neither slow the process for change nor eliminate competition among network members or ensure that all parties will succeed equally. A network should consider developing a super PHO if some of the following conditions exist:

- It has the financial strength.
- It possesses a strong position in the local market.
- It is attractive to payers because of its quality, its cost efficiency, and the geographic area served.
- It provides an adequate primary care base.
- At least one viable, functioning PHO exists among network members.
- A caring vision exists between physicians and management.
- There is a compatible culture and values.
- There is minimal or no overlap in service area.

Organizations probably should not consider developing super PHOs if they are located in mature managed care markets, if powerful local systems already exist, or if major payers and purchasers will not contract with PHOS. (PHOs are discussed in greater detail in chapters 16 and 17.)

Management Services Organizations

An MSO is a legal entity that can provide support services to medical practices. It can be owned by hospitals, MCOs, or outside management companies. Physicians can either purchase services from the MSO or sell their practice to it.

There are many variations in MSO structure, from a wholly owned hospital subsidiary to a physician equity model, to a joint venture between a hospital and physicians' not-for-profit corporations, for-profit corporations, LLCs, and partnerships. Most MSOs are designed as taxable, for-profit corporations that enhance their ability to access capital.

The advantages of MSOs include the following:

- They enable physicians to participate with the hospital (if the MSO is owned by the hospital) without becoming major investors.
- Physicians retain ownership of practice and medical records.
- Physicians may find the joint venture MSO attractive because they have equity interest in it.

- The hospital does not have to negotiate with physicians regarding purchase of practice or goodwill issues.
- The hospital and physicians share regulatory compliance responsibilities.

The disadvantages of MSOs include the following:

- The MSO relationship does not require referrals to a specific hospital.
- MSOs may require a large capital investment, depending on the level of MSO services provided.
- They do not offer a vehicle for physicians and hospital to share in cost savings from managed delivery of inpatient and outpatient care.
- There is minimal integration with physicians' results. They may still only resemble IPAs.

Under MSO arrangements, physicians remain independent practitioners, enabling them to shift loyalties, and this in turn limits the ability of the MSO to shift resources in response to evolving market conditions.

It is anticipated that MSOs will have an increased need for capital and will experience a trend toward a greater degree of participation by physicians as equity shareholders. Moreover, there will likely be a strong demand for professional management of the various MSO structures as they evolve from a business office service bureau to group or network management. (MSOs are discussed in greater detail in chapters 18 through 21.)

Physician Organizations

An emerging form of integration that warrants special attention is the physician-directed network, or PO model. The PO is an unregulated joint venture of physicians organized for the purpose of facilitating their managed care contracting initiatives. Significant capital resources are required to build and operate a PO. These resources primarily come from physician practices. The perceived advantage of a PO is that it offers physicians the opportunity to work together on a collaborative basis without having to merge, which obviates the need to grapple with the political, emotional, legal, and financial considerations that exist in a full-scale merger of a large number of practices. However, many POs often do merge after the physicians reach a comfort level with each other and have a track record of working closely together.

Additionally, the PO is able to introduce advanced information systems without having to take over the detailed office management of every medical practice. Physicians can continue to use their own billing and practice management systems, and the PO typically will contract with a managed care information vendor to connect the detailed information from each physician's office to a master computer system that reaggregates the information and puts it into a managed care format. Because of the physician committee structure, the PO tends to establish its own regulatory provisions.

Although currently not a large number of POs are successful, it is expected that the number will increase. Successful POs require a nucleus of strong physician leaders who are able to take decisive action beyond simply conceptual consideration. It probably is a reasonable hypothesis that, as physicians become more educated in managed care, they will become more receptive to, and realistic about, the PO structure.

Physicians who are part of successful POs tend to:

- Understand the importance of establishing and enforcing credentialing/criteria for participation of prospective physicians
- Select hospitals individually regardless of their perceived network boundaries
- Recognize that health care is delivered on a regional rather than national basis
- Select a core group of physicians or a steering committee to whom they are willing to delegate and who will have power in making decisions
- Be decisive and determined to have the organization continue to make the changes necessary to be a viable entity in an evolving managed care market
- Actively participate in the PO by attending meetings and staying abreast of developments within the organization

FUTURE EXPECTATIONS

The health care industry will continue to undergo major changes that inevitably will result in the ongoing development and redesign of various physician-hospital integrated delivery models. Many of the structures that exist today are at best transitional steps to the ultimate goals: establishing more integrated models and enabling the parties at a minimum to assume risk, exchange information (both clinical and financial), and measure performance and quality.

It is likely that physician-directed managed care will increase and that physicians will more aggressively explore both participation in and development of collaborative contracting models. Single-specialty

POs will likely merge into multispecialty POs in an attempt to respond to market demands. Many POs and group practices will begin evaluating the feasibility of developing insurance products, either on their own or in collaboration with hospitals that are amenable to extending significant control to physicians. Financial gains by these new entities will be the result of managing care appropriately, rather than selling insurance. Moreover, physicians and hospitals participating in these organizations will realize profits by appropriately managing risk for defined populations and simultaneously providing a high standard of medical care.

The changes occurring in the health care industry are prompting physicians to be more inclined to consider becoming part of integrated models that possess certain characteristics, such as:

- Management by dedicated, respected physician leaders
- Member physicians who accept or embrace the realities of managed care
- Possession of adequate capital
- Physician-driven quality assurance and utilization review
- Financial incentives based on success under capitation
- Strong ties between PCPs and specialists
- Proactive alliances with MCOs, insurers, and employers
- Responsiveness to rapidly changing and specific local market needs

As we witness the demise of solo practice, the aggregation of physician groups, the decline of FFS medicine, the decrease in inpatient utilization, and the increase in managed care penetration throughout the United States, certain conclusions can be drawn regarding physician practices in IDSs. These include:

- No single IDS model or formula is applicable for every organization.
- Every geographic market, as well as every physician practice style, degree of managed care penetration, and competition, is different.
- Initiatives by MCO, insurer, and employer vary by market.
- A phenomenon is emerging in some markets whereby MCOs are beginning to resemble providers and, conversely, some providers are developing the capabilities to take on the characteristics of MCOs.
- Increased interest exists in both managing and acquiring physician practices not only by hospitals and physician groups, but also by professional practice management firms.

CONCLUSION

When selecting an integrated model, physician groups will have to make key decisions on which physicians will be permitted to participate, how risk will be managed, and which affiliation option offers the maximum level of professional and personal satisfaction. Although there is much debate, and even ambiguity, in terms of precisely defining the future of medical care delivery, it is reasonably certain that the current integrated structures—IPA, GPWW, PHO, MSO, and PO—will evolve to a much more sophisticated level than currently exists or is even contemplated.

14

Independent Practice Associations

Gordon D. Brown, PhD

The development of independent practice associations (IPAs) is almost synonymous with the development of managed care; IPAs were initiated for the purpose of contracting with managed care companies, and their future will be defined by the managed care market and the competitive forces within it. In the rapidly changing health care marketplace, IPAs have demonstrated their effectiveness and, to a degree, their superiority as organizational forms of practice. They are the most prevalent form of medical practice structure, accounting for about 47 percent of the annual growth in managed care and making up 65 percent of the managed care market.[1]

The popularity of IPAs is due, in part, to the fact that they can be organized around existing physician practices. This enables physicians to maintain their current practice patterns, thus requiring minimal start-up time and capital. However, this strength of building on historic structures and practice patterns might be diminished as managed care organizations (MCOs) begin to redeploy their medical resources. If IPAs are unable to adjust, their strength could become their weakness. However, if they are able to make the transition, they will evolve toward more structured institutions with greater corporate influence on practice. Thus, the challenge for these organizations will be to compete more aggressively for managed care contracts and to change their members' practice patterns while retaining important elements of physician independence. To date, the IPA structure has proved to be adaptable, but also fragile and vulnerable, subject to failure or assimilation into better-structured institutions with more organizational control.

As integrated systems become the predominant structure for health care delivery, IPAs will have to integrate with other providers. For example, IPAs already have partnered with hospitals to form physician-hospital organizations (PHOs). Such partnerships provide IPAs with capital and commitment for investments in primary care clinics, information systems, and their own HMOs. However, these relationships, too, will impose greater organizational influence on IPA institutions and increase their corporate complexity.

This chapter explores the structures of the principal IPA models. It examines each structure's strengths and weaknesses as an organization and discusses how each will need to position itself strategically in the face of ongoing change in the health system.

DEFINITION OF THE IPA

An IPA is an organization of physicians created for the purpose of forming a legal entity through which to negotiate and manage contracts or to enter into joint ventures with other organizations. Originally, IPAs were developed to contract with HMOs and to serve the enrolled population of the HMO plan as a health care provider. They were attractive because they enabled physicians to maintain their independent practice, a strong tradition in the U.S. health system.

IPA growth was greatly stimulated by the Health Maintenance Organizations Act of 1973, which:

- Recognized the IPA as an acceptable form of organized medical practice
- Provided an infusion of money for IPA development
- Greatly contributed to the recognition of managed care as an appropriate form of health care delivery[2]

STRUCTURE OF THE IPA

In an IPA, physician income is derived primarily from the performance of the "individual practice." The specific type of IPA structure depends on the reason for its being organized and the level of competition it is experiencing within the managed care market. There are three basic types of IPAs: the created model, the established model, and the direct-contract model, each with different variations.

Created Model

The created model refers to an IPA that was created by another organization, typically an HMO, for the purpose of risk contracting. The IPA is a separate legal entity that is linked to its partner organization contractually. The IPA can be described as a legal "shell" with little corporate commitment from physician members, little influence over their individual practice behavior, and little corporate power to chart a strategic direction. Physician behavior is influenced in a created IPA through such financial incentives and operating rules as preadmission authorization imposed by the HMO, and not through shared risk and a commitment to corporate goals.

This model has great appeal for physicians because of its minimal interference with their individual practice. Physicians are likely to join more than one IPA in order to retain as many of their patients as possible, wherever their patients are enrolled. Although this increases administrative costs, it is regarded as a necessary condition to retain existing patients and attract new ones. Membership in a plan is viewed by physicians as just another factor that must be considered and managed as part of being an independent practitioner.

Established Model

The established IPA has a structure similar to the created IPA but is organized for an entirely different purpose. An established model is difficult to distinguish from a created model by looking at its organizational structure, membership, or bylaws. However, its mission and corporate culture can be dramatically different. In this IPA model, physicians take the initiative to form an organization for the purpose of contracting with an HMO or a PHO. Member physicians are much more likely to establish an exclusive relationship with the IPA and to become involved in determining its strategic direction. Physicians forming an established model IPA develop more sophisticated medical management systems (information and so on) and a more active governance function. An established model IPA has greater potential influence on the practice behavior of physicians because of their stronger commitment to a set of corporate goals; its physician members are willing to give up a certain amount of autonomy for the good of the corporation. Indeed, the corporation might exclude or remove physicians who do not support its standards of practice.

Direct-Contract Model

The direct-contract model is similar in function to the created model, except that the contract is directly between the HMO and the individual physician. Technically, this model is not an IPA at all because no new organizational entity is formed. In fact, at one time, this model was illegal because the close relationship between the financing agency and the individual medical practitioner was viewed as interfering with the practice of medicine. However, now that it is permitted, it has become popular with many physicians because it allows them to participate in managed care contracts without forming a corporation. Because their commitment to the HMO is minimal, the physicians can participate in many plans. In addition, the model has little influence on individual physician behavior, which is controlled primarily by external incentives and rules.

IPAS CONTRASTED WITH OTHER MODELS

There are three other principal integrated health care delivery models: the staff model, the group model, and the network model. The following subsections discuss these structures and compare them with IPAs.

Staff Models

In staff model clinics, the medical staff consists of salaried employees of the corporation. Salaries are individually negotiated and are not directly based on the volume of clients seen by the individual practitioner. The corporation has the freedom and responsibility to set corporate objectives and strategies and to negotiate contracts. Of course, staff models are still professional organizations and physicians exert much influence within them.[3] These models are considered highly structured corporate forms in that the organization has an employer-employee relationship to the physician staff. Staff model clinics tend to be large and to retain on staff a rather full range of medical specialists, as well as primary care physicians.

Initially, HMOs were based on staff models, in part because they were already formed as corporate entities and could either contract for services or assume risk directly. In addition, physicians who were in staff model clinics already believed in an organizational form of health service delivery; they were not interested in retaining traditional solo practices. Staff model HMOs were considered by many to be inherently superior models because they "eliminated" financial incentives for physicians to increase consultations, referrals, and hospitalization.

However, other models, including IPAs, have proved to be very competitive and in some ways superior. For example, one criticism of staff models is that removal of the financial incentive for physicians to increase productivity makes them less productive. Moreover, staff model practices have greater restrictions than IPA models on patient freedom to select a physician because of the self-contained nature of the medical staff. They also have been criticized for not allowing individuals to select a personal physician on the staff but, rather, to select only the clinic itself. However, while these policies might have characterized staff models, they are not inherent in the model and most practices allow patients to select and see a personal physician within the clinic.

Although staff model clinics have been described as having the greatest organizational control over the physician's clinical practice, this is true only to a limited degree. Although the organization employs the physician, and the physician is subject to its policies and rules, those rules have not traditionally included clinical decision making. Thus, the organization has not fundamentally altered the clinical decision-making process, and physicians function in large part as independent professionals within the organization. An interesting strategic question is whether physicians in staff models will be more receptive to adopting and utilizing decision rules and practice guidelines in their practices. If so, they could achieve a short-term competitive advantage in managing cost and quality.

Group Models

Group model clinics are organizations created by a group of physicians for the purpose of contracting and otherwise conducting business, where physician members specify how revenues are to be distributed. The organization has a corporate mandate to develop a mission and a strategy and to conduct the group's affairs. Its authority is a board of directors consisting of the group's physicians, frequently all of them. Although such large boards tend to be very democratic, they are not always well suited to address the strategic and operational issues of more complex organizations.

Some of the earlier HMOs were linked to group model clinics. The group practice might have existed prior to its affiliation with a health plan, or it might have been created for the purpose of contracting with a plan. The preexisting group might agree to an exclusive commitment to a health plan but probably is more inclined to continue to function independently, providing services to the plan and retaining fee-for-service (FFS) patients. Additionally, the group might provide services to more than one HMO. A created group practice is more likely to have an exclusive arrangement with an HMO and to provide services only to the beneficiaries of that health plan. Group models have characteristics similar to IPA models with regard to their relationship to health plans, but internally, they have a single corporate identity and commitment.

The group model HMO is considered a closed panel because physicians have to be members of the group to be able to participate in the plan. The group selects, evaluates, and rewards its member physicians. It might contract to assume all risk for the plan's subscribers, or it might contract to provide services on a predetermined cost basis.

Group practice models have many of the same operational and strategic advantages and disadvantages as staff models. Their physician panel may be small and perceived as restrictive by the plan beneficiaries. Moreover, these models might require considerable investment in time and capital to develop practices in new markets. However, because of their increased flexibility in income sharing, group practice models have demonstrated the potential for increased productivity.

Network Models

The network model is formed when a series of medical groups are linked together (usually to contract with an HMO) to provide services to the beneficiaries of the health plan across a broader geographic region. Initially, the network might be formed by existing groups but then might create additional groups to fill in its provider system coverage. The groups might initially be multispecialty groups, causing the HMO to encourage primary care physicians to form a group to fill service gaps in its delivery system.

Participating medical groups typically are capitated for members assigned to the group by the HMO, and they manage the risk of those beneficiaries. If outside referrals are needed, they are paid for by the group. The group would represent the HMO in the region and adopt some identity, processes, and quality standards of the HMO but would function with considerable independence.

The network model HMO overcomes many of the disadvantages of a staff or group model. For example, a network model can be more quickly formed and expanded to cover wide geographic areas. In this way, it shares some characteristics of an IPA. Network models also require less capital investment, and can build on the reputations and practices of the groups that participate. The network model's chief disadvantage is that the participating groups might have different orientations, cultures, and management systems.

ADVANTAGES OF IPAS

One of the IPA's greatest strengths is the nature of its structure, which preserves and builds on historical values and patterns of medical practice within the health system. The U.S. health system is deeply rooted in the principles of freedom of individual choice to select health providers and the independence of providers to respond. These values serve to define acceptable social and health policies and are embodied in the doctor-patient relationship, which has been defined as the DNA structure of health institutions and systems.[4] This structure has been characterized by FFS financing, solo practice, and the autonomy of physicians to individually make clinical decisions drawing on their own knowledge base. However, these characteristics are currently being challenged as society addresses major social issues of high cost, access to health services, and rationing technology.

One of the chief strategic and marketing strengths of IPAs is their appeal to patients who want to have greater choice in the selection of physicians, to maintain a relationship with their physician of choice, and to consume medical services outside a multiphysician clinic environment. Clinic medicine has responded to consumers by personalizing practice, such as identifying a single physician within the group to serve as a member's "family physician."[5] However, the culture of physicians practicing independently and consumers being free to select their physician is still deeply embedded in the value structure of patients and their families. Although consumer and provider preferences and convenience certainly have changed over time, the fundamental values of individual choice of physicians and benefits and limited organizational and governmental influence probably have changed little. The history of defeat of federal health reform legislation illustrates the enduring strength of these values.

However, the general consumption patterns of individuals do change over time and health providers need to monitor and interpret them. Rice has noted the changing patterns of consumption of consumer goods—from neighborhood or local community stores to urban shopping centers and "mega marts."[6] These changes in consumer behavior will undoubtedly affect health services consumption patterns as well. Moreover, there is evidence of changing preferences in practice style by physicians, particularly among young physicians and female physicians, due to a desire for lifestyle changes.[7] Although in the long run, this might give rise to increased acceptance of more highly structured group and staff models, changing values and attitudes also support an inherent advantage of the IPA model—its variability and adaptability.

In addition, there are a number of operational and strategic advantages to IPAs, including their flexibility in responding to local preferences and competitive conditions, their ability to achieve economies of operations without interfering with the clinical process, and the speed and economies of expanding into new areas.

Flexibility in Adapting to Local Conditions

A strategic advantage of IPA models of practice is their flexible organizational structure. This allows them to provide different degrees of control over either the business or clinical functions of the practicing physicians. In markets where there is little managed care penetration, physicians can join one or more IPAs to maximize their patient base but have minimal interference with their practice. In this instance, they can function as a very loose confederation but have the corporate ability to contract with HMOs. In contrast, in advanced managed care markets, IPAs can shift to more highly structured corporations, negotiate exclusive arrangements on behalf of physicians, or develop joint venture relationships with other partners, including shared risk contracts. Their uniqueness is their ability to change as market conditions or preferences of the practicing physicians change. This flexibility and adaptability of structure enable IPAs to respond to local preferences and to change over time. This characteristic gives IPAs a strategic advantage in a health care market characterized by continuous change.

Practice management structures vary by the degree of control the organization has over either the business or clinical functions. IPAs initially were created to provide independent physicians an organizational entity for contracting with managed care plans. These "created" IPAs frequently limited their activities to contract negotiations, with the remaining direct clinical support functions of marketing, enrollment, claims processing, utilization review (UR), and provider relations supplied by an outside organization, usually an HMO. The general administrative support activities of purchasing and inventory, personnel recruitment and payroll, and facilities and equipment maintenance were carried out by individual physician practices. The IPA constituted a shell organization only for contracting purposes.

Production Economies

Increased cost competition in the health system has given rise to pressures for increased efficiency in health service production. Economies from consolidating various business functions in medical practice have been demonstrated consistently.[8] Costs of maintaining a medical practice have been rising due to increased investment in expensive technology and information systems, malpractice insurance, and medical supplies. Some rising costs have been associated with the managed care industry itself, such as billing, claims processing, and UR procedures.

When competitive forces necessitate it, physicians have responded by consolidating administrative practices to achieve economies of scale and greater access to capital. The IPA model is an effective structure for consolidating general administrative services for physicians. It has the structure to manage some, or all, of the business functions but still allow relative autonomy of physicians to manage the clinical function. A strength of the IPA model is its ability to make adaptive change without the abrupt and dramatic change necessitated by restructuring as a staff or group model. It can introduce the degree of organizational control in either the business or clinical functions necessary to increase performance.

Moreover, consolidating business activities of physician practices increases the corporation's ability to negotiate favorable contracts with HMOs and suppliers due to bargaining power. The effect of increased influence of the organization is at the expense of individual physician autonomy, including identity, the independence of staffing, and managing other aspects of the business function of the individual practice. This increased organizational presence can be difficult to achieve in some IPAs due to resistance to change. Corporate integration requires considerable managerial skills in communications, negotiations, corporate restructuring, and human resources management.

Strategic Positioning in an Expanding Market

Another of the IPA model's strengths is its adaptability when moving into new markets. This mobility comes from its reduced capital requirements relative to staff or group models.[9] If market expansion is into neighboring regions, the IPA might be able to provide administrative support from existing offices, without additional cost of rent and support systems, and with a marginal cost in manpower. If the movement is into a more distant geographic location, the IPA might create a local office offering provider services but keeping most business activities centralized. In this way, the IPA becomes a very dynamic and flexible structure to meet the needs of each market area and provider system. It takes on the qualities of the "virtual" organization, which has been made famous in popular management writings. The qualities of this structure give it strengths in an expanding market and within a rapidly changing system.

A second strength of the IPA in an expanding market is its use of existing physicians in the market—physicians who have well-established practices. There is no need for major initial investments in facilities and medical staff, so the start-up costs and the pressure to break even are reduced. In addition to far fewer requirements for capital resources at start-up, there are fewer marketing costs and less risk associated with developing service volume while competing with the existing physicians. The disadvantage to building on the established practice patterns of existing physicians is that of accepting those whose practice behavior is not consistent with that of other practitioners in the IPA. In addition, the IPA is taking in physicians who, by their nature, are independent and reluctant to change. It will take a period of time to change behaviors or to select those physicians who will be retained in the system

Conditions for Developing a Provider Panel The strategy of developing a selected provider panel within an established market is based on a number of conditions. Many physicians will be inclined to pursue membership in two or more IPAs. This strategy has several potential advantages to the physician, namely the ability to retain or develop a sizable patient population where patients are members of different HMOs. In addition, participation in several IPAs and HMOs enables physicians to maintain a higher level of autonomy by avoiding becoming dependent on only one plan. That dependence would necessarily result in greater IPA power and control over the individual physician. The downside to physicians is the need to participate in plans having different sets of rules for determining benefits, processing claims, and managing finances. This in itself adds costs and complexity to the physician's office.

The IPA organization has the incentive to develop a more selective and committed panel of physicians in order to manage physician behavior through development of a corporate culture committed to quality and efficiency. This does not suggest that physicians practicing independently, or those in multiple IPA organizations, are not committed to quality and efficiency. Commitment to a "corporate culture" implies a collective or corporate orientation that enables the organization to develop its own standards and style that can be managed and used as a business strategy. This enables the IPA to increase its business potential by increasing marketing leverage and better managing risk. To achieve this, the IPA must create a panel of physicians dedicated primarily or exclusively to it as their organizational home. This is easier to do in an existing IPA than in a created IPA, and most difficult to do in a direct-contract model.

Expansion in the Managed Care Market The IPA model is well adapted to the rapidly expanding managed care market. This market is very differentiated, with some regions achieving heavy penetration and enrollment and others very little.[10] Markets experience different stages of development, from initial penetration of managed care products to rapid expansion to maturity. The acceptance of managed care is now somewhat universal in all regions of the country, although most geographic areas still have less than 20 percent penetration, and some population groups, such as Medicare (8 percent) and Medicaid (8 percent), have very little. The pattern of managed care development has been, and continues to be, one of rapid market expansion. Market expansion in managed care is typically at the expense of traditional fee-for-service insurance. All managed care models have grown in that market. In markets where managed care models compete, the IPA has proven to be a formidable player.

The market dynamics are rapidly increasing because of the development of such capitated public insurance programs as Medicaid, Medicare, and plans for state and municipal employees. These plans bring large numbers of new enrollees into the market at one time and increase the long-term risk to existing plans if they are unable to effectively compete for this new market. To do so, plans must move quickly into new markets, frequently into a new geography, for Medicaid populations. IPA plans are well suited to respond to these market demands because they can rapidly deploy and adapt to new markets. For example, competing for a new Medicaid contract requires expanding into low-income and culturally diverse populations. That requires a provider system that understands the values and culture of the individuals, families, and community that make up this population. An IPA has the advantage of building on the existing provider system in the community, one that is knowledgeable of and accepted by individuals in the market.

VULNERABILITY OF THE IPA

Despite its advantages, the IPA is vulnerable in its resistance to change, and particularly its resistance to change clinical practice patterns. The vulnerability of the created IPA entity is the independent orientation of the physicians and their resistance to policies and strategies of the IPA organization. This resistance results in the HMO gaining power over the IPA as the stronger organizational entity, reflected, for example, in contract negotiations. In addition, as integrated health systems evolve and competitive forces increase, the HMO, as the more aggressive organization, can move quickly to improve its strategic position within the health system. The failure of many IPAs is caused, not by the limitations of the organization per se, but by its unwillingness to change. The IPA's strength is its flexibility to change and its weakness is its members' unwillingness to do so.

MCOs moving into new capitated public insurance markets need to be cautious of the added risk they are incurring. This risk is a result of the large size of the enrollments, the risk of enrolling less healthy populations, and a pattern of overutilization of costly services, such as hospitals and emergency departments. In addition, the size of the populations being enrolled will bring many plans into the market and increase competitive pressures. This will require managed care plans to be more efficient, with increased institutional capacity to negotiate contracts and sell services based on demonstrable quality and efficiency. IPA organizations have the flexibility to effectively manage these areas, but they will need to become more structured and allow less individual physician autonomy in clinical decision making. Their ability to address these issues and make organizational adjustments will define their strengths and determine their success.

As competition in the market increases, IPAs will be challenged by the increased effectiveness of other models to restructure and manage the clinical process. Competition will move from the effectiveness of managing the business function to restructuring and managing the clinical function. This may be the greatest challenge facing IPA models because it will result in the organization increasingly invading the clinical domain, the area most sensitive and most resistant to change by physicians. How IPAs address this issue will likely determine their success, and perhaps survival, in the future.

STRATEGIES FOR SUCCESS

There are a number of strategies that can be used to help ensure IPA success. Following are discussions of three such strategies: integrated health systems, risk sharing, and clinical process reengineering.

Strategies within Integrated Health Systems

A number of structures and strategies are emerging as IPAs position themselves in rapidly forming integrated health systems. Probably the most common development is the response to hospitals as they aggressively move to form PHOs. (See chapter 16.) Hospitals frequently contract with individual physicians through the PHO, which gives them increased organizational influence over physicians in the joint venture. Hospitals have an advantage in setting up new organizations because of their organizational savvy and their ready cash reserves. A PHO with individual physician contracts is similar to the direct-contract IPA model, and provides the hospital greater strategic and operational control than if the physicians formed their own corporation as a joint venture unit. This is true regardless of how the PHO structures the governing board. This form of structure will result in less institutional influence on individual physician practice patterns.

Physicians might elect to form IPAs that serve as the physician organization in the PHO joint venture. These established IPA models are initially organized around the medical staff of the hospital and accept all members of the staff. This is usually politically desirable, if not essential for implementation, and is an appropriate model for managing shared business services, including UR processes. This structure is adequate if the extent of the shared interest between the two parties is joint administration or business activities.

Many IPAs will face increasing competition and cost pressures; others will take on additional risk through capitation contracts. In doing so, they will need to exert greater influence on the behavior of physicians. As IPAs take on additional risk through joint ventures with PHOs, they will need to become more selective in terms of who is in the physician panel and the practice behavior of the panel. Selection will be based on medical specialty, quality of care, efficiency, and practice style. Most IPAs will go outside the existing hospital medical staff to recruit new members, as well as select out some of the existing panel. The goal is to achieve the right mix of physicians, as well as the right values, orientation, and style. This is achievable by an IPA but moves the IPA up the scale of corporate power, requiring greater individual physician commitment to the corporation and thus greater organizational influence. For many physicians, the "pure" IPA form will have been lost; this process of change will have to be carefully managed.

As the physician organization in a PHO, the IPA will have its own board and retain some independent responsibility for strategic initiatives. In the long term, this model might be in the best interest of both hospital and PHO, as providers develop strategies for going at risk and asking physicians to assume more corporate control over the structure and management of the clinical function. Here again, the IPA's potential strength can become its weakness in that the desire of physicians to maintain independence can make them reluctant participants in, or even obstacles to, pursuing these strategic opportunities. When the IPA structure has achieved sufficient corporate identification by the physician members and has developed strong corporate management, they become more strategically aggressive. When this occurs, the strengths of the IPA model can be a strategic asset.

Risk Sharing

IPAs will have the opportunity to address the strategic question of where to place themselves in the delivery system and, within that role, what value they bring to the system. Will they serve as a stage of production within an integrated system, or assume risk and manage the integrated delivery of services?

Traditionally, HMOs have assumed risk in the system and developed external "regulatory processes" to manage risk across independent institutions.[11] They have developed an array of rules and controls over providers to manage access, utilization, and specific medical services and procedures. These rules include financial withholds, bonuses, utilization review, gatekeepers, second opinions on expensive medical procedures, and mandatory outpatient surgery for defined medical problems. These external controls have brought about changes in medical service utilization rates, reduced the need for physicians in many specialties, and contributed to a slower rate of increase in medical costs. Additionally, they have produced some restrictions unpopular with consumers and providers through bureaucratic rules on patient access to providers and on provider choice of appropriate care.

Risk sharing is a concept for distributing financial risk across a number of institutions, typically provider and financing organizations. Institutions that assume risk have the potential to reduce externally imposed rules and accept responsibility for managing services within the per member per month (PMPM) rate. This has an inherent appeal to physician members of an IPA but might fade with the realization that the IPA will need to develop internal decision rules, controls, and sanctions for managing the risk they now assume. Although this might seem a "Catch-22" to physicians who wish to retain their independent practices and practice patterns, others will realize the potential of having the rules and controls set within the organization, by them and for them.

The operational implication of this strategy is that the IPA will have to develop a structure and staff commensurate with the corporate obligation it assumes. This cannot be done within a direct-contract model, or a corporate shell, described for the created IPA model. The IPA assuming risk will need a well-organized corporate board prepared to assume responsibility for the organization strategically, as well as for internal operations. The corporation also will need to develop management systems for providing decision support for both the clinical and business functions. It will need to develop a team to manage the complex financial and other business operations and negotiations and to set strategic direction for the corporation. These IPAs will need much more corporate sophistication, and related complexity, to manage these relationships and processes.

IPAs need to address the strategic question of the role they will take in the reformed system. Will they play a niche provider role and bargain with whoever is integrating and managing services, or will they take the lead, or become a partner, in developing managed care products? Some IPAs might form exclusive partnerships with other providers and assume risk through direct contracts with corporations or business coalitions. These strategies will determine the structure required of IPAs, as well as their importance in the system.

Clinical Process Reengineering

As IPAs and other providers become more involved in assuming risk and managing care by changing practitioner and consumer behavior, traditional externally or internally imposed financial incentives and administrative rules will give way to systems for restructuring and directly managing the clinical process. This technology is currently being developed, typically referred to as *disease management,* or *clinical pathways,* by a number of provider systems as well as suppliers such as pharmaceutical companies. Provider organizations that reengineer and directly manage the clinical process have the potential to challenge traditional financial and administrative controls based on demonstrated efficiencies and quality outcomes.[12] IPAs will have an opportunity to take the initiative to manage risk through restructuring and directly managing the clinical process.

This new technology consists of the development and use of clinical decision-support systems to provide reminders and decision rules that serve as clinical guidelines and protocols for practitioners. In addition to the value added by physicians through the direct provision of clinical services, they have the opportunity to develop "knowledge-based" systems for managing care across the continuum. Services will be "provided" within these systems under the direction of physicians, without their having to deliver the service directly. For example, protocols for providing annual foot examinations for diabetics can be performed under the direction of a medical specialist without the patient seeing the physician for each unit of service. These knowledge-based systems deserve careful consideration by IPAs.

Knowledge-based systems of managed care are only starting to evolve and are slow to develop because they require a fundamental change in how the clinical function is structured and, in turn, how it impacts the structure of health institutions and systems. Current efforts to form integrated systems combine the previously independent institutions but primarily link their strategic and business functions. The fundamental structure of the clinical decision-making process within the system has not been altered. In the future, the structure of the clinical decision-making process itself will be altered as the means of managing care. This model has the potential to return greater clinical decision-making responsibility and control to physicians, depending on how it is structured.

A provider system that is organized as independent providers will not provide an appropriate structure for restructuring and managing the clinical process across the continuum of care. In like manner, many of the new hierarchical, integrated health systems will be no more effective. There is need for a fundamental change in the structure of the clinical process and the development of systems to manage that process. In order for provider organizations to assume and manage risk, they will have to develop internal structures for managing care at the point of the clinical encounter and across the continuum of care. That is the challenge and potential of the managed care concept in the health system. Managed care will move from being just a reformed financing system to a fundamental reform of the health care delivery system. IPAs are positioned to participate in that reform so long as they are well structured and well led.

CONCLUSION

The increased responsibility of provider organizations over the design and management of the clinical function will alter the structure of health organizations within the system and the relationship between the organization and health professionals. Health organizations will likely become part of integrated systems structured around well-articulated protocols that define how health services will be delivered and consumed over the continuum of care.[13] This will decrease the autonomy of individual health professionals and increase the role of the organization in managing the clinical process. The strategic question is, who will manage the process?

As organizations, IPAs can choose whether they will remain as a stage of production within integrated systems or provide the integrator role, particularly for primary care, by creating the knowledge-based systems for structuring the clinical function and managing care. They have an advantage serving as the organizing focus for restructuring and managing the clinical process because physicians retain a high degree of responsibility and control over the clinical process—a process with a primary care orientation. However, their traditional commitment to autonomy and control by individual clinicians is a potential strategic weakness. In addition, IPAs typically do not have the corporate structure, commitment, and management leadership to carry out such strategic initiatives. They can play a role—in fact can be central to the process—if they choose and are willing to put the necessary organizational processes in place.

In IPA models, physicians are faced with the strategic question of their role in developing knowledge-based structures for managing the clinical function. The operational question is the degree of control by the corporation over their independent practices that physicians are willing to accept. Their unwillingness to do this will be a distinct strategic disadvantage when competing with more highly structured practices, such as group practice and staff models, that can commit to this strategic direction. IPAs that become more highly structured will become more like group practice models, with greater organizational influence over strategic direction, including the structure of the clinical process. Although they still have the advantage of practicing in independent practice sites and quickly expanding into new markets by using established practices, they still must selectively choose physicians coming into the network based on how they practice medicine and their commitment to a corporate orientation.

IPA physicians can shift their focus of concern from individual clinician control to corporate control by clinicians as a group. Physicians should focus on retaining control over the organization, and in doing so, regain control over the clinical process. They should also expect to derive financial and other benefits if the organization is successful. Popular literature on organizational control frequently characterizes physicians as practitioners aligned against managers representing the organization. This is a misconception based on the structure of traditional organizations, resistance to change, or lack of understanding. The issue is whether physicians function as independent practitioners or as colleagues within an organized environment, following standards of practice they define. Organizations are not inherently bad or good; they are simply vehicles for carrying out a defined purpose within a set of collective values. The question is, who will define the purpose and develop the collective values?

IPA physicians can take the leadership and reclaim responsibility for defining and managing the clinical process. They must do it collectively, through organizations, not use the organization for preserving past practices of individual autonomy. One can debate the question of whether physicians acting collectively through organizations are less professional that those acting independently. The operative question is whether they will assume responsibility for organizing and managing care or whether some other organizational form does it. It is clear they cannot be rigid in a rapidly changing health system.

References

1. *Managed Care Digest: HMOs and PPOs* (Kansas City, MO: Hoechst Marion Roussel, Inc., 1995).

2. M. R. Soper and others, *Balancing the Triad: Cost Containment, Quality of Service, and Quality of Care in Managed Care Systems* (Kansas City, MO: National Center for Managed Health Care Administration, University of Missouri, 1995), p. 14.

3. H. M. Mintzberg, *The Structuring of Organizations* (Englewood Cliffs, NJ: Prentice-Hall, 1979).

4. G. D. Brown, "Managed Care," in *Merriam-Webster's Medical Office Handbook* (Springfield, MA: Merriam-Webster, 1996).

5. L. A. Robinson and others, "Use Facilitated Case Discussions for Significant Event Auditing," *British Medical Journal* 311 (July 20, 1995): 315–18.

6. B. Rice, "Put Your Practice Where Shoppers Throng?" *Medical Economics* 70 (Jan. 25, 1993): 138–40, 142, 144.

7. N. Dedobbeleer, A. Contandriopoulos, and S. Desjardins, "Convergence or Divergence of Male and Female Physicians' Hours of Work and Income," *Medical Care* 33, no. 8 (Aug. 1995): 796–805.

8. K. E. Boles and S. T. Fleming, "Breakeven under Capitation: Pure and Simple?" *Health Care Management Review* 21, no. 1 (Winter 1996): 38–47.

9. B. J. Smith, R. E. Wilson, and T. P. McCabe, "Financial Options for Integration," *Trustee* 48 (Jan. 1995): 17, 19.

10. *Managed Care Digest.*

11. G. D. Brown, K. Bopp, and M. R. Soper, "Managed Care's Evolving Role," in *The AUPHA Manual of Health Services Management,* ed. R. Tylor and S. Taylor (Gaithersburg, MD: Aspen, 1994), pp. 118–46.

12. E. A. Balas, "Clinical Practice Patterns in Missouri: Cesarean Section," *Medical Practice Research Center* (Jefferson City, MO: Missouri Hospital Association and Missouri State Medical Association, 1993).

13. K. Bopp, G. D. Brown, and R. H. Daugherty, "Continuum of Care," in *The AUPHA Manual of Health Services Management,* ed. R. Tylor and S. Taylor (Gaithersburg, MD: Aspen, 1994), pp. 62–64.

Bibliography

Fisher, E. S., H. G. Welch, and. E. Wennberg, "Prioritizing Oregon's Hospital Resources. An Example Based on Variations in Discretionary Medical Utilization." *JAMA* 267 (Apr. 8, 1992): 1925–31.

Pennings, J. M., "Strategically Interdependent Organizations," in *Handbook of Organizational Design, Vol. I: Adapting Organizations to Their Environment* (New York: Oxford University Press, 1981), pp. 443–55.

Starr, P., "The Coming of the Corporation," in *The Social Transformation of American Medicine* (New York: Basic Books, 1982), pp. 420–49.

15

Group Practice Affiliation Structures

Russell C. Coile Jr.
Peter N. Grant, JD, PhD

This is the era of the consolidation of health care services. Large clinically integrated and economically disciplined physician groups will dominate the health care marketplace of the 21st century. Physician groups of 200 to 500—and some megagroups with 1,000 to 5,000 physicians—will take the lead in capitation contracting and care management for thousands of managed care "covered lives." In the next 5 to 10 years, the rapid rise of partially and fully integrated medical groups will transform American medicine from a cottage industry. This transformation raises many questions about the future of the nation's 625,000 physicians, including:

- What organizational structures and market strategies will these very large medical groups use?
- Will most physicians affiliate with loosely organized independent physician associations (IPAs)?
- How many doctors will be acquired by hospitals and health systems as salaried physicians?
- Will the majority of America's practicing physicians move into fully integrated group practices and group practices without walls (GPWWs)?

This chapter focuses on three types of physician group structures: partially integrated physician organizations, in particular, group practices without walls (GPWWs), primary care networks, and single-specialty network groups; fully integrated medical organizations, including the foundation model, hospital/health system division, and the equity model; and "super-groups," which combine multiple models in a hybrid structure.

'GOLD RUSH' OF PHYSICIAN GROUP ACQUISITION

A modern-day gold rush is occurring in the medical marketplace for entrepreneurs, venture capitalists, consultants, and attorneys who are crisscrossing America to organize physicians for managed care contracting. Their business is "packaging physicians" for wholesale contracting with HMOs, integrated health systems, and self-funded employers to manage thousands of managed care enrollees. In the process, Wall Street–traded companies are paying up to $400 million to acquire physician groups. Some of these transactions include:

- MedPartners of Birmingham, Alabama, acquires Mullikin Medical Centers of Long Beach, California, for $360 million.
- Caremark of Deerfield, Illinois, pays $140 million to the Friendly Hills Medical Group of La Habra, California.
- Caremark also acquires Pacific Physician Services, of San Bernardino, California, a NASDAQ-traded physician management company (estimated price $150–$200 million), to merge some 400 physicians in southern California into the Friendly Hills group.

With a pace Wall Street would admire, physician practices are being bought, sold, and merged at a record rate in the 1990s. Why would successful physicians sell their practices or groups? There are a number of compelling reasons, including:

- To provide an "exit" strategy for older, soon-to-retire physicians
- To take equity out of practice-building investment
- To obtain an investment nest egg for future retirement
- To merge into a larger, more powerful medical group
- To obtain access to capital for growth and development
- To achieve economies of scale that would reduce practice expenses and improve physician net income
- To obtain salary guarantees and economic security
- To improve the quality of work life through fewer hours and on-call demands
- To meet the need to acquire information systems and managed care infrastructure
- To enable others to handle the hassles of practice management

- To improve managed care contracting position
- To "sell while others are buying," if this trend (fad?) should fizzle

All this deal making is creating a heady atmosphere among physicians and medical groups, delighting some and dismaying others. For long-underpaid primary care physicians (PCPs), the growth and sale of PCP-based medical groups is "payback" for years of service at rates far below their subspecialty counterparts. The Wall Street multimillion dollar transactions for managed care physician groups are a source of concern for those who believe the industrialization of medicine has no place. Nobel prize–winning economist Milton Friedman laments: "Depersonalized, doctor and patient as enemies—those are the key phrases in the growing body of complaints about health maintenance organizations and other forms of managed care."[1] But the market is driving medical group integration, and Wall Street is vying with local hospitals and physician management entrepreneurs to provide the capital.

MANAGED CARE DRIVES GROUP FORMATION

The spreading dominance of managed care is the critical force accelerating the industrialization of medicine. On a national basis, more than 50 million Americans are enrolled in HMOs, and another 50 million in preferred provider organizations (PPOs).[2] Already, some 40 percent of the nation's consumers are enrolled in a managed care plan, which is likely to rise above 50 percent by the year 2000. With more than 60 percent of employer-sponsored health plan members signed up with HMOs, the conversion of the employer market to managed care is now nearly complete.[3]

HMOs are taking aim at the 65 million Americans covered by public programs. Government-sponsored insureds covered by Medicare and Medicaid are the next targets for HMO marketing. Senior HMO products are proving very popular with seniors, especially in competitive markets where HMOs are wooing seniors with $1,500 to $2,500 in pharmaceutical coverage and free services such as dental and vision care. Medicare HMOs have converted more than 5 percent of Medicare's 33 million seniors, and enrollment in senior HMO plans is rising by more than 20 percent.[4] State-sponsored Medicaid beneficiaries are rapidly being switched to HMOs and capitated arrangements. More than 25 percent of the nation's 33 million Medicaid beneficiaries have been converted to HMOs, and a growing number of states are converting their entire Medicaid population to managed care.

The rapid rise of managed care is forcing doctors to organize and bargain with HMOs and PPOs for patients and fees. The average U.S. physician has at least one HMO contract and four to six PPO agreements.

Solo physicians and small medical groups have little leverage in HMO contracting or price setting. In more competitive markets, solo physicians and small groups are being bypassed by HMOs that prefer to contract with large medical groups that can provide multisite coverage for an entire medical region.

HMO consolidation is creating national powerhouse plans with millions of enrollees and substantial market clout to discount hospital prices and physician fees. The merger of indemnity giant Aetna with U.S. Healthcare creates the nation's largest managed care plan, with 14 million enrollees.[5] The $8.9 billion affiliation will be managed by two senior U.S. Healthcare executives. The Blue Bell (Pennsylvania)–based HMO is known for its aggressive cost controls and bargaining style. The Aetna/U.S. Healthcare merger is the latest in a series of deals involving some of the largest insurers and HMOs scaling up to compete on a national level. In another blockbuster consolidation, United Healthcare, a Minneapolis-based HMO, acquired MetraHealth, the health business of Metropolitan and Travelers. Physicians hoping to contract with companies such as Aetna/U.S. Healthcare and United must organize large regional and statewide networks of PCPs and specialists to hope to gain any "suppliers' clout" in setting fees or getting capitation.

RATIONALE FOR PHYSICIAN INTEGRATION

Almost 25 percent of the U.S. population was enrolled in an HMO in January 1996. Managed care's economics are driving physicians into groups for self-preservation. Price competition among HMOs will ripple down the payer-provider "food chain" and shrink physician and hospital revenues by 20 to 35 percent, predicts health care consultant Nathan Kaufman, president of the Kaufman Group in San Diego, California.[6] As health plan premiums shrink from $140 down to $100 by the year 2000, physician and hospital reimbursement will drop substantially. (See table 15-1). This financial pressure on provider finances is virtually irresistible because of the momentum of HMO enrollment growth and premium competition. Physicians must organize integrated physician organizations if they hope to successfully contract and partner with these very large health plans.

The rationale for the development of partially and fully integrated physician organizations is driven by managed care economics and contracting. For example:

- Large multisite medical groups provide regional access for a diverse enrolled population.
- HMOs reduce administrative network management costs by contracting with a few large groups.

- Physician groups assume risk for medical services under medical capitation (or total health care costs under global capitation).
- Medical groups must have financial reserves and working capital to assume capitation risk.
- Only large physician groups can afford information systems investment for continuous care management and payer reporting (for example, HEDIS [Health Plan Employer Data and Information Set] data).
- Physicians need sophisticated management expertise in order to control administrative and clinical costs.
- Medical groups must develop utilization management protocols and provider performance assessment profiles.
- Physicians must have the capability to educate, discipline, and, if needed, exclude physicians from the group for below-standards quality or excess treatment costs.

The largest medical groups hold dozens of managed care contracts and may receive more than 75 percent of their revenues from HMO/PPO plans. These group practices have the financial and administrative capacity to engage in at-risk capitation contracting for thousands of HMO covered lives. Some of the largest medical groups are 80 to 100 percent capitated, especially on the West Coast, including the Kaiser-Permanente Medical Group in northern and southern California, Mullikin Medical Centers in Long Beach, Friendly Hills Medical Group in LaHabra, and Sharp/Rees-Stealy and Scripps Clinic in San Diego. The most successful of these physician groups hold global capitation contracts from HMOs that give physicians control over 80 to 89 percent of the premium.

TABLE 15-1. Provider Payments under Managed Care Competition, 1995–2000

	PPO 1995	*HMO 1995*	*HMO 2000*
Total premium	$140	$112	$100
Medical services:			
Primary care physicians	14.00	18.20	16.25
Specialists	42.00	26.60	23.75
Hospital/institutional services	51.80	33.60	30.00
Prescription drugs/other	11.20	11.20	10.00
Subtotal	$119.00	$89.60	$80.00
Plan administration	15.40	10.00	10.00
Profits	5.60	12.40	10.00

Source: N. Kaufman, Distribution of funds as premiums decline. Presentation to the Michigan State Medical Society, Apr. 12, 1996. Unpublished handout, p. 19. Reprinted with permission.

Partially Integrated Physician Group

Partially integrated physician models such as the GPWW represent a compromise between solo practice and being a member of a large, salaried group. These structures offer many of the benefits of a fully integrated group while protecting much of the autonomy of a physician's private practice. Partially integrated groups may be components of hybrid organizations and supergroups that combine GPWWs, management services organizations (MSOs), IPAs, and fully integrated medical group practices.

Health care market observers are changing their minds about fully integrated models. In a remarkable turnabout, the Health Care Advisory Board, a Washington, DC–based market research organization, has shifted away from its bias for fully integrated medical group practices. In 1993, the board gave a "C−" rating to open-panel IPAs and GPWWs. Now it is changing its mind, reflecting recent evidence that large staff and group model plans such as Kaiser Permanente are losing enrollees and experiencing rising costs.[7] Consumers are rejecting narrow-gated HMO panels. Partially integrated models, such as GPWWs and physician networks, are well aligned to meet insistent consumer demands for choice and broad provider networks.

Each of the partially integrated models represents a compromise between traditional independent practice and salaried employment. However, their advantages (flexibility, low start-up costs, and relative autonomy) also are the source of weaknesses, notably a limited ability to retain earnings, make shared capital investments, or exercise cost and clinical self-discipline. Physicians choosing to work in partially integrated structures may find them entirely workable practice structures or only stepping-stones to more fully integrated models. For hospitals and health systems acquiring physicians, partially integrated models may provide transitional vehicles for bringing solo practitioners and small groups into new alignments.

Alternative models for partially integrated physician groups include:

- GPWWs
- Primary care network groups
- Single-specialty network groups

Each of these models is discussed in the following subsections.

Group Practice without Walls The GPWW is a professional corporation (PC) shared by a number of solo physicians and small medical groups that voluntarily merge their practices into a single PC. Also known as the "clinic without walls," this jointly established medical organization is formed to combine for managed care contracting and to share administration expenses. The GPWW bills under a single provider number.

Physician compensation is based on the profit center approach. All revenues flow through the GPWW and then are channeled into the accounts of the profit centers, that is, the participating physicians and groups. Back-office functions such as contracting and billing are centralized and expenses shared as a percent of gross revenues and/or as defined fees for specific administrative services.

Putting a GPWW together is an exercise in diplomacy. The interests, finances, and styles of the multiple physician participants somehow must be brought into alignment. A workable governance structure must be developed that is both representative and businesslike. In terms of legal structure, a GPWW may be established as a for-profit corporation, such as a partnership or limited liability corporation (LLC), or chartered as a not-for-profit entity (for example, a medical foundation). It hires a common administrator, develops a central office, and decides which administrative and clinical services to centralize. The primary task of the GPWW will be to contract as a group with HMOs, insurers, third-party administrators, and other payers such as Medicaid.

Some of the advantages, disadvantages, and legal issues[8] involved in structuring partially integrated "virtual" medical groups and fully integrated physician organizations are as follows:

Advantages: The GPWW can be very attractive to physicians who want to retain autonomy but recognize the need to organize for managed care. Its advantages include:

- It achieves some of the benefits of a fully integrated group practice without requiring physicians to move to a single site.
- Its start-up costs and capital requirements are relatively low.
- Multiple practice sites may be more attractive to managed care payers.
- Physician members can achieve economies of scale by sharing administrative expenses.
- The physicians share investment in information systems.
- The physicians develop joint practice guidelines and utilization review programs.
- The GPWW retains earnings and pools capital for growth and development.
- Members can sell interest in the GPWW to outside investors.
- The physicians participate in capitation and true managed care risk contracting.
- The GPWW produces clinical efficiencies and cost savings under capitation.
- It offers increased leverage in negotiating with payers and hospitals for inpatient risk pool.
- The GPWW is a vehicle for the sale of a practice upon retirement.

Disadvantages: The ease of start-up and flexibility of the GPWW mask real issues in becoming a financially viable medical organization. Some of the GPWW's disadvantages include:

- There are limited economies of scale due to multiple locations.
- There are redundant costs across multiple sites (for example, staffing, office leases, equipment).
- The GPWW lacks group culture and discipline.
- Governance and decision making frequently are diffuse.
- The GPWW may not be cost competitive with fully integrated groups in contracting.
- It is difficult to retain sufficient earnings to capitalize growth internally.
- The GPWW may attract physicians who are incapable of adapting to a group style of practice.
- The GPWW must be able to discipline or expel incompatible physicians.

Legal issues: Due to the limited financial integration and autonomy of the participants, this model is fraught with legal issues, including:

- Antitrust issues arise because the GPWW is a nonintegrated model subject to price setting and group boycott challenges.
- Fraud and abuse problems may result from limitations on the acquisition of intangible assets (such as goodwill of the practices [discussed in chapter 11]).
- Stark II regulations (discussed in chapter 11) prohibit payment for ancillary referrals in the compensation plan.
- Individual/small group pension plans must be closed out, and the GPWW must adopt a common pension plan.

Primary Care Network Group Managed care's emphasis on primary care and use of PCPs as gatekeepers has put a premium on these physicians. By definition, PCPs include physicians trained in family practice, general internal medicine, pediatrics, and obstetrics. The network group is a hybrid, combining a GPWW or a fully integrated group with an IPA. The GPWW or fully integrated group may either provide MSO services to the IPA or own it.

Primary care networks are being aggressively organized for managed care contracting by a variety of sponsors, including hospitals and health systems, HMOs and insurers, and venture capital–backed entrepreneurial physician management companies (PMCs) such as MedPartners of Birmingham, Alabama, and PhyCor of Nashville, Tennessee.

Primary care networks are partially integrated medical groups of PCPs who provide routine medical services and coordinate care for enrolled populations of HMO and PPO covered lives. Common features of primary care networks include the following:

- They are 50 to 100 percent composed of PCPs.
- Their services are reimbursed on a fee-for-service (FFS) or capitation basis.
- There are multisite locations for geographic access.
- They offer extended hours of service for urgent care.
- They offer scheduled appointments and walk-in service availability.
- They provide routine medical, diagnostic, and treatment services, including minor outpatient surgery.
- They may use physician extenders (for example, advanced nurse practitioners, physician assistants).
- They may provide gatekeeping, referral control, and care management.
- They may take on global capitation contracts, subcontracting for physician specialty, hospital, and other services.

With the growth of managed care, the relative shortage of PCPs has fomented a "bidding war" in some markets to acquire these physicians. Although prices range from $100,000 to $150,000 for the average PCP practice, some primary care groups have received as much as $1 million per doctor. Many U.S. hospitals have acquired physician practices, mostly PCPs. A national survey by the Chicago-based consulting firm of Ernst & Young showed that 60 percent of the nation's hospitals had purchased physician practices by 1995, and 80 percent of the remaining hospitals planned to buy physician practices in 1996.[9] The competition for PCPs is driving up reimbursement, with salaries ranging from $120,000 to $160,000. In New York, Aetna Health Plans has quietly postponed, and perhaps abandoned, its plans to spend $15 million to develop a network of primary care clinics in the New York/northern New Jersey market.[10] Aetna actually closed the first two clinics it had opened, dismayed at the skyrocketing costs of purchasing PCPs in the New York marketplace.

It may be easier to purchase PCPs than to make PCP networks successful. Florida-based Coastal Physician Group saw its 120-physician network crumble when it abruptly lost 3,000 capitated lives from Humana.[11] Coastal's recovery required selling 47 of its Florida clinics to Humana for $50 million, leaving Coastal with 14 pediatric and obstetrics and gynecology clinics. Florida has been a hotbed of PCP network development, led by for-profit companies. For example:

- PhyCor purchased the Riverside Clinic, the oldest multispecialty group in the state, which has grown to 100 physicians (with 60 percent in primary care) and plans to grow the network to 150 to 200 physicians.

- MedPartners of Birmingham, Alabama, another physician management company, has 32 predominantly primary care groups in Florida, with 206 physicians clustered in five counties.
- Caremark International recently made its entrance into Florida, acquiring the Diagnostic Clinic, a 95-physician group with six locations in the Tampa/St. Petersburg area.

Advantages: Early-stage managed care markets are experiencing bidding wars among hospitals, insurance companies, and for-profit companies rushing to create physician networks that are solely or predominantly composed of PCPs. Some of the advantages to primary care group networks include:

- They establish a physician organization that is specifically organized to manage the routine health needs of HMO and PPO enrollees.
- They capture a significant share of PCPs in short supply in most markets.
- PCP networks also can be magnets for PPO contracts and patient self-referral.
- Primary care clinics can function as urgent care centers.
- For hospital sponsors, a PCP network can relieve overcrowded emergency facilities.
- Primary care group networks can be gatekeepers under at-risk capitation arrangements.
- They offer the capacity for PCPs to take on and manage global capitation.
- They engage in direct contracting for primary care and global capitation with self-funded employers and business coalitions

Disadvantages: Despite the initial rush of enthusiasm to develop primary care networks, some observers are now noting the limitations of a PCP emphasis. Disadvantages include:

- Primary care group networks tie up capital in physician acquisition.
- PCPs have limited control over expensive inpatient volume/costs.
- PCP acquisition ignores specialists who drive most of the hospital/HMO's costs.
- There are significant capital, equipment, and administrative costs in relocating PCPs into ambulatory care centers and satellite clinics.
- Certain salary guarantees may be made to PCPs without control of revenues.

- PCP productivity may slump after acquisition.
- Salaried status of PCPs may diminish/eliminate incentives for productivity.
- Hospitals and HMOs have little experience in managing physician groups.
- The network may load too much overhead on PCPs.
- Hospital/HMO owners may centralize key ancillary revenues for PCPs (for example, lab, x-ray).
- The PCP network must develop a shared clinical culture and practice parameters.
- It is less capital-intensive to simply "rent" (contract for) primary care services from PCPs in their existing offices/groups.

Legal issues: The legal challenges and issues facing primary care networks are similar to those of other partially integrated groups. These issues may be compounded by the predominance of solo physicians and small, unsophisticated PCP groups that are the building blocks of PCP networks. Moreover, significantly more front-end legal and organizational work may be involved in putting together a PCP network than acquiring larger, more established physician groups.

Single-Specialty Network Group The momentum of physician integration is shifting toward specialists. After more than five years of intensive primary care acquisitions and group development, hospitals, HMOs, and PMCs now are turning their attention to physician subspecialists. Payers and providers are recognizing the strategic control that specialists exercise over expensive inpatient care and ambulatory procedures.

Developing single-specialty network groups has one enormous advantage. There are thousands of existing single-specialty groups that are potential building blocks for regional and statewide network groups. Of the more than 40 percent of physicians in 20,000 group practices today, most are in single-specialty groups. Physicians in single-specialty groups make as much as 100 to 300 percent more than those in multispecialty groups, who average $140,000 to $160,000 per year. The challenges of organizing single-specialty physician groups have some unique advantages and limitations that are significantly different from putting together primary care networks.

Advantages: The many physicians already in single-specialty groups may make them easier to organize into a regional or statewide network group. Some of the advantages to single-specialty groups include:

- Single-specialty physicians share a common training experience and culture.
- There is a focus on a similar set of patients and conditions.

- Specialty physician leaders are already well acquainted with their colleagues.
- There is a natural market opportunity for subcapitation around common diseases/procedures.
- Specialists share a reasonably standard set of fees and reimbursement arrangements.
- Compensation is relatively similar for specialists in the same field.
- The "best and brightest" specialists in a local market area can take leadership in group development.

Disadvantages: Despite the potential for collegiality and cooperation on a single-specialty basis, there are limitations to this approach. These limitations include:

- Some leading specialists may feel the local market is "too small to share" and refuse to cooperate in organizing a single-specialty group.
- Specialists may be more intent on protecting their incomes than forming a true managed care group that must limit costs and utilization.
- Subcapitation opportunities may be limited.
- HMOs may contract with multispecialty groups for convenience and lower prices.
- Single-specialty groups may recruit many more doctors than their contracts will support.
- Specialists may be reluctant to establish or enforce tough cost or quality standards on peers and colleagues they know well.

Legal issues: The legal hurdles to forming single-specialty groups are similar to those for developing other partially integrated groups, but with even more antitrust problems. The Federal Trade Commission (FTC) and Justice Department have indicated they will challenge any physician organization that seeks to organize more than 20 to 30 percent of single-specialty physicians into a group. Physician specialists have been able to get some relief from antitrust limits by redefining their "market" on a broader regional or statewide basis to permit more specialists to join together in a single-specialty network group.

Fully Integrated Physician Group

When it comes to fully integrated physician groups, one must think in terms of "brand name" physician organizations—Kaiser Permanente, Mayo, Cleveland Clinic, Geisinger, Fallon, Virginia Mason, Oschner,

Lovelace, and Marshfield. These fully integrated medical group practices dominate their markets. Fully integrated physician groups are typically salaried, full-time medical practices, either multi- or single-specialty. The best-known fully integrated medical groups are large, most often multispecialty, with 100 to 300 (and more) physicians. A few groups, such as Kaiser and Henry Ford, employ more than a thousand doctors. Physician compensation is heavily dependent on the performance of the entire group, not the individual or clinical department.

The key characteristics of fully integrated physician groups include shared economic risk, pooled revenues and shared expenses, corporate governance, collaborative/collegial medical practice, and a shared information system that links all group members, even those practicing in satellite locations (for example, Mayo Clinic's satellites in Florida and Arizona conduct daily "rounds" via satellite communications). Other characteristics of a fully integrated physician group include the following:

- It is a single legal entity, which can be a professional corporation or general partnership of PC and sole proprietorships.
- There are single tax and provider numbers.
- Its employees, including physicians, nursing and allied health professionals, and administrative staff, are salaried.
- Salaried physicians typically make up the core medical staff, sometimes backed by group-selected community physicians organized as an IPA.
- There is common governance and ownership led by a small, corporate-style board composed mostly, or exclusively, of physicians.
- There is a high level of clinical and administrative cooperation.
- The group may be a single- or multispecialty practice.
- There is a group compensation structure, with a combination of salary plus incentives, often based on organizational (not individual) performance.
- Clinical care is heavily collegial, with peer-to-peer consultation and a willingness to review and critique each other's work.
- Administrative support services usually are centralized and shared by all practitioners.
- Common information systems link all providers, including central office and satellite clinics.

A fully integrated physician group offers a number of advantages. It is an "industrial model," which has the infrastructure, capital, management, and systems to become a large, even dominant, medical organization in a managed care marketplace. Its chief advantages include the following:

- It offers economies of scale and lower practice costs per physician.
- A combined revenue stream from multiple physicians improves financial strength and access to capital.
- There are centralized management and systems.
- It offers managed care negotiation, finance, and administration expertise.
- It provides a collegial environment with easy access to consultation and referrals.
- It offers a high quality of working life, with defined work hours, call coverage, vacations, and continuing education.
- It is attractive for physician recruitment and retention.[12]

However, the fully integrated physician group also has its disadvantages, including:

- There are high fixed costs of administration and salaried physician/support staff.
- Access to capital is limited by cash flow and ability to retain earnings.
- The potential exists for specialty dominance and continued FFS dependence.
- The large partnership structure may be inflexible in a rapidly changing managed care market.
- Productivity-based compensation is antithetical to capitation.
- A centralized clinic site may be unattractive to managed care buyers with geographically dispersed enrollees.
- The salaried compensation structure may diminish physician productivity and customer service orientation.
- The structure presents buy-in/buy-out problems.

There also are a number of legal options and issues available to fully integrated physician groups, described in more detail in the models below. Legal and organizational issues add complexity when the integrated group grows by acquisition of smaller groups, requiring the merging-in of multiple group forms. Mergers of not-for-profit and equity model groups are increasingly common, with the emergence of investor-owned PMCs such as Caremark, PhyCor, and MedPartners.

There are four models of fully integrated physician groups:

1. Medical foundation
2. Medical clinic
3. Hospital/health system division or subsidiary
4. Equity model

Each of these models is discussed in the following subsections.

Medical Foundation As a tax-exempt 501(c)(3) organization, the medical foundation model has a strong appeal for providers who believe that health care should be more of a social institution than a business enterprise. This not-for-profit approach has a long history in American medicine. Many of the nation's largest physician organizations are organized as not-for-profit medical foundations, including Mayo and Kaiser Permanente, which operate as charitable enterprises and engage in teaching and research. The foundation model frequently is found in California, due in part to that state's legal restrictions on the corporate practice of medicine. (See chapter 10.)

Advantages: For physicians who are somewhat dismayed by the invasion of Wall Street–backed companies and the ascendancy of the profit motive in medicine, the not-for-profit medical foundation model may provide a value-compatible setting. The advantages to this model include the following:

- It offers the financial advantages of a tax-exempt organization, especially no corporate income tax.
- It offers access to tax-free bond financing with lower interest costs and longer paybacks.
- Consumers view it as community-oriented provider of care.
- The community benefits from charity care, teaching, and research.
- It appeals to physicians who want to practice medicine with fewer financial pressures than those that exist in for-profit groups.
- It offers financial benefits such as property tax exemption and charitable donations.
- It is a flexible model that may employ physicians or contract with group practice.
- It may purchase or sell both tangible and intangible assets of physician practices.
- It offers business expertise and community linkages of nonphysician (lay) trustees.

Disadvantages: The limitations of the medical foundation model derive chiefly from its tax status and legal structure. The limitations of this model include:

- Nonphysicians control 80 percent of its board seats; only 20 percent of the board may be physicians with an economic interest.
- A board dominated by lay trustees may not act in the physicians' best interests.

- Obtaining IRS (Internal Revenue Service) approval to create a not-for-profit foundation can be time consuming and expensive and is subject to ongoing IRS review.
- A not-for-profit model does not have financial incentives or equity "upside" for physicians as do for-profit structures.
- Administrative management and growth strategies may not be as aggressive under limited financial performance incentives for key managers and physician executives.

Legal issues: The U.S. hospital movement to establish not-for-profit medical foundations in the 1990s has resulted in increased IRS scrutiny of applications to create these tax-exempt physician structures. Legal costs may exceed $1 million, and IRS approval can take 12 to 24 months. This model is more complex, costly, and time consuming to establish. Moreover, not-for-profit foundations are limited in what they can pay for physician practice assets—no more than fair market value that has been independently established. They will receive continuing IRS scrutiny over the next several years, as tax authorities exercise a critical oversight to ensure that this model is not being used as a way for physicians to avoid paying corporate income taxes.

Medical Clinic The freestanding medical clinic is the most common form of fully integrated physician group practice, including regional and nationally recognized groups such as Mayo, Cleveland, Oschner, Geisinger, Scott-White, Lovelace, and Virginia Mason. In the sparsely settled West, medical clinics were the regional referral centers covering hundreds of square miles in settings such as Fargo, North Dakota; Billings, Montana; and Rochester, Minnesota. On the West Coast, medical clinics such as Kaiser Permanente, Ross Loos, and Mullikin Medical Centers were in the forefront of managed care and capitation.

Both single- and multispecialty groups have adopted the freestanding clinic model. Historically, freestanding medical clinics attracted top specialists and drew patients from broad regional markets. As a fully integrated model, the freestanding medical clinic operates with a single provider and tax identification number. Staff, including physicians, are salaried employees. Clinics are legally structured as professional corporations or general partnerships with both a PC and sole proprietorships. In the past, medical clinics grew primarily through recruitment. More recently, however, mergers and acquisitions have accelerated the pace for developing large medical clinics. To satisfy managed care buyers with dispersed regional populations, many large clinics have opened satellites staffed by their own salaried physicians.

Advantages: The medical clinic continues its popularity among physicians because of the many advantages it offers, including:

- The physician partners have a control over the organization similar to that found in other professional group practices such as law or accounting.
- It offers economies of scale in operations and costs, depending on the size of the group.
- Staffing costs for the services of physicians, managers, and support workers are predictable.
- It offers the ability to attract capital through either borrowing against the revenue stream or selling a portion of the ownership.
- Corporate governance is highly flexible.
- The compensation system is set by the group.
- It is attractive for the recruitment of physicians who want secure employment without the costs of starting a practice.

Disadvantages: The freestanding clinic model's flexibility and physician control also can be its weaknesses. For example:

- The physicians in charge may not be good business managers.
- Generating capital internally by retained earnings requires a self-discipline many groups lack.
- Loose corporate governance and "one-doctor, one-vote" policies may limit the ability to make good, quick business decisions.
- The group may be too small for effective economies of scale.
- Small, thinly capitalized groups face greater vulnerability when competing with large, well-capitalized group competitors.
- Small groups may have difficulty "cashing out" a retiring partner.

Legal issues: The legal issues involved in structuring freestanding medical clinics involve choice of legal model (for example, a professional corporation or a limited partnership). Governance structures that do not create a "corporate model" of small-board and tight management may not grow well as the group expands. Legal and governance issues arise when groups are merged, including the restructuring of pension plans, benefits, and other administrative issues. Moreover, Byzantine physician compensation schemes add complexity when groups are merged or acquired.

Hospital/Health System Division Hospitals are prime movers of physicians into group settings. (See chapter 16.) More than 60 percent of U.S. hospitals already have acquired physicians, and most (80 percent) of the rest of America's 5,500 community hospitals planned to purchase physicians in 1996.[13] The goal is to create integrated physician-hospital organizations (PHOs) that can engage in at-risk capitation contracting with HMOs, insurers, third-party administrators, and self-insured employers. Integrating physicians and hospitals offers payers an opportunity to enter into a "single-signature" capitated contract with a provider organization that can deliver both medical and institutional health services.

Acquired physicians may remain in their individual offices, operating much as if they were independent contractors, or they may be relocated by the acquiring hospital/health system to hospital-owned medical offices. To gain the greatest economies of scale, acquired doctors may be merged into a fully integrated group practice setting. However, these "shotgun marriages" to form medical groups do not always work. For example, dissatisfied physicians may exit the group once their noncompete agreement expires, or the hospital/health system may give the physicians one last opportunity to exit. California's Sutter Health System in Sacramento reconstructed a specialty-dominated GPWW into an integrated primary care group, allowing 75 percent of the specialists to leave the group voluntarily.

In the employment model, physicians are offered the economic security of a salaried practice, backed by the capital resources of the hospital/health system. Physicians do not have the worries of operating their own small business, and they can see patients with a minimum of administrative hassle. Management services are provided by the hospital, usually as a separate division or subsidiary. The hospital/health system directly employs the physician, either full- or part-time, under defined terms including salary, benefits, and incentive opportunities. However, it may or may not acquire the physician's medical practice. Employed physicians typically operate in a separate division of the hospital with a distinct administrative staff reporting to the hospital CEO. An internal advisory council of physicians may provide administrative and clinical leadership for the employed physician group.

Advantages: Physician acquisition can position the hospital and doctors as a truly integrated health care organization for managed care contracting. Some of the advantages of this model include the following:

- Creating a joint physician-hospital entity for managed care contracting reduces the problem of a multiplicity of potentially conflicting organizations and governing bodies.
- The model can commit both physicians and institutional facilities as an integrated system with a single signature.
- A hospital-acquired primary care network can service a dispersed population of HMO enrollees.
- PCP network physicians function as gatekeepers for HMOs.
- This model can reduce hospital overhead through the purchase of institution-based physicians, such as radiology or pathology, lowering hospital costs by shifting these physicians' compensation from FFS to salary.
- The acquisition of key specialist groups is a long-term investment in clinical centers of excellence (for example, oncology, obstetrics and gynecology, and so on).

- The model offers a "first-strike" acquisition strategy for the hospital to avoid loss of key PCPs or subspecialists to competitors.

Disadvantages: For many physicians, hospital employment is anathema, and hospitals proposing to employ doctors may create a firestorm of protest in the local medical community.[14] Some of the disadvantages of this model include the following:

- Some key physicians the hospital would like to employ may prefer to remain autonomous.
- If established doctors will not sell their practices, the only physicians willing to become hospital employees may be younger or second-tier physicians.
- Without equity and a sense of ownership, hospital-employed doctors may not be as committed or productive.
- The hospital/health system may pay too much for physician practices.
- Salary guarantees to physicians may be unrealistic or unconnected to productivity.
- The hospital/health system may centralize lab and x-ray revenues that were providing the profit margins in practices prior to acquisition.
- The hospital/health system may have limited administrative capacity, expertise, and systems for managing physician practices.
- The hospital/health system may load too much corporate overhead on the physician division.

Legal issues: Legal issues often drive the organizational structure of the hospital/health system–owned group practice. Depending on each state's corporate practice of medicine statutes, physicians may be employed or independent contractors. The hospital/health system generally becomes the sole corporate member of a tax-exempt foundation or the majority shareholder of a taxable clinic. Thus, the foundation/clinic is the provider of care, and owns and operates both the clinical and administrative aspects of the practice Owning a foundation or a clinic can raise problems with fraud and abuse, private inurement, and benefits to which tax-exempt hospitals are unaccustomed.

Equity Model Medical groups organized on the equity model give physicians the opportunity to be owners as well as employees. Equity-based physician groups achieve both economic and clinical integration. Sharing revenues and expenses compels group physicians to take charge of their costs. Every cost saving goes directly to the bottom line and becomes available as future capital (reserves) or distribution (bonuses).

As a for-profit, entrepreneurial model, the equity-based group practice may own a number of components within an integrated delivery system, including hospitals, ambulatory care centers and surgical centers, medical office buildings, a home care company, durable medical equipment, pharmacies, IPAs, and even an HMO. Large equity groups may establish an MSO to acquire and/or manage other physicians' practices. In some cases, the equity will be created in the MSO, not the group itself. Equity may be closely held by a small number of senior partners, or more widely distributed, with many or all physicians holding equity positions.

The equity model allows the medical group to acquire or merge with other groups on an equity-swap basis, with little or no cash involved in the transactions. The acquired group or physician(s) receive stock in exchange for the appraised value of the practice. Thus, equity-acquired partners become committed to economic and clinical integration. Acquired physicians align their cost structure and pricing with that of the group. The equity model may provide a level of commitment that may be higher than a similar situation where the physician is acquired outright, by a not-for-profit hospital/health system, for example, receiving only cash and holding no equity.

Advantages: The equity model offers a number of advantages over other physician group structures, including:

- The potential exists to sell the group at a substantial multiple of annual net earnings per physician to a for-profit physician management company.
- The equity model provides employment security as well as the upside potential of ownership if the group is sold.
- The equity model provides a sense of ownership by physicians who hold equity stakes in the group.
- Equity-holding physicians may be more committed to cost reduction strategies and collegial practice patterns.
- There is a shared commitment among physician owners to pursue a unified business strategy and to make the group successful.
- The model offers the opportunity for retiring or relocating partners to be cashed out.

Disadvantages: There are definite risks under the equity model. These include the following:

- This model requires substantial entrepreneurial expertise and risk taking.
- The model will limit its growth potential if physician owners are unwilling to reserve significant earnings for growth and development.

- There are high working capital requirements for managed care contracting, capitation, and information systems.
- The costs of capital may be high compared to not-for-profit systems funded by tax-exempt debt.
- Physician owners may bicker over costs, compensation, and strategy.
- The model needs corporate-style governance to make swift, sophisticated business decisions.
- At least one physician partner must devote substantial effort, often full-time, to managing the practice.

Legal issues: In many ways, the equity-model group practice is like any other for-profit corporation, but with some unique factors. These include the following:

- The allocation and pricing of stock to current, and future, partners can be contentious.
- The model must meet SEC (Securities and Exchange Commission) requirements if the group issues or sells shares.
- Investments by the hospital/health system must be fair-market-value transactions to avoid fraud-and-abuse risk and the danger of private inurement.
- Taking MSO public requires substantial SEC compliance.
- Significant costs are involved in buying out partners who are retiring or relocating.

Physician Supergroups

Aggressive physician supergroups are emerging to dominate markets from coast to coast. Very large physician organizations with hybrid structures are rapidly emerging that can provide a one-stop resource for physician services and management. Supergroups such as Mullikin Medical Centers in Long Beach, now merged with MedPartners of Birmingham, and the Leahy Clinic in Boston combine traditional group/clinic models with MSOs and IPAs. The biggest supergroups employ and manage thousands of doctors, and take global capitation from commercial and Medicare HMOs for 500,000 managed care enrollees and more.

Supergroups combine fully integrated group practices with IPAs, GPWWs, and MSOs, operating in single or multiple markets. The largest supergroups have multistate and even national ambitions. These fully integrated groups may merge and consolidate other organizational forms or operate them as subsidiaries through the MSO. Partially integrated groups and IPAs may receive stock in the MSO in exchange for acquisition or may be purchased outright. Supergroups may become hybrids from targets of opportunity, as weaker physician organizations look for a strong, integrated group partner. In other situations, an integrated group chooses to diversify through acquisition of other models, to give it greater flexibility in meeting managed care customers' demands.

On the payer side, supergroup customers include commercial HMOs, traditional insurers, PPOs, third-party administrators, employers and business coalitions, and government agencies such as Medicaid. On the provider spectrum, supergroups own and/or manage physician group practices, primary care networks, and specialty and multispecialty IPAs. The largest supergroups own hospitals or health systems, as well as a variety of continuum-of-care services such as home health, reference laboratories, imaging centers, and long-term care facilities.

The range of services supergroups may provide includes the following:

- Medical group development, including acquisition and mergers
- Practice management, including group and IPA
- Physician recruitment, compensation, and incentive performance systems
- Physician network credentialing (for example, primary care network, IPA)
- Utilization management/provider profiling/quality control
- Practice guidelines and clinical pathways
- Information systems
- Managed care negotiation/contracting
- Capitation arrangements
- Gatekeeping and specialty referral management
- Billing, claims processing, and electronic payment
- Case management (for example, workers' compensation)

Most supergroups have decided not to launch their own HMOs as branded products for fear of retaliation from their HMO and health insurer customers. For example, California's Mullikin Medical Centers recently acquired a standard ("Knox-Keene" in California) HMO license from the state but characterized it as a more limited "wholesale license." The HMO permit will allow Mullikin to take global capitation under California's restrictive insurance laws, but Mullikin has no current plans to go into competition with its HMO customers in "retail" marketing to employers.

Venture capital is flowing into supergroups. Wall Street–backed PMCs such as Caremark of Deerfield, Illinois, PhyCor of Nashville, Tennessee, and MedPartners in Birmingham, Alabama, are purchasing and merging alternative physician groups in the same marketplace into a hybrid supergroup in order to improve the groups' potential to dominate a region. Even large supergroups are getting bigger. Soon after its acquisition by MedPartners, Mullikin was merged with PPS, another large medical group based in San Bernardino, California, creating a supergroup with more than 600,000 covered lives. The deal was quickly matched by Caremark's purchase of the 140-physician Friendly Hills Medical Group, expanded to supergroup status when Caremark purchased Cigna's southern California medical network of more than 200 doctors. Nationally, MedPartners/Mullikin has acquired groups totaling 7,000 physicians. This group will dominate southern California, with more than 3,000 doctors, 15 percent of the physician supply, and 1.1 million capitated HMO patients.

Advantages to Supergroups Supergroups aim to become the dominant physician organizations of their territories. These structures enjoy the following advantages:

- Capital for rapid expansion through acquisition and merger
- Financial strategies of critical mass
- Economies of scale in operations
- Management expertise and systems
- Ability to contract with the biggest customers
- Creation of brand-name recognition as a physician organization
- Geographic accessibility through strategically dispersed satellite locations
- Multiple physician delivery system options for purchasers
- Ability to recruit physicians with multiple options for affiliation

Disadvantages to Supergroups As supergroups grow, the downside of "big" becomes evident. Some of the supergroup's disadvantages include:

- With high fixed costs, a supergroup requires rapid growth of contracts, covered lives, and revenues.
- Physicians perceive a loss of local control.
- A new level of management expertise is needed to manage very large groups.
- Information systems become critical.
- There is potential for failure if not adequately capitalized.
- Physician dissatisfaction/alienation occurs over issues such as compensation, profitability, or "corporate" management policies.
- The danger exists of subgroups breaking away.
- High price-earnings ratios for investor-owned PMCs must be met with sustained earnings performance.

Legal Issues Building supergroups is costly, complex, and risky. Huge capital investments will carry high investor expectations. Supergroups may be professional corporations, medical general partnerships, or equity models. Creating hybrid medical supergroup models will bring high developmental costs in legal assistance. Will governance be centralized or dispersed? Antitrust issues can arise with the less-integrated components, which are not as fully integrated in capitation or economic risk sharing. In addition, deal making at the supergroup level can be complicated and expensive. The affiliation structure may be statutory merger, stock, or asset swap. Moreover, credentialing, peer review, and malpractice issues must be managed. Some acquisitions force doctors into long-term (20 to 30 years) professional service agreements. Physicians acquired in a variety of models must be satisfied, even with multiyear noncompetition agreements, or they will bolt the firm.

CONCLUSION

Given the rapid ascendance of managed care, it is clear that America's 625,000 physicians must restructure: "With health care reform looming on the horizon, providers recognize that they must establish creative and legally acceptable relationships with one another in order to survive in the evolving health care marketplace."[15] First-generation physician group structures such as IPAs and GPWWs now are being strengthened by more centralized management, tough provider credentialing, common care standards and clinical pathways, more clinical discipline, information systems, and shared risk taking in capitation contracts with HMOs.

The need for flexibility is reflected in the evolution of hybrid models that combine partially and fully integrated physician groups into supergroups, which may employ or manage hundreds, even thousands, of doctors. Economic insecurity, HMO administrative requirements, and the need for capital are driving doctors into group practices. Better-capitalized hospitals and venture capital–backed physician management companies are purchasing thousands of solo doctors and group practices. The voluntary merger of physicians into partially and fully integrated groups will provide independence, but the physicians must discipline themselves to retain earnings for growth and development.

Signals of change are everywhere, even in "stage-one" and "stage-two" markets with 5 to 15 percent HMO penetration.[16] Few physicians, even in rural areas or scarce specialities, can afford to go it alone in the age of managed care. Doctors must align their economic and clinical practices to successfully compete for managed care patients and contracts. The strategic implications for the 21st century are clear: Physicians must act now to organize themselves if they hope to own their future.

References

1. M. Friedman, "A Way Out of Soviet-Style Health Care," *Wall Street Journal* (Apr. 17, 1996): A20.

2. Russell C. Coile Jr., "Managed Care Outlook: 1995–2000: Top 10 Trends for the HMO Industry," *Health Trends* 7, no. 5 (1995): 1–8.

3. New York Times/Foster Higgins 1996.

4. R. Hamer, "HMO Industry Report," *InterStudy Competitive Edge* 5, no. 2 (Apr. 1996): 1–133.

5. T. Smart and K. H. Hammonds, "Aetna's Booster Shot," *Business Week* (Apr. 15, 1996): 41–42.

6. N. Kaufman, "Distribution of Funds as Premiums Decline," presentation to the Michigan State Medical Society, Apr. 12, 1996. Unpublished paper, pp. 1–74.

7. The Advisory Board, *Emerging from Shadow: Resurgence to Prosperity under Managed Care* (Washington, DC: The Advisory Board Co., 1995), pp. 1–155.

8. P. N. Grant, "Healthcare Restructuring 1996," presentation to the IPA Association of America, Phoenix, Feb. 23, 1996. Unpublished paper, pp. 1–310.

9. Ernst & Young, *Physician–Hospital Organizations: Profile 1995* (Chicago: Ernst & Young, Feb. 1995), pp. 1–20.

10. J. L. Miller, "Aetna's New York clinic strategy on hold," *Integrated Healthcare Report* 4, no. 1 (Jan. 1996): 10.

11. J. F. Pogue, "Battlefield Florida." *Integrated Healthcare Report* 3, no. 11 (Nov. 1995): 1–6.

12. Grant.

13. Ernst & Young.

14. Grant, p. 144.

15. G. A. Niederman and B. A. Johnson, "Integrated Provider Networks: A Primer," *MGMA Journal* 6, no. 5 (Nov./Dec. 1994): 62–68.

16. Russell C. Coile Jr., "The Five Stages of Managed Care: Organization for Capitation and Health Reform," *Hospital Strategy Report* 6, no. 11 (1994): 3.

16

Physician-Hospital Organizations

Peter F. Straley

Physician-hospital organizations (PHOs) have enjoyed remarkable growth in the past 10 years,[1] yet many critics suggest that most will fail because either they do not link the physicians together in a tight enough alliance or the presumed interests of physicians and hospitals are too diverse to be served by such a vehicle.[2] Because PHOs are still relatively recent—and in their actual implementation, very different—no doubt some have fallen victim to all the faults their critics attribute to them. However, others are serving as integral building blocks in the restructuring of the American health care system, not as an answer in and of themselves but, rather, as vital components in a comprehensive strategy for health care financing and delivery.

Using Baycare Health Partners, the largest PHO in western Massachusetts, as an example, this chapter explores the basic structure of a PHO, outlines the roles it can adopt to play an important part in an overall integration strategy, and suggests the factors that are most likely to lead to PHO success or failure.

PHYSICIAN-HOSPITAL ORGANIZATION STRUCTURE AND GOVERNANCE

A PHO can assume many legal forms. However, most commonly, it is a separately incorporated legal entity formed as a joint venture between a hospital or health care system and a group of physicians. (See chapter 16.) The physicians may be organized formally in an independent practice association (IPA) structure (discussed in chapter 14) or informally in groups that collectively constitute the PHO's physician component.

Figure 16-1 presents the organizational chart of Baycare Health Partners, Inc. As the figure shows, Baycare has two corporate parents: Greater Springfield IPA (the physician component), an organization of approximately 700 physicians who practice primarily in western Massachusetts; and Baystate Health System (the hospital component), a multihospital, multicomponent integrated delivery system (IDS). Formed in 1994, Baycare is incorporated as a not-for-profit, taxable corporation, a very common form of incorporation for a PHO. Because there is no need to issue stock to its owners, this corporate form is very simple to undertake.

FIGURE 16-1. Baycare Health Partners' Organizational Chart

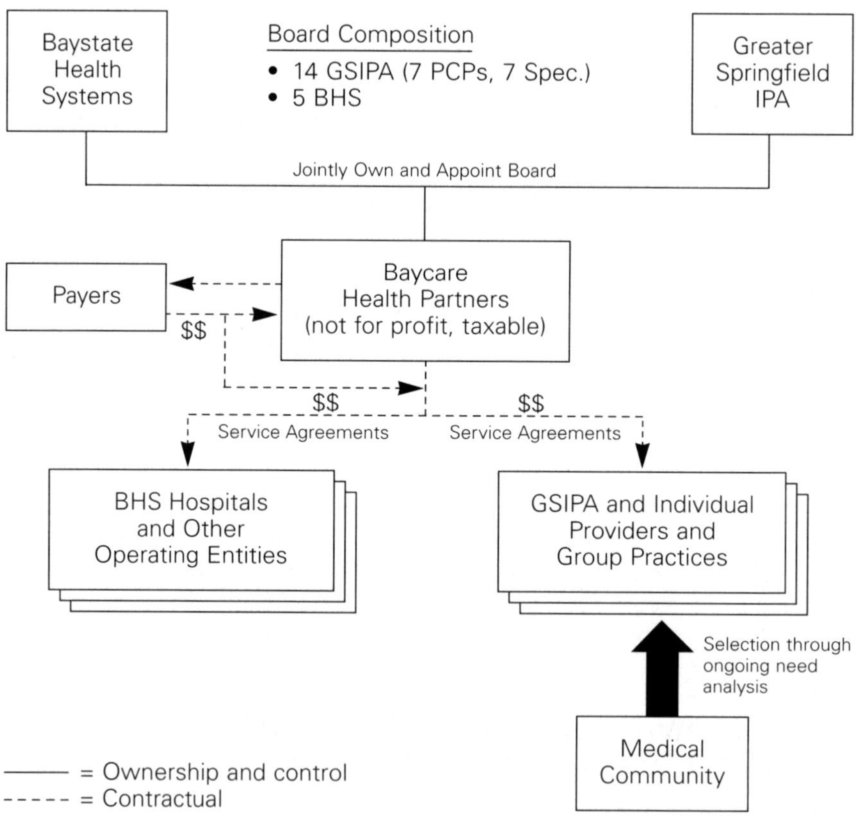

Source: Baycare Health Partners, Springfield, MA, 1994.

More important than corporate form, however, is the form and operation of the PHO's governance. This has been approached in many different ways, but fundamentally the PHO founders are faced with a trade-off among:

- Wanting to have broad representation with ample opportunity for input from its diverse membership
- Needing to be able to conduct business, which in turn implies limiting the number of board members
- Ensuring that the PHO serves as a market vehicle of change, which frequently means that members other than the "same old faces" should serve on its board
- Balancing and protecting the interests of the participants so that no one agenda dominates discussions or overpowers "weaker" components

Although these governance issues create a challenge, they can be addressed successfully in numerous ways. The simplest way is to give each "owner" one vote on all issues. In this format, the physicians vote as a block and the hospitals vote as a block, and both sides must agree for the PHO to take any action. In practice, in a typical PHO, a majority of hospital representatives and a majority of physician representatives must vote in the affirmative for a board motion to pass. Baycare Health Partners is governed in this manner and, furthermore, requires that half the physician representatives be from primary care disciplines. In this manner, all board issues must have both hospital and physician approval while simultaneously ensuring that the physicians build both primary care and specialty care physician support. On paper, this appears more cumbersome than it actually is. At Baycare, it is believed that a fundamental key to future health care delivery success will be for physicians and hospitals to learn to work together in a true partnership in which their interests are balanced. This PHO structure has proved to be an excellent planning forum and ensures that joint actions truly serve the interests of the forward-looking individuals who have dedicated their time and energies to serving on the PHO board and committees.

Typically, the PHO enters into service agreements with providers who agree to provide a full range of health-related services to the PHO. Invariably, the PHO enters into service agreements with its owners who also are providers. However, it can, and frequently does, enter into service agreements with providers who are not owners but who choose to take advantage of the PHO's services without taking an ownership position. As illustrated in figure 16-2, the PHO in turn negotiates global budgets or capitation contracts with managed care plans in the marketplace, serving as a vital intermediary between the plans and the providers of care, integrating their relationships, and ensuring that their interests are realized in their payer relations.

FIGURE 16-2. Role of a PHO

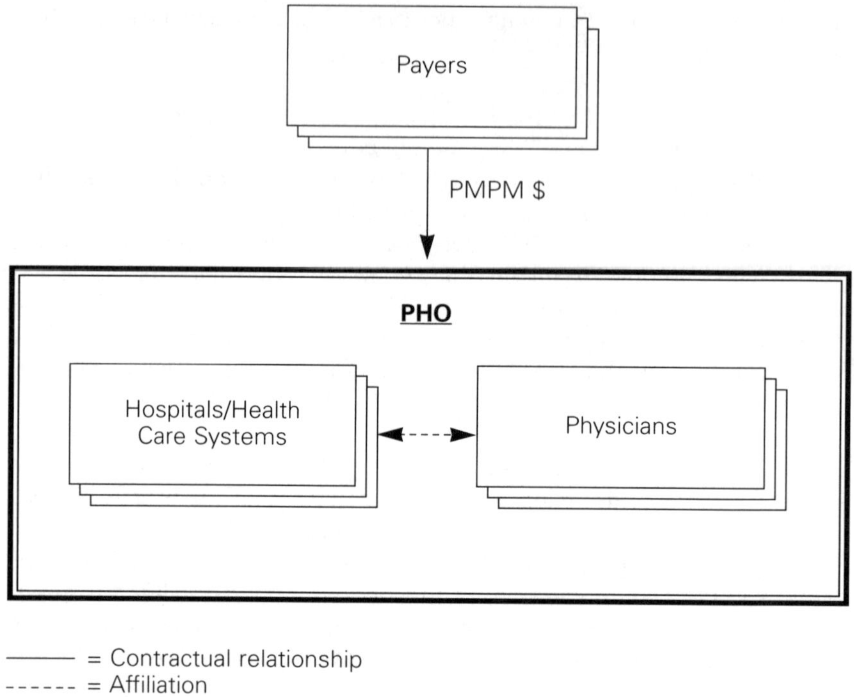

Source: Adapted from Jennings Ryan & Kolb, health care management consultants, Hadley, MA, 1996.

Roles of the Baycare Physician-Hospital Organization

For the purpose of this discussion, the roles of the PHO have been divided into short- and longer-term roles.

Short-Term Roles Figure 16-3 presents a matrix of the roles that were envisioned in the formation of Baycare Health Partners. Baycare is typical of most PHOs. In the short term, its primary functions are related to joint planning between the physicians and the hospitals that participate in the PHO and to entering into risk and non-risk-based contracts with payers in Baycare's market for the provision of health care services by its members and contracted providers.

In some markets, PHOs pursue direct contracts with employers who self-insure, thereby bypassing traditional insurers or HMOs. Although this strategy can work well, at Baycare it is of limited importance because Baycare's market has few large employers whose employees are geographically concentrated enough for the PHO to offer a truly full-service provider panel. Rather, Baycare's experience, and that of many PHOs

FIGURE 16-3. Matrix of PHO Roles

Short Term	*Longer Term*
• Collaboration vehicle • Joint contracting • Joint risk sharing	• Medical management • Demand management • Information collection and analysis

Source: Adapted from Peter F. Straley, ed., *Developing a Successful Physician–Hospital Organization.* Chicago: American Hospital Publishing, 1995), p. 23.

across the country, has shown that working with and through selected health plans is a much better way to serve as the local delivery option within a larger state- or regionwide network of providers assembled under contract to the health plan.

In any case, it is critical that a PHO establish a strong and comprehensive contracting function early in its existence so that it will have an established track record with both the health plans and its members. A PHO must ensure that it is negotiating contracts that meet its members' needs while simultaneously being responsive to the market. Although this is not easy, a "system" that aspires to any reasonable level of integration must achieve this balance. Baycare's experience suggests that a PHO is an excellent vehicle in which to "break ground" in building integration without requiring outright ownership. Baycare's Contract Review Committee, which recommends contracts to its board of directors for approval, must invest the time necessary to educate its members so that they can make informed recommendations about the structure of contracts, assess the risks involved, and ensure that contracts' financial and nonfinancial terms are in the PHO's best interests.

Using evaluation tools: Baycare has developed several tools that aid in this evaluation, two of which have proved to be particularly effective: the Fee Analyzer, whose graphical output is shown in figure 16-4, and the nonrate contract terms analysis, shown in figure 16-5.

The Fee Analyzer, a computer database tool, provides a quick look at the fees paid to physicians in a given contract. (Baycare also has developed separate analysis tools for primary care capitation contracts.) This tool translates the health plan's proposed fee schedule into an "effective conversion factor" of Medicare's resource-based relative value scale (RBRVS) payment methodology. (See chapter 4.) This translation takes place by calculating a weighted average of the payments that would be made to a practice, specialty by specialty, based on the geographically adjusted relative value unit, weighted by the relative frequency of that CPT-4 billing code in practice at Baycare. Thus, it translates a fee schedule that may or may not be RBRVS

FIGURE 16-4. Fee Analyzer Results

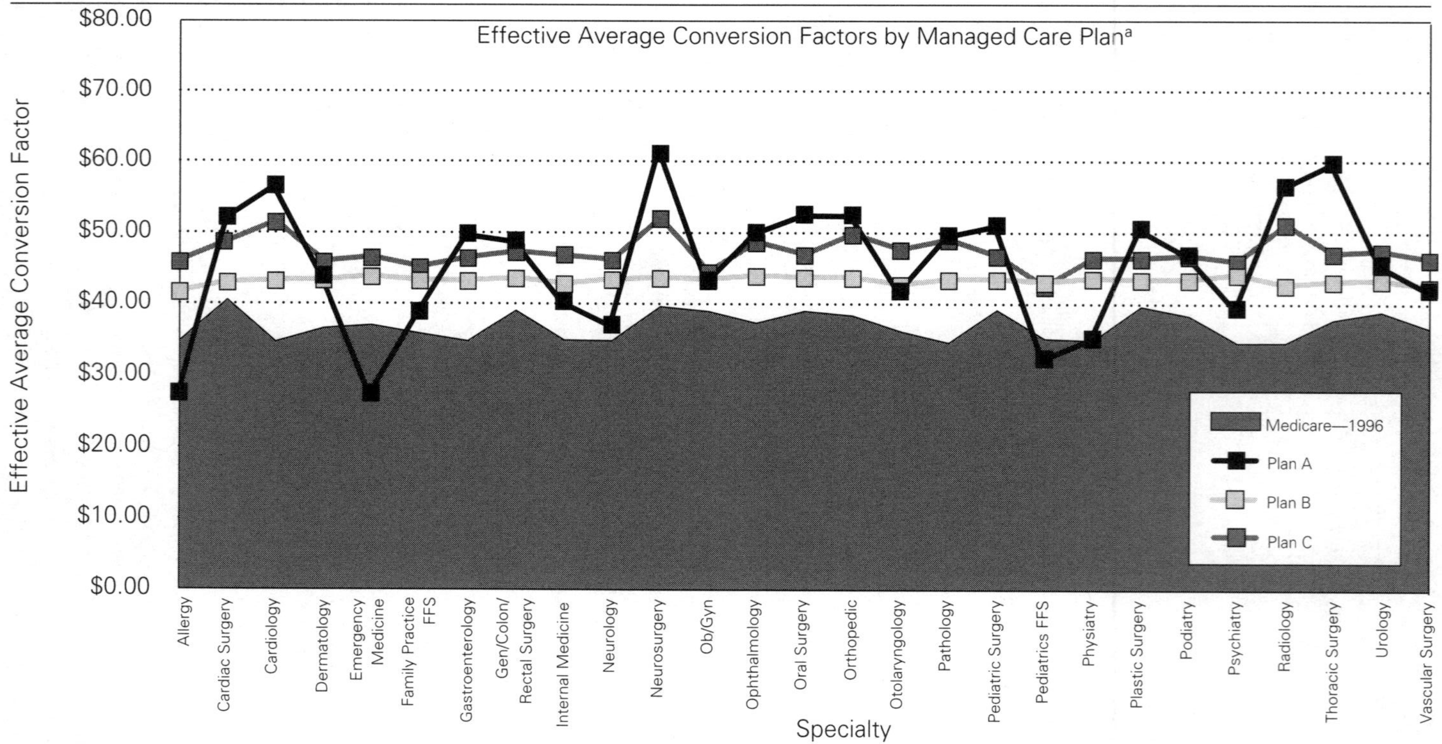

[a]Based on 1996 Medicare RVUs adjusted by the Urban Massachusetts GPCI.

Source: Baycare Health Partners, *Fee Analyzer*, Springfield, MA, 1996.

FIGURE 16-5. Nonrate Contract Terms Analysis

Presented below is Baycare Health Partners' (BHP) rank-ordered checklist of the specific nonrate contract terms that staff members seek to achieve in each contract negotiation.

Hold harmless/indemnification/limitation of liability: Exclude any language that indemnifies the plan against litigation arising out of the provision of covered services. It has become increasingly difficult to separate a plan's utilization review (UR) determination from treatment decisions. This puts clinical staff at greater risk for malpractice litigation based on managed care plans' UR procedures. Also, exclude any language which makes the BHP provider "solely responsible" for the provision of care or otherwise attempts to limit the plan's liability.

Retrospective denial of previously approved care: BHP providers should be able to rely on authorizations (precertifications) even if the plan later determines that the member was not covered for the service or that the service was not medically necessary, unless the authorization was based on inaccurate information given by the provider.

UR issues: The plan should not deny or reduce payment for any care that it considers to have been "medically necessary" if the claim has been submitted on a timely basis, regardless of whether the BHP provider has followed the plan's UR procedures.

At least 30 days prior written notice of changes to UR policies should be provided, and BHP should have the ability to terminate the contract if the changes are unacceptable and the issue cannot be resolved. If BHP gives notice of intent to terminate, new procedures should not go into effect during notice period.

Appeals and reconsideration process should include time limits, a balanced review by providers at both the HMO and provider site, and the possibility to discuss the case with clinical staff from the specialty under review should exist. If the member is an inpatient at the time of appeal, coverage should continue during the appeal period.

There always should be a formal UR appeal process included within the contract, in the case of denied or reduced payment.

Claims submission and payment: "Best efforts" language should be included that states that the provider will submit claims within 90 days.

A clean claim definition with time limits for plan to tell provider it is not a clean claim also should be included.

A plan is required to compensate the provider within 30 days of receiving a completed clean claim. If the plan or plan payer cannot pay within 30 days, it is obligated to pay the provider's usual and customary fees.

Plan should accept electronic claim submission and electronic claim payment.

Retroactive disenrollment: BHP providers should be entitled to rely on plan's verification of a member's coverage even if the plan later determines that the patient was ineligible. This is a business risk the plan should assume. At the very least, the period in which retroactive disenrollment is allowed should be limited to 60 to 90 days. Plan should be responsible for covering claims for

(Continued on next page)

FIGURE 16-5. *(Continued)*

services provided prior to its notice of retroactive disenrollment if the BHP provider attempts to collect from the member or the member's new insurer but is unsuccessful.

New technology: If a new technology, procedure, or drug that was not routinely provided at the time an agreement was negotiated becomes an "expected" part of a service, a separate fee should be negotiated for that new technology, procedure, or drug if it requires the BHP provider to incur significantly more expense than the technology, procedure, or drug it replaces.

Lower of fee schedule or charges: Whenever possible, such a requirement should be omitted, and the amounts in the fee schedule should be the agreed-upon compensation, even when they exceed the amount charged.

Changes in "covered services": When new "covered services" are added to a subscriber's benefit package, BHP should be notified and be able to renegotiate the budget on which risk sharing is based. If the plan and BHP cannot come to terms on a new budget, either party should be able to terminate the agreement.

Misidentification of a covered person: If a member of plan A misidentifies himself as a member of plan B and the BHP provider attempts to verify the eligibility of the individual but is unable to do so, plan A should not deny compensation as long as the services provided are considered "medically necessary" by plan A.

Termination of physician participation by a plan: There should be no termination without cause. When there is termination for cause, the plan should give 30 days notice to BHP, with the physician's authorization. The reason for the intended termination of the physician should be included, giving BHP an opportunity to cure the problem.

Appeals and reconsideration: There should be an impartial mechanism to resolve disputes concerning questions of compensation, fee adjustment, medical necessity, quality of care, UR, or peer review. Appeal procedures should be fair, inexpensive, and expeditious.

Prior written consent for noncovered services: BHP providers should use reasonable efforts to inform patients before providing a specific service the provider knows is not covered by the patient's plan, and the patient should consent to paying for the service if it is not covered by the plan. However, BHP providers should not be required to verify whether the service will be covered (this is a plan/patient responsibility) and should not be required to obtain the patient's written consent (i.e., a note in the medical record should be sufficient).

Medical necessity: Medically necessary or medical necessity should be defined to mean "all health care services required to enhance, preserve, or maintain a covered individual's health rendered in accordance with generally accepted standards of medical practice."

Emergency: The definition of emergency in the BHP agreement with the plan should be consistent with its definition in the federal COBRA "antidumping" provisions.

FIGURE 16-5. *(Continued)*

Paperless referrals: In cases where a plan requires PCPs to authorize referrals to specialists, BHP should encourage the use of a paperless referral system.

Gag rules: BHP contracts should not contain any so-called gag rules, which require providers to refrain from making comments about the managed care plan that could be viewed as being negative or disparaging. Such clauses limit the provider's ability to speak freely with patients about coverage and financial arrangements.

Reinsurance: Under risk-sharing contracts, BHP should retain the right to purchase reinsurance for both inpatient and outpatient services from an outside insurance company. BHP also should reserve the right to purchase reinsurance from the Baystate Health System Insurance Company (BHSIC) at some point in the future, should BHSIC offer such insurance.

Reciprocal assignment language: Neither the plan nor the provider should be able to assign the contract without the other's prior approval. The contract may be assigned to an entity that is owned or controlled by, or under common control with, the plan or provider.

Provider credentialing: Plan's criteria and process for provider initial credentialing and recredentialing must be a part of the agreement with BHP, and the plan must provide BHP written notice of any changes to its criteria or process. Within 120 days of receiving an application, the plan should determine whether a BHP provider is credentialed. In the event the plan is unable to make a determination within this period because of missing or incomplete information, the plan should inform both BHP and the provider. If a provider is not credentialed, the plan should inform both BHP and the provider which of the criteria the provider failed to meet.

Release of medical records: The plan should obtain releases from its members allowing BHP providers to share medical record and other information with the plan. A plan which wishes to review medical records of a patient receiving care for HIV/AIDS, mental health, or substance abuse must obtain and present to the provider a patient release specific to that situation. Plans requesting copies of medical records should pay the provider's copying expense. Those wishing to review records should arrange the review so as not to interfere with the provider's normal business operations.

Billing covered persons for copayments, etc.: BHP providers should have the right to bill covered persons for copayments, coinsurance, deductibles, excess charges, and noncovered services. Providers also should be able to bill for services considered to be not medically necessary or medically necessary services not paid in a timely manner when providing them to patients of self-insured plans.

BHP usage or network access fee: Payer agrees to administer BHP usage fee or to pay a BHP network access fee.

Source: Baycare Health Partners, Springfield, MA, 1996.

based into an equivalent number for evaluation and comparison across specialties.

As shown in figure 16-4, plan A is an HMO in Baycare's market with a "traditional" fee schedule. In general, it pays higher rates (on a relative value basis) to interventional specialists than to noninterventionalists and primary care specialties. Thus, the line shows many peaks and valleys as one looks at the relative value equivalent payment by specialty. Plan B, represented graphically by an almost horizontal straight line, is an HMO that developed its fee schedule directly from the RBRVS payment system with a single conversion factor. The slight deviations from a flat line for plan B are explained by the minor changes in relative value weight resulting from applying the geographic adjustment (a nuance of the RBRVS system that is relatively unimportant to this level of analysis). Plan C is an HMO that also uses an RBRVS-based fee schedule but, like Medicare, applies multiple conversion factors, as illustrated by the line that largely parallels the Medicare line. This comparative information is shared with the health plan during negotiations and with the Contract Review Committee, the board, and, ultimately, each physician as one piece of input to their decisions on whether they want to "opt in" to a given contract.

The second tool, the nonrate contract terms analysis, is a checklist that Baycare developed based on its experience in contracting. It represents the PHO's desired contracting position. (Baycare also has drafted a "standard" or "ideal" contract to support this position.) For each contract under negotiation, it is possible to analyze how closely it meets Baycare's desired contracting position. Again, this is shared throughout the PHO and serves as an equally important input into the Contract Review Committee's and the board's recommendations related to accepting or rejecting contracts and the physicians' decisions regarding their participation.

Creating a template for risk-based contracts: The last piece of information a PHO should create for its members is an understanding of, and a template for, risk-based contracts. At Baycare, this is done by comparing its risk contracts on a per member per month (PMPM) budgeted basis. This gives a more complete financial picture than the one presented solely in the Fee Analyzer. As a PHO assumes more risk in its contracting, a greater percentage of the ultimate income to its members is tied up in the risk share component and less in the actual fees or capitation paid to any individual physician or hospital. Although many other aspects of contract analysis are beyond the scope of this discussion, these specific tools have been outlined to demonstrate how development of this infrastructure and shared knowledge promotes the strategy of jointly sharing risk and designing risk assumption and management tools to allow the PHO to function as an integrated system of care providers without ceding complete control to either party or to outside parties.

In most cases, current legal constraints on PHOs or networks specifically related to their ability to negotiate fees on behalf of their members have not proved to be major stumbling blocks. First and foremost, this is because PHOs are better tools for negotiating risk contracts, and, second, experience has shown that through a rigorous contracting process as outlined above, the health plans have been very competitive in proposing rates that, in turn, can be passed on to PHO members without entering into specific rate negotiations on their behalf. Thus, although the legal constraints can be inconvenient at times, they in no way keep the PHO from pursuing appropriate business relationships with its partners.

Longer-Term Roles As presented in figure 16-3, longer-term yet critical functions of the PHO are likely to include an investment in information systems to support integration and development of medical management and demand management models and infrastructure to ensure that the PHO succeeds in delivering care in a risk environment. The PHO can demonstrate its real value as an integrating tool in implementing these longer-term functions.

Develop medical management capabilities: A mature PHO can play a very important role in the development of medical management capabilities for its owners and its contracted providers. Effective medical management requires a level of coordination and collaboration among diverse parties that usually does not exist unless some organization has taken responsibility for its achievement. By its very nature, the PHO thrives on opportunities for collaboration. Further, development of true medical management activities is a logical strategy for a provider-driven organization to pursue. As with all major decisions made within Baycare, a committee—the Medical Oversight Committee—was convened. The Medical Oversight Committee draws on representatives from many different disciplines in an attempt to bring together the major "provider players" who will be affected by the change implied in managing the delivery of medical care. To succeed in medical management, the PHO simultaneously must:

- *Create a forum:* In such a forum, different points of view can be aired, education can take place, and consensus can be reached on the clinical, financial, and operational aspects of new initiatives.
- *Focus its efforts:* This ensures that results are tangible and significant, rather than trying to effect the entire spectrum of medical and demand management activities providers should be undertaking.
- *Integrate the financial and medical models it generates:* This is done so that, at a minimum, how providers are paid does not remain a barrier to changing the ways in which they deliver care.

Table 16-1 illustrates a construct introduced to Baycare by representatives of Health Partners Ventures as the PHO embarked on its medical and demand management activities. Baycare has found this "three worlds view" useful in creating a forum for activities as outlined above and for ensuring that issues are addressed from many points of view. By striving to assess all new initiatives from a clinical, operational, and financial point of view, participants are reassured that no one agenda will dominate the decision making, regardless of how compelling it may seem for one or more participants at any given point in the process. The discipline this approach imposes on the process supports the PHO's basic short-term roles and helps to deepen the joint planning efforts of the PHO participants.

Baycare chose to focus its medical management efforts in two ways. First, as presented in table 16-2, its Medical Oversight Committee developed an outline for oversight activities. As presented, a broad spectrum of activities could be undertaken for any specific initiative, and no one "silver bullet" would obviate the need for fundamental change in the delivery system. Second, the committee began by focusing on a limited number of initiatives so that early successes could be generated and used as stepping-stones for tackling more difficult issues. Because the PHO decided to take a major initiative with the Medicare risk population, as presented below, the Medical Oversight Committee decided to focus its

TABLE 16-1. Three Worlds of a Health Care Organization

	Clinical	*Operational*	*Financial*
Basic questions	What care is called for? Is it high quality?	What will it take to accomplish care? Is it well executed?	How will care utilize resources? Is it a good value?
Object	Unfolding casework	Systems	Numbers
Process	Actions by clinicians and patients	Operations	Accounting
Outcome	Achievement of health goals	Production	Bottom line
Standard	Technical and service quality and elegance	Efficiency and facility	Price and value

Source: Adapted from C. J. Peek and R. L. Heinrich, "Building a Collaborative Healthcare Organization: From *Idea* to *Invention* to *Innovation*," *Family Systems Medicine* 13, no. 3/4 (1995); 330–32.

TABLE 16-2. Medical Oversight Activities

Activities for Medical Management

Activity in Order of Priority	*Critical to Success*
Risk assessment	• Identify high-risk patients (risk stratification) • Early intervention by appropriate providers
Case management	• Identify and coordinate appropriate interventions for the defined population
Pathways and guides	• Identify achievable goals (clinical and financial) • Provider involvement in development and acceptance and use of pathways • Staff and infrastructure support of pathways • Availability of continuum services to meet goals • Extend beyond inpatient services
Utilization management	• Implement clinical pathways • Limit preventable clinical and resource usage variance • Reduce cost per episode
Continuum of care services	• Identification of needed services • Services available in network through affiliations or preferred relationships
Discharge planning	• Appropriate identification of patient needs (care map) • Timely access to appropriate postdischarge setting • Use of network providers
Demand management	• Identify specific medical conditions that are amenable for successful early interventions • Promote health awareness and self-care through enrollee education
Access to care	• One phone call system for providers and patients requesting services and/or information • Phone triage with well-defined protocols • Referral system to network providers
Clinical outcome measurement	• Identify clinical outcomes for measurement • Provider acceptance

Note: Provider and patient education, communication among involved parties, and information systems for monitoring and evaluating are critical to success for all of the activities.

Source: Baycare Health Partners, Springfield, MA, 1996.

efforts on the highest-volume, highest-cost inpatient diagnoses that occur within this population.

One of the most significant problems facing PHOs is that, frequently, "doing the right thing" medically can cost the providers in real dollars. For instance, it may be appropriate to transfer a patient to a different level of care at a certain point in his or her course of treatment, but if the hospital and the attending physician both lose income as a result of the transfer, the odds of it occurring are lowered. It is for this reason that integrating the financial and medical models is so important. This also is why the "three worlds view" has proved helpful.

Integration can be accomplished in many ways, but Baycare focused its efforts on the Medicare risk market because it offered the greatest opportunity to influence both the payment for, and the pattern of, care for this population. Not coincidentally, this also is the area in which the health plans have the least established infrastructures that would need to be changed to accommodate the emerging delivery system models of care. As a result of this decision, the PHO developed, through its Contract Review Committee, a model of risk and reward sharing for the Medicare risk market that supports the Medical Oversight Committee's medical management activities. In turn, the successes of these activities, developed by the Medical Oversight Committee, can be fed back into the contracting functions, creating more integrated models of alignment and risk and reward sharing in the future.

Ensure a balanced "ecosystem" of providers: A PHO can play many other important roles in a delivery system. Baycare has assumed the task of limiting its enrollment by specialty and geography to ensure that it has a balanced "ecosystem" of providers. This activity, overseen by the Professional Panel Committee, has required Baycare to educate the committee on the most current research in delivery system models and has challenged local thinking on how care should be delivered and by whom. Thus, Baycare is a "mostly closed" PHO in that new physician providers are allowed entry only if they serve a defined need. (See chapter 17 for a discussion of closed PHOs.) Baycare's current challenge relates to the credentialing and monitoring of such nonphysician providers as nurse midwives, mental health providers, nurse practitioners, and many others who provide valuable services in the delivery systems in Baycare's market.

Invest in information systems: A final important role is in the information systems field. Although a discussion of health care information systems is well beyond the scope of this chapter, a PHO can make some investments that may prove valuable in the future. As presented earlier, the Fee Analyzer, which is used for cross-plan comparisons of fees paid to physicians, has proved to be a very worthwhile investment.

Baycare also has installed a claims-reporting system that uses an open-architecture, database format to allow the PHO to report information on its performance across plans. This in turn implies that Baycare must negotiate with each plan under contract that it will provide an electronic copy of every adjudicated claim paid to either one of the PHO's providers (in the case of nonrisk plans) or charged against its budget (in the case of risk-sharing arrangements). Needless to say, this task has not been easy and not all plans can comply with this requirement. However, Baycare has found that, through perseverance, it can get claims information from most of the plans, and it is beginning to use this information for cross-plan comparisons.

Specifically, Baycare providers now are able to look at their claims performance across plans, rather than using the traditional approach where each plan reports its own experience for a particular provider. Although it is early in the process, it is thought that because Baycare will have a database consisting of a broader scope of information sooner than any one plan will, this cross-plan reporting will enhance both physician and hospital ability to more immediately assess their real performance. Further, it has never made sense for each plan to have its own reporting approach. After all, the same providers are treating the same population regardless of which health plan happens to provide their insurance. This claims-reporting system has required a significant investment. Although it is too early to tell whether it will pay off, it is the only place in this market where a database of cross-plan performance for the full medical service budget is being built.

IMPLICATIONS OF STRUCTURE, GOVERNANCE, AND ROLES

As with all organizations, the PHO's structure, governance, and the roles it chooses to play will have an immense impact on its operations and its effect on its owners and participating providers. First and foremost, if a PHO is to play the roles outlined in figure 16-3, its board of directors must be prepared to make a major, ongoing investment in the PHO. Many PHOs have been developed "on the cheap," without appropriate attention to the need for independent staff who can help balance the conflicting needs of its owners. PHOs vary widely in the number and types of staff they employ.[3] However, one of the major reasons PHOs are often ineffective is because they are severely understaffed from the outset and do not have appropriate mechanisms for developing the staff and individuals who serve on their committees. Because few PHOs have a long track record, their staff have to be drawn from related fields. To do so, it is important that the most critical attributes or competencies of the key executives be well defined in advance to assist in the recruitment process. It is Baycare's experience that among the most important attributes for executives are group facilitation expertise, strong interpersonal skills, negotiation and financial skills, and a deep understanding of the clinical aspects of the delivery of care in the PHO's region.

Closely related to the staffing issue is the need to have a consistent and relatively reliable long-term funding source. A PHO has only two viable means of funding: Either its owners must make ongoing direct contributions, or the PHO must take a percentage of the revenues its providers derive from its managed care contracts. Many PHOs use both forms of funding in different combinations. Baycare's financial plan called for two years of contributions by its owners, with a "usage fee" or percent of contract revenues as the longer-term funding mechanism. Any funding approach has strengths and weaknesses, but long term, the PHO needs to have the certainty of a base level of funding if it is to attract and retain high-caliber staff. Thus, most PHOs find it advantageous to collect a percentage of managed care revenues, a recurring source of income, rather than repeatedly trying to seek funds from its founders.

Critics often cite the corporate form of most PHOs (not-for-profit taxable corporation) as a weakness. The logic behind this criticism is that without stock ownership, physicians cannot build equity in the corporation and, as a result, presumably cannot build wealth. However, such critics miss the point: PHOs are not intended to build equity. Accumulation of equity implies a retention of earnings that otherwise would have been paid to providers for the services they offer. Thus, if a PHO builds equity, it is doing so at the expense of the providers themselves. PHOs never were conceived to be equity vehicles; rather, they were meant to be joint planning and collaboration vehicles that return the maximum amount of the health care dollar to the providers that deliver the most value. If equity accumulation is the primary goal, a PHO should not be the primary vehicle employed.

Finally, it should be noted that PHOs are organizations that operate on reaching consensus. The board structure, the fact that board members have competing agendas, and the challenging nature of the issues faced in an increasingly competitive environment all argue for the need to invest substantial time in the operation of the PHO. New skills will be required of its staff and participants. However, regardless of corporate form, the development of such collaboration skills may be required of all providers who wish to succeed in the future.

CONCLUSION

Despite the failures predicted by their critics, PHOs are serving as building blocks in the restructuring of the U.S. health care system, if for no other reason than that they are integral parts of a comprehensive strategy for delivering cost-effective care. Ultimately, PHOs are about trust. Trust takes a great deal of time to build and nurture, and is supported by a consistent track record of shared accomplishments through relinquishing of control. Many believe that the truly successful organizations will be those that learn how to operate outside the traditional, hierarchical, command-and-control management structures common in many for-profit corporations. Command-and-control management certainly is more comfortable for many board members and the entrenched management of health care organizations (including physician group practices and venture capital firms). However, integration involves developing new ways of linking organizations and activities that may prove to be too difficult and expensive to do in anything other than a collaborative way. Although PHOs may not be the vehicle to address all the challenges faced by physicians and hospitals as they retool the delivery system to meet the market's needs, the trust and consensus building fostered by a PHO very well may be precisely what are needed—necessary, if not always sufficient, ingredients for success.

References

1. *1995/96 Profile of Physician-Hospital Organizations and PHO Executives,* survey by the American Association of Physician Hospital Organizations/Integrated Delivery Systems, Inc. and Tyler & Company (Atlanta, GA: Tyler & Co., 1996), pp. 1–3.

2. P. M. Friend, "PHO Growing Pains," *Healthcare Executive* (May/June 1996): 12–16; J. Greene, "Integrated Delivery Looms as Most Significant Issue for System Executives," *Modern Healthcare* 70, no. 15 (Aug. 1996): 91–94; T. Hudson, "What PHOs Know," *Hospitals & Health Networks* 70, no. 17 (Sept. 1996): 54–58; E. Pagnani, ed., "Open Physician-Hospital Organization," in *The Grand Alliance: Vertical Integration Strategies for Physicians and Health Systems* (Washington, DC: The Advisory Board Co., 1993), pp. 161–84; and E. Pagnani, ed., "Closed Physician-Hospital Organization," in *The Grand Alliance,* pp. 189–223.

3. American Association of Physician Hospital Organizations/Integrated Delivery Systems, Inc., and Tyler & Company, pp. 5–10.

17

Physician-Hospital Organizations: Strategy, Structure, and Conduct

Lawton R. Burns, PhD
Darrell P. Thorpe, MD

Since the demise of the Clinton health plan, all eyes have focused on the private sector to control rising health care costs while maintaining (or improving) the quality of care. Partly in response to an anticipated national reform, the private sector has become increasingly engaged in efforts to reorganize the delivery of health care. Horizontal integration via mergers, acquisitions, and strategic alliances has become popular among hospitals, physicians and physician groups, and HMOs.[1] Vertical integration between physicians and hospitals, providers and insurers, drug manufacturers and pharmacy benefit managers, and outpatient surgery centers and rehabilitation clinics also has come into vogue.

Despite all this activity, however, there is little documented evidence to support the promised benefits of integration. With regard to horizontal integration, prior reviews have uncovered few tangible benefits of multihospital systems.[2] More recent studies of hospital and HMO mergers suggest that horizontal integration is often motivated by desires for market power and expanded service networks,[3] with the possibility of achieving some economies of scale.[4] With regard to vertical integration, few benefits have been demonstrated in either industry or health care,[5] although four recently completed studies do suggest that physician-organization integration promotes clinical integration, inpatient productivity, hospital profitability, and physician alignment.[6] However, it may be too early to gauge the success of vertically integrated arrangements. As researchers in the Health Systems Integration Study point out, even the most advanced of these arrangements is in a nascent stage of development.[7] Moreover, these arrangements have not widely diffused.

This chapter focuses on one model of vertical integration, the physician-hospital organization (PHO), as a potential vehicle for delivering cost-effective health care and examines its strategy, structure, and market conduct. First is a brief description of PHOs and their hypothesized advantages and disadvantages. Next, strategy is described in terms of the array of goals articulated and pursued by PHOs. Discussion then focuses on the structure of PHOs, comparing their managed care mechanisms with those used by HMOs. PHOs are intended to accept and manage risk imposed by HMOs in managed care contracts. To be effective, PHOs may need to adopt similar mechanisms. Next, PHO conduct is examined in terms of several behavioral factors that may influence their ability to reduce costs and improve quality: for example, administrative commitment to PHOs, excessive hospital influence in PHOs, and trends away from restrictive provider networks. Finally, a detailed case study of one of the nation's oldest PHOs, founded in 1987, illustrates PHO strategy, structure, and conduct and highlights the difficulty in using this integrative approach to achieve cost-effective care.

PHOs were selected for analysis for several reasons. First, they are widely viewed as a starting point for many integrated delivery systems (IDSs).[8] Second, they often are the initial effort undertaken by physicians and hospitals to manage care and risk under capitated contracts. Third, according to two national hospital surveys conducted in 1993, the PHO is the most common form of vertical integration. The prevalence of community hospital-sponsored PHOs ranges from 13.6[9] to 16.3 percent.[10] Finally, there exist both survey and case study data to assess the cost-effectiveness potential of PHOs.[11]

PHYSICIAN-HOSPITAL ORGANIZATION OVERVIEW

A PHO is a joint venture between one or more hospitals and a group of physicians. Physicians contract individually with a physician entity (for example, a professional corporation) in which they invest and have an ownership stake. This entity then contracts with the PHO, and invests in and owns it together with the hospital(s). (See chapter 16.) Initial capitalization and ownership vary across PHOs, but most strive for equal physician-hospital ownership.[12]

Why enter into this particular joint venture? PHOs are largely a defensive provider reaction to increasing managed care penetration. The

PHO serves as a single provider agent for managed care contracting, presenting a united front to payers. The two parties can exert greater bargaining leverage and respond to purchaser preferences for a single, bundled price. In this manner, the PHO theoretically can resist continued discounting in provider fees as well as obtain managed care contracts by providing value-added services. Additionally, the PHO may be attractive to managed care payers wishing to reduce their transaction costs with multiple providers and to transfer some of the financial risk for patient care. To be seen as cost-effective by payers, the PHO must have active medical management, utilization management, quality assurance (QA), sophisticated information systems, and intensive physician involvement in developing standards of care.

PHOs also may be a proactive hospital strategy to develop a foundation of physician-hospital collaboration for future IDS formation. The PHO serves as a vehicle for collaboration on quality improvement and cost containment efforts on a small scale (for example, capitated contracts negotiated by the PHO). This foundation protects physician autonomy and maintains the separate lines of business for both parties. PHOs typically include an escape clause that permits either side to undertake attractive ventures without the other.

Variations among Physician-Hospital Organizations

PHOs vary in terms of their inclusion and exclusion of physicians. *Open PHOs* are open to virtually the entire medical staff and thus tend to be heavily dominated by specialists (reflecting the medical staff composition). Open PHOs may in fact be instigated by specialists in an effort to circumvent selective contracting by HMOs and obtain some managed care business for themselves.[13] *Closed PHOs,* on the other hand, restrict physician membership by varying means, including (1) limits on the number of specialists by specialty type, thereby increasing the representation of primary care physicians (PCPs); and (2) the use of membership criteria ranging from basic credentials to economic profiling. Due to such mechanisms, closed PHOs may be more attractive to managed care payers.

PHOs also vary in terms of organizational base. According to data gathered in 1995 by the American Hospital Association, the largest proportion of PHOs (25.5 percent) are hospital based. A smaller percentage are developed at the hospital system level (10.8 percent) for their member hospitals.[14] As an illustration of a network PHO, multiple hospitals in different cities may develop a single area- or statewide PHO to pursue contracts with large employers and payers.[15] These network PHOs are distinct from so-called super PHOs, which are joint ventures among multiple PHOs in a local market or state. Super PHOs have formed in Arizona, Florida, and Oklahoma to develop an insurance vehicle (for example, an HMO) that complements the physician and hospital entities.[16] In this manner, the super PHO resembles an integrated health care organization that more closely aligns the incentives of providers and payers.[17]

Physician-Hospital Organization Advantages and Disadvantages

The previous section suggests some of the theoretical advantages and disadvantages of PHOs. The PHO strengthens the providers' bargaining position with managed care payers by presenting a united front; offers the ability to contract for a single, bundled price; and represents a potential cost control strategy. It also serves as an initial step toward aligning the incentives of physicians and hospitals in preparation for further integration efforts. The PHO's chief disadvantage is that it requires a substantial infrastructure (for example, medical and utilization management, information systems) and physician involvement to be effective. Without such an infrastructure, the PHO may fail to improve the contracting capability of its physician and hospital members. Moreover, once this infrastructure is developed, there is no guarantee that managed care payers will contract on a capitated basis with the PHO and pass on the financial risk and reward for patient care. These advantages and disadvantages are considered in greater detail in the next three sections dealing with PHO strategy, structure, and conduct.

Physician-Hospital Organization Strategy

Firms typically pursue multiple goals that reflect both customer demands and competition (for example, low-cost and high-quality products, increased market share). Such considerations are paramount today in the health care industry. Cost and quality have long served as the key objectives of both providers and the federal government.[18] Right-sizing and market share have become increasingly important due to excess capacity and the oversupply of specialists.

Two recent surveys outline goals pursued by PHOs. They indicate that cost and quality are not the PHO's paramount objectives. According to a 1994 survey of 109 PHOs conducted by Hamilton/KSA, the vast majority (88 percent) cite enhanced ability to contract with managed care.[19] Additional rationales include efforts to promote vertical integration (78 percent), ability to risk-contract (67 percent), and cost containment (50 percent). Another 1994 survey of 189 PHOs by Ernst & Young reveals a similar set of objectives.[20] In this survey, 88 percent of respondents rated contracting with managed care organizations (MCOs) as a "very important" reason for starting a PHO. Additional reasons included collaborating with the medical staff (77 percent), enhancing quality of care (63 percent), sharing financial risk (61 percent), and facilitating direct contracting with employers (52 percent).

To fully capture the strategy of PHOs, it also is important to examine how PHOs measure their success. If the goals of PHOs are assessed by performance measures, the Ernst & Young survey results largely substantiate the conclusion above that PHOs exist for managed care contracting. According to the survey findings, PHOs measure performance in terms of number of covered lives (or share of covered lives in a market), number of payer contracts, and profitability of those contracts.

Overall, PHO strategy seems to focus primarily on winning managed care contracts, securing a number of such contracts with a large number of covered lives, and gaining market share in an increasingly capitated environment. A set of secondary goals focuses on developing partnerships between hospitals and their medical staffs in order to jointly manage risk under capitated contracts. The goal of providing cost-effective care appears to lag behind these other objectives, perhaps reflecting providers' realization that their ability to render higher-quality care at a lower cost will require time-intensive collaborative efforts that develop over time.

PHYSICIAN-HOSPITAL ORGANIZATION STRUCTURE

Organization researchers have long argued that a firm's strategy should be reflected in its structure.[21] Where strategies and structures are well matched, the firm's survival prospects and performance are enhanced. It was argued above that PHO strategy centers around winning managed care contracts. Two points follow from this argument. First, PHO structure should reflect and support this strategy. Second, to win managed care contracts, PHOs must satisfy the objectives of managed care payers. Managed care payers seek provider networks that offer comprehensive services across a wide geographic area to their enrollees. Equally important, payers seek networks willing to contract at the lowest price for a reasonable level of quality.[22] Payers also may wish to share the economic risk of care with providers via capitated contracts.

Thus, PHO structures should be designed to accept and manage risk imposed in managed care contracts. To be effective, PHOs may need to adopt managed care mechanisms similar to those used by HMOs. Three types of managed care mechanisms are analyzed here:

- Physician panel selection
- Physician financial incentives

- Nonfinancial systems to monitor and influence physician practice patterns

These mechanisms have been previously identified as the major determinants of HMO success in containing costs.[23]

Physician Panel Selection

A recent survey of 108 HMOs conducted by Mathematica for the Physician Payment Review Commission (PPRC) reports that HMO senior management considers physician selection to be the most important feature in the plan's success.[24] The philosophy adopted by HMOs appears to be "quality in, quality out." That is, the plans attempt to carefully screen physician applicants up front prior to contracting. They take several steps to verify the physician's license and credentials, and review his or her malpractice experience, patient records, practice style, and office. They also set selected requirements for participation, including the physician's ability to obtain privileges at network hospitals, board certification, strong peer references, and willingness to treat Medicare and Medicaid patients.

Various surveys of PHOs show little evidence of physician panel screening. This lack of screening is first apparent from the large panel size of PHOs. Surveys have reported average panel sizes ranging from 262 physicians[25] to 289[26] to 347.[27] The large number of physicians tend to include 95 percent or more of the hospital medical staff.[28] Even in closed PHOs, where greater selectivity is said to be present, more than 80 percent of the medical staff may be members.[29] Thus, it is obvious that PHOs emphasize breadth of membership rather than selectivity. Hospital managers may be reluctant to "freeze out" physicians who are not cost-effective. In contrast to HMOs, their network selection philosophy appears to be "prune later." This philosophy has important implications for the PHO's potential impact. Due to large membership panels, each member physician is likely to see very few PHO patients (that is, patients in managed care plans that contract with the PHO). Consequently, PHO membership and practice will likely have little effect on the physician.

The lack of screening also is evident by the specialty mix of the PHO membership roster. According to the Ernst & Young study, PHOs are specialist dominated: 75 percent of them have more specialists than generalists. This seems odd given the PHO's need to right-size the number of generalist and specialist physicians to attract managed care payers.

Finally, the lack of careful screening is evident by the type of criteria used to select the physician panel. According to the Center for Health Management Research study, 79 percent of PHOs have selection criteria and use an average of 8.4 criteria.[30] These criteria tend to be the same as some of those employed by HMOs, including membership on hospital medical staff (100 percent of PHOs), no revocation or suspension of hospital privileges (91 percent), board certification (82 percent), primary care specialty (72 percent), and immunity to medical staff action (55 percent). Additional criteria mentioned in other studies include current license and liability coverage and satisfactory review of professional history.[31] In-office reviews, chart reviews, and peer recommendations appear to be little used.

Of course, PHOs face barriers to selective physician panel development. For example, hospitals encounter legal barriers in the form of lawsuits filed by excluded physicians who claim restraint of trade. They also face political pressures resulting from physician resentment over their exclusion or their colleagues' exclusion, as well as governing board fear of alienating community physicians. Finally, unlike insurers and HMOs (once contracts are signed), hospitals lack objective data on physicians' office practice patterns, which might be used to evaluate their performance.

Physician Financial Incentives

Altered financial incentives have long been noted as a distinguishing characteristic of managed care organizations (MCOs).[32] According to the 1994 PPRC survey of HMOs, capitation is almost as prominent a method for paying PCPs as fee-for-service (37 versus 43 percent of plans). In addition to capitation, HMOs also utilize withholds and bonuses to share some financial risk with physicians. Additional adjustments are made to PCP payments to ensure that quality and productivity objectives are met. Typically, these are based on utilization and cost measures, patient complaints, quality measures, consumer surveys, and physician productivity.

In contrast, PHOs have not broadly engaged in risk contracting. According to the Hamilton/KSA survey, only 44 percent of PHOs have risk contracts, and of these, three-quarters have fewer than four contracts. Similarly, the Ernst & Young survey reports that only 52 percent of PHOs have risk contracts. However, most of their covered lives are under PPO contracts that involve no capitation and little or no risk. Consequently, it is not surprising that PHO physicians are paid primarily fee-for-service. This appears to be true even when the PHO accepts capitation. The only risk-sharing mechanism used appears to be withholds. However, because the physician group is at risk in the withhold pool, and because the physician panel is so large, the incentive facing the individual physician is diluted.

Moreover, there appears to be little equity participation in PHOs on the part of physicians. Although PHOs are supposed to be 50-50 joint ventures between the hospital and physicians, the hospital typically capitalizes the PHO whereas physicians promise to contribute later. The

Ernst & Young survey shows that 78 percent of PHOs are at least 50 percent owned by hospitals whereas only 5.7 percent of PHOs are majority owned by physicians. The Center for Health Management Research study similarly found that hospitals have an average ownership stake of 71 percent whereas physicians have only an 18 percent ownership. Moreover, only 35 percent of physician partners in the PHO actually invest. This ownership stake tends to be quite small, as little as one or two thousand dollars.[33]

Nonfinancial Systems to Monitor Physician Practice

HMOs have developed several mechanisms and programs to monitor and influence the practice patterns of their physicians. According to the PPRC survey, HMOs use internal mechanisms such as written QA plans, a QA committee, a patient grievance procedure, outcome studies for select conditions, targeted quality improvement initiatives, and consumer surveys. They also employ several utilization management programs (for example, practice guidelines, practice profiling, utilization review), gatekeeper PCPs, a physician recredentialing process, and external accreditation programs.

In contrast, medical management programs in PHOs are "in process."[34] The burgeoning mechanisms appear to include utilization review, case management, gatekeeper PCPs, PCP financial incentives to meet utilization targets, identification of outliers, practice parameters, and clinical pathways.[35] No statistics are available on their prevalence.

What seems clear from the available survey data is that PHOs lack a managed care infrastructure. According to the Ernst & Young survey, the majority of PHOs have no full-time positions in finance, utilization management, management information systems, marketing, or provider relations. Although a majority of PHOs do have a medical director, this individual devotes less than one-quarter of his or her time to the position in two-thirds of these PHOs. PHOs also appear to be severely hampered by a lack of utilization statistics, data to assess profit and loss, and adequate budgets.[36]

Summary of Physician-Hospital Organization Structure

This review suggests a lack of congruence between PHO strategy and PHO structure. To be effective at winning managed care contracts (the strategy), PHOs must demonstrate an ability to reduce costs, control utilization, document quality, and provide comprehensive services. The recent survey evidence indicates that PHO structure currently is underdeveloped in the areas of cost and medical management. Because PHOs are hospital based, they also may be unable to offer a full continuum of services that are both convenient (for example, one-stop shopping) and accessible at multiple sites.

PHYSICIAN-HOSPITAL ORGANIZATION CONDUCT

Several behavioral factors may further limit PHO ability to affect the cost and quality of health care. The first is lack of administrative commitment. Hospital executives may develop a PHO but invest most of their time and resources in the acquisition of physician practices. The Hamilton/KSA survey suggests that practice acquisition activity will accelerate. Executives also may neglect to channel hospital employees into the PHO to gain experience with capitation on a population it knows well, sometimes due to employee resistance to restricted panels of providers (even their own). Finally, hospital executives may continue to view the PHO as a vehicle to bolster inpatient admissions and days in the short term, rather than prepare for managed care and treat the hospital as a cost center.

A second, related limitation may be excessive hospital influence in the PHO. Statistics previously cited reveal that PHOs have few dedicated staff. Rather, PHO staff appear to be borrowed from hospital administration. Coupled with the heavy share of hospital capitalization, physicians may be rightfully wary of the PHO as a vehicle serving the interests of administration. In addition, because such a large percentage of PHO executive directors come from hospitals, it is unclear whether any managed care expertise can be transferred to the PHO.

A third limitation on PHO ability to provide cost-effective health care may be its extensive contracting with "managed care lite" programs.[37] According to the Ernst & Young survey, the single largest market for PHOs (41 percent of payers) are preferred provider organizations (PPOs). Such contracts typically involve little or no risk to providers. Indeed, more than 86 percent of PHOs with PPO contracts did not accept capitation.[38] Future trends suggest greater contracting with point-of-service (POS) options, which have become increasingly popular among employers.[39] Unfortunately, POS options militate against the use of restrictive provider networks.

CASE STUDY

The Physician Hospital Organization of Tucson (PHO Inc.) provides an historical, dynamic illustration of many of the issues identified in the cross-sectional surveys reviewed in the previous sections. PHO Inc. has existed for an extended period, which ensures a sufficient time frame to evaluate its impact on cost, quality, and access to services.

Background

PHO Inc. was formed in 1987 as a jointly owned business corporation by two organizations, TMCare, a tax-exempt parent of Tucson Medical Center (TMC), and Southern Arizona Independent Physicians (SAIP), a professional corporation. The PHO was expressly formed "to maintain the highest quality reasonably possible in the provision of health care in a cost-efficient manner and to review the appropriate utilization of health care services rendered by or through PHO and its programs."[40]

TMC was a 600-bed, general acute care hospital offering a full range of secondary and tertiary services to residents of Tucson and southeastern Arizona. At the time of PHO Inc.'s formation, TMC had a specialist-dominated voluntary medical staff numbering in excess of one thousand members, approximately one-third of which concentrated their hospital work at TMC. Previously, the hospital had worked with a subset of its medical staff (those it identified as future economic partners) in the formation of a joint-ventured PPO and an HMO in which involved physicians participated equally in governance and had an opportunity for ownership. These physicians, representing a range of specialties, had been actively involved in hospital leadership roles (for example, strategic planning). They were selected and viewed by management as natural leaders within the medical staff organizational structure.

SAIP was an independent practice association (IPA) formed by physicians who concentrated their practices at TMC. It was formed specifically to provide physician services and a vehicle for physician participation in the governance of TMC's HMO, Partners Health Plan of Arizona (Partners). The leaders who formed SAIP were generally the same physicians who had played leadership roles in the earlier PPO and, like TMC's medical staff, were mostly specialists. SAIP served as the physician credentialing arm of Partners, and it established, as one criterion for participation, a demonstrated preference for using TMC for hospital admissions. Other criteria for participation included a physician's reputation for delivering high-quality service in a cost-effective manner. Some data were available from the hospital to assist in evaluating physicians on these criteria, but by and large selection was made based on personal experiences of the physicians engaged in the selection process. Although SAIP selected and credentialed physicians for provider contracts with the HMO, the actual contracts were executed between Partners and the individual physicians. SAIP was a shareholder-owned entity with 21 owners initially (more than 100 owners eventually) and many more "members" (more than 400 eventually) participating as contract providers to Partners. The shareholders capitalized SAIP through the sale of stock and, throughout its existence, were predominantly specialists.

In 1986, the Tucson market was an active managed care market (approximately 25 percent of commercially insured individuals in managed care), with the HMO as the dominant managed care product. There were three established group model HMOs competing with Partners, and HMO penetration was high enough for the independent physicians in the community to begin feeling the loss of patients.

PHO Inc. Formation

PHO Inc. was formed as the result of a year-long series of meetings between leaders of SAIP and TMC. The meetings focused on the kind of future relationship between the two organizations that would be most effective in achieving the following objectives:

- Partners Health Plan becoming a major factor in the local managed care market by expanding its membership and becoming profitable
- SAIP and TMC sharing risk and reward in the realization of Partner success
- Preventing interorganizational strife as a result of the hospital "getting into the doctor business" (that is, developing primary care centers) and physicians "getting into the hospital business" (that is, developing physician-owned imaging centers)
- Having a formal vehicle for joint strategic planning and giving physicians more voice in major strategic decisions at the hospital

The two parties agreed that the health care environment in southeastern Arizona would become increasingly penetrated by managed care and, ultimately, price competitive. The parties had earlier agreed that owning and managing the payer part of the system was preferable to simply contracting with payers, and strongly believed that the hospital and physicians working together would be more successful in that type of environment than if they operated independently. They also desired systems of care that were differentiated from each other based on the network of providers involved in the system. It was for those reasons and during these discussions that SAIP and TMC committed to "mutual exclusivity." This involved an agreement that SAIP would be the exclusive physician credentialing arm of TMC's HMO and that SAIP, as an organization, would not contract with any HMO other than Partners, even though its individual shareholders and members could and would. The quid pro quo from the hospital was that the HMO would not contract with any other group or IPA without first obtaining consent from SAIP.

The relationship was embodied in a new joint venture corporation called PHO Inc., owned 50 percent by SAIP and 50 percent by TMCare (the parent of TMC). Governance was also 50-50, with the chair rotating each year from SAIP to TMC. PHO Inc. was thinly capitalized on an equal-share basis with the understanding that money would be borrowed from local lending institutions for projects requiring significant capital and that TMC would guarantee those loans as necessary. It was decided not to hire separate staff initially but, instead, to use TMC staff until there was need for separate management (a need that was never identified). A preincorporation document was developed and approved by the governing boards of both organizations. Important features of this agreement included the aforementioned focus on quality, cost, and utilization; the mutual exclusivity feature; and a "right of first refusal" for PHO Inc. to any project in which either party might be crossing the line into the traditional "business" of the other. Incorporation occurred in early 1987.

PHO Inc.'s initial work plan identified the following activities:

- Shared-risk contracting by PHO Inc. with Partners for all physician and hospital services, with downstream contracts from the PHO to the hospital and individual physicians. Partners retained administrative functions.
- Contracting by PHO Inc. with Partners to provide credentialing, utilization management, and quality management services for the plan. This involved utilization management and quality management committees being established by PHO Inc. and providing services to the plan, such as development and implementation of utilization management policies and procedures, and the conduct of peer review and other QA activities.
- Development of three PHO-owned primary care centers in areas where there was an agreed-upon shortage of primary care for the HMO.
- Development of a PHO-sponsored joint venture imaging center among the hospital, a local radiology group (members of SAIP), and other SAIP members who wished to participate.
- Strategy development for the hospital and SAIP through the PHO board.

Experiences with PHO Inc. Operation

The contract between PHO Inc. and Partners established three separate risk pools, one each for hospital services, specialist services, and primary care services. Expenditure targets were established for each pool based on actuarial projections modified for previous actual expenditures. The hospital pool was funded through a 10 percent withhold from hospital reimbursement. The hospital was reimbursed on a per-diem basis, with different per diems for different levels of service such as general medical and surgical services, intensive care services, and pediatric services. The specialist and primary care risk pools were funded through 20 percent withholds from physician reimbursement, which was based on a fee schedule. Year-end settlement of risk pools was done with physicians, both primary care and specialists, sharing in hospital deficits and surpluses and the hospital sharing in deficits in both physician risk pools, but not in surpluses. The specialists and PCPs each shared in the deficits and surpluses of their own respective risk pools, whereas PCPs also shared in deficits in the specialist risk pool.

It was expected that the combination of this shared risk and reward program, along with the PHO contracting to provide utilization and quality management services, would bring serious shared focus to reducing total costs while protecting or improving the quality of services provided. Those expectations were realized in terms of increased focus, but only to a modest degree in actual reduced costs. Physicians viewed the withhold as simply a second discount, and some responded by increasing units of services provided (churning) to recover that second discount. This resulted in overall increased utilization and loss of some reimbursement to risk pool settlements; those physicians whose utilization was inappropriately high benefited at the expense of those whose behavior was more appropriate.

Controversy also developed between hospital management and representatives of the IPA over in-hospital utilization management decisions. Because the IPA members shared risk for inpatient hospital utilization, and because the hospital was paid different rates for different levels of service, there were frequent arguments over the necessity of a patient's staying an additional day in the ICU rather than in a general medical and surgical bed, or in a general medical and surgical bed rather than in a subacute care unit. Financial incentives had not been fully aligned as had been hoped.

Monthly PHO Inc. board meetings provided an opportunity to discuss the problems created by the compensation and risk/reward-sharing scheme. It was agreed that a provider compensation task force would be formed to make recommendations for change. Several of the most vocally dissatisfied physicians were selected to meet with representatives of the hospital and the HMO, and a new compensation scheme was developed with the following provisions:

1. PCPs would be capitated on an age- and sex-adjusted basis. A target would be established for expenditures on specialist referrals, and PCPs would receive a bonus equal to 50 percent of the

difference between actual and targeted referral cost down to a limit of acceptable rate of referral determined by the plan's actuaries.

2. Specialists would be paid according to a maximum allowable fee schedule with no withhold. They would be eligible for a bonus based on actual-versus-targeted hospital costs.
3. The hospital would be reimbursed on a global per diem and would continue to have a 10 percent withhold at risk based on actual-versus-targeted hospital costs.

Use of capitation payments for PCPs was viewed as a way to motivate appropriate PCP utilization and as a solution to the churning problem. The abandonment of withholds in favor of bonuses was a purely psychological move. It became clear that, rather than recover a withhold, physicians would prefer a guaranteed fixed rate of compensation (even if lower than previously) and then have an opportunity to earn a bonus. Thus, the base rate of compensation was reduced by 10 percent and the bonus program instituted.

The impact of this compensation scheme was substantial. PCPs were initially unhappy with the move to capitation, but Partners agreed to provide reports on a physician-specific basis comparing total reimbursement under capitation to what it would have been on a fee-schedule basis. There was no negative reaction from specialists because those referrals that were avoided were generally inappropriate referrals to begin with (for example, referrals to orthopedic surgeons of patients with minor strains or sprains). The combination of capitation payments and referral bonuses resulted in 80 percent of the PCPs doing better under the new scheme than if they had stayed on the old one. Hospital use rates also decreased, but not as markedly as the rates of specialist referral. The HMO's total medical expense dropped approximately 6 percent.

Although costs were reduced at the plan level as a result of changes in provider incentives, no serious joint effort was made to reduce the cost of actually providing services while enrollees were hospitalized. Attempts by the hospital to get physicians interested in this aspect of the cost issue were unsuccessful. For example, the hospital introduced a computerized methodology for comparing individual physician ordering patterns for specific diagnosis-related groups (DRGs) in an effort to get physicians to consider and discuss why there were wide variations in specific DRG management. However, physicians were unaffected financially by their decisions relative to the bundle of services ordered for their hospitalized patients, and physician-specific information provided by the hospital was not case mix-adjusted and therefore subject to questions of credibility. Thus, physician patterns of ordering diagnostics and therapeutics were essentially unchanged.

Ultimately, the IPA leadership became concerned at the limited ability of their membership to participate directly in discussions regarding their fees because they were not jointly at risk and to do so would be a violation of antitrust law. For that reason, it was agreed that provider contracts would no longer run through PHO Inc. but, instead, would run through SAIP via capitation for all physician services and directly from Partners to the hospital for its services. Since this change in contracting, however, no apparent drop-off in cost reductions has been achieved.

PHO activities directed at improving access to health care services also has shown mixed results. The first initiative, which was to develop three primary care centers in areas of physician shortage, was a failure. Only one center was ever established (physicians could not be recruited to the other two), and it resulted in significant financial losses for the PHO. The problems in recruitment stemmed from the fact that, at that time there still were many opportunities for young PCPs to join existing primary care practices in the community, and the idea of physicians as employees was not viewed as socially acceptable to the medical community. The center's economic failure was due primarily to the fact that it was saddled with too much fixed cost and overhead because of the way it was operated and managed. A management arm of the hospital took operational responsibility for the center and managed it less as a "doctor's office" and more as a hospital outpatient clinic. A broad range of ancillary services was provided, the center was overstaffed, and hospital compensation and benefits policies were utilized.

A much more successful approach to improving access to primary care services came about as a result of the strategic planning activity of the PHO board. An exercise to project future Partners enrollment estimated a future PCP shortfall, more than could be met by the three planned primary care centers. In evaluating the alternative ways of meeting the PCP need, the PHO board discovered a good-sized medical group (60 physicians) consisting mostly of PCPs who were very unhappy in a stafflike relationship with the local Maxicare plan. That physician organization, Group Health Medical Associates (GHMA), had offices geographically well-distributed in Tucson.

Emergence of Group Health Medical Associates

GHMA had started the first HMO in Tucson in 1974 and thus understood how to practice in a managed care setting. Its historical relationships with independent physicians generally were not good because GHMA was viewed as having been responsible for the unwelcome health care changes going on in Tucson. Many independent specialist members and shareholders of SAIP, however, received significant referral business from GHMA because it had few of its own specialists. They attested to the clinical credibility of the group while sharing others' views regarding GHMA's sociopolitical undesirability.

After a great deal of discussion at the PHO board level, however, it was agreed that historical biases should be set aside in favor of what made best strategic sense for the emerging system and that discussions should be entered into with GHMA to determine whether the group would be interested in contracting with Partners. Initial responses were positive, but GHMA's relationship with Maxicare prevented outside contracting. Thus, the PHO board agreed that attempts should be made to buy Maxicare's assets in Tucson. After two years of on-and-off discussions, an agreement in principle was reached wherein TMC would buy Maxicare's assets, which included approximately 40,000 HMO covered lives, the provider agreements with GHMA, and a number of leases for clinical and administrative space in buildings throughout the community. On April 1, 1989, the Maxicare members were absorbed into Partners Health Plan and assigned to the same GHMA doctors who had cared for them under Maxicare.

As expected, the impact of the Maxicare acquisition was immediate and positive. For example:

- An additional 40 PCPs were contracted with Partners, many of whom had substantial excess capacity in their practices. (Maxicare had lost membership over the previous 18 to 24 months, from 72,000 down to 40,000.)
- The additional Maxicare enrollees put Partners over the critical mass of membership necessary for profitability.
- Partners was able to offer the only mixed group–IPA model HMO in the market.

An additional positive impact, not expected by those who negotiated the transaction, was a significant decrease in medical expense in the IPA, primarily as a result of reduced hospital utilization that took place over the next two years. This effect was the result of the fact that those responsible for utilization management at SAIP had the medical group to which to compare their performance and did not want to be "outdone" by GHMA.

Finally, the existence of the PHO per se had little or no effect on the quality of service provided either within the HMO or more broadly in the hospital. PHO Inc. was contracted to provide both utilization and quality management services for Partners and did so with SAIP physicians serving on two separate committees. However, those same physicians had been serving on those committees as plan committees prior to PHO formation, and the review processes used by the PHO committees were the same as those used previously by the HMO quality management committee. Those processes could best be described as QA processes and did not involve active clinical process improvement activities at that time. The general level of quality of service provided, however, was viewed as good and certainly equal to, or better than, that of the competition as measured by employer and consumer surveys done by TMC's market research department. As measured by these surveys, quality appeared to be related to the reputation of the individual physicians who were part of the network rather than to any specific performance factors.

Observations

This case study clearly points out the value and limitations of the PHO as a vehicle for reducing costs, improving access to health care services, and raising the quality of those services. The value comes principally from the PHO serving as a formal mechanism through which hospitals and physicians can jointly and collaboratively see their futures as being inextricably tied to each other and can jointly take specific measures to increase the likelihood of the success of both. It is an excellent transitional model between the traditional, "totally independent while being interdependent" relationship between hospitals and physicians to the more advanced, truly integrated relationships. It allows the two parties to identify those activities and projects in which they wish to share economic risk and reward while leaving other, more potentially contentious areas alone. Moreover, it allows a sense of common purpose, trust, and respect to develop and allows the relationship to expand as the parties agree.

The limitation of this model is directly related to the reasons it makes an excellent transitional vehicle. The economic and operating incentives of the parties in a PHO can be more or less fully aligned as they relate to the activities and projects in which the PHO engages. However, no alignment of incentives occurs across the full array of interactions between them. Thus, PHO Inc. was an effective vehicle through which the physician compensation scheme could be changed, creating incentives for more appropriate utilization of primary care and specialist services. It also was an effective mechanism through which total inpatient medical expense for the HMO could be addressed; and although it did affect hospital utilization rates, it was ineffective in decreasing the cost of producing hospital services. Finally, because improvement in clinical quality was not its specific focus, the PHO had no impact in that area. These limitations were recognized over time by the owners of PHO Inc., and a decision was made to evolve from that model to a fully integrated health care organization. That evolution is now complete with the resulting tax-exempt organization called Health Partners of Southern Arizona.

CONCLUSION

The PHO is a popular form of vertical integration designed to deal with managed care. A joint venture between hospitals and physician groups, the PHO is a defensive action on the part of providers to growing managed care penetration.

However, according to recent studies, neither vertical nor horizontal integration efforts have yet had a positive impact on health care cost and quality. Rather, the PHO strategy appears to center primarily on enhancing its ability to obtain managed care contracts, with the secondary goal of developing hospital-physician partnerships to better manage under capitated contracts. The choice of PHO structure reflects the goals inherent in this strategy, and the mechanisms used to establish the appropriate structure generally encompass three types currently used by HMOs: physician panel selection, physician financial incentives, and nonfinancial systems that can be used to monitor physician practices. Any evaluation of PHO impact on improving health care cost and quality also must include a look at PHO behavior. Three limitations to achieving cost-effective health care through PHOs are limited administrative commitment, excessive hospital influence over the PHO, and trends away from restrictive provider networks.

However, PHOs are still in the early stages of development, and it may be too early to evaluate their ultimate impact on the broad goal of controlling cost while maintaining quality.

References

1. P. Danzon, "Consolidation and Restructuring: The Next Step in Managed Care," in *Health Care Management: Managed Care Principles and Practice,* vol. 2, ed. H. Jolt and M. Leibovici (Philadelphia: Hanley and Belfus, 1995), pp. 221–35.

2. H. S. Zuckerman, "Multi-Institutional Systems: Their Promise and Performance," in *Multi-Institutional Systems,* ed. L. E. Weeks (Chicago: Hospital Research and Educational Trust, 1979); and S. M. Shortell, "The Evolution of Hospital Systems: Unfulfilled Promises and Self-Fulfilling Prophecies," *Medical Care Review* 45, no. 2 (1988): 177–214.

3. R. Feldman, "The Welfare Economics of a Health Plan Merger," *Journal of Regulatory Economics* 6, no. 1 (July 1994): 67–86; and R. J. Bogue and others, "Hospital Reorganization after Merger," *Medical Care* 33, no. 7 (July 1995): 676–86.

4. R. P. Kusserow, *Effects of Hospital Mergers on Costs, Revenues, and Patient Volume* (Washington, DC: Department of Health and Human Services, 1992); and D. R. Wholey and others, "Scale and Scope Economies among Health Maintenance Organizations," *Journal of Health Economics* 15, no. 6 (Dec. 1996): 657–684.

5. J. C. Goldsmith, "The Illusive Logic of Integration," *Healthcare Forum Journal* 37, no. 5 (Sept.–Oct. 1994): 26–31; and S. Walston, J. Kimberly, and L. R. Burns, "Owned Vertical Integration and Health Care: Promise and Performance," *Health Care Management Review* 21, no. 1 (Winter 1996): 83–92.

6. S. M. Shortell, R. R. Gillies, and D. A. Anderson, "New World of Managed Care: Creating Organized Delivery Systems," *Health Affairs* 13, no. 5 (1994): 46–64; D. V. Schulz, L. M. Napiewocki, and D. R. Nerenz, *Measuring Physician Integration in Health Care Systems* (Chicago: Hospital Research and Educational Trust, 1994); L. R. Burns and others, "The Impact of Economic Integration on Physician-Organization Alignment: Results from the Center for Health Management Research Project on Physician-Organization Relationships" (working paper, Center for Health Management Research, Tempe, AZ, 1995); and T. L. Mark and others, "Hospital-Physician Relations and Hospital Financial Performance" (Project HOPE working paper, Center for Health Affairs, Bethesda, MD, 1996).

7. R. R. Gillies and others, "The Correlates and Consequences of Clinical Integration in Organized Delivery Systems" (presentation at the Annual Meeting of the Association for Health Services Research, San Diego, CA, 1994).

8. L. R. Burns and D. P. Thorpe, "Trends and Models in Physician-Hospital Organization, *Health Care Management Review* 18, no. 4 (Fall 1993): 7–20; and The Advisory Board Co., *The Grand Alliance: Vertical Integration Strategies for Physicians and Health Systems* (Washington, DC: The Advisory Board Co., 1993).

9. MACRO International, *ProPAC Final Frequencies* (Burlington, VT: MACRO International, 1994).

10. American Hospital Association, *Hospital Statistics,* 1994–95 edition (Chicago: AHA, 1994).

11. American Medical Association, *Case Study Analysis of Physician-Hospital Organizations* (Chicago, AMA, 1994); T. Hudson, "Growing Pains," *Hospitals & Health Networks* 69, no. 1 (Jan. 5, 1995): 42–45; Ernst & Young, *Physician-Hospital Organizations: Profile 1995* (Washington, DC: Ernst & Young, 1995); and J. A. Alexander and others, "An Exploratory Analysis of Market-Based, Physician-Organization Arrangements," *Hospital and Health Services Administration* 41, no. 3 (Fall 1996): 311–329.

12. P. R. Kongstvedt, *The Managed Health Care Handbook* (Gaithersburg, MD: Aspen, 1996).

13. Kongstvedt.

14. American Hospital Association, *1995 Annual Survey* (Chicago: AHA, 1995).

15. D. Burda, "10 N.C. Hospitals Push to Form PHO," *Modern Healthcare* 25, no. 30 (July 24, 1995): 36.

16. K. Terry, "Super-PHOs: Super Path to a Larger Market Share?" *Medical Economics* 72, no. 17 (1995): 142–50.

17. Burns and Thorpe.

18. W. L. Kissick, *Medicine's Dilemmas* (New Haven, CT: Yale University Press, 1994).

19. Hudson.

20. Ernst & Young, p. 37.

21. A. D. Chandler, *Strategy and Structure* (Cambridge, MA: MIT Press, 1962).

22. L. R. Burns and D. P. Thorpe, "Managed Care and Integrated Health Care," in *Health Care Management: Managed Care Principles and Practice,* vol. 2, ed. H. Jolt and M. Leibovici (Philadelphia: Hanley & Belfus, 1995), pp. 101-8.

23. Lewin-ICF, *Managed Care: Does It Work?* (Washington, DC: Lewin-ICF, 1993); and Physician Payment Review Commission, *Arrangements between Managed Care Plans and Physicians.* (Washington, DC: PPRC, 1995).

24. PPRC.

25. Alexander and others.

26. Hudson.

27. American Association of Physician-Hospital Associations, "Survey of 156 PHOs," *Hospitals & Health Networks* 69, no. 6 (Mar. 20, 1995): 22–23.

28. Alexander and others; AAPHO.

29. Advisory Board.

30. Alexander and others.

31. AMA; Ernst & Young.

32. A. Hillman, "Financial Incentives for Physicians in HMOs," *New England Journal of Medicine* 317, no. 27 (1987): 1743–48.

33. AMA.

34. AMA.

35. AMA.

36. Ernst & Young; AMA.

37. E. Morrison, I. Morrison, and H. Skubik, *Integrated Medical Systems: The Next Generation of Managed Care* (San Francisco: Institute for the Future, 1993).

38. F. B. Abbey and K. M. Treash, "Reasons Providers Form PHOs," *Healthcare Financial Management* 49, no. 8 (Aug. 1995): 38–47.

39. J. K. Iglehart, "Physicians and the Growth of Managed Care," *New England Journal of Medicine* 331, no. 17 (Oct. 27, 1994): 1167–71.

40. PHO Inc. preincorporation agreement, Tucson, AZ, Oct. 23, 1986.

PART VI

Management Services Organizations

Management services organizations have evolved to a central position in shaping the physician services market. This section focuses on these organizations in two chapters. Chapter 18, "Evolution of Management Services Organizations," traces the development of MSOs, explaining their function, structure, and role within the evolving physician services market. Chapter 19, "The Management Services Organization Industry," explains how this industry is currently structured and how it is likely to evolve.

There are many differing views regarding the future of the MSO industry. Two such visions of the future of MSOs are also presented in this section, each from the perspective of an MSO company's CEO. "Fourth-Generation Management Services Organizations" places the evolution of MSOs in a historical context, explaining how these unique organizations will likely appear in the future. "The Future of Management Services Organizations" assesses the long-term viability of these organizations within a framework for evaluation of MSO success.

18

Evolution of Management Services Organizations

Paul R. DeMuro, JD

A management services organization (MSO) may be defined as an organization that provides services to physicians and physician groups; it also may provide services to a hospital or hospitals. MSOs are sometimes called medical services organizations.[1]

MSOs have been around in some form for many years. Their genesis, in part, may have been the medical service bureaus that provided services to physicians as early as the 1910s. Many of these, like Pierce County Medical Bureau in Tacoma, Washington (now Regence Washington Health), became health plans.[2] Their origins also may have been the physician billing companies and companies providing aspects of physician practice management. Initially, such MSO services included billing, collections, and management information system (MIS) functions. Practice management also may have involved some practice development.

County and state medical associations have offered a variety of services to physicians either directly through the association or through related companies. These services included group purchasing of products and services. Groups of physicians and entrepreneurs created companies that offered such services to physicians as utilization management and review, leasing of equipment and space, provision of certain employees, and even the ability to provide physician practice management services on a turnkey basis. These associations and companies providing services to physicians were important in the evolution of the modern-day MSO.

Copyright Paul R. DeMuro.

This chapter provides background for development of MSOs, including medical service bureaus, physician service companies and associations, and modern-day MSOs. Additionally, this chapter explains the functions of the MSO, its structure and relationships, and the role of MSOs in the future. It also sets the stage for discussion of the MSO industry by industry leaders. (See chapter 19.)

HOSPITAL-AFFILIATED MANAGEMENT SERVICES ORGANIZATIONS

Many formal attempts to develop MSOs began in the early 1980s with the proliferation of managed care contracting. Physicians who previously operated all aspects of their medical practices as solo practices, or with one or only a few other physicians, began to join and participate in independent practice associations (IPAs) (discussed in chapter 14), which are groups of physicians organized in a separate corporation who do not combine all their assets and liabilities in a truly integrated practice but come together to access managed care contracts. Many of these IPAs sought management services.

At first, many such IPAs consisted of a majority of the physicians on a hospital's medical staff, and the hospital often was instrumental in the organizing efforts of the IPA. For example, many of the managed care organizations (MCOs) that sought to contract with a hospital also needed to contract with physicians for the provision of services to their enrollees. They often did not want to contract individually with physicians, preferring to have one contract with an IPA or integrated physician group. This was particularly true if physicians were expected to contract on a risk basis, whether capitated, percentage of premium, or in a manner in which the parties shared risk through one or more risk pools.

When managed care contracting grew in significance, hospitals began to employ personnel in this area, giving them responsibility for the managed care contracting functions. Initially, few (if any) of these individuals had training in managed care contracting, and most were not even attorneys but, rather, merely redeployed hospital personnel. These newly minted contract personnel often offered to "assist" IPA physicians with their managed care contract efforts because they were both contracting with the health plans. This assistance was, in part, the genesis of the modern-day MSO.

Types of Services Offered by MSOs

The types of services offered by MSOs included not only managed care contracting, billing, collections, and information systems management, but also network development and administration. They included paying the claims of contract and noncontract providers, credentialing, and overseeing the compensation of IPA physicians.

However, many physicians soon realized that obtaining managed care contracts and other services from the hospital staff, although often at no charge, might not be the best way to obtain them. Hospitals that only maintained managed care contract departments for their own benefit continued to operate them as such. However, hospitals that provided such services to physicians, and an increasing array of other services, began to recognize that they actually were operating an MSO division of the hospital.

As the services rendered by that division began to expand, hospitals began to realize that it might be preferable to establish such companies as separate corporations. This was particularly true for not-for-profit hospitals that might have been concerned about jeopardizing their tax-exempt status through the for-profit MSO operations. In addition, many hospitals wanted to insulate liability for such companies in a separate corporation, not have to allocate as many hospital costs to the MSO operations for Medicare and Medicaid reimbursement reasons, and possibly offer the physicians the ability to buy into part of the MSO.

Many early attempts by hospitals to develop MSOs were failures because of inexperience on the part of the personnel operating those companies and because of physician expectations. Of course, physicians who sought the services of MSOs were looking to decrease their overhead costs and to obtain new services, such as managed care contract services, at as low a cost as possible. Hospital-affiliated MSOs typically wanted to charge physicians, particularly those on a hospital's medical staff, the lowest possible fee without running afoul of the Medicare fraud and abuse laws, and if the hospital was not-for-profit, the prohibition against inurement of benefit. As a result, hospital-affiliated MSOs typically commissioned business plans and feasibility studies and did comparative analyses to determine how low they could set their MSO fees. Often plans for their operations were quite aggressive, assuming that the cost of the MSO services provided to physicians would be equal to or less than the low prices they wanted to charge.

Pricing of Services

To induce physicians to contract with inexperienced start-up hospital-based MSOs, these MSOs charged the physicians low fees for their services. In fact, physicians who might have entered into a turnkey arrangement with an MSO would want to ensure that their overhead would be less than it was currently. As a result, a physician group with a 65 percent overhead factor would be most interested in entering into a contract with a hospital-affiliated MSO if doing so resulted in a reduction of its overhead to 50 or 55 percent.

Obviously, many of the MSOs that charged physicians MSO fees were unable to provide services to the physicians at the price they had agreed to. Consequently, they faced significant losses over the period in which they provided services. Although many might have anticipated initial losses in their business plans and feasibility studies, they could not have predicted perpetual losses because that would have provided documentation for the government supporting claims of payments to physicians for patient referrals, and for tax-exempt providers, allegations of inurement of benefit.

Restructuring of Operations

Significant losses by hospital-affiliated MSOs, as well as fears of government investigations for Medicare fraud and abuse and loss of tax-exempt status for tax-exempt providers, led many hospitals to abandon or restructure their MSO operations. Those MSOs that were forced to charge physicians more to minimize the risk of running afoul of government regulations were in a quandary. If the MSO had an existing long-term contract with the physicians at rates that were favorable to them, the physicians would not want to restructure the relationship. Physicians often seemed less concerned with the Medicare fraud and abuse risk than the hospital. And, of course, inasmuch as they are not tax-exempt entities, the physicians often were uninterested in the hospital's arguments regarding loss of its tax-exempt status. The physicians also questioned whether the rates were too low or whether the hospital-affiliated MSO was inefficient in the provision of its services.

Many hospitals faced the decision of whether to continue to perform under the contract and face the possibility of government allegations of Medicare fraud and abuse and IRS allegations of inurement of benefit, or to seek to repudiate the contract and face a lawsuit by the physicians. Oddly enough, the argument the hospital-affiliated MSO might use most successfully to repudiate its contract was that it was in violation of the Medicare fraud and abuse anti-kickback laws. Of course, such an argument would seem to involve an admission by the MSO that it was in violation of the fraud and abuse laws. Neither alternative was a good one.

EMERGENCE OF ENTREPRENEURIAL MSOS

Entrepreneurial physicians dabbled in MSO development, much of which occurred where a physician group removed its practice management function and placed it in a separate corporation. For successfully operating physician groups, the sense was that they already were operating an MSO for themselves, so why not expand their operations by providing management and other services to other physician groups? If those groups were in some way aligned with the group from which the practice management company was created, synergy could be created, provided the parties were careful to comply with the antitrust laws. If the one physician group was not aligned with the other, the new MSO would have to persuade the would-be managed group that the skills of the parties operating the new MSO have been in place for some time at the first physician group.

Nonphysician entrepreneurs also sought to establish MSOs, many from the springboards of physician billing and management companies that started to perform MSO-type functions. Many such small management companies exist throughout the country providing claims adjudication and managed care functions for IPAs and physician groups.

Hospital-Physician Joint Venture MSOs

Physicians also participate in MSOs with hospitals. Many of these "joint venture" relationships are set up similarly to physician-hospital organizations (PHOs), which generally are owned by both hospitals and physicians and which are entities seeking to jointly negotiate managed care contracts. The PHO also may provide utilization management and review, quality assurance (QA), and information systems management. In an integrated delivery environment, the MSO typically provides the services of a PHO, but also additional services, which may include physician practice management, provision of nonprofessional and nontechnical employees, equipment, space, and possibly even services on a turnkey basis.

Physician-hospital jointly owned MSOs present myriad issues, including who controls the MSO, the MSO's governance structure and decision-making processes, and the degree of capitalization. These issues are discussed in the following subsections.

Control Typically, the shareholders (if the MSO is a corporation), members (if the MSO is a limited liability company [LLC]), or partners (if the MSO is a partnership) have control of the ability to elect or choose the board of directors of the corporate entity or management of the LLC or partnership. Often a percentage of equity follows control. However, hospitals occasionally seek to provide physicians with a greater percentage of control than the equity interest. If the arrangement is not structured properly, Medicare fraud and abuse issues might arise. One way to minimize the risk is for the hospital to divide its interest between preferred and common stock in a corporate entity and to have only as much common stock as the physicians in a 50-50 transaction. Control also can be accomplished in part by reserving certain powers to a majority or super majority of the shareholders, members, or partners.

Governance Typically, corporate MSOs have a board of directors. LLCs and partnerships may have a structure similar to a board of directors, sometimes calling it a management committee. If the hospital and physicians have the ability to choose an equal number of directors or managers, it might be advisable to have the existing directors or managers choose one additional member to ensure that there is an odd number to avoid deadlock.

If there is an even number of board members, it is particularly important to devise a means to break deadlocks. This might be accomplished by appointing a mediator or by delegating substantial authority to management to minimize the number of issues on which the board might be deadlocked.

Management The board of directors, members, or partners should choose the management of the MSO. As in any other organization, management should be given responsibility for performing the functions needed to manage the MSO and should have the necessary expertise to do so.

Capitalization Capitalization is a significant concern. If an MSO anticipates operations and activities that are much greater in scope than a PHO, its need for capitalization will be greater. If the physicians and hospital desire equal ownership in such an entity, it will be necessary for both parties to come up with more capital for their interest in an MSO than they would for a PHO. Often the physician partners do not have, or want to put in, the cash or capital necessary for them to have a one-half interest. With the increasing focus on Medicare fraud and abuse, the physicians must give true value for their equity interests.

ASSETS AND THEIR VALUATION

Probably the assets the physicians might have most easily contributed to the MSO in exchange for equity participation are those associated with their medical practice. The *hard assets* are the easiest to value and transferable into the MSO in exchange for equity. Hard assets typically include real estate, equipment, furnishings, supplies, and inventory. *Soft assets* typically transferred to an MSO include intellectual capital, information systems that can assist in the management of care, practice parameters, protocols, and clinical pathways. Unless a state has no corporate practice of medicine or medical practice act prohibitions, medical records and payer contracts typically have to remain with a physician group or be transferred to a professional corporation related to the MSO for which it has a long-term contract. Such a contract, if it provides for unilateral and perpetual control of the physician group by the MSO, may permit the MSO to account for the value of medical records and contracts.

In many instances, physicians who looked at valuing their hard assets realized their assets did not have significant value. More often than not, the physicians leased their space and often leased their equipment. Generally, their furnishings were depreciated and not worth much, and supplies and inventory did not have a significant value. As a result, the value of their practices consisted primarily of soft assets (such as goodwill and payer contracts) and their ability to continue to generate revenue.

Many hospital-affiliated MSOs typically only sought to purchase the hard assets of a physician's practice and the soft assets capable of being owned by an MSO, such as technical know-how and software. The reasons for doing so included the desire of the physicians to maintain their contracts in their groups, state laws prohibiting the acceptance of risk by MSOs and the holding of such contracts, and the decision of the hospital-affiliated MSO not to establish a related medical group with a physician practice to hold those contracts. (Of course, in states where an MSO might hold such contracts, they might be purchased or contributed to the MSO.)

FULLY INTEGRATED DELIVERY SYSTEMS

Hospitals were not only developing MSOs as a physician integration strategy, but also seeking to employ physicians in those states where they might do so. In addition, where necessary because of applicable state laws, hospitals developed not-for-profit medical foundations to purchase physician practices and employ or exclusively contract with such physicians. Hospitals also developed and operated contractual and equity PHOs to access the managed care market with physicians.

Although many hospitals had the capital to develop such systems, as well as the will to do so, physicians became skeptical of these systems because of the hospitals' desire to exercise a significant amount of control and also because of the fear that a high fixed-cost, asset-based system would seek to cover its costs by ensuring that it allocated sufficient revenue to do so. The physicians feared that such an allocation might be a misallocation necessitated by the hospital's desire to survive.

National Physician Practice Management Companies

Physician skepticism and instability in the marketplace made possible the rapid rise of national physician practice management companies

(PPMCs). The market for physician practice management is approximately \$200 billion per year. Many physicians had traditionally been organized as solo or dual practices. With managed care, they started to seek the "safe harbor" of integrated delivery systems (IDSs), which generally meant employment by a hospital, MCO, or fully integrated health care delivery system. Physicians saw their options increasingly limited and their prospects less bright. Traditional hospital-physician relationships often have been strained. Unsuccessful joint ventures, desire for hospital control, high hospital cost structures, and failure to appropriately right-size led many physicians to seriously consider independent PPMCs as a viable alternative. Wall Street also became very receptive to such companies.

Physician Equity Models

In IDS development, physicians were constantly bombarded with the concept of the physician's equity model being the desired model for their participation in managed care. It was thought to be the "gold" or "platinum" standard where the incentives of the physicians were truly aligned with those of the hospital because the physicians owned the hospital and all means of production. However, very few physicians were organized in a physician equity model. In addition, in such equity models, the physicians who had an equity interest in the hospital were not always all of those who were in the physician group.

Some of the more notable physician equity models were the Friendly Hills Medical Group and the Mullikin Medical Centers in southern California (now all part of MedPartners). Although both groups functioned efficiently in a cost-effective manner and were very efficient in the management of care, the physicians in both models began to realize their expansion efforts were severely hampered by their lack of capital. Physician practices and even equity models did not retain much capital. They generally followed the lead of most physician groups, which for years had distributed most or all of their capital and cash at the end of the year, primarily because of the physicians' needs and desires for that income.

Public Companies

These well-managed, managed care–oriented medical groups wanted to tap into the \$200 billion physician practice management business. However, to do so, they needed access to capital. Many went public (including PhyCor, MedPartners, Sheridan, Pediatrix, FPA Medical Management, and Coastal). Many groups sold to, or aligned with, these companies (for example, Mullikin and Pacific Physicians with MedPartners) or with other public companies that had physician practice management divisions (for example, the Friendly Hills affiliation with Caremark and the Caremark transaction with MedPartners). Table 18-1 lists some of the larger PPMCs and their market capitalization.

STRUCTURE OF NATIONAL PHYSICIAN PRACTICE MANAGEMENT COMPANIES

What is the attraction of these companies for many physicians? Why is it that physicians often will not seriously discuss with a local hospital a sale of their practice or an integration strategy but often will talk to, and gladly affiliate with, a national PPMC?

It is useful to consider a typical national PPMC model in answering these questions. Except in Florida and a few other states, where many such for-profit public companies employ physicians directly, often the PPMC establishes one or more professional corporations in each state with which it intends to conduct business or already conducts business. Generally, the professional corporation is established by one or more of the PPMC's physician employees.[3] In fact, the physician might even be one of the company's founders. The physician shareholder of the professional corporation has restrictions on the transferability of his or her stock, which may be created through a loan or line of credit from the PPMC, or a succession agreement, providing to whom the shares must be transferred in the event of death, disability, termination from employment, or the like.

Physician Practice Management Company Contracts

National PPMCs usually have a long-term or perpetual contract with the professional corporation, often as long as 30 or 40 years, with provisions for automatic renewability. For the PPMC to treat the physician group's revenues as if they were its own, it should have unilateral and perpetual control, a right to net profits, and be able to consolidate financial statements. When that is the case, the PPMC fee is not treated as its revenues but, rather, as all the revenues of the professional corporation it manages. As a result, a PPMC that continually adds more physician practices under management can achieve very significant growth levels and increase value rather quickly in the eyes of Wall Street.

The contract between a PPMC and a professional corporation must achieve a delicate balance between meeting the requirements for unilateral and perpetual control and a right to net profits and not running afoul of the state corporate practice of medicine laws. (See chapter 10.) Operation of

TABLE 18-1. Piper Jaffray Physician Practice Management Comparable Company Analysis

Company	Market cap (in millions)
Multi-Specialty Group/Combination Model	
Advanced Health Corporation	$153
Complete Management, Inc.	$207
FPA Medical Management, Inc.	$846
MedPartners, Inc.	$3,967
PhyCor, Inc.	$2,312
PhyMatrix Corp.	$348
ProMedCo Management Co	$126
Single-Specialty Group Model	
(Oncology)	
American Oncology Resources, Inc.	$723
EquiMed, Inc.	$54
Response Oncology, Inc.	$69
Physician Reliance Network, Inc.	$446
(Cardiology)	
Raytel Medical Corporation	$105
MedCath Incorporated	$174
(Oral Care)	
Coast Dental Services, Inc.	$68
Orthodontic Centers of America, Inc.	$823
(Other)	
Apogee, Inc.	$44
Integrated Medical Resources, Inc.	$14
OccuSystems, Inc.	$627
Physicians Reserve Group, Inc.	$272
Specialty Care Network, Inc.	$160
Hospital Based Group Model	
Coastal Physician Group, Inc.	$37
EmCare Holdings Inc.	$333
InPhyNet Medical Management Inc.	$396
Pediatrix Medical Group, Inc.	$720
Sheridan Healthcare, Inc.	$73

Source: Data provided by Piper Jaffray Inc., Minneapolis, MN, 1997.

the professional corporation with respect to its provision of medical care and its direction with respect to medical decisions needs to be left with the physicians who are at least in nominal control of the professional corporation. The degree of decision-making ability acquired by the professional corporation physicians may differ from state to state, along with laws addressing fee splitting.

Of course, national PPMCs seek to assume the financial risk of the medical practice, but doing so may be problematic in a number of states, from either a corporate practice or medical practices act or a fee-splitting perspective. Thus, it generally is necessary to develop PPMC compensation formulas that provide incentives to the PPMC and compensate it for its efficient and cost-effective practices but preserve some risk of the medical practice in the professional corporation.

Physician Equity

The physicians who sell their practices to such PPMCs or affiliate with them often exchange all or part of the value of their practice for an equity interest in the PPMC, and the remainder may be purchased for cash. Those PPMCs that are already public companies can merely use shares of stock that have been made available for acquisition. For those PPMCs that have not yet gone public, shares in the nonpublic company may be issued with the prospect of such a corporation going public, and the physicians have the possible benefit of participating in a company that may go public.

Benefits of Transactions with Physician Practice Management Companies

Physicians who participate in a transaction with a public national PPMC are attracted to the fact that such companies provide participating physicians with access to capital for expansion and further practice management development. In addition, the physicians who take stock in the public company can participate in the appreciation of such stock. As a result, they have equity in the system, no matter how small.

PPMCs also can achieve or replicate the equity model. Where they own a hospital and lease it to the physicians, such a model can be directly replicated because the physician component can take global capitation, for both the physician and hospital services. In states where physicians can take global capital directly, they might do so. In states where they cannot, and they do not own or lease a hospital, they might be able to replicate global capitation by putting, or having the health plan put, the hospital on a budget. Such a budget may be based on a certain number of patient days per thousand for commercial enrollees. If there is a specific number of enrollees and the days per thousand target is met, the hospital may be paid a predetermined amount for hospital services. If the days per thousand are greater or there are more enrollees than anticipated, the hospital will receive an additional payment. In the event the days per thousand are less than the target or there are fewer enrollees than anticipated, the hospital may have to pay monies to the physicians through the health plans. To minimize some of these complications, the PPMC also can develop or purchase and operate a health plan on a limited health plan license.

With the combination of equity for its physician participants, and an equity model or possibility of replicating same, the public PPMCs have become quite attractive to physicians. These companies seem to be less concerned with lack of control in such situations. They generally seek to leave as many medical decisions with the physician as possible and employ physician practice parameters, protocols, and critical pathways designed to manage care in a cost-effective, high-quality manner, with aligned incentives and with the intention of adding money to the bottom line.

Often PPMCs do not have the costly fixed-asset cost structure of hospital-based systems. Thus, they do not need to cover the same operating costs of such systems. In addition, unlike tax-exempt hospital-affiliated MSOs and IDSs, which often seek to acquire physician practices for debt, the PPMCs typically do it with cash and/or equity.

Growth of Alignments with Physician Practice Management Companies More and more physician groups and their local or regional MSOs are aligning with national PPMCs. Some PPMCs have even been acquired by health plans. For example, Health Spring was acquired by MetraHealth, which in turn was acquired by United Healthcare. Some health plans are spinning off their physician practice companies and practice management companies and divisions to national PPMCs (for example, the sale of the physician division of Cigna to Caremark, now MedPartners).

Continued Consolidation Greater consolidation is expected with respect to PPMCs and physician practices. If the market for PPMC initial public offerings (IPOs) becomes strong, more companies will continue to go public. With a $200 billion potential market, of which less than 5 percent is tapped, the potential for growth and expansion remains great.

However, for those PPMCs that continue to purchase physician practices for large sums and do not receive value (such as the ability to generate net profits) beyond the traditional goodwill of the practice and its lives, such a plan is a fragile one. It may depend on the increasing value for payer lives and the ability of those corporations to continue to expand in the short run; but in the long run, they will have to manage the large PPMCs they have developed and in what will eventually become a mature market. Growth rates of 20 to 50 percent cannot perpetually be the norm. Eventually, the companies will have to tend to the business of managing in a mature market. Moreover, they will have to face the prospect of other companies seeking to acquire them. Like any public company, they will be susceptible to tender offers, even hostile tender offers, by companies that have accumulated significantly more cash than they have accumulated over the years. Such companies seeking to acquire PPMCs are likely to be insurance companies, MCOs, pharmaceutical and laboratory companies, and medical products companies. However, many national PPMCs will remain viable public companies that will operate on their own, and they may not be acquired.

ALTERNATIVE MSO MODELS

In response to the attractiveness of the public PPMCs, hospitals have sought to develop new models and further refine other ones to be attractive to physicians. These models involve ceding some control to the physicians and acting in true partnership with them, not acting with dominance and insistence on control.

Equity Hospital/Physician MSO/PHO Model

The equity PHO or MSO model is one that acts in many respects as a national PPMC. The physicians transfer their practice assets to the PHO or MSO, and the hospital acquires an interest in the PHO or MSO by paying the physicians, in part for their interest in the medical group. The hospital may purchase 50 percent or less interest if the physicians want to have equal or greater than 50 percent control. The PHO or MSO creates an affiliated professional corporation where the physician shareholder is an employee of the PHO or MSO, and ensures that the physician has a shareholder agreement that restricts his or her transfer of the stock and may execute a succession agreement.

The PHO or MSO has a long-term contract on a fair market value basis with the professional corporation where it exercises unilateral and perpetual control, and a right to the net profits of its physician group, to ensure that the physician group's revenues will be treated as the revenues of the PHO or MSO, and to ensure that it has the value of the professional corporation. In such a model, the physicians have access to capital for expansion through the contributions of the hospital to the MSO. The MSO can perform many of the same functions as a national PPMC but may not be able to offer equity interests that are easily transferable.

Comparison with Public PPMCs

Many acquisitions by national PPMCs are for stock of the company or stock and cash, and the stock may not be transferable for a number of years. In addition, when a physician has sold his or her practice to a national PPMC, the covenants not to compete and other restrictions imposed on that physician with respect to his or her ability to regain his or her patient base if the physician were to leave are stringent. Furthermore, as a bottom-line-oriented business, the national PPMC must be concerned with the best interests of its shareholders.

Hospital-affiliated MSO models that are not public are not only concerned with the best interests of the MSO, but also those of the hospital. Although, as noted above, there may be negative connotations for the physicians where there is hospital involvement because of a hospital's high-cost asset base, there also can be positive aspects. For example, a hospital may not be as likely to discontinue its MSO operations in an area where they are less profitable if the physicians who use the MSO are aligned with the hospital. In addition, the hospital may be able to work with the MSO physicians to develop medical management opportunities for combined hospital-physician operations, which can result in substantial savings on the hospital side and which might be shared in an appropriate manner with the MSO through an inventive agreement, generally administered most appropriately through the health plan. Such a model can be quite attractive to physicians and a local alternative to a national PPMC.

Payer Models

Payers also have developed physician practice management divisions and companies to ensure that they remain competitive, have adequate access to physicians, and can combine to participate in the managed care marketplace. A payer may employ a staff-like closed-model relationship with its physicians such that it employs, owns, or contracts with its physician component and operates that component only for the benefit of its enrollees. It may employ a more open or competitive system where the physician component affiliated with it can contract with other payers and provide services to their enrollees. The payer may act as a national PPMC, either directly through a division or through a subsidiary, related company, or joint venture.

However, many payers have sought to spin off their physician practices; for example, CIGNA and FHP. Such actions appear to be a recognition that some health plans would prefer to tend to their core businesses and not worry about the potential conflict issues other health plans may have with being owned by a competitor.

CONCLUSION

MSOs have evolved substantially since their inception and are taking many different forms, including hospital-based, joint venture-based, those operated by nonphysician and physician entrepreneurs on a local or regional basis, and those operated by health plans and public PPMCs. The market for MSOs has barely been tapped by the larger organizations.

The increasing emergence of stronger IPAs and the fractionalization of many IDSs will help fuel the growth of MSOs and make them increasingly significant players in the health care marketplace. National PPMCs will increase in prominence, but their future success will depend on their ability to manage in a mature market. Hospital, payer-affiliated, and regional MSOs may offer alternatives, depending on the market characteristics in an area, to the national PPMC. Other MSO competition will be in the area of hospital-employed physicians, fully integrated delivery systems, and physicians in more loosely affiliated entities such as IPAs and PHOs.

Reference and Notes

1. P. DeMuro, *The Financial Manager's Guide to Managed Care & Integrated Delivery Systems* (Burr Ridge, IL: Irwin, 1996).

2. Pierce County Medical Bureau, Inc., now is a Blue Shield health plan.

3. Increasingly, PPMCs are "buying" contracts to manage other groups as part of their acquisition strategy. This strategy often seeks to leave in place the existing professional corporation, while attempting to achieve unilateral and perpetual control of it.

19

The Management Services Organization Industry

William J. DeMarco
Jennifer M. Marx

Risk brought about by societal change also may introduce opportunity. The shift from fee-for-service (FFS) payment to prepayment for health care services has caused some physicians to reconsider the structure of their practices and to actively seek partners in the management of risk.

This chapter discusses two specific group formation strategies: the management services organization and the physician practice management company. It also identifies their differences and similarities.

DEVELOPMENT OF STRATEGIES FOR GROUP FORMATION

In health care, the ability to anticipate change requires physicians to keep a close eye on their stakeholders (participants in the system) and how each of these groups reacts to change. Active stakeholders and forces of change in the private sector include patients, employers, hospitals, physicians themselves, and HMOs. When a market reaches the point of a loose framework of managed care, for example, physicians might observe the following actions taken by stakeholders:

- Employers form purchasing coalitions to evaluate providers and products present in the market. There are more than 100 health care coalitions in existence today, representing millions of covered

lives. According to Shawn Sullivan, president of the National Association of Employer Coalitions, the number of coalitions formed is increasing rapidly, especially in rural areas.[1]
- Leading HMOs emerge from the pack.[2]
- Hospital provider networks form.
- Physicians form IPAs (independent practice associations) without utilization management and prepaid groups develop to serve HMOs.

From this loose framework stage, the market can go in many directions. The lesson learned by studying market evolution is that the organization or stakeholder that drives the change has the opportunity to set the agenda and thereby derives more favorable opportunities out of the fragmented pieces of marketplace change.

One of the ways physicians create more favorable opportunities in fragmented markets is by carefully selecting partners. They can choose to partner with themselves by forming their own management services organization (MSO) or with a physician practice management company (PPMC). These two products constitute what generally is referred to as the MSO industry. The terms *MSO* and *PPMC* have been used interchangeably in the health care literature, but there are distinctions between the two.

Physicians typically use the MSO strategy to create their own service bureau through which they can partner with fellow physicians. Although some believe that the utility of an MSO generally is confined to providing collective purchasing and related management and administrative services for its owners and participants, many refer to the MSO structure as a transitional one that allows physicians to open doors into a managed care market that were not available to them as solo practitioners.

Alternatively, physicians who are not sure they need to build an MSO or those who simply need a capital source for practice expansion use the PPMC strategy. In this situation, physicians look to partner with publicly traded companies that tailor their business to buying physician assets and offering management services in return. In contrast to physicians choosing to develop their own MSO, the decision by physicians to affiliate with a PPMC means buying a product that has been created by another. Typically, PPMCs provide capital, managed care expertise, information systems, and business management talent in return for physicians signing a management services agreement for 30 to 40 years.

Strengths of the Two Strategies

Although there are differences between the two structures, they share common ground with regard to capabilities, strategies, and functions.

Group formation/acquisition is an increasingly common strategy for addressing physician needs in managed care contracting. Creation of an MSO or affiliation with a PPMC allows physicians to carry out this strategy. However, the motivation behind each is very different.

MSO formation often occurs in conjunction with formation of a physician organization (PO). Some of the strengths of the MSO structure are as follows:

- It accommodates independent physicians unable to affiliate with other entities.
- It establishes educational processes for physicians to recognize and meet their managed care needs.
- It provides a necessary link to permit physicians to take risk as a group and to meet managed care contracting needs.
- It is effective in dealing with core primary care physician (PCP) issues.
- It can stabilize current hospital affiliation and/or add incrementally to hospital medical staff/census.

The group practice acquisition, merger, or joint venture component of a PPMC strategy has certain advantages matching the motivation behind the use of the basic PPMC strategy. These include the following:

- The time to market with a PPMC product is rapid.
- It can stabilize current hospital affiliation and/or add incrementally to hospital/medical staff census.
- It is effective in dealing with core PCP issues such as lifestyle, income stabilization, or enhancement.
- It is a strong vehicle for all managed care contracting needs.

Tools to Manage Physician Practices

One of the strongest links between the MSO and PPMC strategies is their use of critical tools to help manage physician practices—tools that are lacking in so many practices today. Both strategies can address the following variables in physician practices; these variables have been identified by physicians as well as investors in physician-driven enterprises:

- *Managed care expertise:* As physicians seek to participate in the risk and accompanying reward offered through prepayment, they must have expertise and critical mass in contract negotiation and practice management.
- *Information systems:* Useful information is one of the prime resources that successful managed care organizations (MCOs) rely

on to reduce health care costs and improve the quality of care. Data from well-designed and well-maintained information systems can be applied toward development of utilization review, protocol, billing and collection, and the computerized patient record. Management information systems (MISs) will be a point of differentiation between a practice that is well equipped for managed care and one that is not.

- *Practice administration:* Office administration, billing, staffing, recruiting, and so on are business issues of medicine that physicians are glad to turn over to a physician practice management partner.
- *Capital:* Whether a physician group wants to build a new clinic or upgrade its information system, access to capital is a significant part of bringing these goals to fruition.[3]

MANAGEMENT SERVICES ORGANIZATION STRATEGY

The following factors are fueling the growth of MSOs:

- MSOs provide provider revenue compression.
- They consolidate HMOs and hospitals.
- They quell physician frustration.
- They answer the need for capital to expand or meet expenses.
- Strategies are seen as a trend by the popular press.
- Systems are coming into the market with MSOs as an essential component.

Today, the choice by physicians to create an MSO demands that physicians with similar practice patterns and willingness partner with one another to raise capital or choose appropriate investor partners to capitalize the MSO. Whether the physicians finance it themselves or find investment partners, the organization is driven by their leadership and becomes attractive to other physicians in the market because of its physician-driven focus. Figure 19-1 shows the basic structure of a physician-owned and capitalized MSO.

Physician-Owned and -Financed Management Services Organizations versus MSOs Capitalized with Investment Partners

In a physician-owned MSO, physician groups come together to invest in an MSO that operates independently from the day-to-day operations of

FIGURE 19-1. Physician-Owned and Capitalized MSO Basic Structure

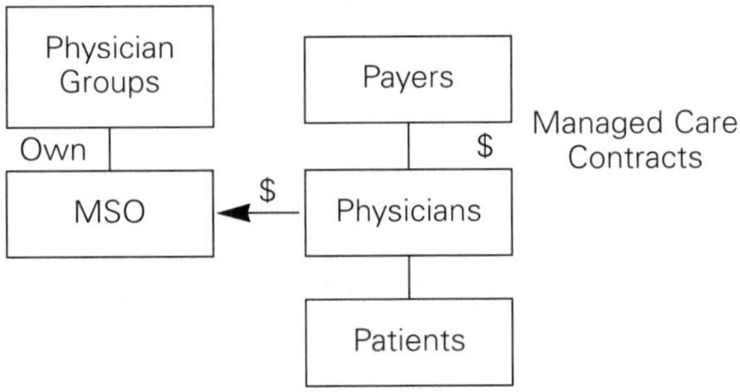

the practices; the MSO has its own administrator and staff who provide the needed practice oversight. The basic deal between the MSO and the physicians is that the MSO receives payment from the physicians with whom it has service agreements. The physicians pay the MSO for its management services through the money they receive from payers for the delivery of medical services. Moreover, physicians can use this MSO structure in their community to contract directly with self-funded employee benefit plans. The MSO provides an efficient way for physicians to coordinate the business resources and the information system technology necessary to administer employee benefit plans.

Physicians in the service area of the MSO can be affiliated with it at a variety of levels. The original physician investors have a high level of affiliation with the MSO through the transfer of their practice administration to the MSO, as well as having a monetary investment in it. Other physicians who are not investors but have developed alliances with the physician investors, perhaps in the form of a specialty physician network, sign a service agreement with the MSO to participate in the direct contracting relationships with employers.

A third level of physician participation can be in the form of a loose affiliation of specialists serving as independent contractors with the MSO. These physicians are not part of a physician network but, rather, contract with the MSO for the purpose of participating in the opportunity to contract with self-funding employers. A physician-affiliated MSO can serve as a service bureau for many types of physicians at different levels of affiliation.

Most physicians who are not in the financial position to capitalize an MSO with their own money can choose an investment partner, often in their medical service area, with whom to share the financial risk and reward of MSO formation. Figure 19-2 outlines the components of a physician-driven MSO capitalized with a development partner. Physicians

FIGURE 19-2. Physician-Driven MSO Capitalized with Development Partner(s)

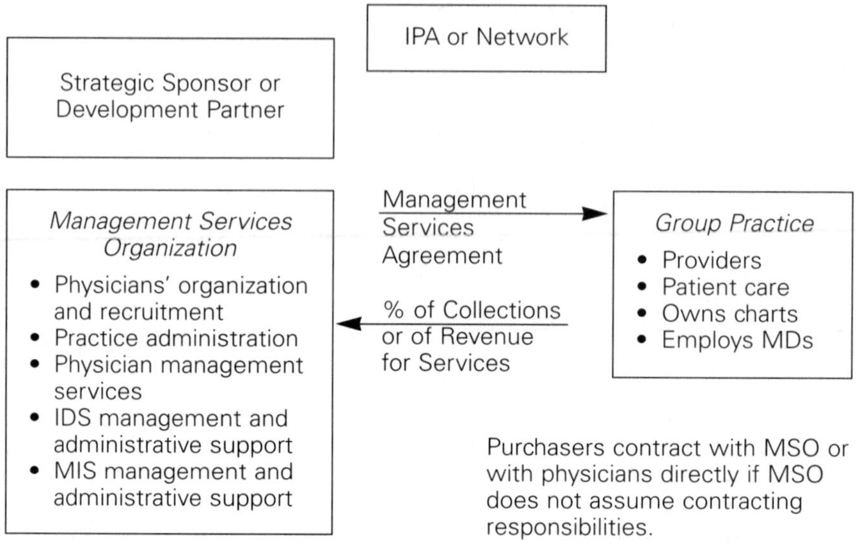

faced with the decision of capitalizing an MSO themselves or selecting an investment partner should consider the following:

- *Price:* Do the physicians have the capital to form the MSO? Is there a partner in the market with whom they can share the financial burden of MSO formation? Are they willing to share the financial rewards with this partner?
- *Autonomy:* Is there a partner in the market they trust and that shares their goals and vision? Will the partner commit long term to the enterprise, or is it in the enterprise for investment savvy? What interest does this partner have in physician-driven efforts? What does it stand to gain?
- *Risk assumption:* Have the physicians assessed how they will take on risk independently and as a group? In general, are they risk adverse or proactive? What is their potential partner's view of risk?
- *Managed care experience:* What experience does their potential partner have in managed care? What experience does it have with managed care? Do their strengths and weaknesses complement those of their partner?

Once these decisions have been made, the focus turns to the MSO itself. Table 19-1 lists the broad categories of services an MSO can offer

TABLE 19-1. Range of Possible MSO Product Services to Physicians

Physician Organization and Recruitment	*Practice Administration*	*Physician Management Services*	*IDS and Administration Support*	*MIS*
1. Organizing physicians into functioning groups (IPAs, PHOs, etc.) 2. Physician communication and education 3. Physician leadership and management development 4. Administrative support for physician recruitment	1. Billing/collections 2. Access to group purchasing/ insurance 3. Fee schedule 4. Legal services 5. MIS support 6. Payroll 7. Accounting/ budgeting 8. Marketing/planning	1. Business/financial management 2. Strategy/planning 3. Integration of communication 4. Managed care contracting 5. Compensation 6. Capitation management	1. Continuum of care development 2. Carve out product development 3. Provider reimbursement 4. Medical management 5. Contracts between IDS and managed care plans 6. Clinical data analysis/reporting	1. Definition of requirement 2. Vendor selection and management 3. Installation and training 4. Technical and operational support

Source: *Integrated Health Care 100 Directory* (Reston, VA: Saint Anthony Publishing, 1996), p. 8.

physicians. Notice that there are physician practice management services included in the gamut of services an MSO can provide. By itemizing all the responsibilities an MSO can assume, it can be seen that the MSO structure affords physicians creativity in product design. An MSO can be what the physicians need it to be at one point in time, yet physicians can adapt its service capabilities to a changing environment.

Physician Perceptions of Management Services Organizations

Many MSOs remain the silent force in the market in which they operate. The public record of successful MSOs is incomplete. The trend in the MSO industry is that there is no guarantee for success, which is reinforced by press given to those MSOs that started as a reaction to managed care and eventually were purchased by a hospital or investment group. With blurred perceptions of MSOs and PPMCs, many physicians view the MSO as an organization destined to consolidate or sell out.

However, this perception does not have to be the destiny of MSOs. By considering table 19-1 as a list of core competencies or aspects of managed care that physicians recognize as valuable to the future of medicine, the market opportunities for physicians involved with the MSO becomes greater than the perceived limitations of the MSO structure.

The reason these physicians succeed is that their involvement in the MSO improves their managed care skills. The MSO strategy becomes limiting when physicians do not view the organization as a business venture. Marc Margulis, managing director with Houlihan, Lokey, Howard, & Zukin, states: "Many IPAs and medical groups simply treat their MSO as a cost center. They charge the system 11 percent, and it costs them 11 percent. There's no profit at this level."[4] One way for physicians to examine costs realistically is to develop a percent of premium charge. This flow of dollars will not provide long-term financing to the MSO, but it is a technique to establish funds for the MSO's day-to-day operations, as well as a basis for developing a profit margin. Table 19-2 shows a breakdown of MSO services and what percentage of the premium is typically maintained by an MSO to provide those services.

Another pitfall for physicians using the MSO strategy is that they do not distinguish development of the MSO from creation of a billing service. If the physicians want to do billing, they need to consider only claims and administration when pricing services. The choice to do billing may seem to simplify the venture, but in the long run it hinders the organization's sustainability. The MSO sustains itself through retaining the current patient market share the physicians represent as well as through creating efficiency in the delivery of care. The value-added services of marketing, provider relations, MIS, medical management, and member services allow the physicians to sustain the MSO strategy and eventually expand on their patient market share and move beyond their current service area.

To make the MSO as valuable as possible, the physician leaders must charge the market rate for its services, between 14 and 16 percent of premium, and keep the cost for these services between 9 and 11 percent. Margulis comments: "On a larger scale, this strategy is—in essence—what the public physician practice management companies are doing. They're really MSOs, not medical groups, that have gone public and the profit is what provides the return to shareholders and the capital to expand."[5] A public MSO as Margulis describes it could result in the arrangement depicted in figure 19-3.

TABLE 19-2. Breakdown of MSO Services, 1995

MSO Services	*Percent of Premium*
Claims	2.3%
Provider Relations	1.0
Marketing	0.2
MIS	1.4
Medical Management	4.6
Member Services	0.5
Administration	1.2
Profit	0.0 to 5.0
Total	11.2 to 16.2%*

*For <10,000 covered lives. For > 10,000 covered lives, the percent can decline by half.

FIGURE 19-3. Public Management Services Organization

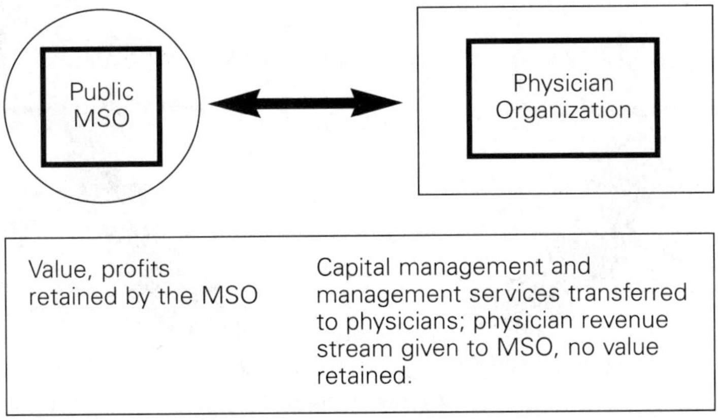

Future Evolution of the Management Services Organization

Where do physicians with managed care expertise and fine-tuned practices developed through affiliation with an MSO go from here? Figure 19-4 shows the potential evolution of an MSO to a physician-owned, private-label health plan. The study of physician-owned health plans across the country shows they are present in markets saturated with commercial HMOs as well as in rural markets. There is no one established path that physicians have taken to develop their own HMO product. Realization that the health care market is not stagnant and that a willingness to join forces through creation of a physician organization are two of the beginning steps that have led physicians down a path that has resulted in creation of a physician-driven health plan. The managed care expertise gained through affiliation with an MSO certainly can be applied to a physician-driven health plan endeavor.

The MSO is a transitional strategy in many ways. It can be a transitional strategy for physicians who want to move away from FFS medicine practiced in an individual setting toward participation in managed care contracts with the administrative support from the MSO. As depicted in figure 19-4, it can be a transitional structure in a market where physicians

FIGURE 19-4. Potential Strategic Evolution of Management Services Organizations

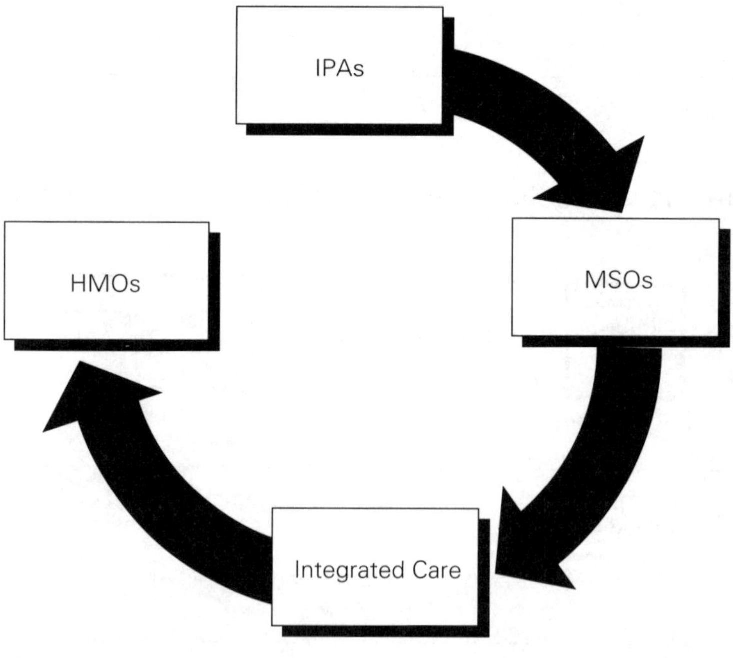

move from membership in an IPA to participation in an integrated care network and eventually to a private-label health plan. Whatever the form of the MSO or the role it plays in the physicians' market strategy, the ultimate function is to bring the critical tools of information systems, managed care expertise, capital, and practice administration to the physician practice while creating an environment for success in managed care contracting.

PHYSICIAN PRACTICE MANAGEMENT COMPANY STRATEGY

Physicians choosing to affiliate with a PPMC can add critical managed care tools currently lacking in their practices and reach a new level of managed care experience, just as physicians who choose an MSO strategy do. However, reaching this goal for physicians who affiliate with a PPMC is a different process than building an MSO.

Just as there are a variety of MSO structures physicians can pursue, there are many different types of PPMCs available to physicians searching for this type of product. The different types include PPMCs defined by the following options:

- Local versus regional versus national focus
- Single-physician specialty versus multispecialty versus primary care physician (PCP) versus hospital-based model
- Publicly held versus privately held
- Physician asset based versus management of practice only

The PPMC industry has been neatly bundled by Wall Street for investment purposes, but upon further examination, John Crawford, CFO of PhyCor, Inc., comments: "There is very little to generalize in the PPMC business except that we all work with physicians."[6] The industry is highly differentiable, and just as no one MSO product has become the template for MSOs throughout the country, there is no one PPMC template.

One way to demonstrate the diversity among PPMCs is to profile several companies. Following are profiles of Pediatrix, First Physician Care, and PhyCor, Inc.

Pediatrix

In the PPMC industry, Pediatrix is a unique organization due to its focus on providing physician management services to hospital-based neonatal and pediatric intensive care units (NICUs and PICUs). Currently, Pediatrix is affiliated with a small percentage of the market that uses its management services: 175 of the 3,000 neonatologists practicing in the United States and 63 of the more than 1,200 NICUs in the country. Analysts predict that the company will become the management company of choice for nearly 25 percent of the neonatologists currently practicing in the United States.

Stakeholders of the Neonatology Industry The neonatology industry breaks into three main stakeholders. One of the strengths of Pediatrix as a PPMC is that it forms a network among the three main stakeholders of neonatology—HMOs, hospitals, and physician stakeholders together—using a comprehensive management approach. Pediatrix achieves success in the market niche by focusing on one medical specialty because the management team is able to carefully balance the needs of the stakeholders.

For HMOs, neonatology is important because enrollees look for superior care for babies before signing up for the HMO product. HMOs need to satisfy their enrollees, yet they experience high cost in this area because of the increased number of inpatient days that neonates require. It is a balancing act for HMOs to offer high-quality care in neonatology in an efficient manner.

For the hospital stakeholders in the industry, the obstetrics department generates high levels of admissions and revenue for the hospital. Demonstrating excellence in the area of newborn and infant care or building a high-quality NICU becomes a competitive variable in the market. A hospital with a highly respected NICU begins to differentiate itself in the market, possibly developing a center of excellence recognized by patients, physicians, and payers in the regional area.

Neonatology as a medical profession is very different from other areas of medicine. Once a patient requires the care of a neonatologist in the hospital, the neonatologist assumes a full attending physician role. For the patient, the neonatologist assumes the role of a PCP, coordinating all his or her care. The neonatologist's role as both physician and manager of care is a key dynamic in this field of medicine. Both hospital and managed care plans rely on the neonatologist to deliver high-quality, efficient care. Some neonatology patients can be hospitalized for two to three months at a time.

Pediatrix brings all these stakeholders together in its management of NICUs. The company has been providing these services to hospital NICUs for more than five years, and the company itself was founded by two neonatologists and a chief medical officer with 25 years' experience in the practice of neonatology.

With the neonatologists as managers of patient care, Pediatrix develops business relationships with them. The typical business arrangement with a group of neonatologists involves the development of a professional association owned by a Pediatrix physician. This professional association transfers all its revenue to the Pediatrix holding company, which pays all the professional association's operating expenses as well as physician salaries. Typically, the physicians accept cash for their assets as they are transferred to the professional association, but because the stock value of Pediatrix remains strong, many physicians are accepting equity as acquisition currency. Figure 19-5 diagrams the relationship that Pediatrix develops with its physicians.

Stakeholder Benefits of Affiliation with Pediatrix Each of the neonatology stakeholders receives certain benefits from its affiliation with an NICU managed by Pediatrix. For a hospital, Pediatrix recruits and staffs neonatologists and formulates schedules. This service includes 24-hour staffing, which many hospitals find important to expand their service base. Pediatrix is able to cross-fertilize its services into PICUs, emergency rooms, delivery rooms, nursery departments, and pediatric units, which means the company generates efficiencies. The efficiencies Pediatrix is able to generate through its comprehensive care model and management and systems infrastructure are attractive to third-party payers. For neonatologists, the exclusive patient record system Pediatrix has introduced allows physicians to readily evaluate treatment patterns and provides them with critical patient data to assist in their clinical decision making. Physicians perceive that Pediatrix is the dominant player in this area of medicine with a solid reputation. Pediatrix has affiliated with some of the most prestigious, highest-quality neonatology groups across the country. The job security and benefits that affiliation with the Pediatrix system offers is attractive to many physicians

Pediatrix has little competition in this market niche. Physicians who have affiliated with them are pleased and speak highly of the management services the company provides. This word of mouth gives Pediatrix

FIGURE 19-5. Relationship between Pediatrix Medical Group, Inc., and Physicians

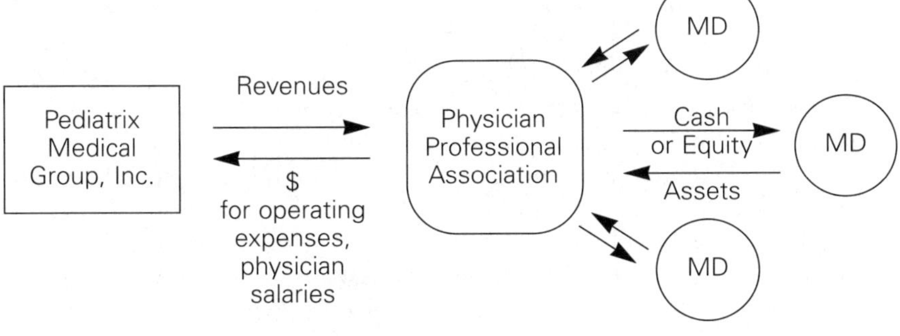

a solid reputation among neonatologists reinforced by the presence of neonatologists at the helm of the organization. Pediatrix's success demonstrates the strategy of hyperspecialization within the PPMC industry, while maintaining a broad perspective on the needs of all of the stakeholders who work in that particular health care niche.

First Physician Care

As a private PPMC providing management services to more than 100 physicians at 25 clinic sites, First Physician Care (FPC) focuses on multispecialty groups that have a strong primary care base and focus. It has an IPA management subsidiary, Precept Healthcare Group, that currently works with 1,700 physicians.

Because it is a private PPMC, FPC has been able to attract physicians who are wary of the large, national PPMCs that some feel will be unable to represent their interests or hear their voice in decision making. FPC has a local flavor that complements its strategy as a private PPMC. Working in south Florida, Atlanta, and St. Louis, the company develops its deals with physicians using a variety of models. (Figure 19-6 shows the stock for assets transaction in all of the markets FPC works.)

In some instances, FPC uses a model in which assets are transferred to the company and, in return, the physicians receive capital from the company, which they use for the growth and expansion of their practice. In other markets, FPC uses the professional corporation/MSO model, where the company becomes an investment partner with the physicians in the formation of a PC the physicians own, and FPC employs the physicians' staff. The PC and FPC become partners in the formation of an MSO that operates in the physicians' local service area. First Physician does use some models where the physicians become employees of the company, but that is not its standard model. Founded by a physician, FPC structures partnerships with physicians as asset purchases or management service agreements to meet the needs and goals of its physician partners.

Recently, FPC announced its entry into the Texas market by merging with Physician Capital Partners, which provides management services for Health Partners Medical Group of Fort Worth. Health Partners Medical Group adds 69 physicians representing family practice, internal medicine, pediatrics, and obstetrics/gynecology to FPC's network of primary care–focused, multispecialty physician groups.

FPC's movement into the Texas market highlights the criteria the company uses in considering physician groups for affiliation. Stephen A. George, chairman and CEO of FPC, stated in the press release of the company's move into the Texas market: "In partnering with community-leading medical groups, FPC looks for entrepreneurial, growth-oriented physician organizations committed to seizing the opportunity of managed

FIGURE 19-6. Organization of First Physician Care, Inc., with Regional, Wholly Owned Subsidiaries

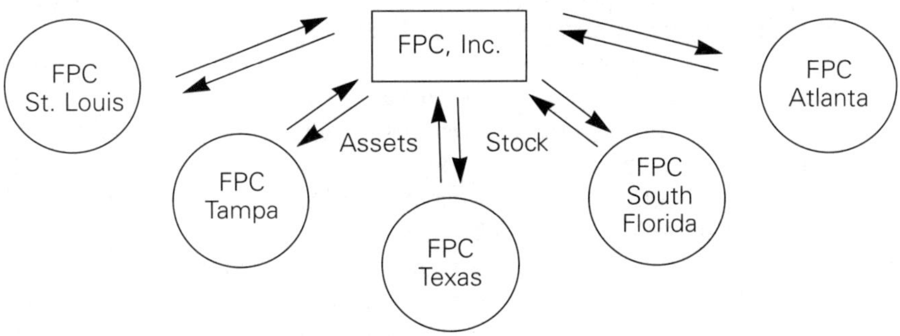

care growth and delivering excellent patient care." The criteria FPC uses to identify physician organizations is different from those of other PPMCs because the company is looking for healthy, growing organizations with physicians who have many years of practice ahead of them. There are PPMCs in the marketplace looking for practices that need to be recovered or rescued, or whose physicians are looking for a way to retire their practice within five years.

Don Smallwood, chief operating officer of FPC, confirmed that one of the most dynamic forces in a health care market is a physician-driven organization, not a physician organization that is management driven. Physician-driven organizations are looking for access to capital and practice management expertise to boost their growth and success. PPMCs have much to offer such physician groups, and, in return, they have much to offer a PPMC.

PhyCor, Inc.

PhyCor, Inc., is a PPMC that operates multispecialty clinics and manages IPAs. The company operates 42 clinics with approximately 2,850 physicians in 24 states, and manages IPAs with more than 8,700 physicians in 15 markets. It is one of two public PPMCs operating in the multispecialty clinic niche, the other being MedPartners/Mullikin, Inc. The appeal of multispecialty clinics to PhyCor is that through one acquisition in the market, PhyCor establishes itself. A multispecialty clinic has referral patterns and relationships within a community that it has built throughout its growth. As *Piper Jaffray* states in its August 1995 assessment of PPMCs: "By acquiring a prominent multispecialty group in a secondary market, PhyCor instantly becomes one of a very small number of sophisticated delivery systems in the market."[7]

When PhyCor purchases a multispecialty clinic, its management team focuses on the administration of the group to expand margins over time by increasing efficiencies and leveraging fixed costs. One of PhyCor's strengths in the market is the physician leadership of the firm and the managed care experience of these physicians. Physician experience and leadership reassures physicians affiliating with the firm.

Once PhyCor has acquired a multispecialty clinic, the physicians remain in control of their own destiny through representation on a joint policy board with physician members as well as PhyCor members and by retaining half ownership of the clinic. PhyCor is noted in the PPMC market for its excellent negotiators who build trust with physicians and work with them throughout the acquisition process.

The standard parts of an offer PhyCor makes to a prospective multispecialty clinic are as follows:

- A 40-year management service agreement with PhyCor
- Noncompete agreements and restrictive covenants for those physicians who later decide to leave the group
- A fee arrangement

Throughout the term of the service agreement, PhyCor receives reimbursement for all clinic expenses from the physician group and shares the excess of net clinic revenues after expenses with them. The physicians receive capital and the right of management over all medical issues; PhyCor retains the right to manage all nonmedical operations. Figure 19-7 shows the general exchange that occurs during the term of the management service agreement.

Although there are standard parts of deals that PhyCor offers physician groups, the company tailors the offers to the various clinic assets

FIGURE 19-7. Basic Transfer within a PhyCor Deal

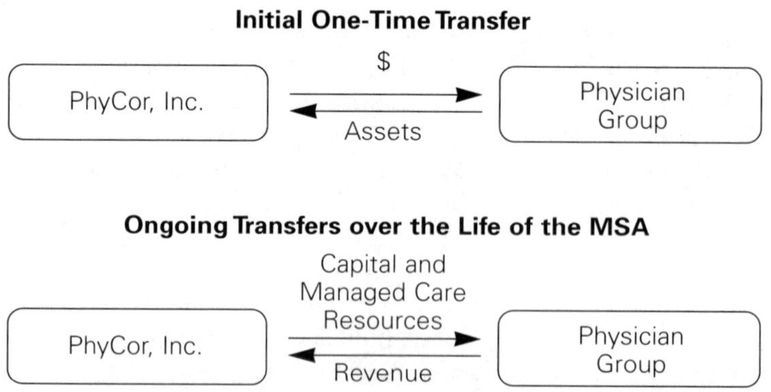

present in each situation, the type of incentive arrangements the physicians prefer, and the information system capabilities of the practice at the time of the proposed deal. The perception of PPMCs is that they offer standard deals to all practices, and that is true about their basic structure. However, the details that make each deal client specific are the pricing, the incentives offered to the physicians, and the information systems that will be used by the physicians. With the number of PPMCs in the market courting physicians, each company is developing its own niche. With a variety of niche players, finding a deal that represents a template for all PPMCs is difficult. Table 19-3 itemizes PPMCs by their market niche and number of physicians they have acquired or networked.[8]

SIMILARITIES AND DIFFERENCES BETWEEN THE TWO STRATEGIES

Although the perception exists that PPMCs are a subset of MSOs, the two strategies have distinct similarities and differences. These are discussed in the following subsections.

Similarities

One similarity is that both strategies can bring physicians to relatively the same point in their practice of medicine: Both sets of physicians can achieve managed care expertise and the introduction of capital, information systems, and administrative efficiencies into their practices. The difference between two physicians following two strategies is the roads they travel to arrive at this point.

Other similarities between the PPMC and MSO strategies include the following:

- *Both have their genesis in local markets.* They are used to developing solutions for local problems physicians face. Because the practice of medicine is a local phenomenon, the strategies that are appealing to physicians considering their practices' growth and development are ones they can craft to fit their particular circumstances.
- *Both broaden the service area of the physicians who use them.* Physicians who take action using an MSO or PPMC strategy are viewed as leaders in the community. Affiliation with these physician leaders is attractive to physicians in neighboring service areas practicing a similar style of medicine or having similar beliefs about the future of physician practice. Suddenly, the

TABLE 19-3. PPMCs by Niche and Number of Physicians Acquired or Networked, 1996

	Acquired Physicians	*Network Physicians*	*Total Physicians*	*PPMC Specialty*
Multispecialty Model				
PhyCor, Inc.	2,300	8,000	10,300	Multispecialty clinics
MedPartners/Caremark	2,893	4,356	7,249	Multispecialty clinics
Single-Specialty Model				
American Oncology Resources	174		174	Oncology group practices
Apogee	74		74	Mental health group practices
OccuSystems	143		143	Provides PCPs and case management services through largest network of occupational centers
Physician Reliance Network	225		225	Eye care professionals
Hospital-Based Group Model				
Coastal Physician Group	170	1,870	2,040	Hospital-based physician services
EmCare Holdings	800		800	Helps hospitals staff and manage EDs
InphyNet Medical Management	1,400			Provides primary care–based physicians services to hospitals, MCOs, and correctional institutions
Pediatrix Medical Group	176		176	Provides physicians with management services to hospital-based neonatal and pediatric ICUs
Sterling Healthcare Group, Inc.	1,000		1,000	Supplies staff and management to hospital EDs; recently diversified into PCP practices
IPA/Primary Care Network Model				
AHI Healthcare Systems		6,946	6,946	Integrates individual and small groups of PCPs and specialists through IPAs; does not purchase the assets of the physician groups; provides administrative functions along with capitated HMO contracting capabilities
FPA Medical Management		2,195	2,195	Organizes PCPs and specialists into IPAs; provides them with range of services: managed care contracting, MIS, claims management, UR/QA, case management, physician credentialing and recruitment

physicians with the leadership role find that their service area has increased through new affiliations with clinics and practices, causing the number of covered lives these physicians represent to increase.

- *Both answer the physician quest and the need for capital.* This is the two strategies' strongest similarity. Physicians contemplating forming a PO or MSO, building a new practice site, or recruiting new physicians to their practice all require capital, whether generated through their own practice revenues or borrowed, contributed, or received from outside sources. The era of group practice formation and the self-organization or market organization of physicians is here. From the 4,026 physicians surveyed for the 1995 AMA study entitled *Physician Marketplace Statistics,* the distribution of physicians in group practices of three to eight members was 49 percent.[9] Figure 19-8 graphs this distribution of nonfederal physicians in group or solo practice. Comparable statistics in 1992 concluded that 36 percent of physicians were in groups of three or more, and it is estimated that in the year 2000, 60 percent of physicians will be members of medical groups of three or more.[10]

Physicians in physician groups have used the MSO or PPMC strategy. What about the 40 percent of solo practitioners remaining? Some will feel the market forces of integration and the need to prepare their practices for the changes of managed care and prepaid health care. These are physicians who will look to the physician leaders in their communities and note where these physicians found their sources of capital and gained their managed care expertise. It is this need for capital and the potential for the formation of physician organizations that drives the MSO and PPMC strategies.

FIGURE 19-8. Distribution of Nonfederal Physicians in Group or Solo Practice, 1996

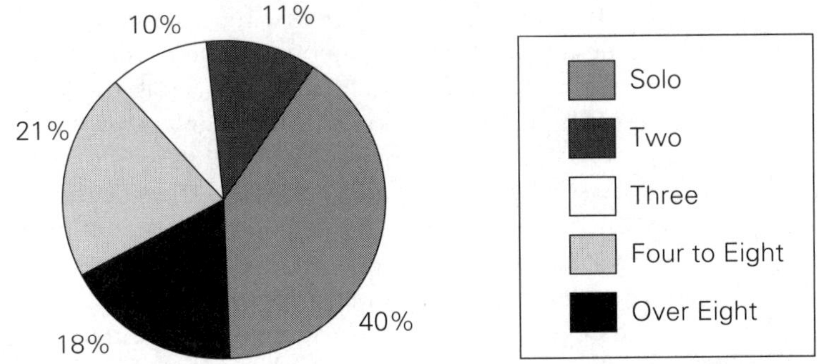

Differences

The two strategies also have their distinctions. One of the distinctions is how long the strategies have existed. Although the ideas of practice management and outsourcing the administrative aspects of a physician practice are not new, the linking of these ideas with a business enterprise is a product of only the past 30 years. Although there is no formal documentation of the first MSO, it is likely that the idea of a management service bureau to coordinate the administrative aspects of medicine appeared on the scene with the direct contracting between railroad employers in the Pacific Northwest and physicians in the early 1900s. (See chapter 18 on the evolution of MSOs.)

The introduction of Medicare and Medicaid into the delivery system also popularized use of the service bureau approach. With forms and regulations, physicians began to streamline their office paperwork, first by pooling office staff and eventually moving these office functions outside their practices into a service bureau. Today, physicians entering practice out of residency have access to MSO services, from practice management to information systems. Often hospitals assist new physicians with the administrative and practice management aspects of managed care. Loyola University Medical Center is one such academic health center that offers MSO services to its residents. The MSO gives physicians an immediate support structure with the resources of a nationally recognized teaching hospital at their fingertips. With that in mind, the MSO is a traditional structure, as opposed to the public PPMC, the first two of which became publicly traded in 1991. The dawning of the age of the PPMC marks a change in the practice of medicine where physician needs for capital and practice management exceeded, in some cases, what they were able to provide through pooling their own resources.

With the dawning of this age of physicians seeking business partners, however, there is the chance that some ventures will result in the pooling of money and assets without pooling value or a sustainable competitive edge. There are PPMCs in the market today that simply keep the cash flowing into the company but do not retain assets to support it. There is the promise of quick capital for physicians willing to sign management service agreements of 40 years; but, without the support of assets, what will these physicians be able to recover if the company should go under or be bought out before the 40 years are up?

There are aspects of the acquisition process of physician practices by PPMCs that are under scrutiny by the IRS and the Office of the Inspector General (OIG). The questions are directed at the goodwill payments PPMCs pay to physicians in the acquisition of their practice to reflect what the IRS describes as goodwill: "total of all those indefinable qualities that bring customers to a business . . . such as a trade-name right, a location, or special know how."[11] Regulators are asking what the PPMCs are really paying for. A PPMC may be paying for the *goodwill* in the purest sense of the word, yet some view these payments as a disguise "for remuneration to physicians in return for future referrals to the acquiring entity."[12]

Attorneys J. J. Sokol and J. I. Zumpano of McDermott, Will, and Emery, specialists in physician practice acquisition, report that actual monetary figures are being paid for goodwill.[13] Primary care goodwill ranges from 30 to 50 percent of the projected gross revenues, and specialty goodwill from 20 to 30 percent of projected annual gross revenues. Are PPMCs paying more than these figures for practices and their associated goodwill? From the press clippings of PPMC purchases from the past four years, the answer is yes. With the rate of consolidation and buyout of PPMCs, what do these goodwill figures really mean? For physicians, this discussion comes down to careful consideration of potential PPMC partners. The partner physicians sign with today may not be the owner of their revenue stream tomorrow.

With the MSO strategy, the question of whether the organization is merely pooling cash or really supporting itself with assets is not necessary for physicians to ask because it is the physicians themselves who are putting the assets of their own practices into the venture; it is a known commodity from the start. For physicians forming MSOs with development partners, the same research and questions have to be asked as when physicians affiliate with a PPMC. With physicians at the helm investing their practices and time in the venture, the investment fundamentals of the homegrown MSO set it apart from the PPMC strategy.

CONCLUSION

In light of the presentation of MSOs and PPMCs in this chapter, an important question for physicians to ask is, What value is the physician or the physician group trying to protect or expand using the MSO or PPMC strategy? Markets that consolidate quickly leave little room for the indecisive physician. Locally grown MSOs with limited capital and a convoluted view of this market are becoming fatalities—selling out to hospitals, insurers, and HMOs. Also, hospital MSOs are looking to companies to take these poorly constructed ventures, turn them around, and maintain some control in the process.

The key element to using the MSO and PPMC strategies so that all participants of the venture reach their goals is the creation of value. This value is ultimately what will improve the strategic position of the various stakeholders. However, to receive the benefit of the value, the physicians, the hospitals, and others considering an MSO or PPMC strategy must be able to take risk and manage it. Those that are able to manage risk, not work to eliminate it, are the ones that will succeed in the MSO and PPMC strategies available today and contribute to the evolution of these strategies in the future.

References

1. Interviews and conversations, 1996–1997.

2. InterStudy, *Competitive Edge* (St. Paul, MN: InterStudy, 1996).

3. B. O'Neil and T. B. Manderfeld, "Physician Practice Management: Just What the Doctor Ordered," *Piper Jaffray Research* 1 (Aug. 1995): 16.

4. M. Margulis, "Preparing for Investment: Part One, Creating Leverage," *Physician Practice Options* (June/July 1996): 13.

5. Margulis.

6. Interview with John Crawford CFO, PhyCor, Inc., Nashville (Nov. 19, 1996).

7. O'Neil and Manderfeld, p. 21.

8. J. Peters, "Strategic/Operational Tactics to Improve MSO Financial Performance" (preconference workshop on profiting with MSOs, Scottsdale, AZ, Oct. 24–25, 1996).

9. M. Gonzalez, ed., *Physician Marketplace Statistics* (Chicago: American Medical Association, 1995).

10. Kenneth S. Abramowitz, "The Future of Health Care Delivery in America" (Bernstein Research, New York, October 24, 1996), p. 21.

11. J. J. Sokol and J. I. Zumpano, "Taking Physicians Public: Understanding Physician Practice Management" (seminar sponsored by McDermott, Will, and Emery, Cambridge, MA, Nov. 21, 1997); K. Terry, "How Much of Your Goodwill Has Evaporated?" *Medical Economics* (Oct. 1991): 28.

12. A. J. Fichter. "Despite Scrutiny, Practice Goodwill Does Have Value." *American Medical News* (Mar. 1994): 34.

13. Sokol and Zumpano.

20

Visions of the Future: CEO Perspectives

Fourth-Generation Management Services Organizations

Steven M. Scott, MD
Jacque J. Sokolov, MD
Kirsten A. Nyrop

A management services organization (MSO) may be defined as a centralized business unit that provides support services—through ownership or management contract—pertaining to the operational and financing needs of solo and group practitioners, provider networks, integrated delivery systems (IDSs), and other entities poised to benefit from economies of purchasing power, contracting clout, managed care expertise, and business operations acumen in an increasingly capitated and integrated health care marketplace. For the purposes of this section of the chapter, MSOs are not distinguished from physician practice management entities.

This section offers a five-stage model to describe the evolving MSO industry. (See figure 20-1.) In it, each succeeding level, or generation, of MSO is characterized by a growing array of services as providers adjust to increasing levels of managed care penetration with new innovations in provider integration and increasingly sophisticated information and medical management systems. This chapter will demonstrate that growing pressures on, and preferences among, providers to move from fee-for-service (FFS) to global risk (the medical loss ratio) are placing a higher and higher premium on effective management not merely of costs and information but, more important, of health outcomes.

FIGURE 20-1. Five Generations of MSOs

Fifth: Managing Population Well-Being

Fourth: Managing Patient Care

Third: Managing Information

Second: Managing Costs

First: Managing the Physician Practice

The section focuses in particular on the evolving near-term future of the MSO industry, which is defined herein as the fourth-generation MSO, whose services are focused on the effective management of patient care and individual health outcomes. Ultimately, the services of future MSOs (the fifth generation) will focus on payer-provider-patient relationships that produce positive health outcomes for entire communities.

FIRST-GENERATION MANAGEMENT SERVICE ORGANIZATIONS

In the MSO model shown in figure 20-1, first-generation MSOs are defined as focusing on managing the physician practice. At this level, MSOs offer services largely to solo practitioners, small group practices, and independent hospitals in a retail FFS marketplace. Information management is primarily for the purpose of securing payments for provider services from payers who are largely indemnity insurers. In this market, there is still minimal FFS discounting, and networks are inclusive, with preferred provider organizations (PPOs) beginning to provide incentives for inner-network utilization. The focus of MSO services is on centralization to improve practice administration and operational efficiency, which includes:

- Providing a higher level of business management expertise
- Addressing human resources challenges through assistance with recruitment and staffing
- Decreasing general overhead through group purchasing and centralized business office support
- Improving cash flow through effective billing and collection systems
- Establishing compatible management information systems (MISs)
- Promoting the development and adoption of standardized operating policies and procedures
- Introducing limited utilization management

SECOND-GENERATION MANAGEMENT SERVICE ORGANIZATIONS

In the model, second-generation MSOs are defined as providing increasingly sophisticated services and systems for managing the costs of health care in a marketplace that has moved toward discounted FFS arrangements and now is moving toward capitation and risk-sharing agreements between (mostly primary care) providers and managed care organizations (MCOs). Leading HMOs are beginning to emerge in this marketplace, with point-of-service (POS) options prompting use of inner-network providers. At this stage, provider networks and hospital affiliations are still loose and largely for the purpose of referrals.

As the health care marketplace evolves into an environment where practitioners can benefit personally from such savings in controllable costs as prepaid arrangements with HMOs, MSOs can assist health care providers in understanding the cost implications of various patient care decisions, with a focus on learning how to provide cost-effective care without compromising quality. For example, MSOs can work with MCOs and capitated physicians, who are increasingly organized into group practices (chapter 15) and independent practice associations (IPAs) (chapter 14), on ways to reduce inpatient hospital days (length of stay), manage specialist referrals, and negotiate pharmaceutical benefits. Expectations for MSO services include:

- To provide a higher level of managed care contracting expertise
- To increase participation in managed care contracts
- To maximize internal savings on prepaid contracts and effective risk management
- To reduce inappropriate utilization through utilization review (UR) and management and use data to provide feedback to providers
- To further develop medical management and practice protocols

THIRD-GENERATION MANAGEMENT SERVICE ORGANIZATIONS

The marketplace for third-generation MSOs is characterized by even deeper FFS discounting and moderate levels of partial and full-capitation agreements with managed care providers. At this stage, physicians and other health care providers are becoming increasingly integrated in order to share risk and provide a continuum in patient care decisions. HMOs and PPOs are achieving critical mass and beginning to consolidate. Large provider groups working with IPAs, exclusivity agreements between HMOs and providers, and the growth of physician-hospital organizations (PHOs) (chapters 16 and 17) and joint ventures also are characteristic of this market.

As provider groups and networks establish systems for managing and monitoring utilization patterns and costs for providing health care services to a specific patient population (generally assigned to primary care providers by MCOs), the need for effective systems to manage growing volumes of information is a particular focus of third-generation MSO services. Increasingly sophisticated MISs are essential to the effective operation of wide-ranging front-office operations and made increasingly complex as providers enter into multiple-payer relationships, each with its own reimbursement rate, patient care protocols, and other requirements. In addition, employers and government entities are requesting data they can use for comparative analyses of provider credentials and the quality of care provided to health plan enrollees. Third-generation MSOs can help IDSs (chapter 13) to collect, analyze, and manage information for a variety of purposes, with MIS resource requirements ranging from relatively low to high sophistication, including:

- Group/health plan contract management and reporting
- Member enrollment and eligibility
- Provider contracting
- UR
- Claims administration
- Member relations
- Premium billing and accounts receivable
- Marketing support

Table 20-1 provides findings from a recent report of the Physician Payment Review Commission (PPRC) indicating the extent to which various MSO services are contracted for by providers.

FOURTH-GENERATION MANAGEMENT SERVICE ORGANIZATIONS

Overriding concerns with controlling health care costs are unlikely to dissipate within the foreseeable future, requiring continued vigilance in finding new and better ways to manage expenditures. Further, the more that can be learned about the capabilities and value of sophisticated MISs, the more this focus is likely to remain in perpetuity. Fourth-generation MSOs, therefore, do not abandon or lessen their focus on enabling providers and IDSs to have efficient business operations, provide cost-effective care, and manage increasingly complex information flows. Rather, fourth-generation MSOs become more and more knowledgeable and expert in these foundation services and add a fourth service focus, managing patient care. This focus entails a fundamental realignment of the incentives of health plan

TABLE 20-1. Services Provided by MSOs

Service	*Percent of Respondents Answering Yes*
Negotiate contracts with health insurers	71.8%
Billing or collection services	69.0%
Management of information/ computer services	68.0%
Management consulting	66.3%
Market physician services	64.9%
Personnel management	58.4%
Utilization review/physician profiling	54.1%
Joint/bulk purchasing of supplies	52.9%
Acquisition/sharing of medical and/or office equipment	52.6%
Leasing of medical office space	43.1%

Source: Physician Payment Review Commission. *Results of the 1994 National Survey of Physicians,* Selected External Research Series, No. 4 (Washington, DC: PPRC, 1995), pp. 2-12–2-13.

administrators and providers to produce positive health outcomes through informed payer-provider-patient interactions.

Production of Positive Health Outcomes

There already are increasingly powerful dynamics in the U.S. health care marketplace pushing for a return to the basics of patient care and the true meaning of "health maintenance," rather than being satisfied with merely "managing care." Driven by perception, reality, or a combination of the two, health plan clients, consumers, and providers throughout the country are increasingly effective in voicing their concern that health care cost reductions achieved by MCOs are occurring at the expense of high-quality care. As a consequence, elected officials—from state legislators to U.S. congressmen—are responding by proposing new laws affecting the managed care industry. That results in such mandated medical benefits as 48-hour maternity stay requirements, networks open to "any willing provider," assurances of direct access to obstetricians/gynecologists and other specialists, and patient protection bills focused on public disclosures of physician credentials and payer-provider contracts. Similarly, growing numbers of state regulatory agencies are seeking additional oversight of methods for compensating network providers, and are developing "report cards" to provide consumers and employers with comparative data on health plans.

More and more, health plans are being asked by their clients (employers and government programs), their members (employees and government program beneficiaries), and the general public (primarily through the press, regulatory agencies, and elected officials) to provide assurances that specific benefit plans, with their restrictive provider networks and effectiveness in reducing health care costs, are nevertheless providing the best results in patient care and clinical outcomes. Reflecting these growing concerns, in the summer of 1996, the National Committee for Quality Assurance (NCQA) released summaries of accreditation reports on MCOs. The six categories of the NCQA's standards for accreditation reflected in these summaries, illustrating the growing demand for up-to-date information on business operations and medical outcomes, are:

- Quality management (quality and improvement of care)
- Physician qualifications and evaluation
- Utilization management ("fair" and quick approval of medical treatment)
- Member rights and responsibilities (member satisfaction)
- Preventive health services
- Medical records (accuracy)

There are concerns within the managed care industry that many of the proposed anti–managed care laws and regulations could quickly become overreaching, violating the basic concept of private contracts, legislating the practice of medicine, or requiring product standardization to the point where HMOs are left to compete only on the basis of price. However, in general, these new public policies are being proposed because there are well-publicized instances where some health plans, at least, appear to have compromised patient health outcomes in the interest of cost containment. It also is possible that these new laws and regulations are proliferating because there is inadequate information—industrywide and often plan specific—with which to refute the contention that cost considerations are invariably at odds with health promotion and the best judgments of health care providers.

Therefore, a crucial role for fourth-generation MSOs is to assist health plans, provider groups, and IDSs to develop and maintain information systems that do not merely track costs, but also monitor treatments and health outcomes for individual patients, specific disease categories, and entire populations. For example, health plan purchasers are increasingly interested in value-based care for their employees and quantitative quality measures that show the effectiveness of various medical procedures and health care services. As a consequence, purchasers are requesting information they can use to analyze and compare MCO capabilities for providing data on the following types of quality measures:

- Preventive care, essential processes, clinical outcome measures, and physician technical skill
- Member health status, satisfaction, and access
- Plan services, procedure frequency, and physician turnover and interpersonal skills

Transition from Contractual to Structural Integration

A second important trend signaling the emergence of fourth-generation MSO services is the marketplace evolution from contractual integration to structural integration. Historically, payer-provider relationships have been largely contractual in nature, where those who pay the health care bills generally have paid little attention to the nature of the health care delivery system. However, as the marketplace evolves toward fully integrated delivery systems and accountable health plans, the sponsors of health plans are becoming more and more intimately involved with the delivery system's actual structure. In fact, in some markets, the sponsors of health plans are changing. Today, health plans are still largely sponsored by insurance businesses, Blue Cross/Blue Shield companies, and MCOs (HMOs and PPOs). But there now appears to be growing interest and efforts on the part of physician- and hospital-driven organizations and PHOs to sponsor their own IDSs and health plans, such as HMOs owned and managed by providers and the Medicare reform–proposed provider-sponsored organizations/networks (PSOs/PSNs).

The most immediate and formidable challenge for these new risk-bearing provider groups is the regulatory arena. In Washington, D.C., and a growing number of state capitals, pitched battles already are being waged between those who believe PSOs and other provider groups that assume global risk should be regulated as HMOs and those who perceive important distinctions between HMOs and provider groups that should be reflected in different regulations. Without digressing too much on this interesting topic—or considering the fundamental issue of PSO regulatory authority resting primarily with the states or the federal government—the authors of this chapter believe that regulations must ensure the financial solvency of these new risk-bearing entities, but also that PSOs are neither HMOs nor insurance companies and that reasonable and rational regulations should reflect their differences.

The point is that as the health care environment makes the transition from contractual to structural relationships, the marketplace will demand substantially more accountability across the delivery system from both those who sponsor health care and those who deliver it. In addition to financial accountability, there must be accountability for the quality of care, which encompasses both health system indicators and health status indicators. Health system indicators include such measurable factors as:

- Length of time it takes to see a physician
- Length of stay for a particular illness or episode of care
- Customer satisfaction survey reports
- Annual disenrollment rates from a plan

Health status indicators, on the other hand, focus on clinical data and clinical quality management measures that can be used to analyze specific clinical care and medical management decisions. Examples of these indicators include information on:

- Clinical outcomes
- Immunization rates
- Procedures for appropriate high-risk screening for certain diseases among certain types of populations

The emerging new provider-direct contracting networks could provide one of the best opportunities to resolve today's provider-patient-payer conundrum by focusing on appropriate care, specifically at the delivery system level. Protocols and guidelines for demand management, disease management, and specialty carve-out capability (going beyond length of stay, pharmaceutical benefits, and specialty referral) could be facilitated significantly. In these new risk-bearing organizations, payers and providers are merged, enabling a coming together of the health plan and the delivery system in a "health care management team." Historically, health plans have managed costs through UR, then utilization management, and eventually through catastrophic case management, largely by superimposing an artificial structure on the clinical delivery capabilities of physicians. As a result, physicians have become resentful of the "micromanagement" of the practice of medicine, first by insurance companies and then by HMOs.

By contrast, what now seems to be occurring in many IDSs across the country is a distancing of the UR/utilization management/patient care management functions away from the fiduciary—the insurance company or HMO—and into the delivery system itself, enabling physicians to reconnect with the clinical decisions they are making. To the extent that these new systems result in improved coordination, integration, and structural as well as functional sophistication, they can lead not only to improved customer service, but also to substantially improved quality of care at substantially lower cost. In other words, when the risk for an entire episode of care actually gets placed on a group of providers, they have a significant financial incentive to manage resources very efficiently. As physicians are charged with managing significantly more and more of the total health experience of a patient, including hospitalization and specialty services, physician management structures have the opportunity to "self-monitor" how physicians practice, why they practice the way they do, why certain diseases are treated in a particular fashion, and so on. New systems that are physician driven, physician led, and physician accountable—that enable and empower physicians to both bear the risks and reap the financial benefits of effective and appropriate managed care—will be the foundation for a new health care paradigm that places providers and payers in a full and equal partnership. Time will tell whether these new systems will be dominated by HMOs, PSOs/PSNs, or a competitive mix of the two.

FIFTH-GENERATION MANAGEMENT SERVICE ORGANIZATIONS

In the final stage of the model describing the evolution of the MSO industry, the fifth-generation MSO marketplace, it is reasonable to expect to see global capitation agreements with large IDSs encompassing full professional and hospital risk as well as pharmaceuticals, mental health, and ancillary services. Moreover, there will be major health systems contracting with one or more MCOs—whether HMOs, PPOs, or PSOs/PSNs.

In the ultimate marketplace of total provider integration and continuously evolving risk-bearing structures, the new health care paradigm alluded to above should then set the stage for effective health maintenance and disease prevention, not only at the level of individual plan members, but also for entire plan memberships and the totality of plan memberships within a community. This will be accomplished primarily through two developments that, at one level, are by no means new or complex but, at another level, will require almost revolutionary changes in the "culture" of several key players that determine health and wellness in the United States.

The first requirement is one that has been discussed and debated for decades—changes at the societal level that impact individual behavior related to various leading causes of death and disability such as smoking, drug abuse, alcohol abuse, gunshot wounds, and traffic fatalities. Public policies are one avenue; another is voluntary efforts at the community level, such as effective initiatives to educate teenagers about the dangers of drug and alcohol abuse or to establish a community watch program designed to discourage gang activity in the neighborhoods.

Society can try to influence certain health-related behaviors but, ultimately, it is up to the individual to pursue or refrain from actions that can have health consequences. What each individual does is a matter of choice, but also a matter of good information. It is possible that the final added service of MSOs is working with MCOs and IDSs to develop information technology systems that enable plan members and patients, with good information (such as computer-based information on nutrition, smoking cessation, exercise, or proper use of medications) with which to make the decision to take care of their own health and the health of their families.

The Foundation for Accountability (FACCT), an offshoot of the Jackson Hole Group, a well-known health policy consortium, endorsed development of a uniform set of quality measures for making comparisons between different health care plans and providers. (See chapter 9.) The framework being developed by FACCT includes information on consumers' health, satisfaction, and risk factors, as well as outcome measures for specific conditions. Fifth-generation MSOs can play an important role in enabling health plans and provider networks to address the total well-being issues that are the focus of FACCT's patient-oriented quality indicators, measuring the following types of relationships:

- The effect of the basic health condition on patients' lives
- The effectiveness of health services in addressing disease progression in affected patients
- Patient satisfaction with the care, service, and information they receive
- The effectiveness and appropriateness of preventive, diagnostic, and treatment services delivered by the health care system
- The extent to which the health care provided to patients enhances the functioning of their work and professional lives

Table 20-2 summarizes the five generations of MSOs, showing the progression of goals, payment mechanisms, and provider and information integration.

CONCLUSION

The evolution of the MSO industry may be viewed in five stages, or generations, of development characterized by a growing array of services offered to meet the demands of managed care penetration. The first three generations of MSOs were designed to manage physician practices, costs, and information, respectively. The fourth-generation MSO, which reflects the near future, focuses on more sophisticated management of the so-called foundation services provided by the first three, with added emphasis on managing patient care and health outcomes through better-managed information systems. The fifth-generation MSO will focus on total provider integration and development of more risk-bearing structures designed to provide effective health maintenance of not only individuals, but whole communities.

TABLE 20-2. Summary of the Five MSO Generations

MSO Generations: Goals	*Payment Mechanism*	*Provider Integration*	*Information Integration*
Fifth generation: Manage population well-being: Take care of sick patients cost-effectively with multiple provider and payer relations focused on individual health outcomes and total population health promotion, disease prevention.	Full global capitation to large IDSs, including professional and hospital risk. Capitation also for pharmaceuticals, mental health, and other ancillary services.	Total provider integration. Major health systems contracting with one or two HMOs. Emerging new health care paradigm—equal partnership of physicians, hospitals, and insurers.	Plan members, providers, and payers seek convenient access to a wide variety of information to promote healthy lifestyles and prevent diseases on a communitywide basis.
Fourth generation: Manage patient care: Take care of sick patients cost-effectively with multiple provider and payer relationships focused on individual health outcomes.	Deep discounting; extensive capitation and full professional risk agreements. Emergence of new risk-bearing organizations, such as PSNs and risk-bearing PPOs. Purchasers contract with IDSs for comprehensive services for beneficiaries.	Managed competition: Physicians and other providers coordinate patient care increasingly proactively, using agreed-upon guidelines. IPAs and PHOs work with many payers. Emergence of PSOs/PSNs. Strong gatekeeping; strict channeling of referrals.	Aggressive utilization management. Plan members (and government officials) seek information on appropriateness and quality of care, provider compensation, etc. Focus on quality of care, individual health outcome measures, and catastrophic case management.

(Continued on next page)

TABLE 20-2. *(Continued)*

MSO Generations: Goals	*Payment Mechanism*	*Provider Integration*	*Information Integration*
Third generation: Manage information: Take care of patients cost-effectively with multiple provider and payer relationships.	Deeper discounting; moderate partial- and full-capitation agreements with providers, including specialists. Lead HMOs and PPOs achieve critical mass, begin to consolidate.	Consolidation: Physicians/ other providers integrate to share risk, provide a continuum in patient care decisions. Large provider groups work with IPAs. Emergence of PHOs, exclusivity agreements, joint ventures. Referrals only within network; loose gatekeeping.	Medium utilization management; utilization data coupled with financial information focused on claims management. Coordination between multiple payers and providers. Employers and governmental entities seeking data on quality of care and provider credentials.
Second generation: Manage costs: Take care of sick patients cost-effectively.	FFS still predominates, but increasingly discounted. Limited capitation and risk sharing. Emergence of lead HMOs. PPO and POS incentives to use networks.	Loose framework: Loose and large provider networks and hospital affiliations; cooperation for referrals. Emergence of IPAs and group practices.	Basic utilization management and review, and financial information focused on controlling overhead and cost accounting. Financial/ expense information.
First generation: Manage the practice: Take care of sick patients.	Retail FFS, minimal discounting. Inclusive networks. Emergence of HMOs. PPO incentive to use networks.	Unstructured: Independent physicians and hospitals; patients self-refer.	Limited utilization management. Information exchanged to secure payment from payers.

The Future of Management Services Organizations

Paul H. Keckley Jr., PhD

For most physicians, the weekly mail includes one or more opportunities to join a management services organization (MSO), especially if the physician practices in a primary care specialty. Unfortunately, each MSO is different, and to further complicate matters, the sponsor of the MSO may be an unknown.

The future for MSO services is enormous simply because the American medical practice industry is still a "cottage industry." Most physicians still practice in single-specialty groups of fewer than four physicians. Most are not immediately challenged by capitated contracts, and most believe their practices perform successfully. In fact, most physicians believe there would be no need for MSOs or physician practice management companies (PPMCs) if insurers were less aggressive, Medicare more profitable, and patients less inquisitive.

This section of the chapter presents a basic format for evaluating MSOs. To begin, a functional definition of the MSO is useful: An MSO is a legal entity that provides administrative services to medical practices. This rather all-encompassing definition evidences the far-flung universe of MSO options available to physicians in most markets. Some MSOs are cooperatives that provide practice support services on an à la carte basis. At the other end of the continuum, there are such companies as PhyCor that provide comprehensive physician practice management services to practices after the purchase of their assets. In between, there are various approaches and models.

MANAGEMENT SERVICES ORGANIZATION MODELS

Most MSOs may be classified in one of three broad categories:

- *Service bureau:* An organization that provides select services to medical practices on the basis of a percentage of practice revenue or fee for service. There are two major service bureau models in most markets: independent billing services, which typically are aligned with local bookkeeping services; and hospital-sponsored programs, which are closely aligned with the institution's physician relations department. In most service bureaus, billing services are the staple. Value-added services often include a group purchasing program or education for the office staff in the practice.

- *Network management:* An organization that provides administrative services for independent practices that have entered into contractual obligations with the network for managed care participation. These networks typically are organized as independent practice associations (IPAs) (see chapter 14) or, in some cases, physician-hospital organizations (PHOs) (see chapter 16). The services usually provided to practices in these networks are claims management, risk management, and contract negotiations. Often ownership of these MSOs is a combination of physicians and hospitals, physicians and outside management companies, or the outside management company alone.
- *Group practice management:* An organization that provides a comprehensive array of practice services and is contractually obligated to the group for a defined long-term period, usually ranging from 10 to 40 years. So-called pure-play practice management companies such as PhyCor and MedPartners typically purchase the assets of multispecialty groups and enter into 30- to 40-year management agreements. Others target certain specialties with a similar transaction.

Table 20-3 shows the primary sponsors, primary services, primary goals, and cost factors associated with each of these models.

DETERMINATION OF THE BEST MODEL

Obviously, each of the three MSO models provides value to physicians, depending on the personal and professional needs of the physicians involved. From a strategic perspective, advisory board studies suggest that the best long-term position for most physicians is as a participant in a primary care–anchored multispecialty group. (See figure 20-2.) Medical groups in which primary care and specialty physicians have parallel incentives have distinct advantages in securing managed care contracts. The major advantage is their ability to accept full risk for a large population (enrollment) and manage the clinical and financial risks *inside the group.* Most physicians, however, are reluctant to make such a dramatic move. The common starting point for most is participating in the physician network model, followed within two years by making a transition to a group practice.

Unfortunately, most physicians lack adequate information about the performance of their own practice or market conditions to accurately discern their best option. Short-term Band-Aid solutions sometimes create

TABLE 20-3. Key MSO Models

	Models		
Model	Service Bureau →	Contracting Network (IPA, PHO) →	Group Practice
Primary Sponsors	Hospitals, medical societies	Hospitals, medical societies, HMOs, PPMCs	Hospitals, staff model HMOs, PPMCs
Primary Services	Billing, credit, collection; purchasing plan; referral service; physician education seminars	Contract negotiations, claims management, provider relations, utilization review, quality assurance, risk management	Medical management, information systems, ancillary service integration, practice management
Primary Goals	Positive physician relations, case management	Full/partial-risk HMO contracting	Practice consolidation for market dominance; multispecialty group formation with 50% primary care; practice cost management
Cost Factors	Information systems for billing, physician relations staff (1 per 60 physicians)	Capitation management information systems, 1 staff person per 1,000 covered lives	Information systems, capital for growth, 4 staff persons per full-time equivalent physician

Note: Contracting Network and Service Bureau functions are typically provided as a component of Group Practice Management services.

larger problems in the future, especially if the physician's decision is to partner with an MSO whose incentives are not aligned appropriately with those of the practice.

Following are some key questions physicians should ask when assessing MSO options:

- What is the long-term economic impact and value of the MSO for the practice?
- What track record does the MSO have in practice management, capitation management, and physician relationships?
- Are the incentives of the MSO sponsor appropriately aligned with the physician's professional and personal needs and goals?
- Is the MSO a quick fix or a long-term solution?
- As a participant in this MSO, will the physician be treated as an employee or a partner?

Each of the major sponsors of MSO services brings distinct strengths and weaknesses to the MSO's position. (See table 20-4.) Strategically, PhyCor believes the most optimal long-term MSO solution for most practices are practice management companies that build primary care–anchored multispecialty groups. Many hospitals are rethinking their MSO relationships with physicians after experiencing massive losses and increased physician frustration with their services. Notably, staff model HMOs are being dismantled because they recognized the need for physician incentives to be aligned more appropriately vis-à-vis an independent relationship with physicians rather than an employee model. In table 20-4, several dimensions useful in comparing MSO sponsorship are presented. One footnote to this table is significant: As hospitals and physician organizations seek meaningful long-term relationships in "virtually integrated systems" wherein the balance sheets of the hospital and group practice are independent, MSOs are being built that align the incentives of hospitals and physicians for managed care contracting.

CHALLENGES FOR THE FUTURE

For all MSOs, there are seven long-term challenges that should fuel massive consolidation and growth among companies that provide these services. They are:

1. *Information systems sophistication:* MSOs that lack the capability to provide purchasers, consumers, and providers access to clinical outcomes data in useful and interactive formats will be obsolete. Those MSO providers that lack access to capital for these purchases and experienced clinical management expertise will

FIGURE 20-2. Ascending Scale of Advantages in Winning Covered Lives

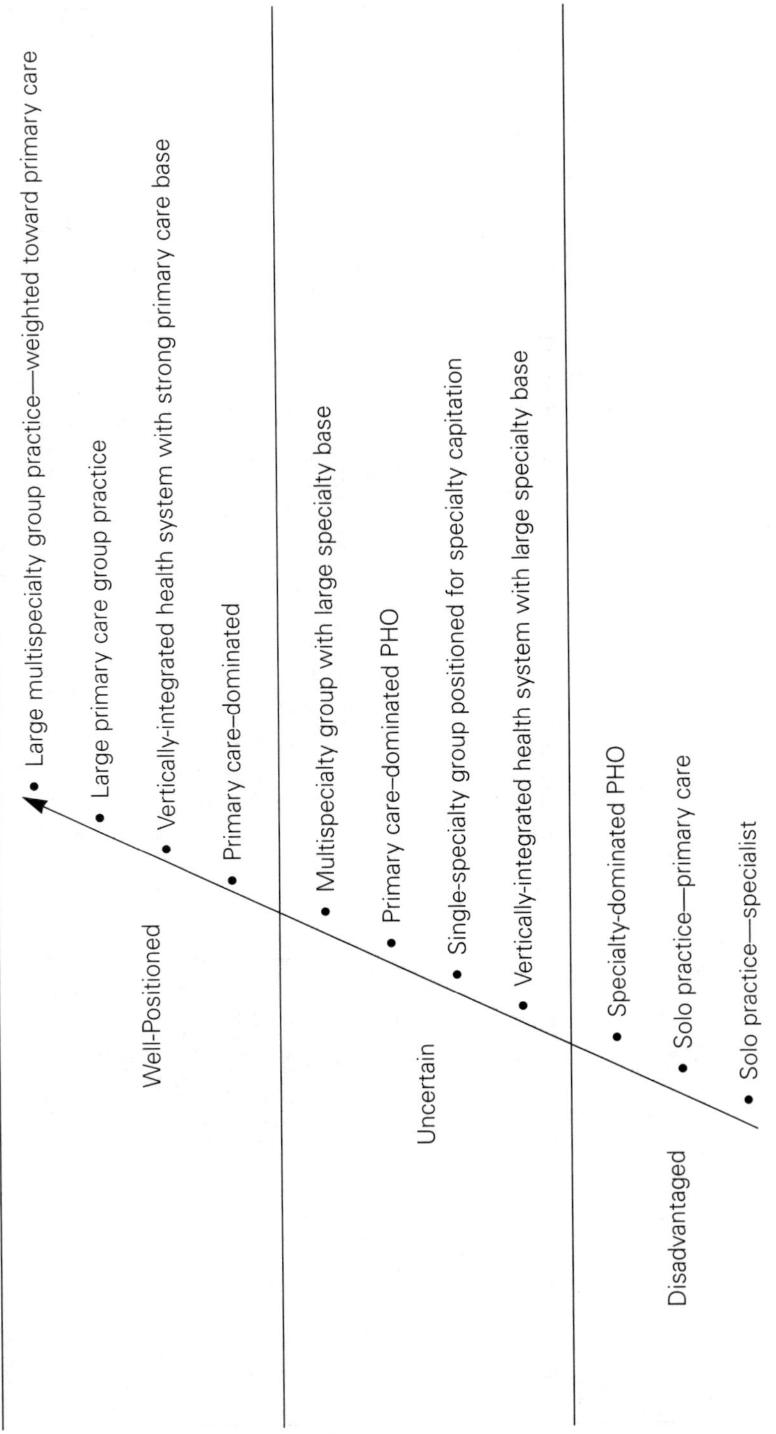

Source: Adapted from The Advisory Board, *Capitation Strategy* (Washington, DC: The Advisory Board Co., 1994), p. 99.

TABLE 20-4. Sponsors of MSO Services

	Hospitals	*Insurers/HMOs*	*Medical Societies*	*PPMCs*
Primary Models	Service bureaus, networks, group practices	IPA networks, group/staff model group practice	Service bureau (purchasing cooperative), open model/IPA network	IPAs, single-specialty carve-outs, multispecialty group
Primary Strengths	Hospital reputation, access to capital	Access to capital, employer relationships, information systems, provider utilization profiles	Physician relationships, physician trust	Management, access to capital, use of stock in practice trans-actions, parallel incen-tives with physicians
Primary Weaknesses	Lack of physician trust; hospital costs; specialist-driven culture; hospital culture; lack of management expertise, incentive misalignment	Lack of physician trust; administrative process hassles, administrative costs, insurance culture, tendency to treat physicians as employees	Orientation to "all members," society politics, access to capital, lack of experience, lack of information systems	Expectation of return on capital
Current Strategy	Purchase PCP practices, create PHO, sustain multiple specialist referrals	Enter partial-risk contracts with IPAs, dismantle staff model, strategic alignment with provider network	Partnering with key plans, IPA development, HMO development	Multispecialty group formation, acquisitions, capitation

fall far short in providing long-term value for physician users of the service.

2. *Appropriate relationships with hospitals and plans:* The successful MSO will be a partner in a managed care organization in which key plans and a partner hospital system play an active role. Those MSOs that lack such alliances will not have access to covered lives. Importantly, the best MSO will be the physician component for a virtually integrated health delivery system in which the physician organization is the hub. In the optimal setting, the MSO will have clinical autonomy and all economic decision making (for example, premium distribution) will be based on independent actuarial analysis.
3. *Access to capital:* The cottage industry of the past will give way to a robust industry composed of five to ten large, multispecialty groups in each market. To appropriately merge these operations and reengineer infrastructures, significant capital will be necessary.
4. *Substantial expertise in managed care:* Success in managed care for most MSOs will be reflected in their ability to provide market-quantifiable measures of cost-effectiveness, clinical outcomes, and patient satisfaction for specific diseases and conditions. It will require most MSOs to assume full risk for populations of citizens and to engage in aggressive prevention and wellness programs and services. Any MSO that stops short of these ambitions within the next three years is certain to deliver suboptimal results.
5. *Physician leadership:* The best long-term MSOs will be those in which physicians maintain an active role in all aspects of the practice—clinical, financial, and strategic. The philosophy of the successful MSO will be central to its success; if less than physician empowerment, it will fail.
6. *Short-term versus long-term strategies:* Many MSOs offer little more than temporary help for practice trouble spots. For physicians expecting to practice five to ten years from now, the MSO must provide long-term solutions. Among MSOs, evidence of this long-term orientation will be evident in three critical areas: the quality and retention of key executives and local talent, the services provided to physicians related to clinical performance improvement, and the structure of the MSO's physician model (multispecialty versus single specialty).
7. *Relationships:* At the end of the day, the test of the MSO will be the strength of its relationship with its physicians. Trust is, after all, the key to all successful businesses, and the trust between physicians and the MSO partner is especially important because they are entrusted with patient care.

CONCLUSION

The future is bright for those MSOs committed to the new realities of medical practice management in sustainable structures. For MSOs lacking capital or those that rob physicians of entrepreneurship, relegating them to employee status, the future is dim. For all, the physician market is alert and receptive. The needs are great. The options for physicians will boil down to which model and sponsor provide the most long-term value. Physicians must be mindful of the long-term consequences of their MSO affiliation.

PART VII

The Future of Physician Services in the Managed Care Environment

Part VII consists of two chapters. Chapter 21, "Speculations on the Continued Growth of Managed Care," assesses the continued impact of managed care on patient care, physician income, and the organization of physician practices. Chapter 22, "Managed Care and the Evolution of Physician Services," takes a comprehensive look at where the physician services market is headed.

21

Speculations on the Continued Growth of Managed Care

Eli Ginzberg, PhD

Any speculations on how the continued growth of managed care in the wake of the failed Clinton health reform proposals is likely to affect patient care, physician income, and the organization of physician services in the decade ahead must be made with certain caveats. This chapter looks at some of the reasons why forecasting the future of medicine is precarious and examines key factors to consider in the forecasting equation. The chapter then explores how changes in the health care environment are likely to affect patient care, physician income, and physician practice organization.

REASONS FOR RESTRAINT IN FORECASTING THE FUTURE OF MEDICINE

Medicine is a dynamic field, and any speculation about its future (even in the near term) is at risk of unknown and unknowable developments. For example, it took less than a decade for the so-called physician surplus of the mid-1930s to turn into the acute physician shortage of World War Two. Few foresaw that shortly after the return of peace the rush to specialization would follow. In *Science: The Endless Frontier*, his seminal

The author would like to recognize his colleague Miriam Ostow for undertaking the task of turning his draft of this chapter into a finished copy.

postwar report advocating the nation's commitment to a continuing research effort, Vannevar Bush, President Roosevelt's senior scientific adviser, stated that medical research could make good use of $5 to $10 million of government funding per year.[1] Current federal outlays for biomedical research are in the $13 to $14 billion range, almost 300 times greater (in constant dollars) than the experts anticipated.

In the late 1960s, this author noted in a volume of essays entitled *Men, Money and Medicine* that the United States had the lowest rate of women physicians of any Western nation with the exception of Spain; at that time, the medical profession was, and presumably would remain, a masculine preserve.[2] However, this was published at a time when the far-reaching implications of the Civil Rights Act of 1964, which had begun to change medical school admissions policies radically, were not clearly recognized. Since then, women have come to account for more than 40 percent of the entrance class. And when President Johnson sought to mollify the leaders of the American Medical Association (AMA) after the AMA's failure to defeat Medicare in 1965 by assuring them that nothing would change in the system of health care delivery (specifically in the patient-physician relationship) except that government would henceforth pay the bills for the elderly and the poor, he did not contemplate that total national health care outlays would increase in the next three decades from about $200 billion to $1 trillion (constant dollars).

To juxtapose the vicissitudes of these speculations of the past with the uncertainties that may be encountered before 2005: If the number of uninsured Americans rises, as some experts have estimated, to 65 million or so during the next five years, and if the public balks at the growing restrictions on choice of physicians that will be imposed under managed care, it is by no means clear that national health reform may not reemerge as a critical issue in the presidential election of 2000 or 2004.

There are at least two more reasons for caution and restraint in forecasting what lies ahead. First, in a short piece entitled "Signs of a Possible Recession," this author noted that sooner or later, a recession, if not worse, is virtually certain.[3] If there should be a deep recession, all forecasts will be off. And second, recession aside, the recent estimates of the Congressional Budget Office (CBO) that total health care outlays for 2007 will exceed $2 trillion annually must be considered.[4] Clearly, the outlays for health care spending cannot double within slightly more than a single decade without major political and economic repercussions.

KEY FACTORS IN THE FORECASTING EQUATION

Key factors in the forecasting equation may be assessed as follows: the likely numbers of physicians and their characteristics and preferences;

the nation's population profile by age and location; trends in hospitalization; changing attitudes toward the individual's responsibility for protecting his or her health and the definition of his or her role in medical decision making, in particular toward the end of life; and the willingness of the citizenry to continue to provide the financing necessary to ensure for themselves—and the poor—access to health care and the quality of care that modern technology can deliver. Following are some "best estimates" about each of these factors.

Likely Number of Physicians

Between 1990 and 2005, the physician workforce will increase by about a third, from 600,000 to 800,000. The steep increase in applications to medical school since the late 1980s has more or less continued, which suggests wide differences in expectations among established members of the profession who have been in active practice for the past 10, 20, or 30 years and those who will first enter into practice after the turn of the century.

Recently, the CEO of a major academic health center in the New York City area confirmed that he has little difficulty in recruiting young physicians, particularly women graduates from prestigious residency programs, to practice in a nearby low-income or suburban area as full-time employees of the hospital's evolving integrated network, earning $100,000 a year plus benefits and the opportunity for incentive pay. Women physicians, especially those with young children at home, are particularly attracted to such arrangements because these arrangements relieve them of responsibility for managing the business aspects of practice.

However, a couple of conditions must be considered. For example, there is no doubt that, as medical school faculty adopt a more positive view of generalist (versus specialist) practice, more physicians in training will opt for primary care, although how long they will find it exciting and challenging is questionable. Because all evidence points to the overproduction of specialists, a serious challenge now facing the nation is how to moderate the numbers of future entrants into the medical profession. Two prestigious leadership groups—the Association of American Medical Colleges (AAMC), the institutional umbrella for the U.S. system of medical education, and the Council on Graduate Medical Education (COGME), the advisory body to Congress on physician personnel—have recommended reducing the number of international medical graduates (IMGs) whose residency training is underwritten by Medicare, a proposal that warrants serious study and possible action. (See chapter 2.)

It is unlikely, however, that the physician supply issue can be resolved solely by focusing on IMGs. Informed sources report that three new osteopathic schools are on the drawing board and, as noted earlier, the applications to medical school remain at a high level. Clearly, the leaders of the medical educational establishment and the profession at large cannot avoid the numbers issue much longer. The recent analyses of Wiener and others are potent reminders that managed care is associated with a greatly reduced need and demand for physicians in comparison to fee-for-service (FFS) practice.[5]

Population by Age and Location

Projections indicate that the nation's population will grow by about 25 million, or more than 9 percent, between 1995 and 2005.[6] And although the population continues to age, the big bulge as the baby boomers reach 65 and 75 is still some time away. The explosive growth in the post-75 age group is expected to begin in 2021.

With respect to location, it is important to note that just under 4 out of every 5 persons in the United States live in a metropolitan area, which certainly suggests the potential of regionalization to provide high-quality medical care at less cost. It is dismaying to find that small cities located within a hundred miles or so of a major metropolitan center with excellent medical facilities (the St. Louis area is an example) should find it expedient to establish not one, but two cardiac surgery units in a town with a population of under 50,000.

In the mid-1970s, regionalization's potential in the face of the fractionalization of power and money among government, the private sector, and philanthropy in the shaping and reshaping of the nation's health care system was distinctly limited.[7] However, the years immediately ahead should see a renewed interest in regionalization as both managed care plans and large hospitals explore how they can restructure themselves and flourish in order to achieve a greater market penetration that is more conducive to economies of scale.

Trends in Hospitalization

Currently, hospitals account for nearly 40 percent of all health care outlays and, in addition, contribute about 40 percent to total physician earnings. However, an apparent trend that will shift the position of the acute care hospital from the center of the health care system to its periphery is setting the stage for a major realignment in how patients, physicians, hospitals, and payers will interact with each other in the future.[8] Episodic hospital and physician treatment will increasingly be replaced by a system of integrated health care delivery in which FFS and procedure-based payment will gradually give way to capitation and salaried employment.

Changing Attitudes toward Individual Responsibility

In the past decade or so, with support from the Rockefeller, Pew, and Robert Wood Johnson foundations, a growing number of medical schools have been participants in an experimental program known as Health of the Public. This program aimed to redirect the medical schools' curriculum from its traditional, individual pathology orientation toward a population-based preventive care approach. And some of the leading centers of health policy research and evaluation, such as the Institute of Medicine of the National Academy of Sciences, have called attention to the fact that important and impressive as the gains from biomedical research and advancing technology have been, something on the order of 50 to 60 percent of all excess morbidity and premature mortality are linked to behavioral patterns such as diet, smoking, physical exercise, substance and alcohol abuse, and sexual practices.

There is considerable evidence that an increasing proportion of the population is attempting to follow a healthier regimen with respect to modifying, and in some cases eliminating, such high-risk behaviors as smoking. Because most of the younger generation now is entering adulthood with at least a high school diploma and more than 50 percent go on to college or graduate studies, the nation can look forward to a citizenry that is likely to pay more attention to protecting its health and behaving accordingly—at least much of the time.

Moreover, in assessing possible changes in the health care arena in the decade ahead, it is important to note that with respect to at least one critical issue—responsibility for medical decision making at the end of life—the public appears to be ahead of the health care leadership. As more and more Americans live into their seventies, eighties, and nineties, a rapidly growing number are drawing up various documents apprising their next of kin and their physicians that they do not wish to undergo elaborate medical treatment unless they have a reasonable prospect of regaining functionality. Extending years of life is no longer the goal; instead, the goal now is to live longer on condition that one is able to function effectively.

Public Willingness to Provide Health Care Financing

The last theme to be considered relates to the ability and willingness of the American people to perpetuate a system of health care that, as Burton S. Weisbrod of Northwestern University has reminded us, commands ever more of our scarce economic resources.[9] Weisbrod believes that this cost-increasing—as well as value-increasing—health care environment reflects the interactive effects of continuing high-technology innovation linked to private and public health insurance coverage. He is pessimistic about reining in future health care expenditures unless this linkage is broken. True as this probably is, breaking this linkage is likely to require putting a cap on the amount of public, if not total, dollars that we are willing to devote annually to the health care sector.

SPECULATIONS ABOUT THE FUTURE

This section looks at the impact of the emerging changes in the U.S. health care environment within the next decade in the areas of patient care, physician income, and physician practice organization. The speculations offered are subject to change in the event of serious destabilization in the international political environment or in the U.S. economy, growing resistance by the American people to the expanded role of the market in the health care delivery system, and a host of other unknowns.

Impact on Patient Care

It seems unlikely that Congress will cut back funding for biomedical research or that American and foreign manufacturers of medical devices and pharmaceuticals will significantly shrink their outlays for research and development because of a prospective erosion in the demand for their products. In short, between now and 2005, there should be continuing significant innovation in medical diagnosis and treatment that most tax-paying Americans believe is their due.

However, there is ample evidence in the medical literature of the ongoing "rationing" of expensive procedures and drugs in the care of the uninsured and Medicaid populations. It is likely that, either overtly or covertly, such rationing will increase as all three buyers of care—government, business, and households—seek to constrain their future outlays.

A growing number of states are moving aggressively to enroll their Medicaid-eligible populations into managed care plans in the hope and expectation that they will be able to both save money and improve the quality of care the poor receive. The best that can be said for this approach is that the facts are not in. Given that in New York City the physician-to-population ratio in low-income minority neighborhoods may be as low as 1 generalist physician in private practice per 5,000 to 10,000 residents, compared to 1 physician for 300 to 500 population in affluent neighborhoods, it is difficult to imagine where the physicians required to treat Medicaid-eligible patients will come from, at least in the near-middle term. In a market-driven system many "essential community providers" may not survive, which would further exacerbate the access problem for the poor.

Shifting focus from the poor to the privately insured, the consequences of continuing managed care growth similarly invite caution. Clearly, there are HMOs and other types of managed care plans that have a good track record, but for the most part, their enrollees have been healthy adults and children. How well managed care plans will do with large numbers of the disabled, the chronically ill, and the elderly remains to be seen.

A more serious challenge is how patients will respond as they find their choice of providers increasingly restricted and as they are informed by the media of the incentives for their physicians to economize in the use of medications, referrals, hospitalization, and other costly measures that could result in more and better care for them. Admittedly, the better managed care plans are working collaboratively to implement reporting systems and other quality control measures. However, it will likely take the intervention of the courts and large damage awards in cases of undertreatment to keep most managed care plans in line.

If changing the behavior patterns of patients is a precondition for improving health status, managed care arrangements can facilitate greater use of simple preventive measures such as timely immunizations of the young and the elderly. Among the many misconceptions that are abroad, however, is the belief that greater reliance by managed care plans on preventive measures will result in better health outcomes for their members and lower total expenditures for the plan. Selectively, that is true. As a generalization, however, it is not demonstrable, at least not in a single decade or generation—and most investments need to pay off within a much shorter period. And the behavioral changes, on which so much of improved health status is conditioned, involve not one or another test or procedure performed by a physician but, rather, profound changes in the lifestyle of the patient.

Another facet of the anticipated interaction between managed care organizations (MCOs) and their enrollees in the decade ahead is that, in a more competitive and cost-constrained marketplace, a key factor in the profitability and expansion of any managed care plan is the extent to which its physicians can be persuaded to practice in a more productive mode by improving their access to information, optimizing the support staff available to them, and, not least, encouraging them to see more patients per hour or per day. However, this last factor is likely to generate increasing dissatisfaction on the part of many patients who already find that their physician spends too little time explaining things to them.

Nor are the managed care plan's rules and regulations aimed at reducing referrals to specialists likely to gain ready approval by most patients, particularly if they do not experience prompt symptomatic relief. Parallel tensions between plan physicians and their patients are likely to arise over admission to a hospital for inpatient care as well as length of stay. Advocates for the further rapid expansion of managed care are convinced that the current enrollment of more than 75 million individuals in such plans is the best evidence that managed care does not lead to disgruntled patients. The skeptics, on the other hand, note that many of the recent enrollees are individuals who have long enjoyed greater degrees of freedom in the choice of their physicians and that many are aging, chronically ill, or disabled, conditions with which most managed care plans have had little or no prior experience. Hence, future patient satisfaction cannot be assumed. Finally, the increasing competitiveness of the marketplace will add to the tensions between the managed care plans' efforts to limit outlays and patients' desire for more and better health care services.

Impact on Physician Income

By way of introduction to this issue, it is useful to cite the report of a 1996 survey by the AMA.[10] Following are some of its highlights:

- Over the 10 years between 1984 and 1994, physician income rose an average of 5 percent per year.
- All technical specialties, except anesthesiology, outpaced the average inflation rate for the period.
- Self-employed physicians had a median income of $176,000 in 1994; employed doctors took home $130,000. However, several important factors were hidden within this sizable differential. For one, employed physicians were more likely to receive fringe benefits. Further, the self-employed are more likely to be older, male, and board certified.
- James S. Todd, former executive vice president of the AMA, commented as follows: "Overhead has been going up steadily, compensation from Medicare has remained stable, and managed care has been leaning on a lot of physicians. Put these three together and you would anticipate income would decline across the board. My answer is, maybe—and for a relatively short time, not necessarily for long. The likelihood that total health care expenditures will double, from one to two trillion dollars annually over the next decade; the prospective increase in the total number of practicing physicians from approximately 600,000 in the early 1990s to 800,000 in 2005; the current surplus of specialists in many fields and in many locations; and the ability of managed care plans to operate with fewer physicians per 1,000 enrollees than the fee-for-service sector all point to increasing pressure on physician earnings, particularly the earnings of specialists."

A number of specialty societies are putting out the word to recent graduates preparing to enter, or already engaged in, the early phase of their residency training to think twice about careers in ophthalmology, anesthesiology, neurology, neurosurgery, and other fields where the evidence suggests "overcrowding." Close observers of the physician environment in California report that increasing numbers of specialists are finding it preferable, if not necessary, to relocate out of the state. With managed care enrollments on the increase, they cannot earn a living, much less the type of living to which they have aspired.

Another perspective on the future bounds of physician earnings is that if analysts at the CBO are correct in estimating that total health care outlays will rise to $2 trillion in 2007 from $1 trillion in 1995, and if the physician supply increases by 200,000, or one-third, one should not anticipate that the members of the profession will suffer serious declines in income (inasmuch as physician earnings currently account for a little more than 20 percent of total health care outlays). On the basis of the foregoing numbers, they might even see an increase in earnings.

Another consideration relates to possible actions by Congress and the medical educational community, fearing an oversupply of physicians, to reduce drastically the numbers of IMGs enrolled in graduate medical education and to effect the downsizing, merger, or closure of medical schools operating under state or voluntary auspices. However, even serious efforts to reduce the prospective physician supply would have at best only a marginal impact by 2005. It is doubtful that any significant reduction in the number of admissions and graduates from medical school and residency training will be seen in the decade ahead. And even if significant reductions in entrants were instituted, their effect would not be felt until some years after 2005. In sum, although the foregoing analysis of the midterm outlook indicates the maintenance of the present average earning levels of physicians, many specialists will likely face significant reductions in their accustomed earnings.

The other factor related to the future supply of physicians is outflow—early retirement or leaving clinical practice. There is considerable anecdotal evidence that many physicians, disgruntled that the practice of medicine they had long known is rapidly deteriorating, are opting for early retirement rather than fight the changes under way, a fight they would most likely lose anyway. There appears to be no solid statistical evidence relating to early retirement, but there are reports that several major insurers have experienced a substantial increase in the number of claims for disability payments from their physician policy holders.

However, based on the author's personal teaching experience at both the Graduate School of Business and the School of Public Health at Columbia University, in recent years more and more younger and even middle-aged physicians have been attending classes on health policy in an apparent search for alternatives to clinical practice. This is a relatively new phenomenon. It would appear that the numbers of physicians exploring and finding alternative careers has multiplied by an order of magnitude. It would be interesting to collect and analyze statistical information on the physicians who now hold administrative positions in the managed care sector.

Impact on Physician Practice Organization

Historically, American physicians have operated as solo practitioners out of their own offices or in group practices composed of physicians in the same specialty or a number of specialties. In the early years of group practice, there were relatively few HMOs, most of them not-for-profit, with differing types of physician organization—from staff or group models to network or independent practice associations (IPAs).

Prior to 1989, there was a limited number of group practice arrangements under for-profit auspices. Since then, however, the organization of physician practices has been increasingly transformed by the rapid growth of for-profit managed care plans under the auspices of venture capitalists (including a few physician-led organizations) and major insurance companies that have recognized the potential of recruiting and managing large groups of physicians by assuring them a steady flow of patients and payments, providing them incentives and bonuses for exceeding specified targets, and imposing rules and regulations on their modes of practice. (See chapter 12.) At the same time, the plans are in a powerful position to expand their enrollments by offering employers lower premium rates and, in turn, to leverage their market power by obtaining discounts from hospitals and other providers. In retrospect, the organization of physician practices in the past decade and a half has shifted increasingly from self-employment to employment in for-profit corporate enterprises.

The question that cannot yet be answered definitively is whether the shift from independent practice to employment in businesses is temporary or permanent. This shift is likely to be an early stage of what will turn out to be a long process of reorganization of physician practice. Why should employers continue to deal with for-profit intermediaries that take 20 to 30 percent or more off the top for marketing, administration, and profits? In turn, why should physicians who have spent 7 to 12 years or more preparing for the practice of medicine agree to take orders from M.B.A.s who know nothing about medicine, however clever they may be about raising and earning money in competitive markets?

As mentioned earlier, the acute care hospital is losing its position of dominance in the delivery of health care to the American people. However, voluntary (that is, not-for-profit) community and teaching hospitals and their physician staffs remain the core elements of the health care delivery system. Both must adapt and change if they are to survive and prosper: The hospital must transform itself into an integrated health delivery system, and its physicians must play a key role in the future management and delivery of health care to the members for whom the integrated system has assumed responsibility. The physician staff has the ongoing challenge of determining how to provide more and better care (for the most part ambulatory) to its enrollees. Physicians need access to improved data systems; they need to work in suitable facilities in close association with mid-level health care personnel; and they need to explore, assess, and redefine protocols for improved and cost-effective treatments.

From today's vantage, one might conclude that physicians have ceded most decision-making power to the lay executives of the fast-growing managed care plans. However, this is unlikely to continue. Although it may be uncertain whether physicians will be able to negotiate an effective partnership with their local hospital, it is reasonably certain that they will not yield their professional leadership and patient responsibilities to a group of businessmen who know nothing and often care little about high-quality medical care. A one trillion dollar sector of the economy on the way to two trillion will not become and remain the exclusive province of venture capitalists and bureaucratic insurance companies.

CONCLUSION

As noted at the beginning of this chapter, it probably is an error to assume that, because the Clinton health reform proposals failed, health policy issues will not reemerge on the nation's political agenda—and soon—if only because of the growing unease and dissatisfaction of both physicians and patients with the evolving system dominated increasingly by businesses in search of profits. It is impossible to assume that the current low level of opposition to the market-driven managed care environment will continue, particularly when the thus-far poorly informed American public learns that almost half the nation's outlays for health care represent government funding (tax subsidies included). At some point, the American public is likely to reassess whether it makes sense to continue an arrangement whereby corporate enterprises are encouraged to make sizable profits from governmental outlays.

Unless physicians find satisfaction in practicing medicine under the auspices of for-profit managed care companies and enrollees have a positive view of the plans in which they are enrolled (a highly improbable scenario), the coming decade is likely to witness a great number of further changes in the financing and delivery of health care.

Despite the hazards of forecasting the future, it is worth the risk to venture the judgment that physicians will seek and succeed in recapturing much of the decision-making power they have recently lost and that privately insured patients will insist on retrieving reasonable degrees of freedom in the choice of their physicians and other providers of care. To the extent that this forecast turns out to be more or less accurate, one can be sure that the organization of physician services in the decade ahead—as well as those that follow—will experience continuous change, if not turmoil.

References

1. Vannevar Bush, *Science: The Endless Frontier* (North Stratford, NH: Ayer Co., 1980).

2. Eli Ginzberg and Miriam Ostow, *Men, Money and Medicine* (New York: Columbia University Press, 1969).

3. Eli Ginzberg, "Signs of a Possible Recession," in *The World and I* 11, no. 2 (Washington, DC: The Washington Post Corp., 1996).

4. Congressional Budget Office, *The Economic and Budget Outlook, 1998–2007* (Washington, DC: U.S. Government Printing Office, 1997), p. 126.

5. J. P. Weiner, "Forecasting the Effects of Health Reform on U.S. Physician Workforce Requirements," *JAMA* 272 (July 20, 1994): 222ff.

6. U.S. Department of Commerce, *Statistical Abstract of the United States, 1995* (Washington, DC: U.S. Government Printing Office, 1995).

7. Eli Ginzberg, *Regionalization and Health Policy,* DHEW Pub. No. (HRA) 77-623 (Washington, DC: U.S. Government Printing Office, 1977).

8. Eli Ginzberg, *Tomorrow's Hospital: A Look to the 21st Century* (New Haven, CT: Yale University Press, 1996).

9. Burton S. Weisbrod, "Democratic Society—Undemocratic Medicine: Limited Resources in Medical Care" (Lecture given at the Congress "Future Medicine," The Center for Arts and Sciences, Northrhine, Westphalia, Düsseldorf, Germany (Nov. 12–13, 1995).

10. "Doctor Pay Slides for the First Time in '94," *American Medical News* (Jan. 22–29, 1996): 13–19.

22

Managed Care and the Evolution of Physician Services

Ronald B. Conners, PhD

Managed care is rapidly and dramatically altering the organization and management of the physician services market. In 1995, 73 percent of all Americans receiving health insurance through the workplace were enrolled in a managed care plan, an increase from 51 percent in 1993.[1] The observed changes to date are truly revolutionary in their depth and breadth, and reflect a profound shift in market power from the producers of health care to its consumers. To a certain extent, the shift to consumer sovereignty could be interpreted as a market-driven response to rapidly escalating health care costs. As early as 15 years ago, Paul Starr, in *The Social Transformation of American Medicine,* foresaw the coming revolution:

> Unless there is a radical turnabout in economic conditions and American politics, the last decades of the twentieth century are likely to be a time of diminishing resources and autonomy for many physicians, voluntary hospitals, and medical schools. Two immediate circumstances cast a shadow over their future: the rapidly increasing supply of physicians and the continued search by government and employers for control over the growth of medical expenditures. These developments promise to create severe strains throughout the medical system. They may prepare the way, moreover, for the

> acceleration of a third development, the rise of corporate enterprise in health services, which is already having a profound impact on the ethos and politics of medical care as well as its institutions.[2]

This chapter describes the present extent of managed care in the United States and outlines the likely impact on the organization and management of physician services.

PRESENT STATE OF MANAGED CARE

Understanding how the physician services market will continue to evolve in the future health care environment begins with an overview of the current state of managed care. There are many definitions of managed care including a succinct version provided by Iglehart:

> Managed care is a system that, in varying degrees, integrates the financing and delivery of medical care through contracts with selected physicians and hospitals that provide comprehensive health care services to enrolled members for a predetermined monthly premium. All forms of managed care represent attempts to control costs by modifying the behavior of doctors, although they do so in different ways. Most forms also restrict the access of their insured populations to physicians who are not affiliated with a particular plan. Managed care organizations contract with or employ more primary care doctors and fewer specialists than now serve the general population, and primary care physicians assume broader roles in these systems. This characteristic of managed care, combined with the restrictions plans use to discourage their members from seeking care from nonparticipating doctors, places specialists at particular risk, because they are more likely than primary care physicians not to be selected by the plan.[3]

This definition implies a market structure that is highly competitive, consisting of winners (those providers who are successful in contracting for comprehensive health care services) and losers (those providers who are not). Ultimately, such contracting might be reimbursed using capitation (a predetermined monthly payment for each enrolled member), but in its earlier formulations, discounted fee-for-service (FFS) methods might prevail. Cost control, the central focus of managed care, is achieved through close management of utilization and the presence of financial incentives to further reduce the use of services.

In terms of managed care provider models, three have emerged: HMOs (health maintenance organizations), preferred provider organizations

(PPOs), and point-of-service (POS) plans. These three models are continually evolving in the details of their organizational forms, but together they have replaced indemnity insurance plans as the dominant form of health insurance used by the American workforce. Table 22-1 shows a dramatic decline in indemnity plan membership by insured workers and the rapid growth of POS plans between 1993 and 1995. (POS plans are similar to HMOs in structure, but they allow subscribers to use providers outside the HMO network with a corresponding adjustment in the reimbursement amount.)

In addition to looking at managed care plan enrollment as a percent of the American workforce, HMO enrollment has been studied as a percent of the resident U.S. population. Table 22-2 shows HMO enrollment from 1987 to 1995. In 1995, HMO enrollment was 67,575,000 persons and it was accelerating rapidly. Based on a 1995 resident U.S. population estimate of 262,755,000 persons, HMOs have enrolled 25.7 percent of the resident population.[4]

TABLE 22-1. Percent of Insured Workers by Plan Type, 1993 and 1995

Type of Plan	*1993*	*1995*	*Percent Change*
Indemnity Plan	48.9	27.4	−44.0
HMO	22.4	27.5	+22.28
PPO	19.6	25.0	+27.6
POS Plan	9.1	20.1	+120.9

Source: Reprinted, in part, from G. A. Jensen and others, "The New Dominance of Managed Care: Insurance Trends in the 1990s," *Health Affairs* 16, no. 1 (Jan./Feb. 1997): 127, with permission.

TABLE 22-2. HMO Enrollment, 1987–1995

Year	*HMO Enrollment (in thousands)*	*Percent Change*
1987	31,024	
1988	33,715	8.7
1989	35,031	3.9
1990	37,538	7.2
1991	40,388	7.6
1992	44,373	9.9
1993	49,095	10.6
1994	55,006	12.0
1995	67,575	22.9

Source: Reprinted, in part, from Hoechst Marion Roussel, *HMO–PPO Digest 1996,* Managed Care Digest Series, vol. 2 (Kansas City, MO: Hoechst Marion Roussel, 1996), data from SMG, p. 7, with permission.

Enrollment in an HMO is not readily accessible to most Medicaid recipients (due to income constraints) nor is it economically sensible for Medicare patients (unless there is an inducement beyond their current Medicare benefits). To control Medicare and Medicaid health care costs, federal and state initiatives are under way to place these population groups in HMOs or other managed care organizations (MCOs). Table 22-3 shows Medicare HMO and Medicaid MCO enrollment in 1994 and 1995, with projections to 1999. Of the approximately 36.4 million Medicare beneficiaries in 1994 (14 percent of the resident U.S. population), 3.1 million (8.5 percent of Medicare beneficiaries measured at year end 1994) were enrolled in Medicare HMO programs.[5] The estimated number of Medicaid recipients in the United States is 34.4 million persons (13.1 percent of the resident U.S. population); about 9.8 million of them (28.7 percent of Medicaid recipients measured at mid-year 1995) are enrolled in a Medicaid MCO program.[6] (Medicaid MCO programs include HMOs, prepaid health plans, health insuring organizations, and primary care case management programs.)

The rapid growth in managed care enrollments will reduce medical care expenditures because of the degree of competition and price pressure that contracting allows. This in turn results in less overall demand for physicians and their services, greater demand for primary care physicians (PCPs, the gatekeepers of the system), and less demand for specialist services. These changes in the physician services market are occurring in the context of a rising population. (See appendix.)

IMPACT OF MANAGED CARE ON THE PHYSICIAN SERVICES MARKET

Managed care is causing rapid change within the physician services market. Following is a series of stylized facts that outline the future impact of managed care on the physician services market, focusing on organization and management changes from an economic and societal perspective:

- *There will be an oversupply of physicians.* In 1970, the physician-population ratio in the United States was 115 patient care physicians per 100,000 population; by 1990, that number had grown to 182 with further growth anticipated to the year 2010. (See chapter 2.) Patient care physicians include PCPs and specialists but not physicians in training or federal employees. In a managed care environment, what will be the impact on patient care physicians, given the anticipated contraction in medical services rendered? There is strong evidence that physician staffing patterns among

TABLE 22-3. Medicare HMO and Medicaid MCO Enrollment, 1993–1999 (projected)

Year	*Medicare HMO Enrollment[a] (in millions)*	*Medicaid MCO Enrollment[b] (in millions)*
1993	2.6	N/A
1994	3.1	7.4
1995	N/A	9.8
1999 (projected)	7.2	14.1

[a]As of year-end

[b]As of midyear

Source: Reprinted from Hoechst Marion Roussel, *Medicare/Medicaid Special Edition Digest 1996,* Managed Care Digest Series, vol. 1 (Kansas City, MO: Hoechst Marion Roussel, 1996), data from SMG, p. 3, with permission.

managed care providers include fewer physicians and specialists.[7] According to Weiner, there will be a surplus of 165,000 patient care physicians by the year 2000, assuming that all citizens will be covered by some form of health insurance and that 40 to 65 percent of Americans will be participating in managed care networks.[8]

- *The physician oversupply will occur mostly among specialists.* The excess supply of patient care physicians predicted by Weiner consists primarily of a surplus among specialists in comparison to PCPs. Because of the emphasis that managed care plans place on utilization control to maintain the required level of financial performance, there is a substantial reduction in the demand for physician services in these programs compared to traditional health care plans. This diminution occurs primarily among specialists whose utilization is managed through the gatekeeping functions of the PCP. Of the 165,000 physician excess supply forecasted by Weiner, 85 percent (139,000 physicians) are expected to be specialists.[9]
- *There will be a continuing debate on physician workforce issues to determine whether government intervention or market forces will be appropriate to adjust physician supply.* From a policy perspective, the forecasted physician oversupply raises questions as to whether the physician labor market should be relied on to adjust supply or whether government intervention is appropriate. Many analysts are concerned about the accuracy of forecasting physician supply generally, and government intervention in particular, preferring instead to rely on the price system within the physician labor market to reduce anticipated excess supply.[10] Woolhandler and Himmelstein go even further, arguing that the number of physicians should not be rationed but, rather, should be allowed to absorb the large reduction in median real income

while being refocused to address the ills of society, particularly to help with the psychological and social problems of patients.[11]

- *The real net income of physicians will decline.* Although the real net income (measured in 1994 dollars) of physicians fell from $186,300 in 1990 to $181,000 in 1994, the decline was not statistically significant. (See chapter 6 for a discussion of trends in physician income.) Simon has shown that the decline in income first reported in 1994 was larger among doctors in the higher income brackets.[12] As more and more physician groups enter into managed care contracts, prices will continue their downward trend, reflecting increased competition for these contracts and the greater importance MCOs attach to price reductions compared to quality. In addition to the impact of rising competition on managed care pricing, there is some evidence of declining health care insurance premiums.[13] As the cost of physician services falls and the profit objectives of managed care plans are met, growth in premiums to the consumer should slow. Ultimately, these changes in premiums will reflect the lowered costs of participating physicians. Although the impact of managed care on physician income probably is in its earliest stages, there is much written anecdotal evidence that physicians' incomes are falling in response to these new economic forces.[14]
- *The shift in practice setting away from solo practice will continue.* There is strong evidence that the number of physicians working in solo practice settings is declining, with the decline significantly predating the advent of managed care. (See chapter 3.) The shift away from solo practice as an organizational model is identified as a decrease in the proportion of physicians engaged in this practice form. In 1991, the proportion of physicians in solo practice was 34.1 percent, compared to 26.5 percent in 1995. (See chapter 3.)
- *Physicians will work increasingly as employees and subcontractors in group practice and institutional settings.* Physicians are moving from solo practice settings to both group practice and institutional (hospitals, HMOs) settings. The proportion of doctors in institutional settings is growing rapidly, from 22.3 percent in 1991 to 30.4 percent in 1995. (See chapter 3.)
- *Large group practices will increasingly dominate the physician services market.* The number of group practices is increasing, as is their average size. Emmons also shows a decrease in the proportion of physicians in practices with two to four members, from 22.0 percent in 1991 to 19.1 percent in 1995. (See chapter 3.)

Why are physicians moving toward larger group practices? Emmons argues that there are at least four important factors:
—Marketing advantages from easier brand-name identification
—Cost advantages from larger practice size

—Productivity advantages due to the ready availability of such practice supports as information systems, insurance specialists, and extensive specialized billing knowledge

—Staffing advantages due to ease of substitution of allied health professionals (See chapter 3.)

In addition to the factors cited by Emmons in chapter 3, larger physician groups should have greater financial resources and geographical coverage, enabling them to engage in risk-sharing contract arrangements covering larger population groups.

- *Managed care will lower aggregate physician productivity until a new, lower physician supply equilibrium is reached.* Physician productivity can be defined in terms of visits per year per physician. Given that the main objective of managed care is to lower visits (or other utilization variables such as admissions, surgical procedures, and length of stay), to the extent that it is successful, the reduction in visits must be compared against the increased number of physicians clinically active (anticipated to rise until the year 2010) and the growth in the number of patients arising from the growth in population.

  Preliminary evidence shows substantial declines in physician productivity related to practice setting. Visits per week and the number of office visits per week both fell sharply from 1991 to 1995. Even greater declines were shown in the number of visits to hospitalized patients, a reduction of 19 percent between 1991 and 1995. (See chapter 3.)
- *Sharp declines in physician productivity will partially offset the excess supply of physicians.* If Weiner's estimate of an oversupply of 165,000 physicians is correct, reductions in aggregate productivity will reduce the impact of this excess supply.
- *Capitation will continue to grow as the reimbursement method of choice by managed care plans.* FFS payment provides financial incentives to increase care—more visits, more procedures, and more admissions. It also increases unnecessary utilization and raises expenditures. Capitation provides financial incentives to reduce utilization, presenting as the limiting case a consumer who seeks no care but is a member of a managed care plan. (See chapter 5 for a discussion of physician reimbursement in a capitated environment.) To guard against the limiting case, utilization, outcome, and quality measures are maintained.

  Reimbursement based on care provided to population groups changes the providers' focus from the specifics of individual cases to the continuum of care and its cost and effectiveness. Outcome and quality measures become the primary focus for review of the care provided as well as a critical marketing tool for obtaining additional managed care contracts.

In comparison to the traditional FFS-driven practice model, the capitation-driven practice model is a higher-cost form.[15] Group practices that are capitation driven have more support staff due to the need to provide more extensive outcome and quality reporting. However, capitation-based groups have the advantage of "selling care" in large volume compared to FFS groups which "sell care" in low volume, often on a per-case basis.

- *Both vertical and horizontal integration strategies are increasing within the physician services market. Horizontal integration* is a strategy to achieve growth by purchasing other providers within the same market, compared to using internal growth to increase market share. An example would be the expansion of the market share of a group practice through acquisition of a competing practice located in an adjoining geographical market.

  The chief benefit of horizontal integration is the increased geographical coverage provided through expansion. That is reflected in the growth of covered lives that can be managed by the group as well as a possible increase in the number of managed care plans active in the larger area. The effect is to raise the potential revenue available to the group.

  Vertical integration is a strategy to achieve growth along the distribution lines of the business. Growth might be toward either the patient or the supplier. These are integrating-type strategies, both intended to lower costs while capturing referrals or controlling supplies. An acquisition of a physician practice that results in an increase in the number of patients referred to the local hospital would be an example of vertical integration. Combining a group practice with a hospital is an example of a specific vertical integration strategy called a physician-hospital organization (PHO).

  Both vertical and horizontal integration strategies are widespread within the physician services market today. However, at present, it is unclear which of these strategies is the most effective.
- *Large group practices with a high proportion of managed care contracts have higher total revenue, and a greater proportion of this revenue is from capitation contracts.* It already is clear that larger group practices are more successful in obtaining managed care contracts. When larger groups are successful in obtaining these contracts, they achieve higher revenue than groups that are still FFS oriented. Moreover, large group practices successful in obtaining managed care contracts will be reimbursed using capitation rather than discounted FFS.[16]
- *Solo practitioners or small group practices will be generally ineffective competitors in the managed care environment without engaging in some form of alliance or joint venture.* MCOs seek

large provider groups to minimize transaction costs. Such provider groups will be increasingly rewarded with contracts as their geographical scope and size increase.

Solo practitioners and small group practices, although not specifically excluded from the managed care marketplace, will find their ability to compete reduced markedly. Increasingly, they will be forced from the market, forced to join an independent practice association (IPA) or some other organization of providers, or relegated to subcontractor status.

- *Standards of care and clinical practice protocols will increasingly dominate physician practices.* Risk-bearing managed care contracts provide physician groups with strong incentives to manage the care process very closely. Care maps and disease management systems will become the focus for large group practice management strategies, enabling provider groups that absorb risk to remain profitable.
- *Hospitals and physician practice management companies will accelerate their acquisition of physician practices.* The consolidation trend occurring in the physician services market is a requirement for successfully competing in large regional health care markets. A very small percentage of physicians practicing in the United States practice in a group setting, and that provides an enormous opportunity for consolidation.
- *Integrating structures may enable alliances of physicians and hospitals to bypass insurers and HMOs, eliminating overhead and profits traditionally removed by these organizations.* Direct contracting between PHOs and employers will, in certain markets, allow a higher-profit product to be sold. Typically, this form of risk-bearing or discounted FFS contracting is effective for large employers in the larger cities, but it also can be effective in rural areas where a self-insured option can be developed with smaller employer groups. Integrated providers will continue to seek this form of direct contracting because it allows them to obtain higher profit levels than contracting with an HMO or other health plan.
- *PHOs have a mixed record of success as a vertical integration strategy.* The purchasers of services offered by a PHO must understand its ability to control costs; otherwise, its effectiveness as a managed care contracting vehicle will be limited. PHOs that focus primarily on obtaining managed care contracts will not have the long-term competitive ability to prosper as components of integrated delivery systems (IDSs).[17]

PHOs are potential competitors to HMOs and other MCOs. Thus, to attract managed care contracts, they need to expand beyond the focus of a single hospital to provide a regional product with a strong PCP base.

- *The economic incentives of capitation will be increasingly questioned.* In the traditional FFS reimbursement model, physicians are given incentives to provide an increasing volume of service for which they often benefit personally. In a capitated reimbursement system, however, physicians are given incentives to provide as few services as possible, raising the possibility of reductions in service and quality.

  Increasingly, the policies and procedures of proprietary managed care plans are being questioned and scrutinized in public forums.[18] One critical unanswered question is the degree of government regulation they will face in the future.
- *Health care is increasingly seen as a commodity.* Traditionally, health care has been viewed as an activity separate from traditional market-type activities. Within a managed care context, health care is seen as a commodity provided to covered lives, there is a population focus, and the transaction becomes economic in nature.[19] Another critical unanswered question is the degree of "deprofessionalization" of the practice of medicine that will follow.

CONCLUSION

Along with the "commodification" of health care, Blumenthal argues that "the restructuring of our health care system likely will accentuate the divisions and inequalities that existed in our society before the transition to a market-based health care system."[20] The United States has undergone a significant shift toward free markets over the past few years. Managed care and the rise of for-profit health care organizations focus our attention on such issues as rural health care and indigent care and how these societal issues might be resolved within this evolving framework.

A last (or first) unanswered question in the evolution of physician services is whether free markets will dominate the provision of these highly unique services or whether society will recognize the special character of health care markets and, in so doing, increase the isolation of this market from the storms of competition. The question asked by Kuttner is whether society is prepared "to discipline opportunistic market behavior in health care."[21] The answer to this question will truly determine how physician services will evolve.

References

1. G. A. Jensen and others, "The New Dominance of Managed Care: Insurance Trends in the 1990s," *Health Affairs* 16, no. 1 (Jan./Feb. 1997): 127.

2. P. Starr, *The Social Transformation of American Medicine* (New York: Basic Books, 1982), pp. 420–21.

3. J. K. Iglehart, "Physicians and the Growth of Managed Care," *New England Journal of Medicine* 331, no. 17 (Oct. 27, 1994): 1167.

4. U.S. Bureau of the Census, *Statistical Abstract of the United States: 1996* (Washington, DC: U.S. Government Printing Office, 1996), table 14.

5. Hoechst Marion Roussel, *Medicare/Medicaid Special Edition Digest 1996,* Managed Care Digest Series, vol. 1 (Kansas City, MO: Hoechst Marion Roussel, 1996), p. 6.

6. Hoechst Marion Roussel, *Medicare/Medicaid Special Edition Digest 1996,* p. 13.

7. J. P. Weiner, "Forecasting the Effects of Health Reform on U.S. Physician Workforce Requirement: Evidence from HMO Staffing Pattern," *JAMA* 272, no. 3 (1994): 222; T. H. Dial and others, "Clinical Staffing in Staff- and Group-Model HMOs," *Health Affairs* 14 (Summer 1995): 168; and S. Gamliel and others, "Managed Care on the March: Will Physicians Meet the Challenge," *Health Affairs* 14 (Summer 1995): 132.

8. Weiner.

9. Weiner.

10. S. A. Schroder, "The Latest Forecast: Managed Care Collides with Physician Supply," *JAMA* 272, no. 3 (July 20, 1994): 239–40; and S. Foreman, "Managing the Physician Workforce: Hands Off, the Market is Working," *Health Affairs* 15 (Summer 1996): 243–49.

11. S. Woolhandler and D. U. Himmelstein, "The Physician Workforce Delusion," *Health Affairs* 14 (Fall 1995): 279.

12. C. J. Simon and P. H. Born, "Physician Earnings in a Changing Managed Care Environment," *Health Affairs* 15, no. 1 (Fall 1996): 124–34.

13. Hoechst Marion Roussel, *HMO–PPO Digest 1996*. Managed Care Digest Series, vol. 2 (Kansas City, MO: Hoechst Marion Roussel, 1996).

14. G. J. Church, "Backlash against HMOs," *Time (*Apr. 14, 1997): 32.

15. Hoechst Marion Roussel, *Medical Group Practice Digest 1996,* Managed Care Digest Series, vol. 3 (Kansas City, MO: Hoechst Marion Roussel, 1996), pp. 18–19.

16. Hoechst Marion Roussel, *Medical Group Practice Digest 1996,* pp. 35, 44.

17. M. C. Jaklevic, "PHOs Fall Short of Expectations," *Modern Healthcare* (Oct. 9, 1995): 77–81.

18. Church.

19. D. Blumenthal, "Effects of Market Reforms on Doctors and Their Patients," *Health Affairs* 15, no. 2 (1996): 170–84.

20. Blumenthal, p. 183.

21. R. Kuttner, *Everything for Sale: The Virtues and Limits of Markets* (New York City: Alfred A. Knopf, 1997), p. 111.

APPENDIX
OVERVIEW OF ANTICIPATED U.S. POPULATION GROWTH

In 1995, the resident population of the United States was estimated to be 262,755,000 persons. Based on the Bureau of the Census mid-level population projections, this population group is expected to continue to grow at least until the year 2020, but after 2000, its growth will slow from 4.5 percent every five years to 4.1 to 4.2 percent every five years. (See table A-1). This slowing in growth of total population masks rapid growth in certain population segments.

The 65-and-over resident population is one group that is expected to grow rapidly. In 1995, this population group was estimated at 33.5 million persons. This group is forecasted to remain at 12.7 percent of the total population until the year 2010, when it will begin to increase its share. Growth is then rapid, as a percent of total, until at least 2020, when the 65-and-over population will become 16.5 percent of the total population.

In 1995, the 85-and-over population included 3,630,000 persons, representing 1.38 percent of the total resident population. By the year 2020, this group is expected to rise to 2 percent of the resident population.

Table A-2 shows the growth in these three population groups over two periods: 1995 to 2005, and 1995 to 2020. The short-run forecast shows that the total resident population will grow at 8.8 percent, the

TABLE A-1. U.S. Resident Population by Selected Age Categories, 1970–2020

Year	*Resident Population (millions)*	*Percent Change*	*65 and Over Population (millions)*	*Percent of Total*	*85 and Over Population (millions)*	*Percent of Total*
1970	203.2		20.0	9.8	1.41	0.69
1980	226.5	11.5	25.6	11.3	2.24	0.99
1990	248.7	9.8	31.1	12.5	3.02	1.21
1995	262.8	5.7	33.5	12.7	3.63	1.38
2000	274.6	4.5	34.7	12.6	4.26	1.55
2005	286.0	4.2	36.2	12.7	4.9	1.71
2010	297.7	4.1	39.4	13.2	5.67	1.90
2015	310.1	4.2	45.5	14.7	6.19	2.00
2020	322.7	4.1	53.2	16.5	6.46	2.00

Source: U.S. Bureau of the Census, *Statistical Abstract of the United States: 1996* (Washington, DC: U.S. Government Printing Office, 1996), table 14.

TABLE A-2. Projected Population Growth in Selected Age Categories, 1995–2020

Year	*Resident Population (millions)*	*65 and Over Population (millions)*	*85 and over Population (millions)*
1995	262.8	33.5	3.6
2005	286.0	36.2	4.9
Percent Change	8.8	8.1	35.0
1995	262.8	33.5	3.6
2020	322.7	53.2	6.5
Percent Change	22.8	58.8	78.0

Source: U.S. Bureau of the Census, *Statistical Abstract of the United States: 1996* (Washington, DC: U.S. Government Printing Office, 1996), table 14.

65-and-over population at 8.1 percent, and the 85-and-over group at 35 percent. The long-run forecast (from 1995 to 2025) shows an increase in the total resident population of 22.8 percent, an increase in the 65-and-over population of 58.8 percent, and an increase in the 85-and-over population of 78 percent.

In the short run, the total population and the 65-and-over population will grow at about the same rate, but the 85-and-older group (which is included in the 65-and-over group) will expand four times faster. In the long run, both the 65-and-over and the 85-and-over groups will grow at rates that are substantially faster than those of the total resident population. The resident elderly population will increase its share of the total population, but the increase will be especially rapid after the year 2005.

INDEX

(continued on next page)

(continued on next page)